The Dirty Secret of Early Modern Capitalism

This book shows how the Dutch accumulation of great wealth was closely linked to their involvement in wars both at home and abroad. In doing so, it ponders the issue of how capitalism has often historically thrived best when its practitioners are ruthless and ignore the human cost of their search for riches. This complicates the traditional Marxist understanding of capitalists as middle-class exploiters in arguing for a much greater agency among lower-class Dutch soldiers and sailors in their efforts to benefit from skills that were in high demand.

Kees Boterbloem is Full Professor in the Department of History at the University of South Florida in Tampa.

Routledge Research in Early Modern History

Spain, Rumor, and Anti-Catholicism in Mid-Jacobean England
The Palatine Match, Cleves, and the Armada Scares of 1612–1613 and 1614
Calvin F. Senning

Firsting in the Early-Modern Atlantic World
Edited by Lauren Beck

Early Modern English Noblewomen and Self-Starvation
The Skull Beneath the Skin
Sasha Garwood

Maurits of Nassau and the Survival of the Dutch Revolt
Comparative Insurgences
Nick Ridley

The Economic Causes of the English Civil War
Freedom of Trade and the English Revolution
George Yerby

Edwin Sandys and the Reform of English Religion
Sarah L. Bastow

Murder, Justice, and Harmony in an Eighteenth-Century French Village
Nancy Locklin

The Dirty Secret of Early Modern Capitalism
The Global Reach of the Dutch Arms Trade, Warfare and Mercenaries in the Seventeenth Century
Kees Boterbloem

For more information about this series, please visit: www.routledge.com/Routledge-Research-in-Early-Modern-History/book-series/RREMH

The Dirty Secret of Early Modern Capitalism

The Global Reach of the Dutch Arms Trade, Warfare and Mercenaries in the Seventeenth Century

Kees Boterbloem

Routledge
Taylor & Francis Group
NEW YORK AND LONDON

First published 2020
by Routledge
605 Third Avenue, New York, NY 10017

and by Routledge
2 Park Square, Milton Park, Abingdon, Oxon, OX14 4RN

First issued in paperback 2021

Routledge is an imprint of the Taylor & Francis Group, an informa business

Publisher's Note
The publisher has gone to great lengths to ensure the quality of this reprint but points out that some imperfections in the original copies may be apparent.

Library of Congress Cataloging-in-Publication Data
A catalog record for this book has been requested

ISBN 13: 978-1-03-208703-0 (pbk)
ISBN 13: 978-1-138-69288-6 (hbk)

Typeset in Sabon
by Apex CoVantage, LLC

Faith in military might is deeply grounded in the national psyche.[1]

A War so long and full of so many and so famous accidents, as thereby, beyond all others of our times, the memory of our age will be innobled to Posterity; and it may be truly said, that Flanders in this present age hath been as a Military Scene in Europe, which for forty years together, till the conclusion of the Truce [of 1609], hath exposed to the Theater of the Universe all the novelties, and most memorable spectacles which were ever seen in any preceding War, or shall ever be seen in any that shall insue.

Cardinal Guido Bentivoglio (1579–1644) on the Dutch Independence War (or Eighty Years' War)[2]

1. Greider, "How Obsolete."
2. Bentivoglio, *Historicall Relations*, 35.

Contents

Preface

Contemporary historians are in the habit of paying tribute to those who preceded them in the profession, even if methods and approaches have changed. I was lucky in being taught by many outstanding scholars, too, and their ideas have left their imprint on the following pages.[1] One of my convictions may precede my exposure to historical scholarship, though: Economics are the prime movers in human affairs. I agree with Bertolt Brecht's maxim "*erst kommt das Fressen, dann kommt die Moral*," which Macheath notes in Brecht's 1928 take of the *Three Penny Opera*.[2] I also believe that until recently military history has been given too much short shrift in postwar scholarship. Finally, an eclectic sampling of analytical insights out of cultural history and critical theory are informing this book.

As part of a somewhat facile praise for the libertine spirit behind soft-drug sales in coffeeshops or legalised prostitution, observers today sometimes imagine a direct link between Dutch contemporary *laissez-faire* culture and the tolerance of the Dutch Golden Age of 400 years ago. A somewhat closer look shows that this broad-mindedness has and had its limits. The death of Adriaen Koerbagh (1633–1669) in jail or the execution of a good number of "sodomists" (homosexuals) in the 1730s illustrates this limitation in the days of the Dutch Republic.[3] In fact, one might suggest a much less wholesome parallel between then and now. Dutch tolerance and affluence in the Golden Age could exist only by virtue of dubious behaviour outside the idyllic "Holland Garden" ("*Hollandse Tuin*"). Similarly, in the case of the Netherlands today, the good life is enjoyed at the expense of others far away about whom few care to know too much. According to the well-reputed Stockholm International Peace Research Institute, the Dutch belonged until very recently to the largest arms exporters in the world; likewise, they were the number one arms exporters in the seventeenth-century world (as much as they were the greatest producers of printed materials).[4]

There is an undeniable nexus between arms manufacturing and capitalist success or, to use another closely related term, economic growth. Arms production for the domestic and export market underscored a good deal of the economic boom of the European empires around 1900, and much of the Soviet Union's breathtaking economic expansion after 1929 was rooted in an extraordinary development of heavy industry, especially through high investment (and at mind-boggling human cost) in arms manufacturing. The economy of Hitler's Germany was jump-started by huge sums of money pouring into the arms sector. And ever since the end of the Cold War, producing and selling arms remain safe bets both for Western countries, the Russian Federation, and the former Soviet satellites. Most of the manufacturing sector of these countries' economies has been outsourced these days, but the weapons industry remains an area of business that continues to blossom at home.

Today's Kingdom of the Netherlands no longer derives its prosperity from slavery or the slave trade as it partially did in the seventeenth century, but its people and government today show little sustained compassion for their fellow human beings brutally exploited in the sweatshops of Asia, Africa, or South America who provide them with dirt-cheap consumer goods. Few questions are raised about the ethics of this sort of economic practice; even fewer questions were raised about the morality of the slave trade, slavery, or, indeed, Dutch war-profiteering in the seventeenth century. In a vile sort of wink to their audience, arms dealers had innocent cherubs or *putti* depicted celebrating the nefarious source of their prosperity, as the Trips did in their opulent houses (today's *Trippenhuis*, headquarters of the Dutch Royal Academy of Sciences) on the Kloveniersburgwal in Amsterdam.[5] Members of the Trip family such as Elias (1570–1636) and his nephews Hendrick (1607–1666) and Louys (1605–1684) were proud of their phenomenal success in trading arms. And their peers applauded their success as well: Louys was elevated to the Amsterdam city council in 1672, a recognition of his business savvy.[6] The wealth of Elias Trip was already phenomenal in the 1630s: It possibly reached one million guilders, which made him well-nigh the richest man in Amsterdam, probably the richest city in the world.[7] The Trips resemble capitalist tycoons and weaponmongers through the ages, such as the notorious Basil Zaharoff (1849–1936).[8]

What is puzzling is that, whereas, starting in the 1960s, some Dutch historians and foreign historians of the United Provinces have focussed on the "embarrassment" of the slave trade, until very recently, hardly any scholar investigated the global Dutch reach in terms of the trade in military means, military expertise, or mercenary warfare, even if researchers have looked at the role the Dutch played in the significant changes in warfare that are said to have amounted to a "Military Revolution."[9] One English-language attempt published during the 1990s to sketch this crucial role is maddingly thin, even if some of this work's information is invaluable and its title, *The Arsenal of the World*, aptly describes the Dutch importance in the arms trade of the seventeenth world.[10] Suddenly, though, since the turn of the millennium, the study of the pivotal role of warfare in the history of the Dutch Republic has taken flight.

In his discussion of the second endless conflict that engulfed the Low Countries, the wars between the Republic and France from 1672 to 1713, Donald Haks reminds us that the "war-and-society" approach is potentially a promising avenue towards a better understanding of war's widespread impact on history outside strictly military developments.[11] Indeed, society was constantly moulded by the permanent war in which the Republic (like many other early modern European countries) was engulfed. How deep an imprint such a crisis leaves on the collective mind might become apparent through looking at more recent history. Long after the Second World War, the Dutch spoke about the period of German occupation (May 1940–May 1945 for the Holland provinces) as the time of "*de oorlog*," "the war," even if actual combat limited itself to four days in May 1940 and, with some exceptions (notably, the Arnhem and Nijmegen area), a mere few days in 1944 and 1945. Nevertheless, in common parlance and in collective memory, all of those five years left an indelible stamp on people's minds as the years of the war (born 17 years after it, even I understood immediately which "war" was meant if people spoke about it).

Undoubtedly, then, in the century and a half from 1566 to 1713, even when armies or navies often clashed in the borderlands of the Republic, or in seas far away from the Dutch coast, the constant presence of warfare deeply affected the Dutch mindset and everyday life, stretching across five generations. And this was all the more so, because since the early days of the revolt against Habsburg rule most men were trained in combat, including that with firearms, while 10,000 served in the field armies and as sailors on merchant ships that could be used as warships, or on specialised naval vessels, built for warfare at sea.[12] During the Middle Ages, armed combat had been a pursuit of the elite; only during its waning were specialised units consisting of commoners (often paid as mercenaries) added as archers or pikemen. In contrast, in the Dutch Republic, almost all adult males were prepared for war, a sort of (male) mass mobilisation, the first of its kind in the country's history.

Indubitably, even for such a hardened lot, incessant warfare occasionally led to a yearning for peace, as can be seen around 1650, and again after 1667, but pacifist rhetoric should not be mistaken for earnest pacifism.[13] Even if there were periods of peace at home in Europe (and most battling occurred outside of the Dutch heartland of Holland, Zeeland, Friesland, and Utrecht after the mid-1590s), fighting at sea and across the globe meant that war, not peace, was the norm. Someone like Holland's political leader Johan de Witt (1625–1672) was cautious not to provoke potentially mighty foes, but he was no dove when prosecuting wars with Portugal, Sweden, England, and Münster. Ultimately, he failed in his attempts to evade the creation of a formidable coalition of foreign Powers against his country. Stadtholder William III (1650–1702), who took over from De Witt as the Republic's leading politician (and doubled as military commander), successfully restored a balance of power through military grit and diplomatic guile, gradually building alliances that forced the French to the negotiation table in the 1670s and fought the French once again to a draw after 1688. While more inclined than De Witt to choose war over peace, William III was no hawk, though. Circumstances forced war upon him in 1672.

This book disagrees with the argument that we should not measure the past by the standards of the moral high ground of today, for, in a country as ostensibly Christian as the seventeenth-century United Provinces, did the sixth commandment not count?[14] The contemporary attitude of the Mennonites, as we will see, proves beyond a doubt that it did matter. Calvinist ministers, too, did condemn the slave trade and slave labour.[15] In various places, my study of the evidence makes an effort to chart how "[Dutch entrepreneurial panache in making money out of war] has been perceived"; altogether, I found little public protest against the ventures or people that harnessed violence for profit.[16] As much as today, most people turned a blind eye to the pain their gain (or the gains of their successful compatriots) caused. They knew, and they knew that it was ultimately wrong. Even if "the past is a different country in which people did things differently," in essence, we should not hesitate to call them hypocrites in the Biblical understanding of the term.[17]

One may detect hypocrisy as well in the absence of a sustained or comprehensive historical investigation before 2000 into the dirty secret behind the early modern Dutch economic miracle. If a link between capitalism and war can be incontrovertibly established, the implications go beyond that of the seventeenth-century Netherlands and may be relevant to much of the history of modern capitalism since. I am not sure how much of today's wealth of the Kingdom of the Netherlands should be ascribed to arms sales past and present, but a crucial part (and a far larger one than any profits derived from selling slaves or sugar plantations) of the spectacular capitalist success of the Dutch Republic is to be attributed to its profitable cornering of the military market.

The production of weapons and the international arms trade conducted from the Netherlands was rooted in the profit principle of the market exchange that went on to become the dominant mode of economic thought and practice. Intriguingly, the evidence about the Dutch Republic suggests that a country can benefit significantly even from a war with an inconclusive outcome, of which there were many in seventeenth- and eighteenth-century Europe. What has been identified by Michael Roberts, Geoffrey Parker, and others as a "Military Revolution" was a key component of the capitalist success story of the Dutch Republic in the seventeenth century.[18] Whereas the very occurrence of a military revolution has been questioned, it is worthwhile to note that, in the essay in which he coined the term, Roberts suggests several landmark changes that heralded the modern age in the manner wars were waged, which very much apply to Dutch warfare in their Golden Age:

> Mass armies, strict discipline, the control of the state, the submergence of the individual . . . [,] the conjoint ascendancy of financial power and applied science . . . in all its malignity . . . [,] the use of propaganda, psychological warfare, and terrorism as military weapons . . . familiar to theorists, as well as to commanders in the field.[19]

Reger sees as an essential component that made the Military Revolution succeed outside of the (Western) European core "vehicles of transmission of military culture, including personnel experienced in command and training, engineering and manufacturing of weapons technology, textual sources conveying military information, and contact with adversaries whose use of innovations was observed and imitated."[20] This applies to the Dutch role in the military realm at home and in much of the world (albeit especially in Europe) in the seventeenth century. In all of the areas identified by Roberts and Reger, the Netherlanders were among the pioneers, and the Republic was singular in combining all of them before the end of the seventeenth century. Outstanding examples are, to name only a few, Maurice (Maurits) of Orange-Nassau's (1567–1625) and William Louis (Willem Lodewijk) of Nassau-Dillenburg's (1560–1620) reforms, the use of *gedelegeerden te velde* (deputies-in-the-field), the forges and manufacturing plants as set up by Louys de Geer (1587–1652) in Sweden, or the largest printing presses of Europe. Perhaps "terrorism" appears most difficult to identify, but two of the more infamous examples of Dutch misconduct may suffice in proving Roberts's point about this: The savagery by William III's armies in Ireland in the 1690s and the brutality of Jan Pieterszoon Coen's (1587–1629) soldiers on the Indonesian Spice Islands during the 1620s.[21]

Academics unleashed a veritable avalanche of writing on the Dutch Republic even before the days of Immanuel Wallerstein's *Modern World System* and its analysis of the emergence of modern capitalism.[22] In standard works on early modern Dutch capitalism such as those by De Vries and Van der Woude or Schama, however, no attention is paid to the key role played by the arms trade.[23] In most of the works appearing before 2000, if the Dutch involvement in such enterprises is noted, it tends to be in passing. Just very recently historians have begun to turn to a key source of Dutch enrichment: War. Not so long ago, it was only Vogel who had dedicated a brief article to the topic of arms manufacturing and export from the Republic.[24] A major overview still is lacking; at least in part, this book tries to fill this gap.

Notes

1. That is in my case, somewhat simplistically, from Johan Huizinga (1872–1945) taught Jan Romein (1893–1962); Romein's last favourite mentee was Maarten Brands (1931–2018), who taught me; Huizinga is, of course, still

famous as a pioneer cultural historian; for Romein, see Romein, *Watershed*, which Brands prepared for print. Most English readers will be unfamiliar with this work, but it was a major source of inspiration for Eric Hobsbawm's best-selling trilogy on the "long nineteenth century" (see Hobsbawm, *Age of Imperialism*, 379).

2. Brecht and Weill, *Die Dreigroschenoper*.
3. See Israel, *Dutch Republic*, 787–9, 919; Schama, *Embarrassment*, 601–6.
4. See www.sipri.org/yearbook/2013/05, accessed 4 February 2019. Guus Kouwenhoven (b. 1942), the arms dealer at large of the vicious Liberian warlord Charles Taylor, proves the survival of the unscrupulous Dutch entrepreneurial spirit: In his efforts to turn a profit, he moved from trading tropical wood to weapons.
5. See www.knaw.nl/nl/de-knaw/het-trippenhuis/overzicht, accessed 18 May 2019. The artist responsible for the ceiling paintings among which the cherubs can be found is Nicolaas de Heldt Stockade (1614–1669), who died in the same year as Rembrandt. The façade of the house has (or had) a number of references to the nature of the Trips' trade as well (De Geer van Jutfaas, *Lodewijk de Geer*, 57–8). Much later, in the nineteenth century, the Swedish Academy of Sciences commemorated the Trips' illustrious relative, Louys de Geer, by casting a medal on which his bust was portrayed along with cannon, sword and the staff of Mercury (ibid., 2fn1).
6. Prak, *Dutch Republic*, 122–5.
7. Klein, *De Trippen*, 35–6.
8. Anderson, "British Rearmament," 17, 21. Already at the time, Zaharoff's behaviour was so notorious that it was lampooned by Hergé (see Hergé, *L'Oreille cassée*).
9. An excellent recent overview regarding the Dutch attitude towards slavery and the slave trade is Vink, "Freedom and Slavery," 19–46. Vink shows how slavery was far from unproblematic to the seventeenth-century Dutch. Vink's suggestion that as "slavery and slave trade [towards 1650] became an established Dutch practice, profit gained the upper hand over principle—if not among all, at least among most Dutchmen," may equally apply to the production and sale of arms or military expertise to those willing to pay (ibid., 30). For a general account on the significance of the arms trade in the age of imperialism, see Grant, *Rulers, Guns and Money*. Elsewhere, Grant writes, "By the seventeenth century, the Dutch became probably the leading arms exporters internationally, with Amsterdam at the heart of the trade" (Grant, " 'Merchants of Death'," 1).
10. Puype and Van der Hoeven, eds, *Arsenal*.
11. Haks, *Vaderland en vrede*, 13–14. See as well Brandon, " 'War and Society'," 51–72.
12. Brandon suggests that the mercenaries were not in it just for the money (see Brandon, " 'War and Society'," 57–8, 61).
13. The contrast he draws between the pacifist Holland regents and the belligerent Oranges is drawn far too sharply (Boogman, "raison-d'état," 384–5).
14. It certainly counted very much for Protestants on the other side of the North Sea (see Willis, *Reformation*).
15. Klooster, *Dutch Moment*, 245–6.
16. Parrott, *Business*, 3.
17. See, for example, Luke 3:8 or Matthew 7:15. The quotation is a version of the maxim by L.P. Hartley (1895–1972) in his novel *The Go-Between* (London: Hamish Hamilton, 1953; although he quoted the historian David Cecil [1902–1986]).
18. Roberts, "Military Revolution"; Glete, *War and the State*, 141, 143, 161; Van Nimwegen, "*Deser landen crijchsvolck*"; Parker, "The Limits to

Revolutions"; Parker, *Military Revolution*; Parker, rev. of *Krijgsvolk* by Swart. The great opponent of the Parker–Roberts school of thought has been Jeremy Black (see especially Black, *A Military Revolution?*).

19. Roberts, "Military Revolution," 217–18.
20. Reger, "In the Service," 13.
21. Also note the slaughter of "Kieft's War" (see Klooster, *Dutch Moment*, 73).
22. See Glamann, *Dutch-Asiatic Trade*; Boxer, *Dutch Seaborne Empire*; Meilink-Roelofsz, ed., *De VOC*; Prakash, *Dutch East India Company*; Wallerstein, *Modern World System*, vol. 2; De Vries, *Economy*; De Vries, *Industrious Revolution*; De Vries and Van der Woude, *First Modern Economy*; Israel, *Dutch Republic*; Israel, *Dutch Primacy*; Schama, *Embarrassment*; Parker, *Dutch Revolt*; Schmidt, *Innocence Abroad*; Schmidt, Stott and Godfriend, eds, *Going Dutch*; Cook, *Matters of Exchange*; Jardine, *Going Dutch*; Postma, *Dutch in the Atlantic Slave Trade*; Dekker, *Childhood*; Emmer, *Dutch Slave Trade*; Van den Boogaart, *Civil and Corrupt Asia*; Lach and Van Kley, *Asia*; Kaplan, *Calvinists and Libertines*; Prak, *Dutch Republic*; Price, *Dutch Republic*; Price, *Dutch Culture*; Burke, *Towards a Social History*; 't Hart, *Dutch Wars*; Van Nierop, *Treason*; Po-Chia Hsia and Van Nierop, eds, *Calvinism*; Adams, *Familial State*; Van Deursen, *Plain Lives*; Goldgar, *Tulipmania*; Davids and Lucassen, eds, *Miracle Mirrored*; Spies and Frijhoff, *Dutch Culture*; Bruijn and Prud'homme van Reine, *De Ruyter*; Barendse, *Arabian Seas*; Ormrod, *Rise of Commercial Empires*; Wills, Jr, *Pepper, Guns and Parleys*, to mention only *some* of the most important books (and mainly *in English*, it should be noted) that have contributed to the debate. There were detractors from the idea that from an economic perspective the Republic was modern, but their voices seem to have been muffled by now by those who argue the contrary (see Klein, "Nederland de eerste moderne economie?"; Krantz and Hohenberg, eds, *Failed Transitions*).
23. De Vries and Van der Woude, *First Modern Economy*; Schama, *Embarrassment*. Typical, too, is the otherwise excellent PhD dissertation by P.W. Klein (Klein, *De Trippen*): Its introduction discusses in lucid manner the pitfalls of the debate in economic history about the astonishing flourishing of the Republic, but even when Klein's topic is the Trip family, he neglects to make the link between war and profit explicit that made them into the equivalent of contemporary billionaires; I argue that it is not just the inventiveness of the seventeenth-century Dutch entrepreneurs that is remarkable but their total lack of scruples about increasing the slaughter on the European and non-European battlefields to which their ventures significantly contributed (cf. ibid., 7–9). More sober and critical is the recent essay collection by Heerma van Voss et al., eds, *Wereldgeschiedenis*.
24. Vogel, "Arms Production."

Bibliography

Adams, Julia. *The Familial State: Ruling Families and Merchant Capitalism in Early Modern Europe*, Ithaca, NY: Cornell University Press, 2007.

Anderson, David G. "British Rearmament and the 'Merchants of Death': The 1935–36 Royal Commission on the Manufacture of Manufacture of and Trade in Armaments," *Journal of Contemporary History* 1, 1994, 5–37.

Arms Trade, available at: www.sipri.org/yearbook/2013/05, accessed 4 February 2019.

Barendse, René. *The Arabian Seas*, Armonk, NY: M.E. Sharpe, 2002.

Bentivoglio, Cardinall. *Historicall Relations of the United Provinces and of Flanders*, trans. Henry, Earl of Monmouth, London: Humphrey Mosely, 1652.
Black, J. *A Military Revolution? Military Change and European Society, 1550–1800*, Basingstoke: MacMillan, 1991.
Boogaart, Ernst van den. *Civil and Corrupt Asia*, Chicago, IL: University of Chicago Press, 2003.
Boogman, J.C. "De Raison-d'état Politics Johan de Witt," *Bijdragen en Mededelingen betreffende de Geschiedenis der Nederlanden* 90, 1975, 379–407.
Boxer, C.R. *The Dutch Seaborne Empire*, London: Hutchison, 1965.
Brandon, Pepijn. "Een 'War and Society'-geschiedenis van de Tachtigjarige Oorlog," *Bijdragen en Mededelingen betreffende de Geschiedenis der Nederlanden (Low Countries History Review)* 3, 2014, 51–72.
Brecht, Bertolt, and Kurt Weill. *Die Dreigroschenoper*, Berlin: Felix Bloch, 1928.
Bruijn, J.R., and R. Prud'homme van Reine, *De Ruyter: Dutch Admiral*, Rotterdam: Karwansaray, 2011.
Burke, Peter. *Towards a Social History of Early Modern Dutch*, Amsterdam: Amsterdam University Press, 2006.
Cook, Harold. *Matters of Exchange*, New Haven, CT: Yale University Press, 2008.
Davids, Karel, and Jan Lucassen, eds. *A Miracle Mirrored*, Cambridge: Cambridge University Press, 1996.
Dekker, Rudolf. *Childhood, Memory and Autobiography in Holland*, Basingstoke: Palgrave, 1999.
Deursen, A.Th. van. *Plain Lives in a Golden Age*, Cambridge: Cambridge University Press, 1991.
Dutch Academy of Sciences, available at: www.knaw.nl/nl/de-knaw/het-trippenhuis/overzicht, accessed 18 May 2019.
Emmer, Pieter. *The Dutch Slave Trade*, New York: Berghahn, 2005.
Geer van Jutfaas, J.L.W. de. *Lodewijk de Geer van Finspong en Leusta (1587–1652)*, 3rd ed., Utrecht: Kemink and Son, 1852.
Glamann, Kristof. *Dutch-Asiatic Trade, 1620–1740*, Den Haag: Nijhoff, 1958.
Glete, Jan. *War and the State in Early Modern Europe*, New York: Routledge, 2002.
Goldgar, Anne. *Tulipmania*, Chicago, IL: University of Chicago Press, 2008.
Grant, Jonathan. "'Merchants of Death': The International Traffic in Arms," *Origins: Current Events in Historical Perspective* 3, 2012, 1–2: 1, available at: http://origins.osu.edu/article/merchants-death-international-traffic-arms/page/0/0, accessed 30 August 2015.
———. *Rulers, Guns and Money: The Global Arms Trade in the Age of Imperialism*, Cambridge, MA: Harvard University Press, 2007.
Greider, William. "How Obsolete, Triumphalist Militarism Is Destroying America," *The Nation*, 29 January 2016, available at: www.thenation.com/article/how-obsolete-triumphalist-militarism-is-destroying-america/, accessed 1 February 2016.
Haks, Donald. *Vaderland en vrede: Publiciteit over de Nederlandse republiek in oorlog, 1672–1713*, Hilversum: Verloren, 2013.
Hart, Marjolein 't. *The Dutch Wars of Independence: Warfare and Commerce in the Netherlands, 1570–1680*, London: Routledge, 2014.
Hartley, L.P. *The Go-Between*, London: Hamish Hamilton, 1953.

Heerma van Voss, Lex, et al., eds. *Wereldgeschiedenis van Nederland*, Amsterdam: Ambo-Anthos, 2018.
Hergé. *L'Oreille cassée*, Brussels: Casterman, 1937.
Hobsbawm, E. *The Age of Imperialism*, New York: Vintage, 1989.
Israel, Jonathan. *Dutch Primacy in the World Trade, 1585–1740*, Oxford: Oxford University Press, 1989.
———. *The Dutch Republic*, Oxford: Oxford University Press, 1995.
Jardine, Lisa. *Going Dutch*, New York: Harper, 2009.
Kaplan, Benjamin. *Calvinists and Libertines*, Oxford: Clarendon Press, 1995.
Klein, P.W. "Nederland de eerste moderne economie? Een kritiek," *Tijdschrift voor Geschiedenis* 109, 1996, 514–20.
———. *De Trippen in de Zeventiende Eeuw*, Assen: Van Gorcum, 1965.
Klooster, Wim. *The Dutch Moment: War, Trade and Settlement in the Seventeenth-Century Atlantic World*, Ithaca, NY: Cornell University Press, 2016.
Krantz, F., and M. Hohenberg, eds. *Failed Transitions to Modern Industrial Society*, Montréal: Interuniversity Centre for European Studies, 1975.
Lach, Donald and Edwin van Kley. *Asia in the Making of Europe*, 3 vols., Chicago, IL: University of Chicago Press, 1965–1993.
Meilink-Roelofsz, M.A.P., ed. *De VOC in Azië*, Bussum: Fibula-Van Dishoeck, 1976.
Nierop, Henk van. *Treason in the Northern Quarter*, Princeton, NJ: Princeton University Press, 2009.
Nimwegen, O. van. *Deser landen crijchsvolck*, Amsterdam: Bert Bakker, 2006.
Ormrod, David. *The Rise of Commercial Empires: England and the Netherlands in the Age of Mercantilism, 1650–1770*, Cambridge: Cambridge University Press, 2003.
Parker, G. "Review of Krijgsvolk: Militaire professionalisering en het ontstaan van het Staatse leger, 1568–1590 by Erik Swart," *Journal of Military History* 4, 2007, 1225–7.
———. *The Dutch Revolt*, London: Allen Lane, 1977.
———. "The Limits to Revolutions in Military Affairs: Maurice of Nassau, the Battle of Nieuwpoort (1600), and the Legacy," *Journal of Military History* 2, 2007, 331–72.
———. The Military Revolution: Military Innovation and the Rise of the West, 1500–1800, 2nd ed., Cambridge: Cambridge University Press, 1996.
Parrott, David. *The Business of War*, Cambridge: Cambridge University Press, 2012.
Po-Chia Hsia R., and H. van Nierop, eds. *Calvinism and Religious Toleration in the Dutch Golden Age*, Cambridge: Cambridge University Press, 2010.
Postma, Johannes. *The Dutch in the Atlantic Slave Trade, 1600–1815*, Cambridge: Cambridge University Press, 2008.
Prak, Maarten. *The Dutch Republic in the Seventeenth Century*, Cambridge: Cambridge University Press, 2005.
Prakash, Om. *The Dutch East India Company and the Economy of Bengal*, Princeton, NJ: Princeton University Press, 1985.
Price, J.L. *Dutch Culture in the Golden Age*, London: Reaktion Press, 2011.
———. *The Dutch Republic in the Seventeenth Century*, Basingstoke: Palgrave Macmillan, 1998.

Puype, J.P., and M. van der Hoeven, eds. *The Arsenal of the World: The Dutch Arms Trade in the Seventeenth Century*, Amsterdam: Batavian Lion International, 1996.

Reger, W.M. "In the Service of the Tsar: European Mercenary Officers and the Reception of Military Reform in Russia, 1654–1667," unpublished PhD diss., University of Illinois at Urbana-Champaign, 1997.

Roberts, M. "The Military Revolution (1560–1660)," in M. Roberts, ed., *Essays in Swedish History*, London: Weidenfeld and Nicholson, 1967, 193–225.

Romein, J. *The Watershed of Two Eras*, Middletown, CT: Wesleyan University Press, 1978.

Schama, Simon. *The Embarrassment of Riches*, New York: Vintage Books, 1997.

Schmidt, Benjamin. *Innocence Abroad*, Cambridge: Cambridge University Press, 2001.

Schmidt, Benjamin, A. Stott, and J. Godfriend, eds. *Going Dutch: The Dutch Presence in America, 1609–2009*, Leiden: Brill, 2008.

Spies, Marijke, and Willem Frijhoff. *Dutch Culture in a European Perspective*, vol. 1, Basingstoke: Palgrave, 2005.

Vink, Marcus P.M. "Freedom and Slavery: The Dutch Republic, the VOC World, and the Debate over the World's 'Oldest Trade,'" *South African Historical Journal* 1, 2007, 19–46.

Vogel, H. "Arms Production and Exports in the Dutch Republic, 1600–1650," in M. van der Hoeven, ed., *Exercise of Arms: Warfare in the Netherlands, 1568–1648*, Leiden: Brill, 1997, 189–210.

Vries, Jan de. *The Economy of Europe in an Age of Crisis, 1600–1750*, New York: Cambridge University Press, 1976.

———. *The Industrious Revolution*, Cambridge: Cambridge University Press, 2008.

Vries, Jan de, and A. van der Woude. *The First Modern Economy: Success, Failure and Perseverance of the Dutch Economy, 1500–1815*, Cambridge: Cambridge University Press, 1997.

Wallerstein, I. *The Modern World System*, vol. 2, rev. ed., Berkeley, CA: University of California Press, 2011.

Willis, Jonathan. *The Reformation of the Decalogue: Religious Identity and the Ten Commandments in England, c. 1485–1625*, Cambridge: Cambridge University Press, 2017.

Wills, Jr., John E. *Pepper, Guns and Parleys*, Cambridge, MA: Harvard University Press, 1974.

Acknowledgments

As always, I will undoubtedly forget some people whose help in writing this book has been instrumental. This will be all the more so as this project has taken more than five years to complete (and some of its research goes back decades, as it was conducted for other projects and then shelved). So before I start to give thanks, my sincere apologies to those whom I have inadvertently omitted while, of course, my gratitude goes out to them as well. Some of those who helped me arrive at this point of my scholarly career have passed away, among whom are my parents, Anne Clendinning, Martin van den Heuvel, Maarten Brands, Jan-Willem Bezemer, and Valentin Boss. Over the years, crucial encouragement, advice, and support were offered in addition by Rudolf Dekker, David Beeler, Michael Swierczynski, Daniel Kaiser, Golfo Alexopoulos, David Goldfrank, William Cummings, Michael Decker, Davide Tanasi, Denise Cali, John Belohlavek, Victor Peppard, Philip Longworth, Marc Jansen, Erik van Ree, Bruno Naarden, Marion Peters, Karel Berkhoff, Carola Tischler, Jan Struys, Bart van Drunen Littel, Klaas-Jan Boterbloem, Martin Stegeman, Nicole van Weeringh, Rubin Ootes, Harry Oomen, J. Scott Perry, Steven High, Barbara Lorenzkowski, David Mooney, David Schimmelpenninck van der Oye, Paul Robinson, Donald Wright, Murat Tuncali, Martha Gould, Rawil Fakhrullin, Igor Osipov, Irina Leifer, Leonid Maksimenkov, Eugenio Bolongaro, Otto Bleker, Lara Campbell, Steven Usitalo, Ben Whisenhunt, Ben Sperduto, Joyce Goggin, Piet van Steenis, Arnoud Jonkhoff, Gerrit Peijs, Susan Rhinehart, Eve Setch, and Max Novick.

Ultimately, though, I have derived most sustenance from the love and support of Susan, Duncan, and Saskia Mooney!

Introduction

> A portrait of war makers and state makers as coercive and self-seeking entrepreneurs bears a far greater resemblance to the facts than do its chief alternatives: the idea of a social contract, the idea of an open market in which operators of armies and states offer services to willing consumers, the idea of a society whose shared norms and expectations call forth a certain kind of government.[1]

The history of the United Provinces from the 1560s to the early 1700s seems to exemplify Charles Tilly's point that happenstance and hard-nosed individuals were the driving forces behind the formation and survival of early modern states. Despite the selective tolerance and the relative diffusion of political power in the Dutch Republic, it was not a haven of human liberty, an idyllic or harmonious place where polite conversation was the norm and the making of the great art and architecture took centre stage, protected by benign armed forces and led by an enlightened patriciate that had the common good at heart. Its independence was an accident of history or, more aptly, was the result of a long-drawn-out and hard-fought war before 1648, which was preserved in another major conflagration that started in 1672 and ended only in 1713. The Republic had not been created with the aim of creating an open society in which the arts and sciences flourished or of the pursuit of happiness.

On the eve of his successful coup in 1917, the Russian revolutionary leader V.I. Lenin (1870–1924) suggested that in the Imperialist Age in which he lived, the working class of the industrialised Western countries had become in effect a part of the exploitative bourgeoisie that suppressed the underclass, or poor masses, in non-Western countries.[2] Lenin's point applies as well to the early modern capitalist empires. In their Golden Age, the comparatively high standard of living of the northern Netherlanders came at the expense of others elsewhere. Many of those others paid with their lives. The country's wealth and opportunities for enrichment muffled any complaints about such dire costs while contributing to the population's ready acceptance for almost two centuries of what in effect amounted to an authoritarian oligarchy.[3] The Dutch rise to political and economic power was achieved by a tough lot.

The nexus between the Dutch economic boom and matters military is staring the historian in the face: One does not have to dig far to find evidence of the Dutch genius in turning to warfare for a profit (or making war profitable).[4] To quote Hoff:

> [T]he Netherlands were the first to establish and maintain a large-scale trade in . . . war materials . . . [with] Dutch models of firearms [dominating] all European armies, and . . . Dutch capital and Dutch production facilities . . . available in the necessary dimensions.[5]

The strange thing is, however, that few scholars ever looked for this link, until quite recently.[6] In popular culture and scholarly works, at most nostalgic veneration of old seadogs could be encountered in a sort of romantic recollection of the Age of Sail.[7] Otherwise, however, the bloody stains on the history pages of the Golden Age, a period more or less encompassing the entire seventeenth century, were even recently, unwittingly or not, scrubbed out of the narrative; historians depicted the country as an innately peaceful place, a victim of circumstances that forced it to fend off many a foreign predator, especially the tyrannical Philip II (1527–1598) and his great-grandson Louis XIV (1638–1715).

In the course of the last half century, English-language histories have detailed the Dutch Republic in all its precociously modern economic and cultural glory. The study of the entanglement of its society and economy with warfare remained strangely muted, however, until after 2000 (or perhaps 2001?). Historians such as Jan Glete, Roger Manning, and, to a lesser extent, Geoffrey Parker did address the remarkable military capacity of the Republic and its ability to harness its resources, capable of holding off all comers even when they combined their efforts, as they did in 1672.[8] In the process, the Dutch built up a vast arms industry, selling to all and sundry.[9] Few, however, recognised the centrality of Dutch military production, Dutch trade in military goods, or the diffusion of Dutch military expertise in this age and the considerable economic benefits or cultural impact that derived from it.[10]

Then, as much as now, waging war was not an uncomplicated affair of a state paying an army with the proceeds from the taxes it raised form its population: For it all to work, ". . . a group of manufacturers, traders, suppliers and financiers" were essential, too.[11] Besides a plethora of Charles Tilly's very wealthy "self-seeking" arms manufacturers and traders, the seventeenth-century Dutch population as a whole was complicit in aiding and abetting the sale of arms abroad, as manifested in their keenness to hire out their expertise in the art of war (on land and at sea) to foreign employers. Soldiers, sailors, politicians, or merchants exhibited few moral qualms about occupying themselves with such lethal pursuits, even if the origins of their country's meteoric ascent could be traced to a conflict over religion. In the early stages of this clash, Catholic fought Calvinist zealotry, but the humanist tolerance in spiritual matters that had influenced the educated classes in the Low Countries since the days of Erasmus prevailed in the United Provinces, the northern polity that emerged as an independent state towards 1590. Such tolerance proved a good business decision.

The period of Dutch hegemony in the European World System as identified by Immanuel Wallerstein coincides almost precisely with the age of the country's great arms manufacturers and traders.[12] But while the historiography was largely silent before 2000, the Dutch genius at channelling violence, productively and profitably, was amply evident to contemporaries who fruitlessly tried to defeat the Dutch on land and at sea, or to King Gustavus Adolphus, Tsar Aleksei Mikhailovich, or his son Peter the Great, who were some of the great empire builders of the age.

Since about 2000, however, the link between Dutch economic prosperity and the expertise and trade in matters military has begun to be vigorously investigated by a number of scholars such as Marjolein 't Hart, Michiel de Jong, Olaf van Nimwegen, Jonathan Grant, Erik Swart, Jeroen Duindam, and Pepijn Brandon.[13] Addressing an audience outside the academy, the journalist Ewald Vanvugt has subjected the smug and amoral pride regarding the production and sale of weaponry that permeated the merchant elite to a withering condemnation, as part of his criticism of the entire Dutch colonial enterprise (and the roaring silence about its misdeeds even after its collapse).[14] Indeed, his history of Dutch imperialism—for compelling reasons—is that of a "Robber State" ("*Roofstaat*"), indicating that its prosperity was gained at gunpoint or swordpoint.[15] It has to be said that historians of the Dutch colonial enterprises and long-distance trading in the early modern era have been more frank about the ruthless side of the Dutch during the Golden Age, although some of the criticism of the Dutch slave trade and use of slaves seems occasionally overly nuanced.[16] In some of this scholarship, an inclination remains palpable to paper over the sheer (and very un-Christian) savagery of the merchants, planters, officials, sailors, and soldiers towards European competitors and non-European enemies and subject peoples.

The better-known Dutch trans-Atlantic slave trade and the ruthlessness of a Jan Pieterszoon Coen in East Asia were undoubtedly symptomatic of the unbound capitalism upon which the Republic thrived, but a far more lucrative business, almost invariably yielding great returns, was that of arms sales.[17] That historians only recently have turned to this topic is odd but might reflect how many people still today operate as "merchants of death," while mercenary military units continue to deploy in conflict zones across the globe as well. It may be more difficult for historians to address the history of chapters that have not yet closed.

The success of the Dutch international arms trade aided the diffusion of the profit principle as the engine of the modern global economy. In the wake of the Dutch seventeenth-century *Wirtschaftswunder*, capitalism went on to become the dominant mode of economic thought and practice. In the middle of the twentieth century, the British historians John Nef and A.H. John fiercely debated whether capitalist boom periods were fuelled by a marked uptick of arms manufacturing and sales by way of the example of England.[18] In a spirited effort, Nef contended that the roots of England's economic advance could rather be found in cost savings of the long period of relative disengagement from European wars under the Tudors and early Stuarts and the absence of serious domestic civil strife between 1540 and 1640.[19] This allowed England to husband its potential for its subsequent flourishing as a capitalist and imperial Power. Nef responded to the many politicians and economists of his day who, in their appraisal of the Second World War's consequences, suggested that there was often no better stimulus for a country's economy than waging war or to prepare for it (as long as one's country was not vanquished). The more sober-minded John countered Nef's hypothesis with a fairly persuasive argument: Available statistics and other evidence indicated that Great Britain's economy did, in fact, receive a marked boost in terms of the production of weapons, profits, wages, and employment from its long-term involvement in European and global conflicts around 1700, the crucial moment when the United Kingdom economically started to forge ahead of the rest of the world. John implied a parallel both with the appearance of the United States as a hegemonic capitalist power during the First and Second World Wars and the priming-the-pump rearmament of the Nazi regime that pulled Germany out of its slump during the 1930s. In looking at the evidence of the United Provinces, the assessment of John seems to be borne out that "the extent of the economic effects of war will be [varied, but] given a favourable conjuncture of circumstances war [can be] an impetus to growth of the victorious power."[20]

In the Preface, we already referred to the Military Revolution, a somewhat nebulous concept despite the dogged efforts of Roberts and especially Parker to define it and assess its significance.[21] The German historian Hahlweg may have given one of the better appreciations of the changes in land warfare of the late sixteenth century in the Netherlands:

> The reforms of the Dutch way of fighting war [*Kriegswesen*] which largely took place in the decade from 1590 to 1600, . . . [entailed s] ystematic education of soldiers, the creation of a modern general staff and an orderly administration and supply (logistics) apparatus for the military; the establishment of a scientifically schooled officer corps; far-reaching application of the sciences for military aims; modern leadership structures (numerous commanders, systematic hierarchy); high accuracy, mobility, flexibility and speed in tactical movement. . . .[22]

As Hahlweg pointed out half a century ago, there were a number of highly influential theorists of warfare and engineers whose ideas shaped the Dutch art of war during the seventeenth century. Among the first group were Justus Lipsius (1547–1606) and Hugo de Groot (Grotius, 1583–1645), while the second group included Simon Stevin (1548–1620)—who founded a school of military engineering in 1600—and Menno van Coehoorn (1641–1704).[23] Not only in fighting their own wars stood the Dutch at the forefront of a significant advance in the production and use of military technology, which encompassed the building of new fortifications; extensive mining of iron and copper ore as materials for arms production; producing on a massive scale cannon, muskets, shot and powder; and building warships and drilling armies to make more efficient use of firearms by way of volley fire.[24] In Russia, for example, the Amsterdam expatriate Andries Denijsz. Winius (1605–c.1661) started the Tula armament foundries and arms manufacturing plant, which for the first time saw Muscovy produce firearms on a large scale. His son Andrei Andreevich Vinius (1641–1716) was not only involved in building a warship for Tsar Aleksei in the late 1660s but also oversaw Tsar Peter Alekseevich's visits to Arkhangel'sk in the early 1690s and started a school for military engineers in the early 1700s.[25]

An exhaustive accounting of each and every episode linking the Dutch seventeenth-century economic boom to warfare would lead to a volume that might be ten times larger than this one. Much of the second part of this book, therefore, will illustrate the crucial role played by the Dutch as conduits for military innovation and as arms traders and producers by way of the example of northern Europe from 1590 to 1725.[26] The example of Russia (straddling both Europe and Asia) to chart the global spread of Dutch military expertise and arms is a particularly illustrative test-case. A case study of the Dutch prominence in this period of Russian history reveals their pivotal role in military modernisation, both globally and in Europe.[27]

Few doubt Russia's great role in global history during the last three centuries; this role has been primarily the consequence of its military might, which became first noteworthy under Peter the Great. But a considerable part of the groundwork for Peter's exploits was laid previously, and this seventeenth-century military and economic transformation was strongly influenced by Dutch actors. Peter's frantic hiring of Dutch naval experts in the wake of the Grand Embassy of 1697 and 1698 was the culmination of a long process, part of which was, for example, his father's great admiration of Dutch army drill: A Dutch manual for military exercise, a version of Jakob de Gheyn's *Wapenhandelinghe* (1607), became the first secular book printed (in 1,200 copies) in Russia in 1647.[28] The publication of this book coincided with the arrival in Russia of a group of experienced officers from the Dutch Republic, led by Isaac van Bockhoven, who trained the Russian cavalry and infantry according to the Dutch innovations in warfare as depicted in De Gheyn's pictures.[29] Throughout the seventeenth century, shipments of weapons arrived at the port of Arkhangel'sk on Dutch vessels. The evidence for the Dutch role in the Russia's military modernisation can be readily adduced, even if it has been underplayed in the historiography.

In addition, the general (European-wide, or even global-wide) waning of the Dutch predominance in military affairs can be nowhere more clearly charted as in Russia, where a disappointed Peter the Great grudgingly turned away from the maritime *hegemon* he had so fervently admired in his formative years. A final pertinent reason to home in on the Dutch influence in Russia is that it has probably had the longest lasting effect on world history, given Russia's subsequent rise to prominence. Without the vast importation of Dutch arms, the establishment of manufacturing and mining industries by A.D. Vinius, Lus Tieleman A(c)kema sr, or Peter Marselis sr, the use of Jacob de Gheyn's work, the constant stream of strategic and other information provided by Dutch merchants, the Van Bockhovens' pivotal role in modernising the army, or the building of the sailship the Eagle *(Oryol)*, Russia might never have become one of Europe's five Great Powers and, subsequently, one of the world's two superpowers.[30] The Russian example will be compared with some crucial episodes out of Sweden's and Denmark's seventeenth-century history in which a kindred Dutch role appears evident.

To contextualise the Dutch-infused Russian rise, the role of the Dutch as conduits of military modernisation (i.e., as arms traders or military experts) in other parts of the world will be outlined in the chapters before those on northern Europe. Because seventeenth-century maps made in Europe still contained some blank spaces (such as much of the African interior, the Amazon region, Australia, Central Asia, and Siberia), Dutch firearms might have been few and Dutch soldiers or sailors entirely absent in those remote parts. But the world known to the Europeans showed a marked presence of Dutch people or the merchandise in which they traded. Usually, they pursued the goal of turning a profit through the sale of arms or the application of their military expertise, while they frequently reinforced their exploring and trading by military means.[31]

The following pages will often home in on individuals who may serve as outstanding exemplars of the Dutch militaristic mindset and activity of the age, such as Koenraad van Klenck (and some of his business partners and relatives), Andries Denijszoon Winius (Vinius), some of the many scions of the De Moucheron, Marselis, De Geer, De Vogelaer, or Trip dynasties, or the Van Bockhoven clan of mercenary officers. But besides those fabulously successful people, I will also revisit the revealing example of Jan Struys and his companions (and their one-time *sputnik* Ludvig Fabricius, who was a military officer), a motley crowd who hailed from Amsterdam and its environs. These typical Dutch sailors, I suggest, displayed bold pluck by embarking for the tsar's realm in the late 1660s, offering their skills as shipwrights and armed sailors to the Muscovite sovereign. They knew how to exploit their scarce skill, which was in part at least military, by selling it to a high bidder.[32] Both Dutch navy and army rewarded deserving non-commissioned officers (subalterns) with commissions: The military offered a way to wealth and a higher status, another sign how traditional customs and ways of thinking about rigidly cordoned-off estates made way for a more capitalist mode, in which rare skill commanded higher rewards.[33] Struys's and others' success was more modest, but their achievements are undeniable.

But the table is first set by an outline of Dutch history since the later Middle Ages. The question why the Dutch were so successful in turning a desperately embattled situation into a roaring capitalist economy is the central topic of the first three chapters. Across much of Dutch society, a mentality was forged that was as entrepreneurial as it was ruthless. A keen awareness spread that, up to a point, benefits derived from a collective endeavour towards freedom and prosperity, which informed the development of a national identity. But the Dutch had no qualms if this came at the expense of others.

The swift creation of the Dutch overseas empire and the Republic's emergence as a Great Power was not merely due to a ruthless search for personal profit or commercial opportunity, for which a remarkable group of enterprising individuals with sophisticated mercantile training and business insight harnessed the Dutch state and found willing participants in the inhabitants of the United Provinces. It was perhaps equally due to great expertise at soldiering, the art of war and everything that should contribute to the operation of a sophisticated army and navy. In some ways, the first four generations of the house of Orange-Nassau were central to this phenomenon. Their military feats became part of the early modern Dutch collective identity, emblematic of its martial spirit that led to the country's paramountcy. It is again not wholly coincidental that the decline of the Republic as a military power and as a militarised bastion in the eighteenth century witnessed a concomitant decline in the ability (or even sheer presence) of the stadtholders and their extended family as military commanders. In order to understand the Dutch rise as military paragons of Europe and the world, this dynasty's role and activities will be a focal part of the following story as well.

Notes

1. Tilly, "War Making," 169.
2. See especially its eighth chapter: Lenin, *Imperialism*.
3. Maarten Prak makes an intriguing case in suggesting that modern societies have moved further away from urban communities' self-determination (see Prak, *Citizens Without Nations*). The towndwellers of Holland likely experienced a decline in the say they had over their government during the 200-year history of the Republic, during which the urban elite—the

regents—closed itself ever further off from its fellow citizens, becoming an oligarchy in the process. Some of the seventeenth-century conflicts between guilds and regents seem to express this growing gap. The Old Regime in the Republic began to be challenged in a coherent and sustained fashion only in the later 1700s (see Schama, *Patriots*). In his dissertation, Rudolf Dekker charted the rare popular revolts that befell the United Provinces in the seventeenth and eighteenth centuries (Dekker, *Holland in Beroering*). Despite Dekker's earnest efforts to depict the country as a much more restless place that suggested previously by the historiography, the incidence and intensity of Dutch rebellions pales in comparison with the frequency and character of the violence recorded in domestic uprisings elsewhere in Europe between 1600 and 1789. Of course, the period from 1566 to 1578 in the northern Netherlands was an exception to this normal social tranquility, when in the north a sort of civil war prevailed; this remained the case for a while after for some of the borderlands of the United Provinces (such as Groningen or Twente).

4. These words, for example, can be found in an unexpected place, a book on Rembrandt's art: "[Around 1626] . . . the art-lover Alphonse Lopez. Lopez had made a journey to Holland in the service of the French king [Louis XIII], in order to negotiate the acquisitions of munitions, cannons, and large ships" (Van de Wetering, *Rembrandt*, 63).
5. Hoff, "Foreword," 7. In his Preface to this publication, the avid Dutch weapons collector H.L. Visser speaks of "an important and heretofore neglected part of . . . Dutch history," (Visser, "Preface," 9).
6. To be fair, that was sometimes because scholars focussed on a different topic, through which the arms trade or arms production only tangentially became part of the discussion (see, e.g., Amburger, *Die Familie Marselis*, 96–7). Werner Sombart, as Amburger notes, firmly established the link between the arms industry and early capitalism first (ibid., 96; see Sombart, *Der Moderne Kapitalismus*, fifth ed., vol. 2, 798–9, 881–2).
7. For some recent examples of (nuanced) sea-hero veneration, see Prud'homme van Reine, *Rechterhand*; idem, *Schittering en schandaal*; idem, *Admiraal Zilvervloot*. It is worth noticing that, until very recently, the Dutch have been unable to face their more recent colonial past dispassionately (see Limpach, *De brandende kampongs*).
8. See for Manning's lucid discussion of the organisation behind the 1688 landing at Torbay, Manning, *An Apprenticeship*, 360.
9. De Jong, "Dutch Entrepreneurs," 36–7.
10. Glete, *War and the State*; Parker, *Military Revolution*; Ralston, *Importing the European Army*; Parker, *Dutch Revolt*. Linked with the innovations in the training and battlefield deployment of infantry, some attention has been paid to the diffusion of Jacob (Jacques) de Gheyn II (1565–1629)'s endeavours; for more on him, see Filedt Kok, "Jacques II de Gheyn-I"; idem, "Jacques II de Gheyn-II"; Swan, *Art, Science and Witchcraft*. See De Gheyn, *Wapenhandelinghe*; see as well www.kb.nl/en/themes/book-history/more-special-books/exercise-of-arms. On the significance of De Gheyn's work, see, too, Feld, "Middle-Class Society," 423–5, 429.
11. Duindam, "Geschiedschrijving," 458.
12. See Wallerstein, *Modern World System*, vol. 2, 54. Looking at a rather different topic, Elizabeth Clare Edwards agrees that this was the "zenith of the Golden Age" (see Edwards, "Amsterdam and William III," 35–6).
13. See Grant, *Rulers*; Duindam, "Geschiedschrijving"; 't Hart, "From the Eighty Years War"; 't Hart, *Dutch Wars*; Brandon, *War*. See as well Swart,

Krijgsvolk; De Jong, "*Staat van Oorlog*; Van Nimwegen, *Dutch Army*. For a more general overview that takes the long view, see Paul, ed., *War*.

14. Vanvugt, *Roofstaat*. Vanvugt notes a slew of contemporary critics who during various periods criticised Dutch rule overseas such as Multatuli (Eduard Douwes Dekker [1820–1887], from whom Vanvugt borrowed the title of his book), or Anton de Kom (1898–1945) and Henk Sneevliet (1883–1942). They, however, always remained a very small minority, mostly ignored by the Dutch public. For a more solidly scholarly treatment of the complications of mixed marriages, racism, gender and so forth in the early modern European world, see Blussé, *Bitter Bonds*. See also another critical account by a non-Dutch historian: Reid, *Southeast Asia*, 2 vols.
15. Vanvugt, *Roofstaat*; Vanvugt reminds of Howard Zinn in his effort to sober up the Dutch and others who are drunk on their magnificent past (see Zinn, *People's History*).
16. In terms of hypocrisy, it seems telling how both the Dutch and English prohibited slavery inside their own countries, but had no qualms about dealing in, or owning, slaves outside Europe. Shame about the ruthless exploitation of fellow men and women therefore did exist (an analysis following Norbert Elias may be illuminating in understanding this peculiar phenomenon, as I suggest elsewhere in these pages; see Elias, *History*). Even if Giles Milton's point is correct regarding the wicked operations of the Dutch in the Indonesian Archipelago, to contrast them with innocently naïve Englishmen reeks too much of modern-day English nationalism (Milton, *Nathaniel's Nutmeg*). For the Dutch in Asia the standard, probably, is Marcus Vink's work, and, for the Dutch role in slavery and the slave trade in Africa and the Americas, that of Postma and Emmer: see Vink, "Freedom and Slavery"; Postma, *Dutch in the Atlantic Slave Trade*; Emmer, *Nederlandse slavenhandel*. Earlier worthwhile scholarly accounts can be encountered in Van Leur, *Indonesian Trade and Society*; Van Lier, *Samenleving*.
17. For a recent take on Coen, see Van Goor, *Jan Pieterszoon Coen*. Coen's life as already exhaustively documented a long while ago (see Colenbrander and Koolhaas, eds, *Jan Pieterszoon Coen*, 7 vols). The Danish historian Lauridsen, for example, mentions the De Geers, Trips, Marselises, and Sautijns (for the Mediterranean), the De Willems (Denmark), Van der Stratens (Mediterranean) as well as Humphrey Bradley and Jan Hoeufft in France (Lauridsen, *Marselis Konsortiet*, 8). Whereas the Dutch West India Company (GWC/WIC) paid out dividends in the late 1620s (not in the least thanks to the capture of the Spanish Silver Fleet in the Bay of Matanzas in 1628), it was most of the time hemorrhaging money, incapable of maintaining a navy and army (in Brazil or North America) without contracting huge debts. Still, this provided an economic stimulus: Twenty-four thousand troops were fielded in Brazil in the 1630s, and 800 ships crewed by 67,000 men served the company in this era (Snapper, *Oorlogsinvloeden*, 77). The building and supplying of this force and employment in the WIC will have stimulated the Dutch domestic economy (perhaps as much as, or more than, the VOC in this era, see ibid., 78).
18. Nef, "War"; John, "War." "[There is a type of] marketing . . . that attempts to influence [politics] to increase the demand for public goods provided by private firms [and t]his is especially true of the armaments industry, which has a vested interest in creating and expanding the demand for weaponry" (Shaffer, "Peace, War and the Market," 641). See also Kaempfert, "War and Technology." The idea that capitalism develops because of warfare goes at least back to Werner Sombart, as I noted in an earlier footnote (see as well

Sombart, *Krieg und Kapitalismus*). Meanwhile, Nef's thesis was to some degree falsified for the Republic (or Holland) by Frits Snapper (see Snapper, *Oorlogsinvloeden*). Snapper overly focussed on trade alone; by ignoring the economic role of manufacturing, the significant number of Dutch soldiers fighting in the Republic's armies, Dutch mercenaries and military experts employed abroad, or Dutch sailors who fought many a battle in declared or undeclared wars, his assessment of the significance of warfare in nurturing the Dutch economic boom and comparative prosperity was far from comprehensive. But he did argue persuasively that Dutch trade between 1580 and 1610 strongly benefitted from the country being at war, and that, for example, the port of Rotterdam began to outstrip Dordrecht and Delft because it was a harbour linked to the war effort (it was the location of one of the admiralties from 1576 onward; see Snapper, *Oorlogsinvloeden*, 48, 50).

19. In a sense, this debate has been reopened as well by Scheidel's work (see Scheidel, *Great Leveler*).
20. John, "War," 329. Although a war of attrition in a sense, this attrition affected the Spaniards far more than the Dutch.
21. Roberts, "Military Revolution"; Glete, *War and the State*, 141, 143, 161; Van Nimwegen, *Deser landen crijchsvolck*; Parker, "The Limits"; Parker, *Military Revolution*; Parker, rev. of *Krijgsvolk* by Swart.
22. Werner Hahlweg, "Aspekte und Probleme," 164. Hahlweg's *magnum opus* was Hahlweg, *Die Heeresreform*, which seems to have become a sort of casualty of the Second World War; long forgotten, it enjoyed a revival after it was republished in 1987. See, too, Van Nimwegen, "Het Staatse leger," 495. I am not sure whether I agree with Van Nimwegen's point that there hardly was a "Military Revolution" around 1600 (or only so in a tactical sense) but instead perhaps rather around 1670 (ibid., 496–501; he especially emphasises as key the far larger size of the armies as well as the demise of the military enterprisers). What strikes me as most significant is not only how the Dutch proved capable of constantly financing an absurdly large army (at least 60,000 in actual strength in the field during the first half of the seventeenth century, bankrolled by a country of two million) but that the country's economy produced vast quantities of arms at the same time with which to supply it. Beyond the 60,000, thousands served on the fleet as well, of course (with the merchant marine and navy not always clearly separated), or in auxiliary units (such as *schutters* and *waardgelders*). This was a "nation in arms," fighting a total war not unlike the belligerents of the First World War. The new martial mindset was so deeply ingrained that it allowed the Republic to be constantly at war from its early days until 1713, for five generations. And the skill at waging war (and surviving or winning war) was so highly appreciated elsewhere that the Republic exported its arms and expertise in astonishing numbers. It is no coincidence that Glete compared Sweden, Prussia, and the Republic in his work on the early modern fiscal military states, for they are the prime examples of how great military skill, an eye for innovation, and economic-financial *nous* could combine to make previously insignificant fringe areas in Europe into Great Powers (see Glete, *War and the State*). Each did it in their own way, and in the Dutch and Swedish cases, dominance did not last all that long (whereas Prussia made a comeback after it was almost destroyed by Napoleon), but each found the formula that was best suited to its conditions, bossing far larger states around. Those states were often forced to copy parts of the formula in order to surpass those pioneers; indeed, the admiration for Prussian-German military organisation and skill has only recently faded.
23. Hahlweg, "Aspekte und Probleme," 161.

24. See Boterbloem, *Fiction and Reality*, 42–52, 69–70, 178. For an excellent outline of the innovations introduced by Maurice, William Louis, and John of Nassau, see Feld, "Middle-Class Society," 425–7.
25. See Boterbloem, *Moderniser of Russia*.
26. For more on the numerous northern wars as such, see Frost, *Northern Wars*; idem, *After the Deluge*; as well as Davies, *God's Playground*, vol. 1; Brian Davies, *Warfare, State*; Belkin Stevens, *Russia's Wars*; Hellie, *Enserfment*.
27. Although Fuhrmann has written on the Tula works (see Fuhrmann, *Origins*), there is very little written in English about the Dutch role in making Russia a significant producer of arms and a Great Power. An exception is Esper, "Military Self-Sufficiency." In Dutch, Jan-Willem Veluwenkamp has written a few small pieces, notably Veluwenkamp, "De Nederlandse wapenhandel," and occasionally turns to this topic in Veluwenkamp, *Archangel*. Jarmo Kotilaine intermittently addresses these topics as well, see Kotilaine, "When the Twain"; idem, *Russia's Foreign Trade*; idem, "In Defense of the Realm."
28. De Gheyn, *Wapenhandelinghe*, which became [Wallhausen,] *Uchenie i khitrost'*; see Driessen-van het Reve, *De Kunstkamera*, 28; Kurskov, *Vedushchee napravlenie*, 110; Malov, *Moskovskie vybornye polki*, 55, 288; Hosking, *Russia and the Russians*, 154; the first English translation was De Gheyn, *Exercise of Armes*. See, too, Reger, "In the Service," 144–54.
29. Even though Brian Davies suggests that De Gheyn (and Wallhausen's version of it) had become outdated by that time, given the developments during the Thirty Years' War (Davies, *Warfare*, 136).
30. On the information provided by Karel du Moulin, Jurriaan van Klenck, Isaac Massa, Peter Marselis, and others, see Waugh and Maier, "Muscovy," 84–6, 89–90. See later in the chapter on Russia for Van Keller's and Witsen's roles in this.
31. Even if Dutch writers and researchers in particular, such as Olfert Dapper (Africa) or Nicolaas Witsen (Siberia) began to describe these regions (see below).
32. One should be careful in generalising an attitude such as Struys's (who ended his life a rather well-off man), but it is just as dubious to proffer that "sailors' ambitions were modest" (Klooster, *Dutch Moment*, 126). Undoubtedly, many spent their wages faster than they earned them, but many clearly looked further ahead and tried to save their money, and so forth, as Klooster himself indicates (ibid., 126–7).
33. Manning, *Apprenticeship*, 34.

Bibliography

Amburger, E. *Die Familie Marselis*, Gießen: Wilhelm Schmitz, 1957.

Belkin Stevens, Carol. *Russia's Wars of Emergence, 1460–1730*, London: Routledge, 2007.

Blussé, L.J. *Bitter Bonds*, Princeton, NJ: Markus Wiener, 2009.

Boterbloem, K. *The Fiction and Reality of Jan Struys: A Seventeenth-Century Dutch Globetrotter, Houndmills*, Basingstoke: Palgrave, 2008.

———. *Moderniser of Russia: Andrei Vinius, 1641–1716*, London: Palgrave, 2013.

Brandon, Pepijn. *War, Capital and the Dutch State (1588–1795)*, Leiden: Brill, 2015.

Colenbrander, H.T., and W.P. Koolhaas, eds. *Jan Pieterszoon Coen, bescheiden omtrent zijn bedrijf in Nederlandsch Indië*, 7 vols., Den Haag: Nijhoff, 1919–1953.

Davies, Brian. *Warfare, State and Society on the Black Sea Steppe, 1500–1700*, London: Routledge, 2007.
Davies, Norman. *God's Playground*, vol. 1, New York: Columbia University Press, 1979.
Dekker, R. *Holland in beroering*, Baarn: Amro, 1982.
Driessen-van het Reve, J.J. *De Kunstkamera van Peter de Grote*, Hilversum: Verloren, 2006.
Duindam, Jeroen. "Geschiedschrijving en oorlogvoering: de metamorfose van een klassiek genre," *Bijdragen en Mededelingen betreffende de Geschiedenis der Nederlanden* 4, 2003, 455–66.
Edwards, E.C. "Amsterdam and William III: The Role of Influence, Interest and Patronage on Policy-Making in the Dutch Republic, 1672–84," unpublished PhD diss., University College London, 1998.
Elias, Norbert. *The History of Manners*, Oxford: Blackwell, 1994.
Emmer, P.C. *De Nederlandse slavenhandel*, Amsterdam: Arbeiderspers, 2000.
Esper, Thomas. "Military Self-Sufficiency in Muscovite Russia," *Slavic Review* 2, 1969, 185–208.
Feld, M.D. "Middle-Class Society and the Rise of Military Professionalism, the Dutch Army 1589–1609," *Armed Forces and Society* 4, 1975, 419–42.
Filedt Kok, J.P. "Jacques II de Gheyn: Engraver, Designer and Publisher-I," *Print Quarterly* 3, 1990a, 248–81.
———. "Jacques II de Gheyn: Engraver, Designer and Publisher-II: A Catalogue," *Print Quarterly* 4, 1990b, 370–96.
Frost, Robert. *After the Deluge*, Cambridge: Cambridge University Press, 2004.
———. *The Northern Wars: War, State and Society in Northeastern Europe, 1558–1721*, Harlow: Longman, 2000.
Fuhrmann, Joseph T. *The Origins of Capitalism in Russia*, Chicago, IL: Quadrangle Books, 1972.
Gheyn, J. de. *The Exercise of Armes for Caliures, Muskettes, and Pikes*, The Hague: n.p., 1608.
———. *Wapenhandelinghe van roers, musquetten ende spiessen*, 's Gravenhage: n.p., 1607.
———, available at: www.kb.nl/en/themes/book-history/more-special-books/exercise-of-arms, accessed 11 June 2019.
Glete, Jan. *War and the State in Early Modern Europe*, New York: Routledge, 2002.
Goor, Jur van. *Jan Pieterszoon Coen (1587–1629). Koopman-koning in Azië*, Leiden: Brill, 2015.
Grant, Jonathan. *Rulers, Guns and Money: The Global Arms Trade in the Age of Imperialism*, Cambridge, MA: Harvard University Press, 2007.
Hahlweg, Werner. "Aspekte und Probleme der Reform des niederländischen Kriegswesens under Prinz Moritz von Oranien," *Bijdragen en Mededelingen van het Historisch Genootschap* 86, 1971, 161–77.
———. *Die Heeresreform der Oranier und die Antike*, Berlin: Junker und Dunnhaupt Verlag, 1941.
Hart, Marjolein 't. "From the Eighty Years War to the Second World War: New Perspectives on the Economic Effects of War," *Tijdschrift voor Sociale en Economische Geschiedenis* 2, 2014a, 261–79.
———. *The Dutch Wars of Independence: Warfare and Commerce in the Netherlands, 1570–1680*, London: Routledge, 2014b.

Hellie, Richard. *Enserfment and Military Change in Muscovy*, Chicago, IL: University of Chicago Press, 1971.

Hoff, Arne. "Foreword," in E. Yablonskaya et al., eds, *Dutch Guns in Russia*, Amsterdam and Zwolle: Rijksmuseum and Waanders, 1996, 7.

Hosking, G. *Russia and the Russians*, Cambridge, MA: Harvard University Press, 2001.

John, A.H. "War and the English Economy," *English Historical Review* 3, 1955, 329–44.

Jong, M. de. "Dutch Entrepreneurs in the Swedish Crown in Copper and Iron, 1580–1630," in Hanno Brand, ed., *Trade, Diplomacy and Cultural Change*, Hilversum: Verloren, 2005a, 36–57.

———. "*Staat van Oorlog*," Hilversum: Verloren, 2005b.

Kaempfert, W. "War and Technology," *The American Journal of Sociology* 4, 1941, 431–44.

Klooster, Wim. *The Dutch Moment: War, Trade and Settlement in the Seventeenth-Century Atlantic World*, Ithaca, NY: Cornell University Press, 2016.

Kotilaine, J. "In Defense of the Realm: Russian Arms Trade and Production in the Seventeenth and Early Eighteenth Century," in M. Poe and E. Lohr, eds, *Military and Society in Russia*, Leiden: Brill, 2002, 67–95.

———. *Russia's Foreign Trade and Economic Expansion in the Seventeenth Century*, Leiden: Brill, 2005.

———. "When the Twain Did Meet: Foreign Merchants and Russia's Economic Expansion in the Seventeenth Century," unpublished PhD diss., Harvard University, 2000.

Kurskov, Iu. *Vedushchee napravlenie obshchestvennoi mysli i proekty gosudarstvennykh preobrazovanii Rossii 40–60-kh godov XVII veka*, Chita: Gosizdat, 1973.

Lauridsen, John T. *Marselis Konsortiet: En Studie over Forholdet Mellem Handelskapital og Kongemagt i 1600-Tallets Danmark*, Arhus: Jysk Selskab for Historie, 1987.

Lenin, V.I. *Imperialism, the Highest Stage of Capitalism*, Petrograd, 1917, available at: www.marxists.org/archive/lenin/works/1916/imp-hsc/ch08.htm, accessed 8 May 2017.

Leur, J.C. van. *Indonesian Trade and Society*, Den Haag: Van Hoeve, 1967.

Lier, R.A. van. *Samenleving in een grensgebied*, Den Haag: Nijhoff, 1949.

Limpach, Rémy. *De brandende kampongs van Generaal Spoor*, Amsterdam: Boom, 2016.

Malov, A.V. *Moskovskie vybornye polki soldatskogo stroia v nachal'nyi period svoei istorii 1656–1671 gg*, Moscow: Drevlekhranilishche, 2006.

Manning, Roger B. *An Apprenticeship in Arms: The Origins of the British Army, 1585–1702*, Oxford: Oxford University Press, 2006.

Milton, Giles. *Nathaniel's Nutmeg*, London: Picador, 1999.

Nef, John U. "War and Economic Progress," *English Historical Review* 1–2, 1942, 13–38.

Nimwegen, O. van. *Deser landen crijchsvolck*, Amsterdam: Bert Bakker, 2006.

———. "Het Staatse leger en de militaire revolutie van de vroegmoderne tijd," *Bijdragen en Mededelingen betreffende de Geschiedenis der Nederlanden* 4, 2003, 494–518.

———. *The Dutch Army and the Military Revolutions, 1588–1688*, London: Boydell Press, 2010.

Parker, Geoffrey. "Review of *Krijgsvolk: Militaire professionalisering en het ontstaan van het Staatse leger, 1568–1590* by Erik Swart," *Journal of Military History* 4, 2007, 1225–7.
———. *The Dutch Revolt*, London: Allen Lane, 1977.
———. "The Limits to Revolutions in Military Affairs: Maurice of Nassau, the Battle of Nieuwpoort (1600), and the Legacy," *Journal of Military History* 2, 2007, 331–72.
———. *The Military Revolution: Military Innovation and the Rise of the West, 1500–1800*, 2nd ed., Cambridge: Cambridge University Press, 1996.
Paul, Jeff-Lynn, ed. *War, Entrepreneurs and the State in Europe and the Mediterranean, 1300–1800*, Leiden: Brill, 2014.
Postma, Johannes. *The Dutch in the Atlantic Slave Trade, 1600–1815*, Cambridge: Cambridge University Press, 2008.
Prak, M. *Citizens Without Nations: Urban Citizenship in Europe and the World, c. 1000–1789*, Cambridge: Cambridge University Press, 2018.
Prud'homme van Reine, R. *Admiraal Zilvervloot*, Amsterdam: Arbeiderspers, 2003.
———. *Rechterhand van Nederland*, Amsterdam: Arbeiderspers, 1996.
———. *Schittering en schandaal: Biografie van Maerten en Cornelis Tromp*, Amsterdam: Arbeiderspers, 2001.
Ralston, David. *Importing the European Army: The Introduction of European Military Techniques and Institutions into the Extra-European World, 1600–1914*, Chicago, IL: University of Chicago Press, 1990.
Reger, W.M. "In the Service of the Tsar: European Mercenary Officers and the Reception of Military Reform in Russia, 1654–1667," unpublished PhD diss., University of Illinois at Urbana-Champaign, 1997.
Reid, Anthony. *Southeast Asia in the Age of Commerce*, 2 vols., New Haven, CT: Yale University Press, 1988–93.
Roberts, M. "The Military Revolution (1560–1660)," in M. Roberts, ed., *Essays in Swedish History*, London: Weidenfeld and Nicholson, 1967, 193–225.
Schama, S. *Patriots and Liberators*, New York: Knopf, 1977.
Scheidel, Walter. *Great Leveler: Violence and the History of Inequality from the Stone Age to the Twenty-First Century*, Princeton, NJ: Princeton University Press, 2017.
Shaffer, Edward H. "Peace, War and the Market," *The Canadian Journal of Economics/Revue canadienne d'Economique* 29 [Special Issue: Part 2], 1996, 639–43.
Snapper, F. *Oorlogsinvloeden op de overzeese handel van Holland, 1551–1719*, Amsterdam: Ellerman Harms, 1959.
Sombart, Werner. *Der moderne Kapitalismus*, vol. 2: Das europäischen Wirtschaftsleben im Zeitalter des Frühkapitalismus, 5th ed., München and Leipzig: Duncker and Humblot, 1922.
———. *Krieg und Kapitalismus*, München: Ducker and Humblot, 1913.
Swan, Claudia. *Art, Science and Witchcraft in Early Modern Holland*, Cambridge: Cambridge University Press, 2005.
Swart, Erik. *Krijgsvolk: Militaire professionalisering en het ontstaan van het Staatse leger, 1568–1590*, Amsterdam: Amsterdam University Press, 2006.
Tilly, C. "War Making and State Making as Organized Crime," in Peter B. Evans, Dietrich Rueschemeyer, and Theda Skocpol, eds, *Bringing the State Back in*, Cambridge: Cambridge University Press, 1985, 169–91.

Vanvugt, E. *Roofstaat*, Amsterdam: Nijgh and Van Ditmar, 2016.

Veluwenkamp, J.W. *Archangel: Nederlandse ondernemers in Rusland, 1550–1785*, Amsterdam: Balans, 2000.

———. "De Nederlandse wapenhandel op Rusland in de zeventiende eeuw," *Armamentaria* 31, 1996, 71–6.

Vink, Marcus P.M. "Freedom and Slavery: The Dutch Republic, the VOC World, and the Debate over the World's 'Oldest Trade,'" *South African Historical Journal* 1, 2007, 19–46.

Visser, H.L. "Preface: The History of this Catalogue," in E. Yablonskaya et al., eds, *Dutch Guns in Russia*, Amsterdam and Zwolle: Rijksmuseum and Waanders, 1996, 8–9.

Wallhausen, Johann Jacobi von. *Uchenie i khitrost' ratnogo stroeniia pekhotnykh liudei*, Moscow: Moskovskii pechatnyi dvor, 1647.

Wallerstein, I. *The Modern World System*, vol. 2, rev. ed., Berkeley, CA: University of California Press, 2011.

Waugh, Daniel, and I. Maier. "Muscovy and the European Information Revolution," in Simon Franklin and Katherine Bowers, eds, *Information and Empire: Mechanisms of Communication in Russia, 1600–1850*, Cambridge: OpenBook Publishers, 2017, 78–112.

Wetering, Ernst van de. *Rembrandt: The Painter Thinking*, Amsterdam: Amsterdam University Press, 2016.

Zinn, Howard. *A People's History of the United States*, New York: Harper, 2005.

1 War in the Low Countries, 1566–1713

Beginnings, Victories, Glory

"*Maak van de nood een deugd*"
("Make a virtue out of necessity")
Old Dutch saying

The Netherlands, Erik Swart writes, were used to war as the normal state of being long before the outbreak of their Eighty Years' War in 1566; as elsewhere in Europe,

> War was seen as inevitable in the sixteenth century. Observers during those days considered this to be the consequence of the ambition of the princes and nobility, for whom war meant glory and fame, and of the nature of human beings as political animals. Such views were framed into cyclical theories, which showed how war and peace continually interchanged.[1]

The violent conflict that began in 1566, however, proved to be relentless, linear rather than cyclical.[2] It was to stop only for a fairly brief hiatus in 1609, after which it resumed in 1621. By the time of the Peace of Münster (the Dutch-Spanish part of what is more commonly known as the Peace of Westphalia) in 1648, no one in the Low Countries knew otherwise than having lived in a region that had been constantly at war. Even during the twelve-year armistice, Dutch soldiers and sailors still engaged in armed clashes overseas, and the Dutch almost immediately began to pay substantial subsidies to the Protestant forces in the Thirty Years' War after its outbreak in 1618. And 1648 did not mean enduring peace. A number of wars at sea or overseas with various European rivals marked the 1650s. Meanwhile, fighting occurred outside Europe with local and European foes between 1640 and 1662.

The 1660s saw various violent conflicts: The Dutch lost Taiwan in 1661 to the Chinese warlord *Koxinga* (Zheng Chenggong) and New Amsterdam to the English in 1664 (even if by 1667 Surinam was received in exchange from the British). This decade saw fighting along the West

African coast, eventually yielding the Dutch their most notorious slave station, at Elmina (there were others). In Indonesia, the Dutch engaged in a ruthless expedition to Makassar on Sulawesi. In the mid-1660s, Münster's bishop Bernhard von Galen (1606–1678) briefly invaded Dutch territory, a move he repeated in 1672 when he allied with France and England as well as Cologne. That latter war, which almost led to a comprehensive Dutch defeat (at least on land), ended in 1678. A few years of uneasy peace followed, but ominous clouds began to pack when the Catholic James II became king of England in 1685, in which year Louis XIV issued the Edict of Fontainebleau, ending the last vestige of tolerance of Protestants in France. Another round of war began with William III's successful invasion of England in the fall of 1688, which came to a definitive close only in 1713 at the Peace of Utrecht. Throughout the conflict with Louis XIV's France, fighting occurred between French ships and Dutch bottoms on the oceans and along their shores, while a completely unrelated but equally lengthy war was waged on Java.

In addition, the Dutch contributed money to the precarious survival of the Protestant cause in in the first half of the Thirty Years' War, while Dutch soldiers and sailors were sometimes recruited with the explicit help of the Dutch government by foreign-government agents for the Swedes, Danes, or Russians. They were just as often recruited by foreign recruiters without permission from the Dutch government. Dutch sailors and soldiers fought on ships in the Mediterranean Sea, the South China Sea, or the Baltic Sea, as well as along the shores of these seas, or in Ireland. And Dutch-produced arms were found across Europe, the Americas, Africa, and Asia, shipped from the Republic's ports and sold by covetous Dutch merchants.

1.1 Warfare and the Arms Trade in the Low Countries Before 1600

While Dutch skill at warfare at sea or shipping commodities on water might seem unsurprising for a people living along a lengthy seashore, it is less obvious why the Dutch excelled at the art of war on land or the production of weapons, introducing within a brief period a slew of improvements in "small arms, artillery, siegecraft and fortifications, [and improved] drill, tactics and logistics."[3] Roots of this development can be traced to various parts of especially French-speaking Wallonia (the southeast and east of what is now Belgium) in the later Middle Ages. At that point, small-scale local suppliers (such as blacksmiths) could no longer sufficiently meet the demand of armies that used an increasingly diverse assortment of arms. Rudimentary or all-round skill was no longer adequate once ever more sophisticated weaponry was required, such as cannons or arquebuses, instead of swords, shields, longbows, or crossbows. Using the iron ore and coal mined in this region, a more complex division of labour emerged in response. The virtually autonomous territory of Liège (ruled by a prince-bishop whose suzerain was the Holy Roman Emperor) and the Mons and Namur regions to its south-west became in the fifteenth century centres of iron and lead mining and firearms manufacturing (using blast furnaces), while the demand for mercenaries from these territories in the south of the Netherlands concomitantly increased.[4] The production of gunpowder (out of charcoal, sulphur, and saltpetre) had taken flight in the late Middle Ages, too, with the Burgundian-controlled Flemish port of Bruges pivotal because of its access to overseas supply routes of the raw materials necessary for its production.[5]

The Walloon skill at forging arms cast a long shadow, still leaving an imprint on the Dutch Republic. Walloon skilled arms manufacturers moved to the United Provinces not just as Calvinist refugees in the 1570s or 1580s, but also long thereafter, in search of lucrative opportunities in the north. From the 1610s onward, the Liège-region native Louys de Geer favoured hiring Walloon experts for his Swedish plants, as did contemporary Dutch arms producers in Russia. They were put on the payroll in Amsterdam, a popular market to hire labour of all sorts.[6]

Towards 1500, the trade of arms between the Low Countries and other parts of the Empire was stimulated by the ever intensifying trading between urbanised Flanders and its eastern hinterland. The Walloon arms industry and mercenary profession received a boost from the election as Holy Roman Emperor (in 1519) of Charles V (1500–1558), who had been born in Flemish Ghent and who was to spend his life mainly on the battlefield.[7] Already Charles campaigned with significant numbers of Walloons among his elite fighting units of *tercios*.

There was a broader economic context within which the Walloon arms industry and mercenary profession developed. In the later Middle Ages, the various regions of the Low Countries increasingly grew complementary in economic terms, with metal products of the Walloon region or Flemish cloth first shipped from Flemish Bruges and then from Brabantine Antwerp overseas. All of the Netherlands had since the High Middle Ages been part of the northern end of what economic historians have dubbed the "Blue Banana," the part of Europe that stretched from the delta of the Rhine and Meuse rivers in the north to Florence in the south, a stretch of land distinguished by a specific economic profile.[8] This region had a comparatively high population density, a significant number of towns, and a high degree of trade and artisan activity. While trade and manufacturing flourished in the sixteenth century, agricultural specialisation emerged in Flanders, stimulated by sufficiently high demand from the urban population. This has led historians to suggest that the "Agricultural Revolution" that overtook England in the eighteenth century occurred even earlier in the Low Countries. In the less developed and populated northern maritime provinces (Zeeland, Holland, and Friesland), other key developments that prepared the ground for the later boom can be traced to the late Middle Ages, as in the herring fishery, or the ever greater share Amsterdam shippers acquired in transporting Baltic (primarily Polish-Lithuanian) grain to the markets of Western Europe. By 1500, Amsterdam, albeit still a small town, survived on Baltic rather than Netherlandic grain for its bread and beer.

Rivers such as the Rhine, Meuse, or Scheldt were navigable for long stretches, as were many smaller streams, and the coastline was lengthy. This made trade and communication between the various provinces often easier than elsewhere in Eurasia, and although flooding (of the sea and of rivers) was a threat in most parts, the natural environment of the region was comparatively friendly: There were no mountain passes to traverse or extreme temperatures threatening to ruin crop cultivation, for instance. Shared social and economic traits and certain common legal traditions informed a political effort to forge closer ties between the provinces. This effort truly began with the Burgundian duke Charles the Bold's (r. 1467–1477) strategy to resurrect a sort of Lotharian monarchy (a recreation of one of Charlemagne's grandsons' kingdoms) located in the borderlands between the Holy Roman Empire and France. The Emperor Charles V, his great-grandson, brought under his control all 17 provinces that made up the Low Countries, the northernmost part of Charles the Bold's imagined realm.

The move towards a unified polity was underlined when, after 1550, Charles V began to reflect on the division of his vast empire among his heirs. Charles wanted to preserve his recently created "Burgundian Circle" intact, linking their continued prosperity to maintaining the common government he had begun to set up. Despite hindsight efforts from Dutch historians such as Pieter Geyl (1887–1966) to argue for the historical unity of this area, the Low Countries had, however, little in common culturally or historically, even if the provinces were all Christian, or uniformly Catholic before 1517, and even if there was a certain geographic logic to their organisation as a unified polity.[9]

In his multiple roles as emperor, king, duke, or count, Charles V had not been able to exert control over his disparate territories in the manner that he would have liked. He never had sufficient time to reorganise at least one of his many lands into a coherent political entity, whether Spain, his German lands, his Italian possessions, or the Low Countries. To a considerable degree, this was due to the enormous distance between those parts in an age of horses. But his failure at accomplishing any meaningful political unification of the Netherlands, or of the other geographically linked and culturally affiliated territories of which he was formally the overlord, was to a significant degree due to his incessant preoccupation with warfare. He poured his energy into fighting his foes but proved unable to defeat any of his major enemies definitively, despite the vast resources he could command, such as the gold and (growing supply of) silver of the Americas, or the mercantile wealth of the Low Countries, as exemplified by the bustling port of Antwerp. He battled endlessly and inconclusively with the king of France, the German Protestant princes, the Turkish sultan and his allies, mostly on land, sometimes at sea.[10] In the Low Countries, he defeated Duke Charles of Guelders (1467–1538), but it took Emperor Charles long enough to overcome even this minor player opposing him, and this conflict sapped Charles V's strength further.

Towards the end of his life, Charles V concluded that it was best to divide up his realm between the lands located around the old Habsburg core in Austria (which now included both the kingdom of Bohemia and the rather truncated kingdom of Hungary), possessions supporting the perennial Habsburg claim to the throne of the Holy Roman Empire, and the Spanish or western Mediterranean part, which was to include the Americas. In making this division, however, the Low Countries—historically largely a part of the Empire, but closely linked to the bustling long-distance Spanish and Portuguese trade—were difficult to apportion: It probably would have been better if Charles had identified a third heir, next to his brother Ferdinand and his son Philip, to succeed him in the Burgundian Circle, which at the time still included the Free County (Franche-Comté) of Burgundy, located to the south of the Low Countries. A ruler who from Brussels (the city in which gathered the Estates-General, the meeting of representatives of all the seventeen provincial estates) exerted full sovereignty over this realm might have been able to stave off the calamity that began to unfold in the Low Countries in the middle of the 1560s. There may not have been much of a common past that the seventeen provinces shared, but there may have been a common future, if Charles had chosen differently in bestowing his empire on his successors.

In the end, Charles decided to add the Low Countries and the Free County to the share he bequeathed to his son Philip II. This, unfortunately as it turned out, did not solve the problem of ruling parts of Europe that were geographically very far apart, which had plagued Charles's rule and contributed to his failed efforts in destroying any of his main opponents. The poor state of communications of the age (not in the least the prohibitive distance from the Iberian peninsula to the Netherlands) that had already frustrated Charles V was in a considerable degree to contribute to the loss of the northern Netherlands by Philip II. The split between north and south was nonetheless not a foregone conclusion, and an interminable war was to be fought before in 1648; finally, Philip II's descendant Philip IV (r. 1621–1665) was willing to surrender his sovereignty over the northern Low Countries. As much as the rebels in the northern Netherlands began to identify their foe as "Spanish" by the 1570s, as little was Philip II considered a foreigner when he succeeded his father in the 1550s.[11] He ruled the Low Countries without encountering much opposition for a decade. But Philip, in his younger years a warrior-king like his father, chose, after the victory over the French at St. Quentin in 1557 (and a concomitant bankruptcy!) and the subsequent Treaty of

Cateau-Cambrésis of 1559, to reside almost exclusively in Castile and never personally saw his north-west European territories again. From Madrid (and the nearby Escorial), he tried to control his vast empire but proved in many respects even less successful than his father in commanding the obedience of his lands' inhabitants.

Solidly Catholic Spain with its pronounced martial (indeed somewhat archaic) culture appealed to Philip. Spanish (Castilian) was his first language. In Sevilla, the silver fleet arrived from the Americas every year. And vividly embedded in the collective memory of Spain was the centuries-long *Reconquista* on the Muslims, which now might see a new glorious chapter in chasing the Ottoman sultan from his territories along the shores of the Mediterranean Sea. Philip's campaigns against the sultan were seen as crusades, but he could never win this contest with the Ottomans, who stood at the height of their power in the sixteenth century. Even the resounding victory in the sea battle of Lepanto in 1571 did not dislodge the Ottomans from any of their territories. And the warfare with the Turks and their allies was a continual drain on the Spanish treasury. For Philip, it would have been better to accept the stalemate with the Ottoman sultan that had ensued after the failed Turkish siege of Vienna in 1529 and refrain from costly adventures in the eastern Mediterranean or North Africa.

In hindsight, it appears obvious that Philip made a mistake in choosing Castile as his sole base. While Geoffrey Parker rightly debunks the image of Philip II as a "prudent" king, however, Philip's behaviour or world-view was by no means out of step with his times.[12] That his choice to reside in Spain was wrong is much easier to identify for us today than for Philip, who still thought to live in a heroic, medieval, world, where sword and honour still counted, and who almost seems a precursor to Miguel de Cervantes's *Don Quixote* of 1605.[13] The martial mindset of the Dutch, too, was both an enduring legacy of the violent medieval world and a response to an equally violent contemporary environment.

Seen from today's vantage point, though, Philip II would have been wiser to choose his headquarters to be in the wealthy Low Countries. There much of the wealth of the Americas ended up, fuelling a burgeoning "European world economy," the early capitalism of which Antwerp was the hub before 1585. If Philip had chosen Brussels rather than Madrid as his capital, the Netherlandic nobles might never have dared to throw down the gauntlet, as they did in 1566 before his half-sister, Margaret of Parma (1522–1583). He might have been able to deal much more effectively with the then suddenly erupting Calvinist movement. Lutheranism in the Low Countries had hardly flourished in Charles V's reign, while Anabaptism had been largely suppressed, to a considerable degree because Charles had paid these matters personal attention. Philip's church reform (inspired by the Council of Trent, held from 1545 to 1563) might have been easier to implement if he had been present in the region to enforce it. And by personally visiting the provincial estates and the most important towns, he might have been able to raise taxes without causing a rebellion. With money thereby raised, he could have avoided some of his bankruptcies and fielded an army that might have capitalised on the chaos that enveloped France after 1559.

Philip II might even have become a popular sovereign in the mould of his contemporaries Henri IV of France (1553–1610) or Elizabeth I of England (1533–1603). Of course, he was, at least in Castile. The popularity of Charles V before him, and William of Orange after him, proved that the Netherlands were far from solely populated by diehard republicans, and the Habsburg monarchy might have survived in all of the Netherlands if Philip had preferred Brussels over Madrid. Much of the stubborn unity of the northern Netherlands was forged in opposition to a remote "*koning van Hispaniën*," who became a hateful, alien figure after his departure in 1559.

In the king's absence, the nobles of the seventeen provinces, who had been firmly loyal when Philip moved among them in the 1550s, became restless and defiant. They chafed at what seemed to be an effort by the king's deputies to increase his power by centralising his administration and supporting a reorganisation of the Catholic church that was firmly subordinated to Philip. As elsewhere in Europe, conflict erupted between a monarch with absolutist ambitions and an aristocracy jealous of its traditional independence.[14] The town population of the Netherlands harboured a long-standing tradition of challenging overbearing and impecunious sovereigns, but its rebellions had been mostly in vain (as the harsh treatment of revolting Ghent showed in 1539, for example), lacking outside support. An alliance between local nobles and towns would be hard to suppress, however, as Philip found out.

The arms manufacturing and iron-ore mining industry of the bishopric of Liège and other French-speaking areas nearby in ever greater quantities supplied the armies of Europe with state-of-the-art weapons after 1500. This region remained important far into the seventeenth century, as did the Rhineland (such as Solingen and its environs), both linked to the province of Holland thanks to the navigable rivers Rhine and Meuse. The waterways allowed finished arms or materials out of which weapons were made to be shipped in bulk from both Wallonia and the Rhineland to the Republic. In the seventeenth century, many arms arrived as half-products only to be assembled and finished in the Republic.

After 1566, the maritime provinces (Holland and Zeeland as well as Flanders and Brabant) witnessed swift developments in shipbuilding, while the Flemish and Dutch skill at naval warfare (whether authorised or not by sovereigns with letters of marque) acquired increasing fame in the second half of the sixteenth century.[15] All these developments combined to create an extraordinarily fertile environment for the increasing technological sophistication and expertise in the production and use of arms that were to make the Dutch Republic a pivotal centre of the international arms trade and a locus of military know-how as well as a popular recruiting ground for officers (for land and naval forces), soldiers, and sailors after 1600.

The burgeoning demand for Walloon mercenaries after 1500 was linked to these soldiers' knowledge about the use of the more sophisticated arms that were produced in their neighbourhood. The very fact that the region of what is now eastern Belgium, north-eastern France, Luxembourg, and the southern Rhineland was a permanent battlefield encouraged some of the local population to make the best of a bad situation and exploit the opportunities this constant state of war offered. Walloon mercenaries continued to be hired by many military campaigns but in the Dutch Revolt began to be joined by increasing numbers of Flemish and northern Dutch soldiers.[16] Even though Walloons were popular on the battlefields of the Low Countries, some soldiers who earned their stripes there hailed from England, Scotland, Ireland, France, the Holy Roman Empire, or, indeed, Switzerland, as was the Genevan François Lefort (1656–1699), who gained experience in the Dutch war with France in the 1670s, on which he managed to cash in once in Russia.[17] Some served as soldiers, others served as officers. Among the latter was Henri de la Tour d'Auvergne (1611–1675), the viscount of Turenne, who gained his first experience at the side of his relative Prince Frederick Henry of Orange-Nassau (1583–1647) at the siege of 's-Hertogenbosch in 1629.[18] He went to become marshal of France and almost vanquished the Republic's land forces in 1672.

Vogel depicts the outcome of all these developments by the middle of the 1650s:

> The Republic was, in addition, a suitable market for the recruitment of troops. Numerous foreign princes received special permission to recruit soldiers for their military operations. Of course, there was an extra advantage to raising troops in the Netherlands because they could be completely equipped and armed with products of the Dutch armaments industry. Once assembled and equipped, the troops could be immediately dispatched to the war theatre that they were destined for.[19]

1.2 War and Peace

As for almost all Europeans in the seventeenth century, war was the normal state of being for the Dutch. Oddly, however, for them it became the source of their affluence as well. Thomas Hobbes's notorious aphorism that life was "nasty, brutish and short," remained nevertheless true for most Dutch men and women, even if warfare was only one cause of this, next to the impact of harsh climatic conditions, malnutrition, diseases, and a dreadful state of healthcare.[20] Although battles were becoming bloodier and armies increased in size towards 1700, while civilians continued to be targetted, war was still not the sort of massacre that became all too familiar in the twentieth century. More often than not for civilians, the greatest problem of warfare was roaming soldiers on campaign, who not merely plundered, beat, raped, and killed people but also spread disease. The population of the northern Netherlands, different from their southern Netherlandic neighbours, managed to avoid the impact of such marauding for a lengthy spell (from the 1590s to 1672, and then again after 1675), which explains in part how they thrived in the midst of this permanent state of war.

Still, young Dutch-born men (and women who worked in the train of the armies) answered the beat of the tocsin in significant numbers and joined the land army (often fighting shoulder-to-shoulder with soldiers of fortune from a welter of regions) and fought at sea with even greater alacrity. Their military outlook on life explains in some measure the prominent role and sometimes quasi-monarchical mystique of the stadtholders (who personally commanded their troops in the field), while the almost perpetual state of war explains the—often overlooked—continued importance of the Dutch nobility, who frequently served as army officers.[21]

Dutch genius in martial matters was found more in such scarce expertise required of a military officer or engineer in seventeenth-century armies than in providing cannon fodder as regular soldiers. Even at sea (where the nobility hardly played any role), Dutch-born sailors were joined by natives from the Holy Roman Empire and Scandinavia in manning the warships, with the Dutch frequently occupying a more privileged position in the on-board hierarchy than their foreign comrades.

Most economic and cultural historians who marvel at the Dutch Republic's prominence have underplayed the effect of the constant state of war in which the country was embroiled from its genesis in the 1560s to the Peace of Utrecht of 1713.[22] Tellingly, this 1713 treaty ushered in several decades of peace (even if some skirmishes in which the Dutch were involved were recorded outside Europe) that served to hasten the Republic's decline towards a secondary political (and eventually economic) status within the Concert of Europe.[23] Previous to 1713, though, the Republic had done rather well waging war: Not only did it win many an epic battle on land and at sea it even succeeded in landing more than 20,000 troops at Torbay in November 1688, undoubtedly one of the most successful amphibious operations in history.[24]

In this era, the record of the Dutch in matters military, in fact, is stunning. The Eighty Years' War against the mighty Spanish empire (stretching from the Iberian peninsula and Italy to Mexico, Peru, and the Philippines) looked like a lost cause at its onset in the 1560s, especially after *El Duque* D'Alba (Alva, 1507–1582) led his Army of Flanders into the Low Countries in 1567. Somehow the Dutch managed to defy this reputedly invincible military and stall its progress in the early 1570s. Eventually, they not only pushed the Spaniards back from the northern Netherlands but also captured a number of their overseas properties from Brazil to the East Indies while bankrolling the Protestants in the Thirty Years' War who were at war with the Central European branch of the Habsburg family. Having checked the Habsburgs, the Dutch faced the combined forces of German bishops and the kings of England and France in 1672 but survived this onslaught as well. All this fighting made the Low Countries a "school of war," as Cardinal Bentivoglio called it, where one might observe the most advanced ways of waging war with infantry soldiers on the battlefield, in (withstanding) sieges, or in sea battles.[25] A marine corps was founded in the 1660s Republic. Weapons were modernised, firepower increased and became more precise, and mortars and field cannon as well as bayonets were introduced on a wide scale. Combat became more lethal as a result.

In 1667, the Dutch navy commanded by Michiel de Ruyter (1607–1676; accompanied by Cornelis de Witt [1623–1672], the brother of the Dutch political leader Johan) sailed up the Thames, broke the chain hanging across the river at Chatham, and hauled off the English flagship, the *Royal Charles*. After taking a heavy drubbing in Africa, North America, and the Caribbean in the immediately preceding years, the Dutch sought and found revenge on the English and appeared at the pinnacle of their power, economically and militarily, in 1667 when the Treaty of Breda was signed.[26] Overconfidence, though, may have seeped in: The country let itself be surprised by the coalition of the kings of Britain and France and the bishops of Cologne and Münster in 1672. Johan de Witt's pro-French policies had failed to prevent this terrifying alignment of enemies, while the *raadspensionaris* had not prepared his country's defence adequately to face a concomitant assault on land and at sea (even though it is questionable whether anyone could have done so). He was blamed for this calamity and together with his brother Cornelis brutally murdered in the streets of The Hague in the summer of 1672. Astonishingly, the Republic defied the odds and managed to deflect the foreign attack, both on land and at sea. Luck was part of the story, but good fortune alone cannot adequately explain this escape. Pushing back an enemy coalition that could draw on the resources of a combined population that was more than ten times as large, this was testimony to the Republic's lingering military strength, economic power, improving skills and adaptability, and staunch collective resolve. A few more rounds were to be fought before Dutch power faded.

In 1672, with war seeming inevitable, in the province of Holland all men between 18 and 60 were called to arms.[27] An astonishing two thirds of them was expected to arm themselves with a musket or similar type of firearm *(vuurroer)*, whereas the remainder had to use pikes, and all needed to equip themselves with sidearms. Evidently, several hundreds of thousands of firearms were available for this purpose. This seems the equivalent of the call up of a modern conscription army. As Van Deursen wrote in his microcosmic study of a village in Holland, "[The village of] Graft temporarily became a militarily organized society, in which everyone took their place in the ranks."[28] Although few troops called up in this part of the country saw combat on land in the 1670s, warfare did leave a sorrowful imprint on this region's villages, for a good number of men served and died in the navy.[29] Meanwhile, the Dutch land army showed its mettle against the French in a variety of clashes. The willingness to fight was as strong then as it had been at the beginning of the Dutch independence war a century earlier.[30]

The Republic recovered and restored its military reputation for another generation after 1672: Redoubling its efforts, under the command of stadtholder William III as the chief strategist, Louis XIV was kept in check. Until 1700, Dutch military expertise continued to be highly valued, from shipbuilding and sailing to fortification-construction. The Danish king in the mid-1670s was as eager to recruit Dutch sailors and officers for his cause as Tsar Aleksei Mikhailovich was in 1667 and 1668, or his son Peter the Great seemed to be in 1697 and 1698 (even if Peter preferred to hire Dutch craftsmen and sailors above gunsmiths or soldiers).

It seems to us no surprise that the Dutch regents welcomed peace in 1713 after almost five generations of warfare that had beset their country, but this was as much due to financial considerations as to a desire for peace in Christendom or war fatigue. Fighting caught up with the Dutch where it mattered, hitting them in their pocket: The continual state of war had not merely begun to drain the state's coffers, but Dutch entrepreneurs, military officers, and many in the labouring underclasses of town and country no longer benefitted from perpetual warfare as much as they had before.[31] Certainly, warfare itself had become more costly, for the more sophisticated technology used in battle was more expensive, while the increasing mortality of soldiers and sailors in combat depleted ranks and officers more quickly. Replacements took longer to train, risk of injury or death for the warriors increased. Having developed a much more diversified and maturing economy, investments were spread, concomitantly; to place one's money into peaceful economic pursuits became more common among the affluent Dutch. Many had bought stock in a VOC (*Vereenigde Oostindische Compagnie*, the East India Company) that began to consolidate rather than expand towards 1700 but at least yielded often enough dividends, as did government bonds, especially of Dutch debt. A government default did, however, appear more plausible, and was not an attractive prospect for such share-holders, who were soon treated to the implosion of the Mississippi Bubble and the collapse of the South Sea Bubble that wrecked the French and British investment climate. Nonetheless, being at war rather than at peace had been the normal state of being for the Dutch. The prospect of a prolonged peace must have been somehow daunting.

Despite their stockmarket troubles, the British surge that originated in Cromwell's days left the Dutch ever more emphatically behind, while the Dutch investment in impregnable but woefully costly border fortresses in Belgium against future French encroachments was probably not the best method to stop French expansionism after 1713. Indeed, it was a strategy that looked backward at the fighting of a previous age, in which city walls had been almost unbreachable, as they still had been at Vienna in 1683. It shows how the Dutch were no longer at the cutting edge of military invention, as they had been a century earlier in the days of Maurice of Orange-Nassau and his relatives and, at least at sea, still a generation later, during the heyday of the famous admirals such as Maarten Tromp (1598–1653) or Michiel de Ruyter. Outside of Europe, too, Johan Maurits van Nassau-Siegen (1604–1679) or Rijckloff van Goens sr (1619–1682) had not found successors who could boast of comprehensive victories over sometimes formidable enemies, from Brazil to Sri Lanka.[32] The last great Dutch inventor of military technology was Menno van Coehoorn, the Dutch answer to Sébastien Le Prestre de Vauban (1633–1707) as a genius of fortress-building.[33] Van Coehoorn received the mathematical grounding for his work as an army engineer in his native Friesland, indicative of the diffusion of the systematic study of fortification that went back to Simon Stevin and the year 1600, when for the first time military engineering courses were taught at Leyden University.[34] Van Coehoorn, though, was a versatile thinker, who built as well on the ideas of Vauban's disciples, some of whom moved to the Republic after the 1678 Nijmegen peace, and his own experience at sieges in the previous war, both as defender and as attacker.[35]

On the battlefield, the last great commander was William III, who died in 1702, and who, rather symbolically, had exchanged the Republic for Britain. The great military-industrial businessmen who had made their mark around 1630 such as the Trips, the Marselises, Andries Winius, or Louys de Geer found few counterparts after 1700. The alleged disappointment of Peter the Great in 1697 about the obsolete manner in which the Dutch built their ships is revealing in this respect. After about a century being in the ascendancy, the Dutch military advantage had disappeared. Soon after, its prolonged economic *hausse* irrevocably ended. By 1800, few remembered how the Seven Provinces had ruled the Seven Seas, or how Dutch officers, shipbuilders, and engineers had modernised European warfare. And even fewer recalled that some of the origins of Swedish or Russian manufacturing of modern arms could be traced to the activities of a bunch of ruthless, innovative, and querulous Dutch entrepreneurs.

The Dutch themselves suffered from a sort of collective amnesia regarding their seventeenth-century economic hegemony and military proficiency until, from about 1970 onward, especially foreign scholars rekindled the interest in the Republic as a locus of modern capitalism, the modern middle class, and the Western or capitalist mindset. But few concentrated on the link between Dutch prosperity or riches and the large-scale manufacturing and selling of weapons, the diffusion of Dutch cutting-edge expertise regarding the building of well-nigh impregnable fortresses, the efficient use of firearms of the battlefield, the creation of a marine corps, or the building and navigating of state-of-the-art warships.

1.3 Orange-Nassau Glory

Not unlike the subsequent success of Great Britain as a capitalist world power, "the selfish interests of political and commercial classes" fused in a felicitous manner in the Dutch case.[36] Next to the quantum leap of business *nous* and success that occurred in the late sixteenth-century northern Netherlands, a remarkably successful noble dynasty, that of the Orange-Nassaus, burst onto the scene. As the country's military and political chiefs, they spent for generations the wealth channelled into the Dutch state's coffers, which bankrolled the army and the navy that fought for independence and then maintained it forcefully.

The Oranges clearly started out (and maintained a good amount of this outlook until 1702) as traditional warrior chiefs, representatives of the second of the three estates into which society had been divided in the Middle Ages, whose *raison d'être* was warfare. Such a bellicose outlook was shared by many in their retinue, scions of the lesser or lower nobility of the Low Countries (and often from elsewhere) who threw their lot in with the Orange-Nassaus.

For a republic, Dutch national pride contained a remarkable amount of deferent loyalty to the Orange-Nassau dynasty. Such deference was undoubtedly a legacy of the more traditional, medieval, view of society, but it was, of course, not automatic. If it had been, Orange-Nassaus would never have replaced Habsburgs in Dutch hearts. And it was not unconditional: Orange-Nassau pre-eminence was twice in serious jeopardy, from 1650 to 1672 and again after 1702.

In the first decades of the Dutch revolt against Habsburg rule (1560s–1590s), the Dutch aristocracy led by William the Silent and his relatives concluded a happy marriage with the traditionally equally prominent towndwellers in the region and, especially, the urban merchants and entrepreneurs.[37] Beginning in the 1590s, both groups firmed up their alliance in their involvement in the Dutch imperial project and eagerly capitalised on the opportunity to manipulate the affairs of many parts of Europe. For the Orange-Nassau clan, the cause for which they fought was a combination of Protestantism, noble freedom, and family prestige, whereas for the urban elite, business usually came before religion, but there was sufficient common ground to maintain the alliance. And both parties developed a sentimental attachment to the Republic.

Oranges and regents fell out with each other on several occasions but never fully broke off their pact (at least not before 1702). Dutch ascendancy in Europe was brief, but nevertheless yielded the house of Orange a royal crown, a substantial prize for a family who in the 1560s seemed to have rather more in common with average Italian *condottieri* than with royal houses. Concomitantly, many scions of the Dutch elite gained a wealth that was unprecedented in history (and for some, such as the Marselises or De Geers, it came with a noble title). Warrior chiefs (that is army and naval officers) and merchants could be clearly distinguished from each other in the sixteenth century but had blended into a largely unified elite towards 1700, with many aristocratic families becoming extinct (not in the least through their continued engagement in warfare), their estates either bequeathed to the Oranges or bought up by the gentrifying merchants.[38] Some nobles even entered on their own the world of business, such as the Van Klencks, who had started as noble retainers in the Nassau household in Germany but ended up among the wealthiest tycoons of Amsterdam in the Dutch Golden Age. For Jurriaan (George) van Klenck (c. 1581–1643), or his son Koenraad (1628–1691), the business of war (which saw them both engaged in delivering arms to Muscovy on a grand scale) was perhaps not much of a stretch, given their aristocratic ancestry. Other merchants, bereft of such forefathers, involved themselves in the arms trade for the sheer profits it promised, sometimes enticed through their friends and relatives in a network or clan, as did the champion of the "True Freedom," the stadtholderless age from 1650 to 1672, Pieter de la Court (1618–1685). A Leyden cloth merchant, he seems to have eagerly participated in the international arms trade of his in-laws, the Van der Voorts, who delivered arms for hundreds of thousands of guilders to the province of Holland during the 1660s.[39] And in large merchant families (such as the Witsens), younger sons often took an army commission. While this appealed to their aristocratic aspirations, acquiring an army commission was often the result of a desire for monetary gain. Such posts combined military with business skill, for troops were equipped and fed by their officers (who were remitted by government paymasters).[40]

Businessmen (and women) and common folk as well as nobles rallied behind the house of Orange-Nassau. While William I became the Father of the Fatherland, it was the resolute military leadership of his sons Maurice and Frederick Henry that cemented this relationship. In 1672, the Orange myth was strong enough to return William III to Holland's stadtholderate. His death in 1702 diminished the popularity of the Oranges, but fond memories of them lingered long enough in local lore to welcome them back as Dutch monarchs in 1813.

More than a hundred years ago, the great Dutch historian Pieter Geyl wrote that "Maurice's name resounded throughout Europe [and t]he fame of the Dutch warriors was no less great."[41] Since Geyl's words, historians have frequently enough reiterated Maurice's merits as military innovator, but the appreciation of his significance has become more nuanced. It is clear that he did not operate in a vacuum, and others next to him played important roles as well. In this vein, about a decade ago, Erik Swart restored Prince William I of Orange-Nassau's reputation as a skilful military commander of the Dutch rebels between 1568 and 1584.[42] Previously, the historiography had criticised William I for his responsibility for a number of painful defeats on the battlefield, such as at Heiligerlee in 1568 and the Mookerhei in 1574, and the sort of general retreat of his military northward before the armies of Don Juan and Parma around 1580. Swart suggested, however, that Maurice, William's second son,[43] and William Louis, his nephew, had not been true pioneers in their efforts to improve the way in which their military fought, but followed in the footsteps of William I. They were, in fact, part of a tradition of the House of Orange-Nassau as open-minded and bold military chiefs that spanned across several generations, from the last third of the sixteenth century until the early 1700s.

The Nassaus were undoubtedly a family of considerable military talent, even if its exact scope will remain a matter of debate. William Louis's brother, Johan (VII) von Nassau-Siegen (1561–1623), founded in 1616 the first modern military academy in Siegen (in today's Germany) in 1616. He was the father of the most accomplished Dutch field commander after Frederick Henry's death (1647), Johann Moritz (Johan Maurits) von (van) Nassau-Siegen, the one-time governor of Brazil. An older son of Johann VII, Johann Ernst (1582–1617), served as a commanding officer in the Venetian army (leading several thousands of Dutch mercenaries whom he had hired as a military enterpriser) in the Uskok War against the Austrian Habsburgs, where he died of disease in 1617; his brother Wilhelm (1592–1642) survived this campaign, eventually dying of wounds sustained fighting the Spaniards in the Republic.[44] The French Marshal Turenne, the formidable foe of 1672, was a grandson of William the Silent as well.

Turenne learned his trade as an officer at the side of Maurice's successor as stadtholder of the majority of the United Provinces, Frederick Henry (Maurice's half-brother), who was an equally famous general in his day.[45] Frederick Henry's reputation was such that he received the nickname of "*de Stedendwinger*," ["the forcer of towns"] for his deftness at capturing towns in sieges. Frederick Henry's martial abilities may have been a tad exaggerated by contemporary and later boosters of the Orange-Nassau cause, for, like his father or half-brother, he did not really inflict any decisive blow on his Spanish opponents. The Dutch printing presses, art, and architecture were all harnessed on his behalf, becoming a fine propaganda machine that trumpetted his martial accomplishments wide and far. Frederick Henry aimed at elevation in status, seeking to become more of a true sovereign rather than the mere chief administrator and supreme military commander of the United Provinces that he actually remained. His son, William II, may have harboured similar ambitions and was something of a martinet, but he was stadtholder of Holland and Zeeland for too short a time to display any great military talent. His rash actions in the few short years that he was stadtholder seriously undermined the carefully cultivated prestige of his dynasty in the Republic and left Holland's stadtholderate vacant until 1672. Frederick Henry's grandson, William III, still saw himself as much as a military commander as a political leader.[46] Of all Oranges, William III won the greatest military victory in 1688, which yielded him the English, Irish, and Scottish thrones in 1689.

William II's cousin Willem Frederik (1613–1654), stadtholder of Friesland and Groningen, wrote diaries that reflect the Nassau attitude towards the Republic, which in some ways foreshadows the idea that they were "first servants of the state," as Peter the Great or Frederick the Great of Prussia were to think of themselves. The crucial difference was that in the Republic the Nassaus (both the senior branch and the cadet branch in the north) never were monarchs, unlike the Russian and Prussian rulers.[47] With the exception of William II, the stadtholders understood that they needed to tread carefully so as not to arouse the regents against them.

As traditional aristocrats, the Nassaus had initially sought military glory. Nobles from the central parts of the Holy Roman Empire, such as the sixteenth-century counts of Nassau or the contemporary rulers of the principality of Orange in what is now southern France, were members of the second estate, whose task in life had been to fight since times immemorial. When William I became heir to both the Nassau and Orange inheritance, and entered the court of the Emperor Charles V, he, like most of his peers, could expect a future of political rule and military combat, for both of which he had been previously groomed, as a high-ranking member of his sovereign's retinue. At first, he loyally honed his military skills further at the side of the emperor and his son Philip, who succeeded his father in 1556 as ruler of the seventeen provinces that Charles had united under his rule by the 1540s.

Had William the Silent not thrown in his lot with the Dutch rebels in the 1560s, he and his descendants might very well have become the sort of *condottieri* that would later roam Central Europe during the Thirty Years' War, such as Ernst von Mansfeld (1580–1626).[48] But perhaps this became unlikely once his rather humble patrimony of Nassau was significantly augmented after he became, somewhat felicitously, prince of Orange, succeeding his cousin René de Châlon (1519–1544) as such. The 11-year-old page was all of a sudden a ranking nobleman, something akin to being a peer of the realm in England. Indeed, the small principality of Orange along the Rhône, although still formally part of the

Holy Roman Empire, was considered an independent state. Young William also inherited a number of territories in the Low Countries, which explains why he was eventually considered a "Dutch" noble. Charles V stood as regent over most of William's territories in the seventeen provinces until he came of age, and Prince William was weaned from his originally Lutheran upbringing under the auspices of Charles's sister Mary of Hungary (1505–1558), the regent of the Low Countries on Charles's behalf in the 1540s.

Having groomed the prince of Orange as a warrior, Charles V had William command a detachment of the Habsburg army by the mid-1550s. In the ceremonial proceedings that involved Charles's abdication in 1555, William stood at his side, a sign of his high status. Initially, Philip II favoured William as well, which is evident from his appointment of the prince of Orange as stadtholder of Holland, Zeeland, and Utrecht in 1559.[49] But William of Orange began to resent the advisors on whom Philip's governor Margaret of Parma relied, believing that the voice of the natural leaders of the Low Countries, the native nobility (which he joined by choice rather than through his ancestry), was ignored. The conflict that arose between the cardinal de Granvelle (Antoine Perrenot, 1517–1586) and his allies, on the one hand, and William of Orange and his allies, on the other, was caused by the latter group's opposition to the centralising policies followed by Granvelle's circle, which was backed by Margaret and Philip II. As noted before, these included a church reorganisation inspired by the decisions of the Council of Trent. This reorganisation sought to exert better pastoral care over the Catholic population, which became a pressing issue due to the growing Calvinist movement in the Netherlands. William styled himself a Catholic in the early 1560s, but he was a sort of *politique*, as it was called in contemporary France, one of a tolerant kind that did not believe in religious persecution.[50]

Granvelle, meanwhile, as primate of the Dutch church province and cardinal, as well as the key political advisor of Margaret of Parma, seemed the ideal candidate to spearhead the political centralisation and enforce the religious orthodoxy desired by Philip II. Unfortunately, Granvelle's and Philip's strategy took far too little into account the culture and historical traditions and privileges to which the Netherlands had become accustomed. This was not just an economically advanced area of Europe but also one of cultural vibrancy and a relatively open and tolerant mindset. It was perhaps the genius of William of Orange that he recognised the strength of this culture and rose to its defence; at the same time, he seems to have genuinely been immersed in it himself. He proceeded to become the unrivalled leader of the rebellion because he subsequently knew how to combine political acumen with an incessant willingness to take to the field, taking up arms to defend the revolt and what it stood for against a formidable enemy. He remained stoic through the death of several of his brothers on the battlefield. And for this stamina, as well as for his political skill and military prowess, William became an iconic figure in the northern Netherlands even during his lifetime. Meanwhile, in fighting the Army of Flanders that took the field on behalf of Philip II, William became an innovative military leader, even if his military successes were paltry. His determination to defend his ideals to the bitter end steeled the resolve of the denizens of his adopted "fatherland" from the late 1560s onward. The almost saintly status William (who eventually was indeed nicknamed "Father of the Fatherland") acquired laid the groundwork for the great popularity of the Oranges among broad layers of Dutch society until 1702 (when the direct line of male descendants of William I ended with the death of William III) and beyond.

As soon as another prince of Orange took the reins, leading the Dutch armies into battle, this popularity was rekindled. When William I's brothers Adolf (1540–1568) fell at Heiligerlee and Lodewijk (1538–1574) and Hendrik (1550–1574) died on the Mookerheide in the early years of the struggle against Spain, their battlefield deaths were read as proof of the Nassaus' unwavering dedication to the Dutch cause (as did the murder of William I).[51] Even members of the cadet lines and illegitimate Nassaus aided the military aura surrounding the dynasty.[52] Ernst Casimir (1573–1632), the stadtholder of Frisia and Groningen, fell at the siege of Roermond, another martyr to the cause. At the time of his death, he had been a field marshal in the Dutch army for a quarter century. His son and successor Hendrik Casimir (1612–1640) was mortally wounded at a battle near Hulst. One of the last great generals of the Dutch field army was Henry of Nassau-Ouwerkerk (1640–1708), a grandson of Maurice, who fought at the battles of Ramillies and Oudenarde in the War of the Spanish Succession.

The Dutch never thought of themselves as a peace-loving people. Even in their largely invented tradition of Claudius Civilis, the Batavian commander who successfully rebelled against the Romans in the year 69 AD and in this struggle apparently forged the Dutch nation, war in the name of independence defined them. The Dutch aristocracy by no means died a quiet death in the Dutch Revolt.[53] Indeed, even if tempered by a civilisation process à la Norbert Elias (and the addition of a good number of parvenus, well-off burghers who bought a manor if not a title), nobles played their part in the Republic, and the noble tradition of military prowess lingered and was prevalent even far down among the lower reaches of society.[54]

William III, whose stadtholderate closes out the Dutch Golden Age, seems to have been most comfortable among noble retainers, not a few of whom were (bastard) relatives. Manning suggests,

> Focused as they were upon the military life and dedicated to the struggle against Louis XIV, this small coterie dominated the Orange

> court and officer corps, which still retained the reputation of being the best nursery of arms in Europe.[55]

It is from this perspective, too, intelligible why William III would have wanted to have Koenraad van Klenck, whose grandfather had been a noble retainer of the Nassaus at Wittenberg, join the Amsterdam City Council in 1672.[56]

William III was the last stadtholder of Holland (and most of the other provinces) of the direct line descending from William the Silent. He was also the last of the Orange-Nassaus to personally take the field.[57] Indeed, he was formally the admiral commanding the expedition that landed at Torbay in 1688, whose troops marched unopposed to London and made James II flee. William III's reign in England was brief, but his significance was large, larger than any of his direct predecessors or successors. And it was rooted in his military accomplishments. Focussing especially on the military aspect of this importance, Roger Manning notes how

> William III re-established contact between the military worlds of mainland Europe and the British Isles, fostered the growth of a fiscal-military state on the Dutch model and, through a shared military experience, presided over the emergence of a British state and an integrated army that went on to acquire great-power status.[58]

The Orange-Nassau dynasty, in sum, exemplified or symbolised for many of the Dutch population the martial image with which they identified. The stoic and unwavering comportment of William I, Maurice, Frederick Henry, and William III steeled their resolve in various times of crisis, enhanced morale on the battlefield, and informed their boldness in business. Clearly, as we will see again, reverence for the Oranges was part of early modern Dutch nationhood.

Notes

1. Swart, *Krijgsvolk*, 175. Ewald Vanvugt suggests likewise that the Dutch were well trained in the art of war before they set out on their overseas ventures (Vanvugt, *Roofstaat*, 34). See as well C. Schmidt, *Om de eer*, 19–20.
2. Parker, *Army of Flanders*.
3. Ricklefs, *War*, 20.
4. For a detailed study of cannon production in the late Burgundian era in Dutch, see Decuyper, "De Bourgondische artillerie"; Awty, "Development and Dissemination." Decuyper points out that in the era of Philip the Good and Charles the Bold (1417–1477), cannon manufacturers followed their clients around or settled in major towns that were traffic hubs because of the prohibitive cost of shipping artillery (Decuyper, "Bourgondische artillerie," 174). See also Singleton, "Arms Industry," 160; Amburger, *Die Familie*, 102–3; Goodman, "On the Progress," 494–506. Walloon mercenaries (then called "*stalbroeders*" in Dutch) already fought in the northern Netherlands in the late fifteenth century, see Janse, *De sprong van Jan*, 47–9.

Nonetheless, once the Dutch Revolt broke out, the Walloons became much more sought after, partially because of their skill with the arquebus; by 1570, William I of Orange-Nassau preferred them over German *Landsknechte*, who relied more on the pike (see Swart, *Krijgsvolk*, 144). It stands to reason to link the rise of the Walloons (who fought both of the side of Philip II and on those of the rebels) with the(ir exposure to/proximity to the) burgeoning arms manufacturing of these French-speaking parts of the Netherlands and the continual violence that engulfed their native region. The fighting in their native territory preceded the Dutch Revolt, for they lived in Burgundian-Habsburg territory on the border of the French kingdom of the Valois, opponents of the Habsburg-Burgundians since the fifteenth century.

5. Decuyper, "De Bourgondische artillerie," 195. Especially Rijssel (Lille) was an important centre of powdermaking for the Burgundian dukes.
6. Amburger, *Die Familie*, 102–4, 111–12.
7. In English, a new scholarly biography may be due, but see Alfred Kohler, *Karl V, 1500–1558*, Munich: C.H. Beck, 2001.
8. For more on this term, see Davids and Lucassen, "Introduction," 11–12.
9. Christians in the Low Countries were at the time critical of the misdeeds that plagued the Catholic Church and peculiar, as can be seen in the Modern Devotion or Erasmus, but heresy was relatively uncommon. After 1517, it was not so much Luther as Anabaptism that found an audience (which was harshly repressed, even if pockets of it survived). Geyl's key work in this regard was *De geschiedenis van de Nederlandsche stam*, in which he argued for the common historical and cultural heritage of a Dutch "tribe" *(stam)*, using a term that has become rather pejorative in contemporary Dutch; Geyl, however, was not some sort of ultranationalist in the Nazi style but much more of a liberal (see Geyl, *De geschiedenis van de Nederlandse stam*).
10. Apart from Kohler, *Karl V*, see Espinosa, "Grand Strategy."
11. Many biographies of Philip have been written, but Geoffrey Parker's is one of the most readable and compelling (see Parker, *Imprudent King*).
12. Parker, *Imprudent King*.
13. Cervantes Saavedra, *El Ingenioso Hidalgo*.
14. Charles V, too, had fought several campaigns in the Low Countries to reduce the independence of the Duke of Guelders, after all.
15. See Boxer, *Seaborne Empire*, 69.
16. See, for instance, Manning, *Apprenticeship*, 33.
17. On his curious arrival in the company of a motley crew of Dutch, Polish, and German soldiers of fortune at Arkhangel'sk in 1675, see Myshlaevskii, "Vyezd v Rosiiu Frantsa Leforta." In the late 1610s, both Louys de Geer (for the Swedish crown) and Albrecht von Wallenstein (for the Emperor) were recruiting in the Spanish Netherlands what appear to have been Walloon mercenaries (see De Geer van Jutfaas, *Lodewijk de Geer*, 20fn.4).
18. Bérenger, *Turenne*.
19. Vogel, "Arms Production," 198.
20. See Porter, *For the Greatest Benefit*; Van Deursen, *Plain Lives*, 238–9.
21. See Van Nierop, *Nobility of Holland*. On the stadtholders as commanders, see Swart, *Krijgsvolk*; Troost, *William III*. On the proportion of Dutch natives among those fighting on land and at sea among rank-and-file and officers, see also De Bruin (De Bruin, *Geheimhouding*, 107), who suggests that the soldiers were more often than not Dutch, perhaps more so than those serving in the navy; the land army's officers were possibly least Dutch. Van der Linde, though, suggests that many recruits for the stadtholder's regiments in Frisia and Groningen were born in the Holy Roman Empire (Van der Linde, *Das Leibregiment*, 272–4). But Van der Linde concentrates rather

on the eighteenth than the seventeenth century. In the only calculation he could make of the stadtholder's regiment for the seventeenth century, about half was a native of one of the Dutch provinces (see ibid., 285).

22. Norman Davies provides a good overview of the wars engulfing Europe from the 1648 Peace of Westphalia onward (see Davies, *Europe*, 1282–3). See also Brandon, *War*, 4.
23. On the significance of the peace, see Onnekink and De Bruin, *De vrede*.
24. One can agree with Jan Glete's astonishment at the concerted effort in the historiography to "minimis[e] the military and naval achievements of the Republic" (Glete, *War and the State*, 143). See, for a positive evaluation of the 1688 expedition, Manning, *Apprenticeship*, ix.
25. Bentivoglio, *Historicall Relations*, 35; Duindam, "Geschiedschrijving," 464.
26. Klooster, *Dutch Moment*, 101–6.
27. Van Deursen, *Een dorp*, 290.
28. Ibid. See as well (on the earlier mobilisation of 1629), ibid., 288.
29. Van Deursen, *Een dorp*, 291. See as well ibid., 288.
30. Snapper, *Oorlogsinvloeden*, 149.
31. One can quibble about the timing and reasons for Dutch decline, which at first was relative only to other countries and perhaps for a while more apparent than real, see Brandon, *War*, 264–5, or Israel, *Dutch Primacy*. Brandon does state something quite revealing about the Dutch decline (which he sees occurring after the middle of the eighteenth century), for "in contrast to France or Britain, where major attempts at financial and military reform preceded the age of revolutions and revolutionary war, it was the failure to instigate such reforms that radicalised Dutch opposition movements" (Brandon, *War*, 264). Note the key role military matters play in Brandon's view.
32. On Johan Maurits, see Van den Boogaart, ed., *Johan Maurits*. Van Goens sr, though, was equally active on Java, Sumatra, in India and on Sri Lanka. A recent look at Van Goens is to be found in Gommans, "South Asian Cosmopolitanism." And, of course, the dissertation by Erik Odegard that has been recently defended fills a gap, see Odegard, "Colonial Careers."
33. See Lynn, *Wars of Louis XIV*, 202, 223–6, 235, 248–9. In the Netherlands, even a foundation exists commemorating Van Coehoorn, but he is little known elsewhere. Two recent works on him are Reinstra, *Een veldheer*; Van Hoof, *Menno*. Van Hoof's article is a good summary of Van Coehoorn's activities as a fortification and siege expert (Van Hoof, "Nieuwe manieren"). See on his design for the Namur fortress, Manning, *Apprenticeship*, 408, 413.
34. Van Hoof, *Menno van Coehoorn*, 27.
35. See ibid., 28–30. There were still some very capable officers, of course, such as Godard van Reede (1644–1703), who signed the Treaty of Limerick in 1691 (see Manning, *Apprenticeship*, 372, 397).
36. Hobson, *Imperialism*, 196.
37. On the early Dutch (Republican) arms producers, see De Jong, "Militaire hervormingen," 485–92.
38. Two works are especially useful in charting the evolution of the Dutch nobility: Van Nierop, *Nobility of Holland*; Price, "Dutch Nobility." An enlightening set of case studies on this gentrification is Kuiper and Olde Meierink, *Buitenplaatsen*. Note as well how one scion of the modest Berkhout family, regents of the small towns of Hoorn and Monnickendam in northern Holland at the time of the Revolt's outbreak, by the late seventeenth century became ennobled in the Empire and married at Kensington Palace in 1694, symptomatic of this gentrification (see Schmidt, *Om de eer*, 78–9).
39. Kernkamp, ed., "Twee 'niet ter drukpersse bereide'," 158–60; Kernkamp, ed., "Brieven uit de correspondentie," 95–108.

40. Again, the Teding van Berckhouts fit the pattern as well, with a number of their clan serving in the army, navy or VOC in the seventeenth century, which contributed to the family's prestige as dutiful sons of the fatherland (see Schmidt, *Om de eer*, 39, 43, 75–6).
41. Geyl, *Christoforro Suriano*, 18.
42. See Swart, *Krijgsvolk*.
43. His older brother Filips Willem (1554–1618) had been taken hostage by Philip II, a captivity from which he was not to return.
44. He plays a prominent role in Geyl's doctoral dissertation, see Geyl, *Christoforro Suriano*. Johann Ernst had been mentored in the art of war by his uncle Willem Lodewijk (ibid., 15). Geyl admired the negotiation skills of Johann Ernst, who not only was to receive a high wage himself but also had the Venetians pay his troops a wage higher than enjoyed by contemporary Swiss mercenaries and made sure the Venetians rewarded him handsomely for the ships that transported the soldiers (see ibid., 20–2).
45. For one useful discussion, see Kunzle, *From Criminal*, 481–6.
46. See, too, Manning, "Prince Maurice's School," 12–13.
47. Frederik, *Gloria Parendi*.
48. Although there are indications that he may have been groomed to be a diplomat as well, as he was taught a number of foreign languages (besides his native German) when he resided in Brussels as a teenager.
49. This was not just because William was well liked; his uncle René de Châlon had been stadtholder of the same provinces. In other words, it was to a degree William's due.
50. A new biography has recently appeared in Dutch, in which William is depicted as an utterly scheming character who held few principles dearly and was especially interested in his own power (see Brouwer and Wouters, *Willem van Oranje*). William appears as a ruthless warrior, typical of the high nobility of his age. Compare the more balanced Swart, *Willem van Oranje*.
51. Certainly, Ludwig (Lodewijk) von Nassau enjoyed a fierce reputation as a fearless military commander during his life and posthumously; various others Nassaus fell on other battlefields in the later sixteenth and seventeenth centuries (see Broomhall and vanGent, *Gender*, 18–19, 215–17).
52. Broomhall and van Gent, *Gender*, 21, 26–7. See for the many bastard lines Dekker, *Observaties*, 135. Dekker notes how these families remained loyal retainers of the stadtholders.
53. Van Nierop, *Van Ridders*, 2nd ed.
54. Elias, *History*.
55. Manning, *Apprenticeship*, 352–3.
56. For a discussion of William III's favourites, see Troost, *Stadhouder-koning*, 105–8. See as well De Bruin, *Geheimhouding*, 347; Manning, *Apprenticeship*, 352–3.
57. "King William . . . saw himself as a soldier-king" (Manning, *Apprenticeship*, 401). See also ibid., 438: "Court and camp were indistinguishable in the Netherlands."
58. Manning, *Apprenticeship*, 346. Even if he was not the greatest of generals in the field (see ibid., 439).

Bibliography

Amburger, E. *Die Familie Marselis*, Gießen: Wilhelm Schmitz, 1957.

Awty, Brian G. "The Development and Dissemination of the Walloon Method of Ironworking," *Technology and Culture* 4, 2007, 783–803.

Bentivoglio, Cardinall. *Historicall Relations of the United Provinces and of Flanders*, trans. Henry, Earl of Monmouth, London: Humphrey Mosely, 1652.

Bérenger, Jean. *Turenne*, Paris: Fayard, 1987.

Boogaart, Ernst van den, ed., *Johan Maurits van Nassau-Siegen*, Den Haag: Nijhoff, 1979.

Boxer, C.R. *The Dutch Seaborne Empire*, London: Hutchison, 1965.

Brandon, Pepijn. *War, Capital and the Dutch State (1588–1795)*, Leiden: Brill, 2015.

Broomhall, Susan, and Jacqueline van Gent. *Gender, Power and Identity in the Early Modern House of Orange-Nassau*, London: Routledge, 2016.

Brouwer, Aron, and Marthijn Wouters. *Willem van Oranje: De opportunistische Vader des Vaderlands*, Amsterdam: Nieuw Amsterdam, 2017.

Bruin, G. de. *Geheimhouding en verraad: De geheimhouding van staatszaken ten tijde van de Republiek (1600–1750)*, 's-Gravenhage: SDU Uitgeverij, 1991.

Cervantes Saavedra, Miguel de. *El Ingenioso Hidalgo Don Quixote de la Mancha*, Madrid: Juan de la Cuesta, 1605.

Davids, Karel, and Jan Lucassen, "Introduction," in K. Davids and J. Lucassen, eds, *A Miracle Mirrored: The Dutch Republic in European Perspective*, Cambridge: Cambridge University Press, 1995, 1–25.

Davies, Norman. *Europe: A History*, Oxford: Oxford University Press, 1996.

Decuyper, Pieter. "De Bourgondische artillerie onder Karel de Stoute (1465–1477)," unpublished Universiteit Gent thesis, 2007.

Dekker, Rudolf. *Observaties van een zeventiende-eeuwse wereldbeschouwer. Constantijn Huygens jr. en de uitvinding van het moderne dagboek*, Amsterdam: Panchaud, 2013.

Deursen, A.Th. van. *Een dorp in de polder*, Amsterdam: Aula, 2003.

———. *Plain Lives in a Golden Age*, Cambridge: Cambridge University Press, 1991.

Duindam, Jeroen. "Geschiedschrijving en oorlogvoering: de metamorfose van een klassiek genre," *Bijdragen en Mededelingen betreffende de Geschiedenis der Nederlanden* 4, 2003, 455–66.

Elias, Norbert. *The History of Manners*, Oxford: Blackwell, 1994.

Espinosa, Aurelio. "The Grand Strategy of Charles V (1500–1558): Castile, War and Dynastic Priority in the Mediterranean," *Journal of Early Modern History* 3, 2005, 239–83.

Geer van Jutfaas, J.L.W. de. *Lodewijk de Geer van Finspong en Leusta (1587–1652)*, 3rd ed., Utrecht: Kemink and son, 1852.

Geyl, P. *Christoforro Suriano, Resident van de Serenissime Republiek van Venetië in Den Haag, 1616–1623*, Den Haag: M. Nijhoff, 1913.

———. *De geschiedenis van de Nederlandse stam*, 1947 [1st ed., 1930], available at: www.dbnl.org/tekst/geyl001gesc01_01/, accessed 28 July 2017.

Glete, Jan. *War and the State in Early Modern Europe*, New York: Routledge, 2002.

Gommans, Jos. "South Asian Cosmopolitanism and the Dutch Microcosms in Seventeenth-Century Cochin (Kerala)," in Catia Antunes and Jos Gommans, eds, *Exploring the Dutch Empire*, London: Bloomsbury, 2015, 3–25.

Goodman, J.D. "On the Progress of the Small Arms Manufacture," *Journal of the Statistical Society of London* 4, 1865, 494–506.

Hobson, J.A. *Imperialism: A Study*, rev. ed., London: Allen and Unwin, 1938.

Hoof, Joep van. *Menno van Coehoorn, 1641–1704: Vestingbouwer, belegeraar, infanterist*, Den Haag: Matrijs, 2004.

———. "Nieuwe manieren, sterke frontieren. Het bouwconcept van Menno van Coehoorn en zijn aandeel in de verbetering van het verdedigingsstelsel," *Bijdragen en Mededelingen betreffende de Geschiedenis der Nederlanden* 4, 2003, 545–66.

Israel, Jonathan. *Dutch Primacy in the World Trade, 1585–1740*, Oxford: Oxford University Press, 1989.

Janse, Antheun. *De sprong van Jan van Schaffelaar: Oorlog en partijstrijd in de late Middeleeuwen*, Hilversum: Verloren, 2003.

Jong, M. de. "Militaire hervormingen in het Staatse leger en de opbouw van het wapenbedrijf, 1585–1621," *Bijdragen en Mededelingen voor de Geschiedenis der Nederlanden* 4, 2003, 467–93.

Kernkamp, J.H., ed., "Brieven uit de correspondentie van Pieter de a Court en zijn verwanten (1667–1683), met bijlagen (1657–1685)," *Bijdragen en Mededelingen van het Historisch Genootschap* 72, 1958, 3–195.

———. "Twee 'niet ter drukpersse bereide' geschriften van Pieter de la Court," *Bijdragen en Mededelingen van het Historisch Genootschap* 56, 1935, 151–214.

Klooster, Wim. *The Dutch Moment: War, Trade and Settlement in the Seventeenth-Century Atlantic World*, Ithaca, NY: Cornell University Press, 2016.

Kohler, Alfred. *Karl V, 1500–1558*, Munich: C.H. Beck, 2001.

Kuiper Y., and B. Olde Meierink. *Buitenplaatsen in de Gouden Eeuw: De rijkdom van het buitenleven in de Republiek*, Hilversum: Verloren, 2015.

Kunzle, David. *From Criminal to Courtier: The Soldier in Netherlandish Art, 1550–1672*, Leiden: Brill, 2002.

Linde, B. van der. *Das Leibregiment der friesischen Staathalter: Kriegsgeschichte, Offizierslaufbahnen und militärische Lebenswelten in den Garnisonsstädten Leeuwarden, Groningen und Emden 1666–1752*, Berlin: Duncker and Humblot, 2016.

Lynn, John A. *The Wars of Louis XIV, 1667–1714*, New York: Longman, 1999.

Manning, Roger B. *An Apprenticeship in Arms: The Origins of the British Army, 1585–1702*, Oxford: Oxford University Press, 2006.

———. "Prince Maurice's School of War: British Swordsmen and the Dutch," *War and Society* 1, 2006: 1–19.

Myshlaevskii, A.Z. "Vyezd v Rosiiu Frantsa Leforta (Sovremennaia perepiska)," *Russkaia starina* 3, 1898, 635–49.

Nierop, H.F.K. van. *The Nobility of Holland*, Cambridge: Cambridge University Press, 1993.

———. *Van Ridders tot Regenten*, 2nd ed., Amsterdam: De Bataafsche Leeuw, 1990.

Odegard, Erik. "Colonial Careers: Johan Maurits van Nassau, Rijckloff Volckertsz. van Goens and Career-Making in the Early Modern Dutch Empire," unpublished PhD diss., University of Leyden, 2018.

Onnekink, David, and Renger de Bruin. *De vrede van Utrecht (1713)*, Hilversum: Verloren, 2013.

Parker, Geoffrey. *Imprudent King: A New Life of Philip II*, New Haven, CT: Yale University Press, 2014.

———. *The Army of Flanders and the Spanish Road*, Cambridge: Cambridge University Press, 1972.

Porter, Roy. *For the Greatest Benefit of Mankind*, New York: Norton, 1999.

Price, J.L. "The Dutch Nobility in the Seventeenth and Eighteenth Centuries," in H.M. Scott, ed., *The European Nobilities in the Seventeenth and Eighteenth Centuries*, London: Longman, 1995, 82–113.

Reinstra, Albert. *Een veldheer in Wijckel, Menno baron van Coehoorn*, Franeker: Van Wijnen, 2009.

Ricklefs, M.C. *War, Culture and the Economy of Java: Asian and European Imperialism in the Early Kartasura Period*, Sydney: Allen and Unwin, 1993.

Schmidt, C. *Om de eer van de familie: Het geslacht Teding van Berkhout 1500–1950: een sociologische benadering*, Amsterdam: De Bataafsche Leeuw, 1986.

Singleton, John. "Arms Industry: Historical Overview," in Joel Mokyr, ed., *The Oxford Encyclopedia of Economic History*, vol. 1, Oxford: Oxford University Press, 2003, 159–65.

Snapper, F. *Oorlogsinvloeden op de overzeese handel van Holland, 1551–1719*, Amsterdam: Ellerman Harms, 1959.

Swart, Erik. *Krijgsvolk: Militaire professionalisering en het ontstaan van het Staatse leger, 1568–1590*, Amsterdam: Amsterdam University Press, 2006.

Swart, K.W. *Willem van Oranje en de Nederlandse Opstand 1572–84*, R. Fagel et al., eds, Den Haag: SDU, 1994.

Troost, Wouter. *Stadhouder-koning Willem III*, Hilversum: Verloren, 2001.

———. *William III, the Stadtholder-King*, Aldershot: Ashgate, 2004.

Vanvugt, E. *Roofstaat*, Amsterdam: Nijgh and Van Ditmar, 2016.

Vogel, H. "Arms Production and Exports in the Dutch Republic, 1600–1650," in M. van der Hoeven, ed., *Exercise of Arms: Warfare in the Netherlands, 1568–1648*, Leiden: Brill, 1997, 189–210.

Willem Frederik, Gloria Parendi. *Dagboeken van Willem Frederik, stadhouder van Friesland, Groningen en Drenthe, 1643–1649, 1651–1654*, Den Haag: Nederlands Historisch Genootschap, 1995.

2 The Early Modern Dutch and War, Part 1

Economy, Society, and Culture

As we saw in the previous chapter, the seventeenth-century Dutch were not rank military amateurs who did their best to imitate the achievements of the absolute monarchies. No seventeenth-century state was able to surpass the United Provinces in channelling their resources for war. They never suffered a decisive defeat against the most formidable of enemy forces. Dutch chartered companies, organised for trade and warfare overseas, were also routinely victorious in combat.[1]

2.1 Opportunity Knocks

Even if used to sporadic outbursts of violent conflict, the outbreak of the rebellion in 1566 altered the population's collective mindset, because of the blanket militarisation of Dutch society.[2] The Low Countries' inhabitants began to see war as the normal state of being. By the 1570s, the northern Netherlands (the part that morphed into the Dutch Republic) had some 70 garrisons stationed across their territories, who could call on auxiliary support from the town militias. Almost the entire adult male population was by then enlisted in some sort of military unit (with some serving in the nascent navy). Whereas garrisoned troops initially were feared and resented for their potential misbehaviour, the Dutch adapted to their presence, despite occasional violent clashes between unruly or dissatisfied units and the civilians among whom they were stationed.

The possibility of such conflicts was quickly reduced once it became evident that that soldiers would be a fixture of everyday life. First in Holland and then in the other provinces, a funding system was developed that guaranteed soldiers' regular pay. And, thus, the civilian population began to explore the opportunity for profit the presence of numerous troops in their towns offered rather than fear them. Apart from those who joined the ranks (which meant regular pay, shelter, and nourishment), civilians benefitted from the purchases made by soldiers for their upkeep or nutrition, while housing troops became another rewarding business.[3] Local authorities (rather than the soldiers themselves) paid towndwellers financial compensation for accommodating soldiers. And the building and maintenance of fortifications "had a considerable positive economic effect."[4] Indeed, the peace of 1648 impoverished many a household.[5] This may in part explain why surprisingly few minded that the war with the Spaniards dragged on for generations.

For much of the core of the United Provinces, the acute threat of ending up in a combat zone receded after 1600, even if the war with Spain concluded only in 1648 (and with the short-lived exception of the crisis of the years 1672 to 1674). But that does not mean that the military became invisible in daily life. Around 1700, in Leeuwarden, the Frisian capital, some 500 men served in the stadtholder's guard, approximately 3 to 4 per cent of the total number of residents of the town, whereas in the cities of Groningen and Deventer, almost 10 per cent of the population served in the military.[6] The soldiers lodged with citizens in private homes rather than in barracks.[7] In the cities, the soldiers performed guard duty alongside the civic militia.[8] They were posted as sentries at the city gates, sometimes guarded the houses of local dignitaries, while soldiers usually occupied a guardhouse in the centre of the town near the city hall.[9] They also protected services at the Dutch reformed churches.[10] As far as the example of Leeuwarden or Groningen goes, according to Van der Linde, relations between soldiers and civilians were usually good, and soldiers lived among the civilians in a rather integrated fashion, fully part of the city's social fabric.[11] Discipline was harsh in the military, but civilians who committed crimes were often treated as brutally as soldiers.[12] No great difference between civilian and military life can be discerned in this or several other respects. It is true that after 1600, the territory of the northern Netherlands was largely spared the devastating consequences of military campaigns (with the exception of the 1670s), but in his discussion of the Dutch and Javanese in Indonesia in the late seventeenth century Ricklefs is surely right in discerning an equally pronounced "military ethos" then prevailing among both Dutch and Javanese, whether warriors or not.[13]

Another most obvious early example of a lucrative opportunity, of course, was that of privateering.[14] At sea, the Dutch showed a belligerent spirit from the moment the first sea beggars *(watergeuzen)* left port. In 1572, these maritime rebels reignited the revolt against Philip II by their capture of Den Briel in Zeeland. Klooster suggests that privateering dramatically expanded after the alliance with the English in 1585, somewhat inspired by the example of Drake and Hawkins.[15] Eventually, after 1621, northern Dutch privateers were matched by pro-Spanish pirates *(kapers)* hailing from Dunkerque.[16] Dutch licensed piracy was already clearly on the wane before the 1648 peace with Spain, but that did not mean that fighting at sea significantly diminished.[17] Service in the regular navy replaced licensed piracy.

In 1621, a contemporary observer reflected on the resumption of the war with Spain in the following characteristic fashion:

> . . .; and as the saying goes: *Dulce bellum inexpertis* [war is sweet to those who have not seen it]. This made hearing the drums and trumpets not just an awakening but also an entertainment: to hear news and tidings about the army, and of the campaign. Thus in the previous and current year [1619 and 1620] the curious have received the news from Bohemia, Austria, Hungary and the Palatinate. The common man has tired from the truce: *Multis utile bellum* [war is profitable for many]. Many still remembered how in war a pretty penny could be made, convinced that . . . all domestic commerce had been greater during the war than during the truce.[18]

Heirs of the entrepreneurial spirit that originated in the High Middle Ages in the case of the Flemish and Brabantine towns as well as the Hanseatic outposts along the IJssel river, in the United Provinces capitalism blossomed through the belligerent prism with which the world was seen. From the 1570s onward, the often new arrivals in Holland's and Zeeland's towns, as well as some of the indigenous traders and artisans of a city such as Amsterdam that overtook its Hanseatic competitors in the Baltic Sea, began to cash in on the opportunities that emerged.[19] The permanent state of war offered exceptional profits to the intrepid entrepreneur and many a more moderate artisan or merchant as well as to those whose profession was combat.[20]

Within a generation or so after 1566, the Dutch Republic did not only become a formidable bastion fruitlessly besieged by Europe's most feared professional army, that of the Spanish king, but its population succeeded in generating an astonishing economic boom that made it into the leading capitalist country in the world. A significant part of this involved the Republic producing a surplus of arms in its domestic enterprises, which it either used itself or sold abroad.[21] As De Jong states, "between 1585 and 1621 Dutch merchant-entrepreneurs managed to build up a domestic arms industry in the Republic," triggered by the rapidly increasing demands of the army during the early decades of the Dutch revolt.[22]

This was what economists following W.W. Rostow call the "take-off period" of this and many other branches of the economy, which made the Dutch into a global economic leader.[23] It was truly remarkable that the northern provinces of the Burgundian Circle could embark on such an astonishing wave of expansion in armament production, for they lacked most of the raw materials (e.g., metal ore, wood, sulphur, saltpetre) to manufacture firearms.[24] But resources from different areas far and wide were imported. For example, at first Danzig was the source for saltpetre (potassium nitrate) but was eventually replaced by Hoogli in Bengal, while Muscovy supplied potash (used in manufacturing gun powder as well as for other purposes) through Arkhangel'sk.[25] Sweden became a particularly important supplier of copper (used for forging bronze cannon) and iron.[26] Elias Trip's earlier ventures during the 1600s involved the importation of English-made cannon, while his in-law Louys de Geer succeeded in producing superior cannon with the help of locally found resources in Sweden, after he expanded his arms manufactories there.[27] Labourers skilled at making arms moved to the Republic, while some of its industry began to flourish as a result of import substitution, as De Jong suggests.[28] Rather than using the weapons against the Spaniards, the Republic just as likely served as the collection and distribution point, or staple, for imported (not in the least Swedish) foreign-made arms (and skilled craftsmen!) that went elsewhere.[29] Cold weapons (such as rapiers or daggers) were often imported from Westphalia (the region around Solingen), while Liège's role as a centre of arms production remained important throughout the seventeenth century.[30] As De Jong points out, arms importation from Solingen or Wallonia strongly contributed to the burgeoning of the Republic's domestic arms industry, often using semi-processed or raw materials from there in making weapons.[31]

Amsterdam became the centre of this thriving business. To quote the Dutch historian Vogel at some length:

> During the seventeenth century, the Dutch Republic boasted an impressive and varied arms industry. Most weapons and military equipment were produced locally, especially in Amsterdam and a number of other cities. While Amsterdam was the major center of production, noted for a variety of articles such as muskets, pistols, armour, guns, and gunpowder, other cities had a narrower range of specialties. . . . Apart from guns, small arms, match and gunpowder, Dutch cities manufactured practically everything else needed for fighting wars: pikes, musket and cannon balls, swords, halbards, drums, spades, picks, wagons, and gun carriages.[32]

To which Roger Manning adds:

> . . . a considerable part of the great wealth of the Dutch Republic during the Golden Age derived from the profits of the arms, armour and munitions trade. Indeed, it was very difficult to carry on a war if one could not buy from the Dutch. . . .[33]

And, finally, Glete's summing up is useful in this respect:

> The late sixteenth- and early seventeenth-century Netherlands was a hotbed of entrepreneurial efforts in industry, technology, foreign trade and finance, and in this context, radical reforms of the Dutch way of warfare fit nicely. Most obvious, the large Dutch armaments

> industry could quickly supply the army with modern and standardised weapons.[34]

The cynicism of some of those who took advantage of the crisis engulfing their homeland is remarkable, even if we reckon with the context of its time and place. Already before J.H. Kernkamp's dissertation of 1934, it was evident to historians that Dutch merchants had few qualms about trading with their Spanish opponents in the Dutch independence war, including during its most harrowing phases in the 1570s and 1580s, when a full Spanish victory remained feasible.[35] At the time, such behaviour was lamented. Whereas an economic boycott of the southern Netherlands and Spain might have merely allowed others to pick up the slack, many decried the fact that supplies shipped on Dutch vessels to Spanish-controlled ports kept Philip II's armies in the field and enabled him to build the ships he used against his rebellious subjects.[36] Some attempts were undertaken to prohibit such trade (as in 1586), but this led to unabashed smuggling, while the export fees raised on the goods transported to the Spanish territories were then lost to the United Provinces, handicapping their war effort.[37] Thus enforcement was lax, and prohibitions were quickly (or conveniently) forgotten.

As De Bruin suggests,

> The Hollanders [, too] with their global trade enjoyed . . . quite a dubious reputation and did not refrain from supplying all their enemies with weaponry, ammunition, naval stores and grain, regardless of the desperation the Republic might face in the fight against Spain, England, or France. In the 1630s and 1640s in the Mediterranean Sea, Amsterdam merchants even rented out and sold fully equipped naval vessels to Spain, which surfaced at the Battle of the Downs [of 1639].[38]

It was, of course, not an exclusively Dutch sin to undermine their own cause by trading on the enemy. Louys de Geer, for example, faced difficulties in moving arms from areas under control of the Spaniards to the Republic but move them he did in the 1620s and, remarkably, with the Estates-General mediating on his behalf.[39]

Before 1590, the Dutch arms trade to friend or foe was not yet a large or sustained operation. Indeed, in the late sixteenth century, the rebels remained net importers rather than exporters of arms, which included ordnance and guns from England.[40] The relative novelty of the various skills involved in manufacturing arms is evident from the fact that the artisans (in Amsterdam at least) engaged in it were not organised in guilds, different from many other crafts who traced their beginnings to the pre-Revolt era.[41] Ultimately, here, too, as in other areas of trade (as exemplified by the foundation of the Dutch East India Company in

1602 or the sudden growth of the trade on Russia or the Americas) and manufacturing, a sort of Great Turn (or Rostowian take-off) can be identified around 1600, when concomitantly offence overtook defence in the war against Spain.[42] Then the nascent Republic became a producer and exporters of arms rather than a consumer of such goods manufactured elsewhere.[43]

The centre of this trade and production became Amsterdam, but it is evident that a flourishing commerce in arms went on elsewhere, a considerable part of which was locally made. De Jong, for instance, has detailed the arms industry and trade in Zeeland province.[44] This province's export of arms became a thriving business soon after the anxious 1570s.[45] The foremost customers were the navy and army, but the VOC and (after 1621) the WIC (*Westindische Compagnie*—sometimes *Geoctroyeerde Westindische Compagnie* or GWC—the West India Company) equally bought arms from the Zeeuwish merchants and manufacturers.[46] Even a significant trade in arms from enemy vessels that had been captured by Zeeuwish privateers developed before 1609.[47]

Formally, strict regulations guided such business, but weapons were exported in greater amounts than permitted by the Zeeland Admiralty and, in the Zeeuwish case, too, delivered to clients who used those very arms against the Dutch in the Eighty Years' War (or against the Protestant cause in France).[48] Zeeland's arms export experienced a veritable boom when the British civil wars erupted around 1640.[49] A perhaps unexpected client of the Zeeland arms industry were the Barbary corsairs, Muslim pirates who raided around the Mediterranean and into the Atlantic Ocean; although they took many a Dutch sailor prisoner (some of whom became renegades), the ostentatiously zealously Protestant Zeeland businessmen had no qualms in supplying arms to these pirates.[50] During the 1620s, Zeeland traders delivered arms to both sides engaged in a war between two Moroccan chieftains.[51] Collusion between Zeeland shippers and Barbary pirates even had Dutch ships transporting plundered goods from North Africa to Livorno (Leghorn) in Italy, after first unloading arms on the southside of the Mediterranean Sea.[52] Meanwhile, as elsewhere in the Republic, it appears as if large-scale manufacturing and trade in arms was the domain of a relatively small group of merchants, such as the Buys and Van Best family, who belonged to the most prominent traders in Zeeland between 1579 and 1625.[53]

Much of the Dutch expertise in warfare was a consequence of the acute necessity to fight the Spaniards: Once they narrowly escaped a total defeat by the Duke of Alba and his son Don Fadrique in early 1573, they were clever enough to both borrow skills from their enemies and build on their own proven strength in developing a formidable defensive industry and armed force. At sea, they likely had an advantage from the beginning in the use of vessels that manoeuvred quickly and were capable of navigating shallow coastal waters, by a merely slight adaptation of fishing boats and short-haul trading ships.[54] They nonetheless were bold enough to develop ships able to engage in long-distance journeys, which were to end the dominance of Spaniards (and the Portuguese under Spanish rule) in Asia, Africa, and the Americas after 1600.

On land, Dutch commanders trained and deployed their forces eventually in a manner that was as good as, or even superior to, the Spanish Army of Flanders. An important boost to the arms industry was given by the offensive strategy followed by Maurice of Orange-Nassau, who succeeded his assassinated father (after one of the first political assassinations committed with a pistol) as stadtholder in 1584.[55] Maurice, who was the commander-in-chief of the army and navy for all except the northernmost provinces, and his cousin William Louis, stadtholder of Friesland, Groningen, and Drenthe, went on to become famous for the military reforms they introduced into the Dutch army, the significance of which has been hotly debated by military historians.[56] Michael Roberts discerned in them signs of an unfolding military revolution. The growing consensus today seems to be that what looks to us as significant change in the art of war happened rather incrementally than in one fell swoop. It is also evident that some of the changes worked well in certain theatres of war, whereas they proved ineffective elsewhere. Still, the Dutch moment in forging a new way of warfare looms large and is linked to the great demand for Dutch arms and expertise inside Europe and elsewhere in the seventeenth century. The Dutch were called in everywhere for their talent at building fortifications, at waging war at sea, at manufacturing firearms, at supplying gunpowder, or at drilling troops in making more effective use of their muskets than before. Indeed, even their skills in fighting on horseback were highly valued by the Russian tsar around 1650.

By the end of the seventeenth century, Europeans hardly fought with heavy sword, lance, or pike on the battlefield.[57] Instead, rifles with attached bayonets had appeared.[58] After 1700, the combined effect of these changes, as Geoffrey Parker has underlined, allowed European colonisers to shore up their control over non-European territories, even if their foes (as the Dutch had already found out about Java during the seventeenth century) often proved quite adept at adopting European methods in warfare and using European (or European-style) weapons against European armies.[59] Although developments were perhaps then not as revolutionarily swift as Roberts implied, the Dutch were exceptional in their "ability to mobilize capital to pay for troops, their munitions, and supplies, which private enterprise did better than the clumsy bureaucracy of the early modern state."[60] The Dutch wars, at the very least, proved to be a school of modern warfare for the many officers and soldiers from the three kingdoms of the British Isles who were deployed in them.[61]

Irrespective of both the effect of the changes in military drill and infantry deployment on the battlefield and the success of anti-Spanish offensive (which was middling, perhaps, as the northern armies never dislodged the Spaniards from what is now Belgium), the stepped-up military effort gave an enormous stimulus to Dutch arms manufacturing and trade.[62] Apart from being insatiable clients, the Dutch political authorities stimulated quality, production, and sales of the arms industry in various other ways: Standardisation of guns or cannons at the behest of Maurice was introduced, for example, while the government provided storage for weapons readied for export.[63] High demand was increasingly met by standardisation; besides cannon or muskets, pickaxes, spades, grenades, and so on were also uniformly produced.[64] Production was maintained at high levels as the manufacturers were remunerated in a timely manner thanks to the regular pay of the Dutch army by the Dutch state. Meanwhile, the Dutch provinces were capable of paying for an ever-increasing army: Around 1590, the land army may have amounted to some 20,000 troops; a century later, the Republic deployed a force five times its size.[65]

Maurice in some ways displayed stereotypical Dutch traits in his command of his forces, as Roger Manning suggests, for

> [he] appears to have been one of the few military commanders of this period who husbanded military manpower—preferring sieges to pitched battles. This was because sieges, properly conducted, were more sparing of the lives of soldiers, who, Maurice understood, represented a substantial investment of time and money in training and maintenance.[66]

In addition, as Louis Sloos writes:

> The [war] against the Spaniards [was] essentially a siege war [and] the need to train fortress builders [became] apparent. Prince Maurice saw the need of training in calculation and surveying to be given in Leiden. On 9 January 1600, Simon Stevin . . . ordered the teaching [of] "Dutch Mathematics."[67]

By the 1620s already, fortress builders such as Cosimo de Moucheron, Jan Cornelisz van Rodenburg and Cornelis Claesz were working in Muscovy; Dutch-constructed fortresses across the globe were in high demand throughout the seventeenth century.[68]

Finally, with war such a constant in people's lives, Jan Glete has suggested that labour relations acquired a new, modern trait, affecting the way war was waged by the Dutch:

> A high degree of respect for contractual relationships—including a soldier's right to be paid and receive regular provisions—was typical of the growing capitalist society. Dutch bourgeois and "middle-class"

> society (. . .) had in the decades around 1600 an open and changing socio-economic elite, ...[69]

The vast amount of documents in the Amsterdam notarial archives that are currently being digitised are testimony to this explosion of contractual relationships; even common folk such as the wives and widows of the crew of the ill-fated *Oryol* ship turned to notaries to ensure payment of arrears, showing the widespread faith in such legal writs.[70] In appreciating the novelty of all of this, Glete has probably been more discerning than most in pointing at not merely the development of a highly diversified arms industry churning out massive amounts of standardised weapons but also the Dutch meticulousness in honouring the terms of the contracts with their soldiers or the obligation to feed them.[71] Prior to Glete's study, Klein argued that "the uncertainty of the international rule of law (through wars or piracy) [undermined] the principle of respect for contracts, [which was] at the most existing in embryonic form, both among peasants and among [state] authorities."[72] But Glete is closer to the mark than Klein, it appears: Both contemporary observers and military historians unfailingly remark on the reliability of the Dutch payment of their armed forces.[73] And the vast size of the surviving Dutch notary archives seems to negate Klein's point as well; even among those of modest station, a visit to the notary to record key financial and other agreements became the norm in the seventeenth century.

As elsewhere in Europe, the Dutch army was in practice run by officers who owned their companies, as it was more efficient to have captains and other officers pay and equip fairly small contingents of soldiers, for which they were remunerated by state officials. Capitalism and war met here, again: Officers were businessmen, too, and they did not have to be of noble extraction in the Dutch military.[74] But those officers were paid by the government: Capitalism works best, one might suggest, if contractual terms are honoured. The Dutch showed undeniable brilliance at financing what Parrott calls

> [t]he characteristic pattern of European warfare . . . [,] military organization on the basis of contracts with private suppliers, whether these are for the recruitment and maintenance of fighting soldiers, for the provision of military hardware and munitions, or for military support systems.[75]

This sort of private capitalist endeavour sustaining European militaries was trumped only by the mass (often conscript) armies that began to take to the field by 1750, faced by "radically increased killing power."[76] By then, though, the Dutch had faded, with financiers from other countries often taking over: In this, as in other capitalist ventures, the Dutch had lost their edge.

2.2 Coping With Everyday War: People and Government

Even before 1600, the Dutch authorities established a surprising amount of control over their armed forces, largely avoiding the sort of marauding episodes that became notorious during the Thirty Years' War in the Holy Roman Empire, such as the sack of Magdeburg. This may have been partially due to the vigorous response by the Estates-General to the woeful tenure of the Earl of Leicester as military commander in the United Provinces in the 1580s.[77] Fearful of a repetition of his unruly behaviour and the lack of control over his troops, after his departure in 1587, military commissioners were dispatched by the provincial estates to keep a close eye on the disbursements of funds to the army and navy as well as the loyalty of commanders and the potential for mutinies by the troops. These deputies-in-the-field resemble the political commissars in the Soviet Red Army, making sure that the military did the state's bidding.[78] This innovative system of checking proved effective: After the war with the Spaniards resumed in 1621, the Dutch were spared the worst of the excesses of military enterprising that plagued Central Europe at the same time. After 1650, most European governments began to exert greater control over the (still predominantly mercenary) armies in their pay.[79] Here, too, the Dutch example made school, although the effort to bring the mercenary forces to heel was at least to a considerable extent forced upon the German rulers as well by the logic of the anarchic circumstances they had witnessed during the Thirty Years' War. Certainly, though, most tried to emulate the Dutch example of paying their troops in timely fashion, a rather obvious means by which the Dutch kept their soldiers in check.

The seventeenth century has been considered by historians part of an "Age of Crisis," somewhere beginning in the 1590s and fading towards 1740.[80] Recently, Geoffrey Parker charted convincingly how the climax of the crisis may have occurred around 1650, at least in most of Europe and Asia.[81] Weather colder than usual probably caused repeated misharvests; epidemic and other diseases led to high mortality and even marked population decline, especially if combined with interminable wars that laid waste to large stretches of territory before the 1720s. This prolonged economic downturn seems linked to a key shift of the economic momentum in Europe from the Mediterranean area to northwest Europe. And Dutch and British capitalist flourishing on the basis of business of war appears connected to this shift of the centre of gravity of the European economy.

Historians have for half a century investigated the link between this economic crisis and the simultaneous age of Dutch affluence. Some, like Van Deursen, have questioned this prosperity as such: Certainly, the standard of living in the United Provinces, even if remarkably high for the times, was nothing like that of the postwar Western Europe in which this eminent Dutch historian wrote.[82] He suggested that the Golden Age was far from an age of affluence for most people in the Republic. The grim toll especially of waves of epidemic disease and the macabre death rate of infants and young children, or women giving birth, are hard to deny and might speak at best of a period of mere relative wealth and well-being. But the history of the Western world since the 1970s has shown how a bustling economy does not necessarily translate into the diffusion of wealth and universal individual prosperity. And so it was in the seventeenth century: A high mortality did not stop the Dutch economy as a whole from thriving, even if its sustained boom was ended in 1672.[83] And the Dutch *volk*, the mass of the population, was not unduly fazed by hardship, seeking their luck in a plethora of ventures to better their lot. Life was harsh, but it was not wholly without prospects; with some luck and prudent husbanding, one might overcome grinding poverty. Pepijn Brandon finds strong support for A.H. John's argument that a rise to global prominence is linked to the productive way by which a great variety of people responded to an almost permanent state of war.[84] And Marjolein 't Hart details the often positive effects of war on many countries' economies, with the Dutch Republic serving as a fine example.[85] And, finally, Frijhoff and Spies suggest that contemporaries note how the livelihood of a great variety of people, from sutlers to brewers or ship's captains, was jeopardised by the Westphalian Peace of 1648.[86]

As is obvious from modern-day arms races (such as between the Great Powers before the First World War or the remarkably fast obsolescence of Mussolini's armed forces during the 1930), it is often exceedingly difficult to stay ahead in them. Even brief moments of complacency or budgetary cuts may transform a vanguard military into a second-rate one. Around 1650 in the Dutch Republic, anxiety brought about by signs of an economic downturn added to warnings about the decadence of the soldier and the general neglect of the land forces, which were rooted into an awareness of this danger. By then, the viciousness of direct exposure to acts of war, such as the Spanish butchery of the population of Haarlem or Zutphen in the early 1570s, towns that had been defended by their men, women, and children, receded from collective memory.[87] Soon war resumed, however, and the economy of the northern Netherlands was again on an upswing.

When after the Peace of Utrecht of 1713 the Dutch did enter a very long period of peace at home and overseas (even if skirmishes in the colonies—as in Surinam or Java—were not quite a thing of the past), their leading role as arms traders and military experts quickly crumbled. At that point, it seems, any adverse economic consequences of peace were not as strongly felt as in 1648, perhaps because prosperity had been stagnating for some years, and a sort of economic realignment was occurring that preceded the Utrecht peace.[88] Arms production declined and military preparedness flagged throughout much of the eighteenth century. The dangers of these developments were brought home to the Republic in its final days, when, without meeting any serious armed resistance, the Prussians restored William V as stadtholder in the 1780s, followed by the French revolutionary armies who invaded and occupied the Republic during the 1790s. At sea, too, Dutch illusions about their prowess were ended in the 1780s, when the Fourth Anglo-Dutch War witnessed crushing British victories over Dutch fleets.

Prior to the Peace of Utrecht, though, war and economic expansion were closely linked. As Frijhoff and Spies write:

> The war [with Spain] had boosted the country [economically] . . ., in the first place because of the great expenditure on the land army and navy, on ordnance, weapons and ammunition, on the building of ships and fortifications, on the crews [and] the garrisons and the fighting itself, in which shipwrights and contracters, arms traders and all sorts of suppliers had a great stake. The relocation of Europe's economic centre of gravity and of its financial hub to Amsterdam had been a side effect of the European struggle for power . . . the interaction between warfare and economic development had rendered a positive effect on the war's result for the Republic. . . .[89]

The immediacy of war echoed in the conversations of the country's elite: Political and military affairs were a regular topic of conversation among the well-to-do, of whom there were more than in any other European state, because of the decentralised nature of the state.[90] Even the renowned pioneer of international law, Grotius (Hugo de Groot), considered war as the normal state of being.[91] His peace-loving convictions were not quite the same principles as adhered to by the International Court of Justice in The Hague today, as the critic Louis Menand noted:

> Grotius [in 1625's *De iure belli ac pacis*] argued that wars of aggression are legal as long as states provide justification for them, but that even when the justifications prove to be shams the winners have a right to keep whatever they manage to seize . . . might makes right.[92]

Such a cynical and predatory mindset underscores much of the Dutch government policies and people's behaviour in the Golden Age. From its inception around 1580 until 1713, the Dutch Republic built its remarkable prosperity in great measure on the use of military force. Part of this involved the supply (through its proto-military-industrial complex) of its own rapidly growing armed forces and of foreign armies and navies and the capitalisation of its unique knowledge of warfare. Ninety per cent of state expenditures went to defence during the seventeenth century.[93] The Dutch imported raw materials such as saltpetre, metal, or wood and half-finished goods, from which they managed to produce such an abundance of certain military products after 1600 that they rapidly moved into exporting the surplus for which there was an incessant demand in this war-like age (and not just in Europe).[94] Despite occasional enforcement of the formal prohibition of such practices, Dutch merchants did not hesitate from vigorous trading on the enemy, as we saw, a practice that can be observed in later conflicts in which the country was involved as well.[95] In addition, the Dutch exported arms manufactured elsewhere, as in the Holy Roman Empire or Sweden; as Clé Lesger points out, they even re-exported Swedish-made arms back to Sweden.[96] And some entrepreneurs grew so wealthy (as did the Trips, De Geers, Marselises, or Jean Deutz [1618–1673]), that they bankrolled the armies of various European monarchs, such as the Danish and Swedish kings, or the Holy Roman Emperor.[97]

The Dutch managed to produce state-of-the-art firearms, ordnance, ships, and fortresses as well as crucial literature on warfare by way of their vast printing industry. De Jong sums up the outcome of this historical process as follows:

> During the Dutch Revolt (1568–1648) entrepreneurs managed to build up a burgeoning arms industry in the Dutch Republic, an industry that was driven by both foreign and domestic demand, and that comprised one of the largest markets for mass-produced articles in the Republic. The Dutch army, the admiralties, merchant companies, the expanding merchant fleet, as well as many foreign states—examples being Denmark, England, France, Muscovy and Venice—and individuals, all procured arms and ammunition in the Dutch market.[98]

After experiencing a few growing pains in the late sixteenth century, the Dutch state proved remarkably efficient at waging war; all historians who have plunged into the debate regarding the occurrence of a military revolution in this period agree that that the Dutch army and navy performed as well as they did because of the unfailing regularity of the state's paymasters' remuneration of soldiers and sailors.[99] And it bears remembering that war was the main occupation of the central government and, to a considerable extent, the provincial and town authorities in the Republic, as it was elsewhere in early modern Europe.[100]

The rational manner of the Netherlandish way of warfare and economic efficiency is reflected by the establishment of a military hospital at Mechelen (Malines) in the late sixteenth century (even if by the opponents of the Dutch).[101] Such hospitals were soon after founded across the northern Netherlands. Surgeons appeared on larger ships, such as those of the VOC. This military medical practice made school: According to an American historian, the first initiatives towards establishing military hospitals in Russia in the later seventeenth century can be traced to Dutch expatriates.[102] While some sort of compassion for one's suffering fellow human being was not altogether absent in founding these establishments or training medical personnel, their prime aim was to serve Mars. Battle-hardened veterans were cured from their wounds to fight again. Expert soldiers or sailors were costly, and the losses suffered from poorly treated, or neglected, injuries suffered in battle, or diseases contracted outside of battle, were higher than the deaths of those who lost their lives immediately on the battlefield. An attempt at proper treatment might pay off.

Besides a plethora of creative ways in which the population dealt with the wartime conditions at home, "perhaps the greatest of all European military enterprises, the creation of joint-stock trading companies and their colonial military activities" was another response to the state of war.[103] Actively encouraged by their boards of directors, the activities of the VOC and WIC routinely involved the use of coercion by military force.[104]

Arms manufacturing and sales received the active support of the Dutch government at central, provincial, and city levels, forging a well-operating "federal-brokerage state."[105] This extreme entanglement of government and business (often through family networks who moved between the "private and public sectors") suggests that even before strong modern governments developed, capitalism could very well benefit from government support, a point first cogently argued by the German economist Friedrich List (1789–1846).[106] Despite the absence of an absolutist monarch and though highly federalised, government was comparatively strong in the Dutch Republic.[107]

2.3 Hypocrisy

The global scale of their aggressive trading activities led to cultural diffusion of the precocious Dutch capitalist mindset to a variety of far-flung locales. Offers of trade combined with the threat and use of brutal military force in enabling the Dutch to establish footholds or bridgeheads in Asia, Africa, and the Americas in the search for further profits. The most notorious chapter of this effort is the significant role played by the Dutch West India Company and others in making an inroad into the trans-Atlantic slave trade and in introducing the Caribbean to the sugar plantations that they had found in north-eastern Brazil during the first half of the seventeenth century.[108] As noted earlier, while the nefarious Dutch role in this chapter of human suffering has been charted, the Dutch role as aiders and abetters (and even catalysts) of warfare in countries far and abroad has been neglected, although in recent years the military history of the Republic in itself has finally been given the attention that it deserves.[109]

Those who gained untold riches from this business, many of whom were pious Christians, did so without showing much remorse about their involvement in, or responsibility for, killing people. One may suggest that some orchestrated their affairs with the aim to have solely "papists" killed with their weapons, but few consistently maintained this selectivity in taking care of business. In how far was this inclination to profit from the arms trade and manufacturing, or the sale of unique military skills a source of shame or guilt, as it seems an undeniable contradiction of the Sixth Commandment in this, still oh so Christian, age?

Norbert Elias's brilliant insights into the development of modern "civilisation" may provide a straightforward answer to this question: Before the modern age, violence was such a normal part of life that any moral scruples about war profiteering, or forcing people at gunpoint or swordpoint to submit, trumped Christian morality as displayed in the Ten Commandments or the New Testament.[110] The Trips (who followed the motto that they sold arms to achieve peace!) or Van Klencks did not think of themselves as amoral murder-mongers. Whereas a forward mind such as Grotius at least theoretically conceived of a peaceful world, in Europe, the Republic was formally at peace (if one disregards the Twelve Years' Truce) for less than a quarter of the seventeenth century.[111] Beyond Europe, the Dutch (or their trading companies on the East and West Indies) were continually at war. Brandon provides a table indicating the VOC wars in Asia that is telling enough, even if not quite accurate.[112] In the West Indies, war with the Portuguese (who became independent of Spain again only in 1640) and Spaniards lasted well-nigh 100 years (1566–1662), initially through piracy, but subsequently over territorial possessions in Brazil as well. Surinam was conquered on the English in the 1660s, after which fighting between the local Amerindians and the Dutch remained endemic.[113] In the Guyanas, Dutch soldiers battled maroons, slaves who had fled the sugar plantations. There were battles with native Americans in North America (e.g., Kieft's War) and with the English in the New York region. And raids on the Barbary Coast in North Africa occurred in order to liberate enslaved Dutch sailors and curb the activities of corsairs in the Mediterranean (and sometimes even west of the Straits of Gibraltar). In other words, the state of war was the norm, even during the brief spells when no armed conflict in northwestern Europe was occurring. War was constant. Only when violence began to be seen as truly abhorrent did involvement in the arms trade become an ever more shady, or shameful, business. Only then did military officers check their uniforms at the door when they participated in civilian life.[114] But the use of violence was not as uncomplicated as this thesis makes it out to be.

Criticism and condemnation of Dutch war-profiteering, colonialism, or their practice of other dark arts are not wholly anachronistic and cannot just be dismissed by a simple adoption of Elias's analysis. Clearly, the Republic was born of war, and in seventeenth-century Europe, war was normal; there was no escape from this vicious cycle. Most of the government's revenue was spent on warfare, as we have noted.[115] From all evidence, it does indeed appear that seventeenth-century Dutch businessmen had few moral qualms about making profits dealing in death. Besides Elias's argument of people being accustomed to violence since time immemorial, it has become the conventional wisdom among scholars that this was due to a mindset that considered "others" (distinguished through inferior race, class, or gender) as not fully human, and thus unworthy of empathy. But this latter point about dehumanising or demonising others does not quite pass muster either.

Dutch church ministers and others fulminated against slavery. Actually witnessing slavery itself provoked such revulsion that it was outlawed in Western Europe.[116] Even before 1600, the diffusion of the Black Legend about Spanish atrocities committed against the native American population suggests indignation at the maltreatment of other human beings. Indeed, Dutch sailors took the *nom de guerre* of Sea Beggars ("*Watergeuzen*") in the early days of the Dutch Revolt, intimating, in a somewhat ambiguously levelling manner, that even beggars remained human despite their humble existence. The Dutch public was furious at the sacking of Bodegraven and Zaltbommel by Louis XIV's armies in 1672; civilian casualties were not just considered inevitable collateral damage.[117] Nor was unscrupulous war profiteering a vice common to all members of the hegemonic elite, which shows further ambivalence. Laurens Reael (1583–1637), for example, predecessor to the ruthless Jan Pieterszoon Coen as governor-general of the VOC, seems to have raised grave doubts about violent attempts to increase the Company's clout in East Asia.[118]

The moral imperative to condemn war was nowhere expressed more clearly than among the Anabaptists, predominantly Mennonites, who rejected violence and refused to bear arms.[119] They already appeared in the Netherlands in the very first decade after Luther's theses were published in 1517 and survived often heavy persecution before they benefitted from the religious tolerance that became the norm in the northern Netherlands after 1566. While not a large religious sect in the seventeenth century, Van Deursen suggests that in Holland, by far the most populous and richest of the seven provinces, they may have constituted at least 5 per cent of the population.[120] The Dutch, seemingly inured to violence and warfare through having been exposed to them since times immemorial, were challenged in their warlike mentality by this community, which was large enough to be conspicuous. Any facile declaration that those were violent times and that war was seen as the normal state of being was challenged by the Mennonites' presence. Dutch arms traders and others keenly benefitting from the permanent state of war were more cynical than naïve or oblivious to the morally objectionable essence of their trade. Making money overrode pangs of conscience, one is led to surmise, and in that sense the Dutch were very modern, somehow squaring the circle between the pacifist essence of the Christianity in which they professed to believe and the lucrative albeit immoral options war offered them. Only the Mennonites stood out as not being hypocritical, and even then not always: The curious case of Lus Tieleman Akema problematises too simplistic a reading of *doopsgezinde* virtue. In the mid-seventeenth century, this Frisian entrepreneur, a Mennonite, seems to have had no qualms about running arms manufactories in Muscovy.

On the other hand, some were unhesitatingly blunt: The Trips openly celebrated the handsome profits made out of the business of war in all its aspects, apparently believing this to be unproblematic from a moral perspective. Their thinking may have been akin to Bolshevik moral relativity: On the road to the radiant future, some casualties were inevitable, but the prosperity they created with their business compensated for those victims. Hobson's point about what are nowadays called "special interests" in politics seems pertinent in this light:

> If the [vast amount of money expended] on armaments . . . were subjected to a close analysis, most of it would be traced directly to the tills of certain big firms engaged in building warships and transports, equipping . . . them, manufacturing guns, rifles, ammunition, . . . supplying horses, wagons, saddlery, food, clothing for the services. . . . Through these main channels the millions flow to feed many subsidiary trades, . . . Here we have an important nucleus of commercial Imperialism. Some of these trades . . . are conducted by large firms with immense capital, whose heads are well aware of the uses of political influence for trade purposes. These men are Imperialists by conviction; a pushful policy is good for them.[121]

Hobson's arguments apply to the Dutch Republic, where the peace party among the regents usually was drowned out by the war party. Killing people might be bad, but the going was too good to forgo the massive profits that could be made from the arms business, which benefitted as many or more people.

Those involved in this nefarious enterprise found allies in the stadtholders, whose most significant task was that of commander-in-chief of the armed forces on land and at sea. Tellingly, in 1672, the Amsterdam city council, purged by stadtholder William III (1650–1702), saw a remarkable influx of people involved in the business of war who replaced the anti-Orangist faction.[122] Many of those entering the government, who included Louys Trip (1605–1684), Koenraad van Klenck, and Gillis Sautijn (1635–1689), had reaped the fruits of their heavy involvement in the arms trade and war industries in the previous decades, which had seen the height of the European and worldwide crisis.[123] These people knew how to supply a huge military machine, and, because William III led his country out of its biggest political crisis in a century, few dared to challenge him after 1672.

For the rest of Europe, too, war was the normal state of being (and, unfortunately, this seems to have been almost everywhere the case in recorded history).[124] No doubt, then, that someone needed to supply belligerents with the proper wherewithal to defend themselves. However, one cannot quite shake the suspicion that, even though universal peace is no longer seen as an utter impossibility, similarly convenient moral relativity has sustained arms dealers ever since. Indeed, it is difficult to square the Calvinist sermons to which a trader such as Koenraad van Klenck piously listened on Sundays on his mission to Moscow in 1675–1676 with the habit of selling arms to all and sundry.

This immoral quest for material gain was not limited to a hegemonic elite. It could be found in most layers of Dutch society, truly providing a common bond that may be seen as a core part of early modern Dutch national identity. Or, adopting Jan Glete's phrasing, while "socio-economic interest groups behind the [Dutch R]epublic shaped its military and naval policy to suit economic ends," a pervasive militaristic ethos affected groups without any political clout and informed *their* attempts to "get ahead" in the brave new world of opportunity that was early modern capitalism.[125] The Dutch subalterns had agency, and highlighting cases of their unscrupulous enterprising spirit shows how capitalism is not some sort of moloch in which the individual is object rather than subject.[126] The considerable role of personal agency in developing Dutch capitalism rejects the Marxist caricature of the historical process being determined by impersonal forces (Marx, by the way, acknowledged the importance of Dutch "merchant capitalism," but had little to say about the role of individuals in forging this new historical stage of economic development).[127] People like Jan Struys (c. 1629–1694) subscribed to the capitalist ethos, willing to take calculated risks to "make good," and capable of unrestrained brutality.[128] Struys and his friends (equally lucky and successful was Karsten Brandt [d.1692], the builder of Peter the Great's first vessel, the *botik*, still proudly displayed today in Russia) worked the angles, becoming artful dodgers in their attempt to escape from their ascribed station in life.[129] Before the economic stagnation that started after the Peace of Utrecht, the Dutch Republic was a land of opportunity and a magnet to many across Europe in search of a better lot in life.[130]

No doubt, many (probably most) who tried to cash in failed. But a hallmark of those trying to make their fortune was a shared belief that the gamble was worth taking, while too many moral scruples hindered more than helped. The failures were numerous, while some who struck it rich (or started out rich) were just as vulnerable as some who dwelled at a more modest station in life. Like Rembrandt the artist, a profligate spender, Karel du Moulin, who had made his riches in the Russia trade (including that of weaponry), went bankrupt. And lethal diseases struck all indiscriminately. Meekly accepting this likely grim fate (or Hobbes's "solitary, poor, nasty, brutish and short" lives) was not the response for the seventeenth-century resident of the Dutch Republic (and the immigrants flocking to it). Struys or Brandt did not give up, Rembrandt started again.

These days, the advantages of capitalism for the benefit of humanity are often enough taken for granted.[131] Few in the West dwell too long on its cost (the prevalence of child labour in the developing world, unbridled environmental destruction, etc.), either in the past or in the present. A charting of the seventeenth-century Dutch and their involvement in the international arms trade and mercenary warfare reflects similar wilful ignorance.[132]

2.4 Early Modern Warfare and Capitalism, Dutch-Style

As Pepijn Brandon writes, "[T]he Dutch cycle formed a crucial point in the development of the capitalist world-system, transferring the logic of capital accumulation from the primarily regional scale [of the] Italian city states to the world at large."[133] Amsterdam was the center of Dutch arms trade and manufacturing so crucial to this Dutch economic paramountcy. A century after its heyday, Wagenaar rendered a good illustration of this dominance:

> [In 1641, t]he collegium of the Amsterdam Admiralty issued, . . . so many permits for the export of arms and the necessities of war, that it caught the attention of the other provinces. It was understood at The Hague as well that issuing permits was the prerogative of the Estates General, which was thought to know best whether such an export could occur without a disadvantage to the country's arsenals. The [Amsterdam] Admiralty, however, was of the opinion that the city housed the largest arsenal of military means, and that nowhere better than [t]here one knew whether such means were sufficiently available in the country.[134]

The Amsterdam Admiralty rejected the idea that the central government at The Hague should decide on such matters, as arms sales needed to be handled expeditiously in order not to lose trade to competitors working from Hamburg and from ports along the Baltic shores.[135] The Estates-General accepted this reasoning and declined to curb the Amsterdam Admiralty's activities in this regard.

That the Dutch had an advance over potential competitors and that they had readily available what was needed was commonly accepted. In 1645, for example, an emissary of the "emperor" (sultan) of Morocco, with permission of the Estates-General, was in Amsterdam to purchase a warship with 20 cannon.[136] This was an unusual client for the arms industry but shows how customers even from (perhaps) rather peripheral regions found their way to the Dutch arms market. In 1666, not long before Louis XIV definitively turned against the Dutch, the French king ordered the building of several warships in Amsterdam and gained permission from the Estates-General to hire crews to man the vessels, while his envoy, Godefroy d'Estrades (1607–1686), investigated the possibilities of the establishment of a gun factory in the same city, even if this last project was aborted.[137]

Masters of the Universe in an early modern setting, Amsterdam's businessmen and city councillors carved up much of the world's wealth in the antechambres and corridors of their town hall ever more decidedly after 1650.[138] The regents were almost all scions of, or married into, families who had made a fortune in the previous half century. They often enjoyed meals at their city's expense, during which they decided matters of substance, which "succeed[ed] each other with disconcerting rapidity."[139] As Dutch ambassador Koenraad van Klenck professed to do before the tsar's advisors in 1676, these oligarchs ostensibly adhered to ideas about fair competition for the market, but only as long as it benefitted them.[140] With arguments that echoed those of the outstanding Dutch champion of free trade, Pieter de la Court, Van Klenck unsuccessfully tried to convince the Russians in 1676 of the benefits of the free trade of Iranian silk across Muscovy. But those arguments were clearly grounded in the conviction that because of Dutch expertise, shipping, and superior knowledge about markets, this silk trade would be dominated by Dutch merchants.

In truth, Dutch domination over the global European economy was based on mechanisms rather different from the pure unadulterated competition in a free market. To increase their spoils, business tycoons used patronage networks and nepotism (the seventeenth-century rate of intermarriage among the Amsterdam patricians is staggering) and established cartels while artificially creating and stimulating market demand for items of dubious utility to their fellow human beings, such as tobacco, tea, sugar, or arms.[141] Testimony to John Ralston Saul's suggestion that all capitalism is "crony capitalism," most of the Amsterdam councillors weren't even genuine businessmen by the 1670s: Heading huge patronage networks, they reaped the fruits both from the investments and hard work of their more entrepreneurial ancestors and of all those they employed, the managers, factors, stewards, and clerks, as well as thousands of faceless artisans, sailors, serfs, or slaves.[142]

Immanuel Wallerstein and Fernand Braudel raised the question of what exactly "capitalism" meant in practice, rather than the theoretical *idealtypus* of a free market in which entrepreneurs fairly compete to provide cheaper and better products (and an ever greater variety of them) to ever more discerning consumers. Braudel suggested that global capitalism is run by monopolies that dominate an "anti-market," the operation of which remains opaque to contemporaries or historians.[143] As much as in the American Gilded Age, the entanglement of business, society, and politics among this small elite of the *über*-rich and its unscrupulous exploitation of the "Great Unwashed" were indeed crucial elements underscoring seventeenth-century Amsterdam's success as the centre of the global economic system centred on Europe. The involvement of many Amsterdam councillors, directly or indirectly, in the arms trade reveals its importance in the city's staggering economic success.

In their debate regarding the rise of capitalism, historians follow in the footsteps of Adam Smith and Karl Marx.[144] Immanuel Wallerstein proposed in his magisterial four-volume work the emergence of a "European World-System" after 1500.[145] Wallerstein suggested a period of Dutch hegemony within the European World-System in the middle of the seventeenth century. Wallerstein's vision has come under heavy fire from postmodernist criticism, as he tried to impose a neo-Marxist metanarrative on European (and World) history that may indeed be too schematic in part.[146] Thus, it is hard to make the actual Dutch Republic of the seventeenth century fit Wallerstein's scheme when he writes about it that "from time to time, it needs actually to use its military forces [, which] is costly and diverts finance from economic investments."[147] This completely contradicts Dutch economic flourishing in the course of their Eighty Years' War, in which they constantly deployed their armed forces on land and at sea.

Wallerstein goes on to suggest as well that

> . . . [a] rising sea-based power has tended not to have a significant land army, which would be constructed only at a later stage. The absence of an army at this early stage had one clear advantage: it saved a great deal of money, money that was invested instead in the economic infrastructure of the country, enabling it to win the crucial struggle to be the most competitive power in the sphere of production for the world market.[148]

This is not what occurred in the United Provinces. The Dutch fielded a formidable land army (or land armies) from 1566 to 1609 and 1621 to 1648, the era identified by Wallerstein as that of their "rise." It was so large, technologically advanced, and well organised that it became the example for other European land armies in the seventeenth century, such as that of Gustavus Adolphus. Indeed, the Dutch land army ended the leading role played by the Spanish (Habsburg) army, which had been considered for several decades in the sixteenth century to be the strongest in the world. Besides vast expenditure on the navy, much money was spent on the land army by the Dutch government, but this was not detrimental to the country's economy; on the contrary, it was highly beneficial to burgeoning Dutch capitalism. Wallerstein, then, is correct in noting the significance of the Dutch phase in early capitalism but errs in arguing how the Republic became hegemonic.

Hobson presents perhaps a more compelling argument regarding the link between capitalism, imperialism and war:

> The economic root of Imperialism is the desire of strong organized industrial and financial interests to secure and develop at the public expense and by the public force private markets for their surplus goods and their surplus capital. War, militarism, and a "spirited foreign policy" are the necessary means to this end. This policy involves large increase of public expenditure. If they had to pay the costs of this policy out of their own pockets in taxation upon incomes and property, the game would not be worth the candle, at any rate as far as markets for commodities are concerned. They must find means of putting the expense upon the general public. . . . Taxation [is] indirect and [falls] upon such articles of consumption or general use as are part of the general standard of consumption and will not shrink in demand. . . .[149]

Initially, the Dutch capitalists of the Golden Age may not have consciously harnessed the capacity of the government to tax the population through indirect taxes (*convooien en licenten*, etc., the first word of which tellingly meant "convoy," as the merchant marine was convoyed to defend it against enemy ships) to augment their own wealth; a comparatively high level of such taxes was justified in financing a struggle for survival of the Republic against the Spaniards. After the truce with Spain was concluded in 1609, however, the navy was in significant part purposely maintained to protect the burgeoning Dutch overseas empire and its trade routes, which benefitted primarily the mercantile elite of the country. Capitalism began to overshadow the national (or national-religious) interest once the security of the northern provinces was attained. Without such an outlay to protect the interests of Dutch trade (not only through warships but also through military expeditions both in Asia and the Americas), the Dutch might not have captured so much of the world trade and established their imperial footholds at Java, Taiwan, Sri Lanka, the Cape, Brazil, Manhattan, Curaçao, or Elmina. In the end, even the high level of Dutch taxes, though, did not allow the country sufficient means for a navy strong enough to enforce free trade (benefitting Dutch short- and middle-haul shippers) in Europe or protectionism in Asia and the Americas (benefitting the VOC and the WIC).

The English seriously began to test the Dutch maritime strength in the Anglo-Dutch wars of 1652–1654 and 1664–1667, of which the first ended in an unmitigated Dutch defeat in military terms. It had the outcome of leaving the 1651 Navigation Acts in place, which banned much of the Dutch carrying trade on Britain. The second war may be seen as a qualified Dutch victory, although the Navigation Acts were not abolished. The subsequent assault by the French, with support from Cologne, Münster, and England in 1672, even if deflected, heralded a prolonged period of enormously costly defence outlays, which not even the relatively wealthy Dutch could cover through consumer taxes and import and export fees. The national debt, financed by issuing government bonds, drastically increased, reaching almost unsustainable levels by the 1710s.

The more ingenuous and better connected mercantile conglomerates (often linked through family ties) had already diversified their investments at the dawn of the Dutch miracle and established branches of their business outside the nascent Republic. Many investors, though, began only after 1672 to cast about for investment opportunities abroad. For that "year of disaster" brought home how precarious Dutch survival remained, given the country's puny geographical size and comparatively small population. In case the country collapsed altogether, they began to develop scenarios allowing them to migrate elsewhere in a crisis. It seems not entirely a coincidence that the most open-minded types in this regard were refugees from the southern Netherlands (although not a few hailed from the Empire) or their descendants, uprooted in the 1570s and 1580s and willing to follow the adage of "*ubi bene, ibi patria.*"[150] These were flexible characters, cosmopolitan in outlook. For the first generation that had fled the southern Netherlands, religion may have been the main marker of their identity, but their descendants were often far less rigid in this respect and willing to adapt to a new religious environment, whether Lutheran, Anglican, or Catholic, if it meant that they could thereby continue the standard of living to which they were accustomed.

The originally Flemish Marselis family may be a typical example, with its links to Hamburg, Denmark, and Russia.[151] As Amburger wrote about them, "The Marselis showed as little loyalty to the state in Hamburg as in Holland."[152] The expatriate Liègois Louys de Geer, likewise, made his greatest fortune in Sweden. Even outside of acute crises, a good number of Dutch merchants and entrepreneurs went native: Some of the De Geers became Swedish, whereas Winius chose to become a Russian. Eventually, a fair number of capitalists made their way to Britain, especially after 1688. Other investors stayed put in the Republic, but their money found its ways elsewhere, eventually sheltering their descendants even against the calamity of the French occupation that began in 1795. As we will see in the case of the Salés and others, going native was not exclusive to the upper crust, reflective of the trickling down of the capitalist outlook on life; already before 1600, several people born in the Low Countries had settled in the Americas and served the Spanish regime in a variety of capacities.[153]

The Dutch "primacy in world trade," as Jonathan Israel called it, did not last very long (although it is worthwhile to recall that American economic supremacy has also lasted for a mere century); Israel himself is generous, awarding it a duration of some five generations.[154] Wallerstein is more miserly, giving Dutch economic hegemony a lifetime of about one generation at most (c. 1648–1672).[155] It is true, though, as De Vries and Van der Woude or Brandon point out, that even far into the eighteenth century Dutch primacy had merely faded in relative terms.[156] Competitors would eventually surpass it by far, however, in terms of economic production (especially Great Britain in the late eighteenth century) and even occupy it (France by 1795).

In the middle of the seventeenth century, though, Amsterdam was the financial centre of the world and the foremost global trade hub. Dutch entrepreneurs and frontiersmen, often with the support of their government, struck out across the globe, using blunt methods that included the use of copious acts of violence. Although at times territorial control was surrendered, as it was in Brazil, the New York region, or at Taiwan, this usually did not mean any lessening of Dutch economic activity in, or near, those areas that had to be given up. Conventional wisdom in the Netherlands even today holds that Surinam was seen as a bigger prize than New York when the two were exchanged in 1667. There is more than a whiff of truth about that idea: The Dutch slave trade and plantation economy just began to acquire substantial proportions, and Dutch-ruled Surinam and Guyana were for a long time the only significant non–Hispano-Lusatian territories held by Europeans on the South American mainland.[157] Thus the Guyanas provided an alternative to lost Brazil, too.

Taiwan fell to a rogue Ming admiral in early 1662, but the Dutch responded to its loss by dispatching embassies to Beijing to persuade the (Qing) Kangshi emperor (r. 1661–1722) in an attempt to open mainland China's borders to trade with the VOC.[158] This effort failed, but the Dutch remained the only Europeans to trade with Japan until the mid-nineteenth century. Substantial territorial conquests were made in Sri Lanka and south India to increase the Dutch control over the overseas trade from that region, while they strengthened their commerce with Bengal during the second half of the seventeenth century.[159] The trade with Iran, Mocha, and the Ottoman Empire (especially through Izmir/Smyrna) remained stable as well, and the Dutch firmed up their colony at the Cape in Africa while they acquired slave stations on the West African coast. In hard-fought conflicts on Java and Makassar, the Dutch were advancing while they controlled the strategic point of the Malaysian peninsula (Malacca) for a considerable time after their initial conquest of it (on the Portuguese) in 1641.

In Europe, the Dutch were the shippers who supplied Western Europe with Polish grain or Russian furs and naval stores. They were active in arms manufacturing, mercenary warfare, and trade in Russia, while they enormously beefed up the Swedish arms manufacturing branch after 1600. In the Thirty Years' War, they financed the Danish and Swedish armies (as well as some of the German Protestants' forces), and, half a century after the fruitless efforts by Christian IV to support the Protestants against the Catholics in Germany, they lent Christian V a number of ships sailed by 5,000 sailors and commanded by Admiral Cornelis Tromp (1629–1691); this aid proved instrumental in defeating the Swedes during another round of warfare between the Scandinavian rivals.[160] Dutch ships and their enterprising sailors, too, provided considerable aid to Venice in its long-drawn-out effort to stop the Ottomans from conquering Crete (1645–1667), although a not inconsiderable number of Dutch renegades served in the Turkish fleet (and some even in the sultan's armies).[161] Even before the Dutch marine corps was formed, most sailors were adept at using weaponry, not in the least because of the constant threat of pirates; during the wars of the second half of the seventeenth century, dozens of Dutch vessels were licensed by letters of marque to engage in piracy, their crew legal searovers.[162]

Peaceful and harmful business were closely entangled: A comparison with today's United States may be illuminating, given the presence of US troops in more than 100 countries and of US-owned businesses in every country except North Korea as well as the scale of the American arms trade. What was different was that the Dutch hardly ever made an attempt at giving their efforts some sort of positive spin but produced, traded, invested, and fought almost purely for their own self-interest. In this sense, the Dutch differed from the Spaniards, whose plunder or trade was often accompanied by efforts to convert the locals and save their souls. The most compelling moral justification of Dutch rapacity seems to have been the argument that it came at the expense of non-Christians or non-Protestants.

The Dutch Republic benefitted from its economic lead over almost any other country throughout the seventeenth century. It has remained a mystery, and it will probably remain so in the light of the absence of precise statistics, how much precisely Dutch arms trade and know-how contributed to the Dutch economy, as no comprehensive accounting of the gross national or domestic product can be rendered for the period.[163] But there is no doubt that vast fortunes were made by military officers, gunpowder manufacturers, arms traders, and so on, and that part of the secret of Dutch success derived exactly from the enormous profits made in this sector, as some of the country's leaders realised at the time.[164]

Technological progress and rare military skill alone cannot, of course, explain the emergence of the Dutch as the foremost military specialists or arms merchants of the seventeenth century. Technological and military advance coincided with business savvy, which was the product of generations of expertise in trade and artisanry in Brabant, Flanders, Zeeland, and Holland. The Dutch success in combining such forces led to the "Dutch Moment in World History," when this speck on the map of the world appeared to control global trade and reached extraordinary levels of affluence.[165]

Notes

1. Glete, *War and the State*, 141.
2. See 't Hart, *Dutch Wars*, 82–4. Further attesting to the paramount role war began to play in people's lives in the second half of the 1560s are De Jong, *Staat van Oorlog*; Swart, *Krijgsvolk*.
3. 't Hart, *Dutch Wars*, 87–91; see also Van der Linde, *Das Leibregiment*, 290.
4. 't Hart, *Dutch Wars*, 95.
5. Ibid.; see also Israel, *Dutch Republic*, 614. Van der Vlugt suggests that even the Bickers, who were leading the "peace party" in 1650, had happily benefitted from the war and made a good amount of money (see Van der Vlugt, *Wij zijn*, 111).
6. For Groningen and Friesland, see Van der Linde, *Das Leibregiment*, 77. For Deventer, see Kunzle, *From Criminal*, 596–7.
7. Van der Linde, *Das Leibregiment*, 88.
8. Ibid., 79–81.
9. Ibid., 98.
10. Ibid., 105.
11. Ibid., 107.
12. Klooster, *Dutch Moment*, 127–8. See for a detailed discussion, Spierenburg, *Judicial Violence*. Whereas, in general, "subalterns" undoubtedly were brutally treated in this age, I cannot quite agree with Klooster's suggestion that soldiers' lives resembled those of slaves; the Brazil veterans' militancy he describes indicates people with agency and a clear sense of entitlement to pay for work rendered (Klooster, *Dutch Moment*, 142–3).
13. Ricklefs, *War, Culture*, 130. Ricklefs draws an interesting parallel between warlike mindset of the Javanese after 1670 and that of the Dutch in the same period.
14. See van Loo, "Kaapvaart, handel," 349–68.
15. Klooster, *Dutch Moment*, 25–6. Given that the sea beggars continued to raid after 1572, I am not sure if his point is accurate that the English example was inspirational. While it is true that their operation radius was smaller before 1585, this was in part because their ships were smaller and not capable of long-distance sailing. Long-distance privateering expeditions in Drake's style were undertaken to the South-America for the first time in the 1590s (ibid., 28).
16. Klooster, *Dutch Moment*, 44.
17. Ibid., 69. Ibid., 87–8, appears a bit contradictory in this respect.
18. Van Aitzema, *Saken*, 5–6.
19. On the significance of the "*moedernegotie*," the "mother-trade" with the Baltic see, for instance, Boxer, *Dutch Seaborne*, 6.
20. It is interesting, again, to note how this genius at supplying the military was not necessarily circumscribed by the geographic borders that separated the Republic from the Spanish Netherlands after the mid-1590s (nor was that the case for the knack for painting, as Rubens or van Dyck show): One of the most curious cases of a spectacularly successful war financier and merchant is Hans de Witte (see below and Parrott, *Business*, 216–19, 231–3; see as well Brulez, "De Diaspora," 295–6). Ultimately, De Witte overextended himself and committed suicide. The Calvinist De Witte was linked with the Verpoorten merchants, Hamburgers from Netherlandic stock who traded on Russia (they were represented by their Dutch colleagues and even Dutch ambassador Boreel in his parlays with the tsar's government in 1665).
21. Klein, *De Trippen*, 195–200.
22. De Jong, "Dutch Entrepreneurs," 57; see also Duindam, "Geschiedschrijving," 464–5; De Jong, "Militaire hervormingen," 467–93.

23. Rostow, *Process*.
24. Klein, *De Trippen*, 207–8; De Jong, "Militaire hervormingen," 489. Sulphur was shipped from Sicily and Elba, see Scholten, "Arms Trade and Industry in Groningen," 25.
25. Breedvelt-van Veen, *Louis de Geer*, 40; see as well Mostert, "Chain," 35–6. Mostert notes here how in the course of the seventeenth century saltpetre from Asia substituted for the earlier importation of saltpetre from the Baltic, because saltpetre manufactured in warmer weather was of higher quality. It is interesting to see that Dutch traders in Russia tried on occasion to supply the Dutch market with both grain and saltpetre but aborted these efforts fairly soon (and only went back to grain imports from Muscovy on rare occasions): Saltpetre from Bengal was of higher quality, while the tsar only occasionally was willing to export grain.
26. Breedveldt links the sale of copper concessions by the young king Gustavus Adolphus to the desperate financial and economic situation Sweden faced after the loss of the war against Denmark in 1613 (see Breedvelt-van Veen, *Louis de Geer*, 47). The Dutch at the same time began to expand their copper works, especially for casting cannon (ibid., 48).
27. Klein, *De Trippen*, 211–14, 217–18; see as well a description of Trip's ventures in 1610s Dordrecht (with cannon-barrels cast in England, saltpetre descending down the Meuse, and shot produced in Namur or Liège), which sold to both the Estates-General and to the VOC (see Breedvelt-van Veen, *Louis de Geer*, 8). Breedveldt suggests that De Geer's first involvement began with the importation of Swedish firearms and bullets into the Republic in 1615, triggered by the Liègeois expatriate De Besche (ibid., 8–9). De Geer moved to Amsterdam, as it facilitated doing business with Sweden. See also De Jong, "Militaire hervormingen," 489–90.
28. De Jong, "Dutch Entrepreneurs," 51; De Jong, "Militaire hervormingen," 467.
29. Klein, *De Trippen*, 204–5; De Jong, "Dutch Entrepreneurs," 54.
30. Klein, *De Trippen*, 210. Other significant areas were Cologne, Aix-la-Chapelle, and Namur (see Breedvelt-van Veen, *Louis de Geer*, 79–80).
31. De Jong, "De Zeeuwse wapenhandel," 33.
32. Vogel, "Arms Production," 197. See also Scholten, "Arms Trade," 25; Martines, *Furies*, 92–3; De Jong, "Dutch Entrepreneurs," 36–7.
33. Manning, "Prince Maurice's School," 5–6. Pepijn Brandon notes how Dutch merchants and entrepreneurs derived much of their fairy-tale–like prosperity in the destitution of the "Age of Crisis," or "Mini Ice Age," through the unscrupulous and highly effective trade in arms and the manufacturing of weaponry, while many another fortune was made by Dutch military experts who sold their rare skills to the highest bidder (Brandon, *War*, 1–3).
34. Glete, *War and the State*, 161. Nevertheless, some arms were imported from abroad; both Walloon and German (Imperial) expertise remained popular, not merely in the Republic (see Kernkamp, ed., "Twee 'niet ter drukpersse bereide'," 158–9).
35. Kernkamp, *De handel*. See also De Boer, "Amsterdam," 3–6.
36. Kernkamp, *De handel*, vol. 1, 3.
37. Klein, *De Trippen*, 199.
38. De Bruin, *Geheimhouding*, 72.
39. Breedvelt-van Veen, *Louis de Geer*, 79–80.
40. Kernkamp, *De handel*, vol. 1, 33–4; Klein, *De Trippen*, 211–14, 217–18; Breedvelt-van Veen, *Louis de Geer*, 80.
41. Neither the saltpetre-refiners nor the sulphur-refiners nor the ironcasters were organised in such manner, judging from Wagenaar (Wagenaar, *Amsterdam*, vol. 1, lxxix–lxxx).

42. See, for example, Lesger in identifying the take-off period in the 1590s (Lesger, *Rise of Amsterdam*, 139).
43. See, for example, Klein, *De Trippen*, 195–6.
44. De Jong, "De Zeeuwse wapenhandel"; for Maastricht and Groningen, see Scholten, "Arms Trade"; Hanssen, "The Arms Industry in Maastricht."
45. With France, embroiled in its civil war, as a prime destination (ibid., 43–4).
46. De Jong, "De Zeeuwse wapenhandel," 40.
47. Ibid., 41.
48. Ibid., 43–5.
49. Ibid., 46.
50. Ibid., 46–7.
51. Ibid., 47.
52. Ibid.
53. Ibid., 52–3.
54. See Unger, *Dutch Shipbuilding*.
55. De Jong, "De Zeeuwse wapenhandel," 35; De Jong, *Staat van Oorlog*, 316; 't Hart, *Dutch Wars*, 180–1.
56. Roberts, "Military Revolution"; and essential is Parker, *Military Revolution*. Snapper details how William Louis was inspired by his understanding of both the battle deployment of the Roman and Greek armies in the Classical Age and the writings of the Byzantine Emperor Leo VI (866–912), but that he and Maurice did take into account the technological impact of firearms or grenades (see Snapper, *Oorlogsinvloeden*, 39–41). The Dutch standard work for the changes was until recently Wijn, "Het krijgswezen."
57. From 1708, pikemen were no longer part of the Dutch army (see Van der Linde, *Das Leibregiment*, 57). Already in the previous decade, many pikemen were retrained to use firearms (guns that used a flintlock; Van der Linde calls them "snaphanen," although the original snaphances had become obsolete by then). Some have suggested that the introduction of the removable bayonet, another important change on the battlefield with momentous consequences, should be attributed to Menno van Coehoorn.
58. Ibid. Soldiers did have a foil, that is, a light sword.
59. See also Andrade, *Lost Colony*, 13–15. Like Merle Ricklefs, Andrade suggests that, at first, some Asian military leaders managed to catch up quickly with any European advances.
60. Hall, review of *Business of War* by Parrott, 622. Manning notes how even Italians, who had been at the cutting edge of warfare in the fifteenth century, were eager to serve in Maurice's forces to find out about his innovative ways of fighting (see Manning, "Prince Maurice's School," 14–15). See as well 't Hart, *Dutch Wars*, 148.
61. Manning, *Apprenticeship*, 5–7, 28–31, 40.
62. As Parker points out in various places, the nexus between the Military Revolution and military victories on the West European and Central European battlefields is not straightforward. This seems due to a sort of arms race that developed among the warring parties, which kept any advantages because of superior drill or deployment on the battlefield in check (while no army was continually capable of bringing sieges to a victorious conclusion). Even Gustavus Adolphus of Sweden might have been checked (as his generals subsequently were) had he not fallen at Lützen in 1632 (and he certainly did not excel in siege warfare). Both Maurice (at Turnhout in 1597) and Gustavus Adolphus proved to be very adept at the use of light cavalry *(Reiter/ruiters)*, not usually seen as an important component of the Military Revolution. Parker suggests that the effect of the European advance becomes much more evident in the establishment of the north-western European maritime

empires (and even the Spaniards had already benefitted from their use of sail and guns in the Americas). Interesting in this respect is Den Heijer and De Jong, *Oorlogen overzee*. One Dutch historian suggests that Parma could have won the war against the rebels (commanded by young Maurice!) in 1587–1588 had he not been ordered to wait for the Armada (and prepare for an invasion of England; see Jansen, *Kalendarium*, 95). William Louis and Maurice did gain important victories, even if aided by the failure of the Armada (in 1588), the renewed turbulence in France surrounding the assassination of the Guises and King Henri III (which led to the Duke of Parma's troops moving into France, among other things), and Parma's death in 1592. Maurice and his cousin managed to shore up the northern military effort, chasing (pro-)Spanish forces from the east and pushing them (slightly) back in southern direction as well during the 1590s. They meanwhile never faced the sort of periodic mutinies that befell the English expeditionary army that Leicester had brought to the Low Countries in 1585: It is a sign how well the northerners managed to organise their finances, guaranteeing the regular pay of the troops that fought under the command of the stadtholders. In how far Maurice or William Louis were military geniuses in combat situations, though, remains moot.

63. 't Hart, *Dutch Wars*, 182, 184.
64. Ibid., 182; for more on this standardisation (even of siege tools), see De Jong, "Militaire hervormingen," 474–6, 482–3. Here, too, De Jong suggests that the watershed period was between about 1590 and 1620, the era often associated with the "Dutch stage" of the Military Revolution (of Maurice, William Louis, John of Nassau and De Gheyn's drill book); more reliable muskets, too, began to replace the arquebuses. And more and more troops were fielded (ibid., 476–8). Key, of course, was regular pay of the soldiers, which had not been the case before 1590 or so (ibid., 483–5). Certainly, a lot of pieces fell into place at once, setting the table for seventeenth-century warfare, in which the Dutch excelled.
65. See Snapper, *Oorlogsinvloeden*, 39; Haks, *Vaderland*, 9.
66. Manning, *Apprenticeship*, 92.
67. Sloos, "The Ministry of Defence's Treasury," 25.
68. For Van Rodenburg in Russia, see Davies, *Warfare*, 74, 80, 88. He developed plans for a city wall at Rostov (the Great), among other things, see Reger, "In the Service," 182n94.
69. Glete, *War and the State*, 161.
70. See www.amsterdam.nl/stadsarchief/organisatie/projecten/alle-amsterdamse/, accessed 20 February 2019; see *Stadsarchief Amsterdam Notarieel Archief* 4304 (Notary Nicolaes Hemminck), 227–7 verso and 247.
71. Glete, *War and the State*, 161.
72. Klein, *De Trippen*, 10n17.
73. Parrott, *Business*, 111–13, 224. However, this reliability seems to have firmed up only towards 1600 (see as well Manning, *Apprenticeship*, 36).
74. Van der Linde, *Das Leibregiment*, 58, 200, 204–7, 220–5, 273. At least for Frisia and Groningen, Van der Linde suggests that the aristocratic resurgence noticeable elsewhere in Europe (especially in France) is hardly apparent among those occupying officer rank in the military (of course, even in France, commoners became eligible for commissions in the second half of the eighteenth century, in part a consequence of the growing professionalisation and specialised education of the officer corps; see ibid., 207). And it is noteworthy that among the Frisian nobility, something like two thirds of the noble families in the eighteenth century had no sons serving as officers (ibid., 209).

75. Parrott, *Business*, 2.
76. Ibid., 2.
77. See 't Hart, *Dutch Wars*, 42, 46.
78. A comparison made by Manning, too, see Manning, *Apprenticeship*, 33.
79. Parrott, *Business of War*, 309.
80. See De Vries, *Economy of Europe*.
81. Parker, *Global Crisis*. It is probably no coincidence that Parker does not dedicate a specific section in his hefty volume to a discussion of the impact of this crisis on the Dutch Republic.
82. Van Deursen, *Plain Lives*.
83. For the significance of 1672, see, for example, Brandon, *War*, 225; as well as Panhuysen, *Rampjaar*.
84. John, "War"; Brandon, *War*.
85. See 't Hart, "From the Eighty Years War"; 't Hart, *Dutch Wars*. See as well Van Deursen, *Plain Lives*, 211–12; Snapper, *Oorlogsinvloeden*, 32.
86. Frijhoff and Spies, *1650*, 17.
87. It is pertinent as well that, as Roger Manning writes, "a shared martial culture among the polyglot armies of continental Europe contributed to the movement to limit the destructiveness and cruelty of war which began to emerge during the seventeenth century" (Manning, *Apprenticeship*, 8). Manning adds that the Dutch armies began to be held to a code of conduct that markedly improved their behaviour (see ibid., 59, 205). This code ("*Het Krijgsrecht*") was formalised in 1590 and further specified in 1602.
88. See De Vries and Van der Woude, *First Modern*, 681.
89. Frijhoff, Spies, *1650*, 18. The same authors suggest here that arms manufacturing and trade consisted of 5 per cent of the Republic's economy, a percentage not very well explained (of the value of gross domestic product?). Their source is the all-too-brief article by Vogel (translated into English as Vogel, "Arms Production"). Meanwhile, how does one estimate the value of merchantmen that could be rigged as warships?
90. De Bruin, *Geheimhouding*, 53. See also his discussion of the number of newspaper readers in the seventeenth and eighteenth centuries, already reaching well-nigh 10 per cent of the towndwellers of Holland in the mid-seventeenth century (ibid., 409). Far more people read (or had read to them) pamphlets, meanwhile (ibid., 411).
91. On the significance of Grotius, see Mowat, *History*, 298–9. See, for Grotius's pleading for civilised behaviour in war, Manning, *Apprenticeship*, 208–9; see, too, Parker, *Success*, 147–8.
92. Menand, "Drop Your Weapons," 63; Grotius, *De iure*.
93. Martines, *Furies*, 244; see also Klooster, *Dutch Moment*, 4.
94. On the initial stages, see De Jong, "Militaire hervormingen," 485–92.
95. See, for example, Lesger, *Rise of Amsterdam*, 146.
96. Ibid., 208–9.
97. Ibid., 209. Deutz was married into the Bicker family (see Van der Vlugt, *Wij zijn*, 162, 166). Vogel compiled an impressive list of arms traders active between 1600 and 1650 that he encountered in Dutch sources, which is far from exhaustive: It does not include either of the Van Klencks, any of the De Vogelaers, or Andries Winius (see Vogel, "List of Arms Traders," 76).
98. De Jong, "Dutch Entrepreneurs," 36–7.
99. For a succinct and very lucid discussion of the operation of the Dutch government, see Boxer, *Dutch Seaborne*, 10–13. This, by the way, became the rule only after about 1600; prior to the turn of the century, when the front was much more in flux and the Dutch republican government still in its infancy, payment arrears occurred (see Manning, *Apprenticeship*, 33).

100. De Bruin provides an excellent detailed discussion, see De Bruin, *Geheimhouding*, 30.
101. See Parker, *Military Revolution*, 72–3.
102. Bennet, "Idea of Kingship," 228–33; Kozlova, "Obshchestvennoe prizhrenie," 160–4, 167–8. Thus, see Schouten's employment by the VOC (e.g., *Oost-Indische voyagie*, 17), or that of Jan Termund by the Russians (Boterbloem, *Moderniser*, 106).
103. Parrott, *Business*, 19. See as well Brown, *Merchant Kings*.
104. For example, Klooster, *Dutch Moment*, 146.
105. Brandon, *War*, 20–2.
106. See, for his comprehensive views, List, *Das nationale System*.
107. I am not sure therefore whether I agree with Bert Hall, who writes, "The real engines of transformation are found in the ability to mobilize capital to pay for troops, their munitions, and supplies, which private enterprise did better than the clumsy bureaucracy of the early modern state" (Hall, review of *Business of War* by Parrott, 622). The Dutch use of a sort of the "*gedelegeerde te velde*" to supervise the expenditures and the campaigns in general operated rather well.
108. Among those others were Balthasar Cooymans (1652–1686), a grandson of the notorious arms trader Elias Trip (1570–1636) and a nephew of the WIC director Balthasar Cooymans (1618–1690). The Cooymans family had fled from Antwerp in the late sixteenth century and were among the pioneering investors in the VOC (see Lesger, *Rise of Amsterdam*, 161). For their early forays into the slave trade, see Klooster, *Dutch Moment*, 175–6, 185.
109. See the incisive criticism by Remco Raben on the related absence of a "New Imperial History" in Dutch historiography (Raben, "New Dutch Imperial History?" 8 and *passim*). Raben does predominantly focus on modern imperialism; I am not sure about the meaning of Raben's suggestion that the "'*raison d'être*' of the Netherlands was not grounded in any imperial motivation [and that t]he Netherlands themselves were never perceived as an empire and Dutch colonialism retained a strong business-oriented and technocratic bent" (ibid., 9). Economic imperialism as tracked by André Gunder Frank or Immanuel Wallerstein does not count? What to think about the almost per-definition anti-colonial United States (even despite the Philippines, etc.) and its global domination in the twentieth, "American," century? And, especially in the early modern era, did imperial states/countries always rationalise their existence from the premise that they were first and foremost an empire? For an excellent overview of the effect and role of European imperialism in the modern era, see Berger and Miller, eds, *Nationalizing Empires*.
110. Elias, *History*, esp. 161–72.
111. Grotius, *De iure*.
112. See Brandon, *War*, Table 2.4, 105. I am not aware of a war with the Chinese emperor over Formosa/Taiwan; in fact, it was with Zheng Chenggong, who pledged allegiance to the Ming dynasty that the Qing had deposed in 1642. The short sea war with Iran of 1644–1645 is also omitted, as is the long-term struggle with the Portuguese in India; does Brandon mistake them for the Spanish (see the mention of Cochin, which in this case means South India, not South-East Asia)?
113. Van Lier's work remains a fine overview (Van Lier, *Samenleving*).
114. This was still much later, probably, and is not everywhere even today the case, given the ceremonial dress of much male royalty, for instance. Public condemnation of arms traders really began to spread after the First World War, as can be even be seen in comic books such as those by the Belgian

Hergé (see especially Hergé, *L'Oreille cassée*) as well as the once very popular books by the American writer Upton Sinclair in which the fictional protagonist Lanny Budd meets entrepreneurs such as Basil Zaharoff (e.g., Sinclair, *Dragon's Teeth*, which won a Pulitzer Prize).

115. Duindam, "Geschiedschrijving," 459; see De Vries and Van der Woude, *First Modern Economy*, 100, 102.
116. Klooster, *Dutch Moment*, 240.
117. Haks, *Vaderland*, 21–57.
118. Vanvugt, *Roofstaat*, 134–5.
119. In times of crises, as in 1672, they bought off their duty to defend their country by paying a fine and helped dig ditches (Van Deursen, *Een dorp*, 290). For the moral question in general, see, for example, Martines, *Furies*, 195.
120. Van Deursen, *Plain Lives*, 306.
121. Hobson, *Imperialism*, 48–9.
122. William III dismissed 11 councillors (out of 36) in September 1672: Among their replacements were Sautijn, Trip, and Van Klenck joining the Russia travellers Nicolaas Cornelisz Witsen and Jacob Boreel (Wagenaar, *Amsterdam*, vol. 12, 314–15). For much of the seventeenth century, meanwhile, the number of those on the council having had some involvement in (Dutch-) Russian affairs is remarkable.
123. On Sautijn, see Brandon, "Marxism," 138. Sautijn appears to have delivered arms to the French in 1671, on the eve of Louis XIV's invasion, which did not stop him from being appointed to the council (Amburger, *Die Familie*, 41–2). His relatives also heavily invested in the licensed privateering in wartime in the late seventeenth century (see Bruijn, "Kaapvaart," 416–17).
124. Gregory Carleton's recent book on Russia's infatuation, or obsession, with war is intriguing, but he ignores the fact that, no different from Russia, most countries have been at war for most of their existence and have had to adapt to this reality (see Carleton, *Russia*).
125. Glete, *War and the State*, 143. On the military ethos, see as well Kunzle, *From Criminal*, 577.
126. Most forceful in arguing for a sort of proto-proletarian mindset among seventeenth-century subalterns has been Marcus Rediker (see, e.g., Rediker, *Outlaws*; Linebaugh and Rediker, *Many-Headed Hydra*). The groundwork in this respect was laid by Eric Hobsbawm (see Hobsbawm, *Primitive Rebels*; and, as well, see Hill, *World Turned Upside Down*). Brandon argues that, while we may not know enough yet about the mindset of the regular soldiers, they were obviously not just simple-minded cannon fodder (Brandon, " 'War and Society'," 71).
127. See Marx, *Capital*, vol. 3, 751–5; see as well Smith, *An Inquiry*, 479–88.
128. See Boterbloem, *Fiction and Reality*; Boterbloem, "Inleiding." Note the savage treatment of the highwaymen in Iran whom Struys's caravan captures; Struys unhesitatingly used "we" in describing the terrible retribution to which he and his companions treat the robbers (see ibid., 355–6).
129. See *Kniga ustav'* (in Russian and Dutch), 29; *Svedeniia o botike*, 6–9; Bogoslovskii, *Petr I*, 144.
130. Lucassen, *Migrant Labour* (and other works by the same author); Van Gelder, *Het Oostindisch avontuur*; Van Gelder and Roeper, *In dienst*; Eßer, "From Province"; Van de Pol and Kuijpers, "Poor Women's Migration"; Sommerseth, Ekamper, and Sogner, "Marriage Patterns"; and (like van Gelder using the Prize Papers at Kew) Brouwer, *Levenstekens*. Obviously, the Republic was also a sanctuary for religious refugees: Not all

immigration was economically driven, and some of those refugees met with considerable hardship (see, e.g., Van der Linden, *Experiencing Exile*).

131. On the issue whether the Dutch Republic and its economy were capitalist at all, see Brandon, "Marxism."
132. One of the first latter-day critics of the nefarious quality of capitalism's "primitive accumulation" with the aid of state power was Charles Tilly (see, e.g., Tilly, "War Making and State Making"; originally, the concept of "primitive accumulation" was a Marxist concept). But Tilly rather downplayed the Dutch Republic as a minor, or temporary, player of no great historical consequence.
133. Brandon, *War*, 23–4; like Pepijn Brandon, I do not agree with those historians who suggest that the Republic's economy was somehow proto-, or non-, capitalist (see Brandon, *War*, 22–3). It was primarily a competitive market economy, with labour, services, and goods paid in money. As always in capitalism, though, in many branches of the economy, competition was rarely fair, and the most successful traders and entrepreneurs (or companies such as the VOC) sought to acquire monopolies.
134. Wagenaar, *Amsterdam*, vol. 5, 43.
135. Ibid., 43–4.
136. Ibid., 57–8. The sultan at the time was Mohammed esh-Sheikh es-Seghir (d. 1655).
137. Ibid., 273–4. This came at a time the French were still allied with the Republic and were tempted to join the second Anglo-Dutch War (1664–1667) on the Dutch side.
138. Wolfe, *Bonfire*, 9, 11.
139. Kernkamp, "Inleiding," xxviii.
140. *Nationaal Archief, Archief der Staten-Generaal* 8586 folios 93, 97–8, 358–69; De la Court, *The True Interest* [originally, *Het Interest van Holland*, 1662].
141. Veluwenkamp is one of many to notice that most Dutch trading companies were family businesses (Veluwenkamp, *Archangel*, 63). This is true, too, for manufacturing enterprises.
142. Saul interview.
143. Wallerstein, "Braudel on Capitalism," 354, 361; see also Adams, *Familial State*; Adams, "Trading States"; Prak, *Dutch Republic*; Lesger, *Rise of Amsterdam*, 139–80. Earlier than Braudel or Wallerstein, Karl Polanyi convincingly argued that the notion of an entirely free market is utopian (Polanyi, *Great Transformation* [originally, 1944], 71–80). And, of course, so did Karl Marx and Lenin (see especially Lenin, *Imperialism* [originally, 1917]).
144. See Marx, *Capital*; Smith, *Inquiry*.
145. Originally, Wallerstein, *The Modern World-System*, 4 vols. The earlier three volumes have been revised since their first publication between 1974 and 1989. Wallerstein conducted a fruitful debate with Fernand Braudel regarding the rise of capitalism in the early modern period; Braudel's view is elaborated in Braudel, *Civilization and Capitalism*. Wallerstein's main opponent in the debate has been Robert Brenner, who downplayed the significance of mercantile capitalism and suggested that modern (industrial) capitalism was rooted in what historians have called the Agricultural Revolution and proto-industrial developments within England (see, e.g., Brenner, "Agrarian Class Structure," 61–8, 71–2).
146. For example, the differentiation of people involved in agriculture in early modern France is of a bewildering complexity in terms of their title to the

land (from full ownership, to tenancy, share-cropping, and landless labourers and much in between, rather than a "triadic model"; see Wallerstein, *Modern World-System*, vol. 2, xix); to introduce "*kulaks*" in the Western European Middle Ages seems a rather odd choice of terms (ibid., xvii).

147. Ibid., xxiv.
148. Ibid.
149. Hobson, *Imperialism*, 106.
150. For more, Gelderblom, *Zuid-Nederlandse kooplieden.*
151. As Jensen and Maier suggest, almost all Hamburg merchant families in Moscow had originally immigrated to Hamburg from the Low Countries (Jensen and Maier, "Orpheus," 165n42). Besides Marselis, both Philip Verpoorten and Heinrich Butenant (eventually the Danish resident in Moscow) were among the more prominent ones. And the Marselises ventured elsewhere, although it is remarkable that they hardly operated beyond Europe (see Lauridsen, *Marselis Konsortiet*, 8).
152. Amburger, *Die Familie*, 41.
153. Klooster, *Dutch Moment*, 13.
154. See Israel, *Dutch Primacy*.
155. See for more on his ideas later in this section.
156. Brandon, *War*, 124–31.
157. See Postma, *Dutch in the Atlantic*. Slave trade was conducted elsewhere by the Dutch (and prior to the trans-Atlantic shipping of Africans), as in Asia; not all slaves were Africans either (see Klooster, *Dutch Moment*, 238–40).
158. For the fall of Taiwan from the Dutch perspective, see Lach and van Kley, *Asia*, vol. 3, 1818–1824; Wills, Jr, *Embassies*; idem, *Pepper, Guns*; and for a sober assessment (despite its somewhat grandiose title), Andrade, *Lost Colony*.
159. Prakash, *Dutch East India Company*, 257–8. On Sri Lanka, see Wagenaar, *Sri Lanka*.
160. Prud'homme van Reine, "De Republiek," 125; see also Brugmans, *Geschiedenis*, vol. 3, 13; Breedvelt-van Veen, *Louis de Geer*, 22–5. As supplier of Mansfeldt and Braunschweig, De Geer appears very much the counterpart of Hans de Witte, who supplied Wallenstein. The bills for De Geer's deliveries were largely paid by the Dutch Estates-General, which subsidised the German commanders.
161. See for more on this below in the section on the Dutch activities in the Mediterranean.
162. See Bruijn, "Kaapvaart," 415.
163. But some general conclusions may be drawn from discrete statistics, as Michiel de Jong, Pepijn Brandon, and Marjolein 't Hart do. Earlier, I already expressed my doubts about the 5 per cent estimate of Frijhoff and Spies.
164. Kunzle, *From Criminal*, 8–9.
165. For his use if this term, see also (Poe, *Russian Moment*); (Klooster, *Dutch Moment*).

Bibliography

Adams, Julia. *The Familial State: Ruling Families and Merchant Capitalism in Early Modern Europe*, Ithaca, NY: Cornell University Press, 2007.

———. "Trading States, Trading Places: The Role of Patrimonialism in Early Modern Dutch Development," *Comparative Studies in Society and History* 2, 1994, 319–55.

Aitzema, L. van. *Saken van Staet en Oorlogh*, vol. 1 (1621–32), Den Haag: Veely, Tongerloo en Doll, 1669.
Amburger, E. *Die Familie Marselis*, Gießen: Wilhelm Schmitz, 1957.
Andrade, Tonio. *Lost Colony: The Untold Story of China's First Victory over the West*, Princeton, NJ: Princeton University Press, 2011.
Bennet, D.J. "The Idea of Kingship in 17th Century Russia," unpublished PhD diss., Harvard University, 1967.
Berger, Stefan, and Alexei Miller, eds. *Nationalizing Empires*, Budapest: Central European University Press, 2015.
Boer, M.G. de. "Amsterdam ten onrechte van verraad beschuldigd," *Tijdschrift voor Geschiedenis (Land- en Volkenkunde)* 27, 1912, 1–16.
Bogoslovskii, M.M. *Petr I. Materialy dlia biografii*, vol. 1, Moskva: Ogiz, 1940.
Boterbloem, K. "Inleiding," in Jan Struys and Kees Boterbloem, eds, *Rampspoedige reizen door Rusland en Perzië in de zeventiende eeuw*, Amsterdam: Panchaud, 2014, 7–47.
———. *Moderniser of Russia: Andrei Vinius, 1641–1716*, London: Palgrave, 2013.
———. *The Fiction and Reality of Jan Struys: A Seventeenth-Century Dutch Globetrotter, Houndmills*, Basingstoke: Palgrave, 2008.
Boxer, C.R. *The Dutch Seaborne Empire*, London: Hutchison, 1965.
Brandon, Pepijn. "Een 'War and Society'-geschiedenis van de Tachtigjarige Oorlog," *Bijdragen en Mededelingen betreffende de Geschiedenis der Nederlanden* 3, 2014, 51–72.
———. "Marxism and the 'Dutch Miracle': The Dutch Republic and the Transition Debate," *Historical Materialism* 3, 2011, 106–46.
———. *War, Capital and the Dutch State (1588–1795)*, Leiden: Brill, 2015.
Braudel, F. *Civilization and Capitalism*, 3 vols., Berkeley, CA: University of California Press, 1992.
Breedvelt-van Veen, F. *Louis de Geer, 1587–1652*, Amsterdam: H.J. Paris, 1935.
Breet, M., ed. *De Oost-Indische voyagie van Wouter Schouten*, Zwolle: Walburg Pers, 2003.
Brenner, Robert. "Agrarian Class Structure and Ecomic Development in Pre-Industrial Europe," *Past and Present* 70, 1976, 3–75.
Brouwer, Judith. *Levenstekens: Gekaapte brieven uit het Rampjaar 1672*, Hilversum: Verloren, 2014.
Brown, Stephen. *Merchant Kings: When Companies Ruled the World, 1600–1900*, New York: Thomas Dunne, 2009.
Brugmans, H. *Geschiedenis van Amsterdam*, vol. 3: *Bloeitijd, 1621–97*, 2nd ed., Utrecht: Het Spectrum, 1973.
Bruin, G. de. *Geheimhouding en verraad: De geheimhouding van staatszaken ten tijde van de Republiek (1600–1750)*, 's-Gravenhage: SDU Uitgeverij, 1991.
Bruijn, J.R. "Kaapvaart in de tweede en derde Engelse oorlog," *Bijdragen en Mededelingen betreffende de Geschiedenis der Nederlanden* 90, 1975, 408–29.
Brulez, W. "De Diaspora der Antwerpse kooplui op het einde van de 16e eeuw," *Bijdragen en Mededelingen betreffende de Geschiedenis der Nederlanden* 15, 1960, 273–306.
Carleton, G. *Russia: The Story of War*, Cambridge, MA: Harvard University Press, 2017.
Court, Pieter de la. *The True Interest and Political Maxims of the Republic of Holland*, London: n.p., 1746.

Davies, Brian. *Warfare, State and Society on the Black Sea Steppe, 1500–1700*, London: Routledge, 2007.
Deursen, A.Th. van. *Een dorp in de polder*, Amsterdam: Aula, 2003.
———. *Plain Lives in a Golden Age*, Cambridge: Cambridge University Press, 1991.
Duindam, Jeroen. "Geschiedschrijving en oorlogvoering: de metamorfose van een klassiek genre," *Bijdragen en Mededelingen betreffende de Geschiedenis der Nederlanden* 4, 2003, 455–66.
Eßer, Raingard. "From Province to Nation: Immigration in the Dutch Republic in the Late 16th and early 17th Centuries," in S.G. Ellis and L. Klusakova, eds, *Imagining Frontiers, Contesting Identities*, Pisa: Pisa University Press, 2007, 264–76.
Elias, Norbert. *The History of Manners*, Oxford: Blackwell, 1994.
Frijhoff, W., and M. Spies, *1650: Bevochten Eendracht*, 2nd ed., Den Haag: SDU, 2000.
Gelder, Roelof van. *Het Oostindisch avontuur*, Amsterdam: SUN, 1997.
Gelder, Roelof van, and Vibeke Roeper, *In dienst van de Compagnie*, Amsterdam: Atheneum, Polak en Van Gennep, 2002.
Gelderblom, Oscar. *Zuid-Nederlandse kooplieden en de opkomst van de Amsterdamse stapelmarkt (1578–1630)*, Hilversum: Verloren, 2000.
Glete, Jan. *War and the State in Early Modern Europe*, New York: Routledge, 2002.
Grotius, H. *De iure belli ac pacis*, Paris: Buon, 1625.
Haks, Donald. *Vaderland en vrede: Publiciteit over de Nederlandse republiek in oorlog, 1672–1713*, Hilversum: Verloren, 2013.
Hall, Bert. "Review of the Business of War by David Parrott," *Renaissance Quarterly* 2, 2014, 621–2.
Hanssen, J.H. "The Arms Industry in Maastricht in the Seventeenth Century," in H.L. Visser and D.W. Bailey, eds, *Aspects of Dutch Gunmaking*, Zwolle: Waanders, 1997, 146–94.
Hart, Marjolein 't. "From the Eighty Years War to the Second World War: New Perspectives on the Economic Effects of War," *Tijdschrift voor Sociale en Economische Geschiedenis* 2, 2014, 261–79.
———. *The Dutch Wars of Independence: Warfare and Commerce in the Netherlands, 1570–1680*, London: Routledge, 2014.
Hergé. *L'Oreille cassée*, Brussels: Casterman, 1937.
Heijer, Henk den, and Michiel de Jong. *Oorlogen overzee. Militair optreden door staat en compagnie buiten Europa*, Amsterdam: Boom, 2015.
Hill, Christopher. *The World Turned Upside Down*, New York: Viking Press, 1972.
Hobsbawm, Eric. *Primitive Rebels*, Manchester: Manchester University Press, 1959.
Hobson, J.A. *Imperialism: A Study*, rev. ed., London: Allen and Unwin, 1938.
Israel, Jonathan. *Dutch Primacy in the World Trade, 1585–1740*, Oxford: Oxford University Press, 1989.
———. *The Dutch Republic*, Oxford: Oxford University Press, 1995.
Jansen, H.P.H. *Kalendarium. Geschiedenis van de Lage Landen in Jaartallen*, 4th ed., Utrecht: Het Spectrum, 1979.
Jensen, Claudia, and Ingrid Maier. "Orpheus and Pickleherring in the Kremlin: The 'Ballet' for the Tsar of February 1672," *Scando-Slavica* 2, 2013, 145–84.

John, A.H. "War and the English Economy," *English Historical Review* 3, 1955, 329–44.

Jong, M. de. "De Zeeuwse wapenhandel en wapenproductie, 1572–1648," *Archief: Mededelingen van het Koninklijk Zeeuwsch Genootschap der Wetenschappen* 1998, 33–56.

———. "Dutch Entrepreneurs in the Swedish Crown in Copper and Iron, 1580–1630," in Hanno Brand, ed., *Trade, Diplomacy and Cultural Change*, Hilversum: Verloren, 2005, 36–57.

———. "Militaire hervormingen in het Staatse leger en de opbouw van het wapenbedrijf, 1585–1621," *Bijdragen en Mededelingen voor de Geschiedenis der Nederlanden* 4, 2003, 467–93.

———. *Staat van Oorlog*, Hilversum: Verloren, 2005.

Kernkamp, G.W. "Inleiding," in G.W. Kernkamp, ed., *Hans Bontemantel, De regeeringe van Amsterdam, soo in't civiel als crimineel en militaire (1653–72)*, Den Haag: Nijhoff, 1897, iii-ccxxxiv.

Kernkamp, J.H. *De handel op den vijand 1572–1609*, 2 vols., Utrecht: Kemink en zoon, 1931.

———, ed. "Twee 'niet ter drukpersse bereide' geschriften van Pieter de la Court," *Bijdragen en Mededelingen van het Historisch Genootschap* 56, 1935, 151–214.

Klein, P.W. *De Trippen in de Zeventiende Eeuw*, Assen: Van Gorcum, 1965.

Klooster, Wim. *The Dutch Moment: War, Trade and Settlement in the Seventeenth-Century Atlantic World*, Ithaca, NY: Cornell University Press, 2016.

Kniga ustav' morskoi o vsem' chto kasaetsia dobromu upravleniiu, v' bytnosti flota na mor', St. Petersburg: Sankt' piterburgskaia Tipografiia, 1720.

Kozlova, N.V. "Obshchestvennoe prizhrenie i ego gosudarstvennoe regulirovanie v dopetrovskoi Rusi," in Iu.M. Eskin, ed., *Paleobureaucratica: Sbornik statei k 90-letiiu N.F. Demidovoi*, Moscow: Drevlekhranilishche, 2012, 153–70.

Kunzle, David. *From Criminal to Courtier: The Soldier in Netherlandish Art, 1550–1672*, Leiden: Brill, 2002.

Lach, Donald, and Edwin van Kley. *Asia in the Making of Europe*, 3 vols., Chicago, IL: University of Chicago Press, 1965–1993.

Lauridsen, John T. *Marselis Konsortiet: En Studie over Forholdet Mellem Handelskapital og Kongemagt i 1600-Tallets Danmark*, Arhus: Jysk Selskab for Historie, 1987.

Lenin, V.I. *Imperialism: The Highest Stage of Capitalism*, New York: International Publishers, 1933.

Lesger, Clé. *The Rise of the Amsterdam Market and Information Exchange*, Aldershot: Ashgate, 2006.

Lier, R.A. van. *Samenleving in een grensgebied*, Den Haag: Nijhoff, 1949.

Linde, B. van der. *Das Leibregiment der friesischen Staathalter*, Berlin: Duncker and Humblot, 2016.

Linden, David van der. *Experiencing Exile*, Farnham: Ashgate, 2015.

Linebaugh, P., and M. Rediker. *The Many-Headed Hydra*, Boston, MA: Beacon Press, 2000.

List, Friedrich. *Das nationale System der politischen Ökonomie*, Stuttgart: Cotta, 1841.

Loo, I.J. van. "Kaapvaart, handel en staatsbelang: Het gebruik van kaapvaart als maritiem machtsmiddel en vorm van ondernemerschap tijdens de Nederlandse

Opstand, 1568–1648," in C. Lesger and L. Noordegraaf, eds, *Ondernemers en Bestuurders*, Amsterdam: NEHA, 1999, 349–68.

Lucassen, Jan. *Migrant Labour in Europe, 1600–1900*, London: Croom Helm, 1987.

Manning, Roger. *An Apprenticeship in Arms: The Origins of the British Army, 1585–1702*, Oxford: Oxford University Press, 2006.

———. "Prince Maurice's School of War: British Swordsmen and the Dutch," *War and Society* 1, 2006, 1–19.

Martines, Lauro. *Furies: War in Europe, 1450–1700*, London: Bloomsbury, 2013.

Marx, K. *The Capital*, F. Engels, ed., vol. 3, New York: International Publishers, 1967.

Menand, Louis. "Drop Your Weapons: What Happens When You Outlaw War," *The New Yorker*, 19 September 2017, 61–6.

Mostert, Tristan. "Chain of Command: The Military System of the Dutch East India Company, 1655–1663," MA thesis, Universiteit Leiden, 2007, available at: http://vocwarfare.net/thesis/, accessed 25 November 2018.

Mowat, R.B. *A History of European Diplomacy, 1451–1789*, New York: Irchon Books, 1971.

Panhuysen, Luc. *Rampjaar 1672*, Amsterdam: Atlas, 2009.

Parker, G. *Global Crisis*, New Haven, CT: Yale University Press, 2013.

———. *Success Is Never Final: Empire, War, and Faith in Early Modern Europe*, New York: Basic Books, 2002.

———. *The Military Revolution: Military Innovation and the Rise of the West, 1500–1800*, 2nd ed., Cambridge: Cambridge University Press, 1996.

Parrott, David. *The Business of War*, Cambridge: Cambridge University Press, 2012.

Poe, M. *The Russian Moment in World History*, Princeton, NJ: Princeton University Press, 2003.

Pol, Lotte van de, and Erika Kuijpers. "Poor Women's Migration to the City: The Attraction of Amsterdam Health Care and Social Assistance in Early Modern Times," *Journal of Urban History* 1, 2005, 44–60.

Polanyi, Karl. *The Great Transformation: The Political and Economic Origins of Our Time*, Boston, MA: Beacon Press, 2001.

Postma, Johannes. *The Dutch in the Atlantic Slave Trade, 1600–1815*, Cambridge: Cambridge University Press, 2008.

Prak, Maarten. *The Dutch Republic in the Seventeenth Century*, Cambridge: Cambridge University Press, 2005.

Prakash, Om. *The Dutch East India Company and the Economy of Bengal*, Princeton, NJ: Princeton University Press, 1985.

Prud'homme van Reine, R. "De Republiek als grote en kleine mogendheid ter zee (1648–1763)," in J.R. Bruijn and C.B. Wels, eds, *Met Man en Macht: De Militaire Geschiedenis van Nederland 1500–2000*, Baarn: Balans, 2003, 105–39.

Raben, Remco. "A New Dutch Imperial History? Perambulations in a Prospective Field," *Bijdragen en Mededelingen van de Geschiedenis der Nederlanden* 1, 2013, 5–30.

Rediker, M. *Outlaws of the Atlantic*, Boston, MA: Beacon Press, 2014.

Reger, W.M. "In the Service of the Tsar: European Mercenary Officers and the Reception of Military Reform in Russia, 1654–1667," unpublished PhD diss., University of Illinois at Urbana-Champaign, 1997.

Ricklefs, M.C. *War, Culture and the Economy of Java: Asian and European Imperialism in the Early Kartasura Period*, Sydney: Allen and Unwin, 1993.

Roberts, M. "The Military Revolution (1560–1660)," in M. Roberts, ed., *Essays in Swedish History*, London: Weidenfeld and Nicholson, 1967, 193–225.

Rostow, W.W. *The Process of Economic Growth*, Oxford: Oxford University Press, 1953.

Saul, John Ralston. Television interview, broadcasted on USA C-SPAN, 19 November 2005.

Scholten, F.J. "The Arms Trade and Industry in Groningen in the First Half of the Seventeenth Century," in H.L. Visser and D.W. Bailey, eds, *Aspects of Dutch Gunmaking*, Zwolle: Waanders, 1997, 24–72.

Sinclair, Upton. *Dragon's Teeth*, New York: Viking Press, 1942.

Sloos, Louis Ph. "The Ministry of Defence's Treasury of Books: 10,000 Volumes from the 16th to the 18th Century," in L.Ph. Sloos, ed., *Warfare and the Age of Printing: Catalogue of Early Printed Books from Before 1801 in Dutch Military Collections*, vol. 1, Leiden: Brill, 2008, 22–83.

Smith, Adam. *An Inquiry into the Nature and Causes of the Wealth of Nations*, Oxford; Oxford University Press, 1976.

Snapper, F. *Oorlogsinvloeden op de overzeese handel van Holland, 1551–1719*, Amsterdam: Ellerman Harms, 1959.

Sommerseth, Hilde L., Peter Ekamper, and Sølvi Sogner. "Marriage Patterns and Residential Behaviour Among Norwegian Women in Amsterdam, 1621–1720," *Continuity and Change* 2, 2016, 175–209.

Spierenburg, P.C. *Judicial Violence in the Dutch Republic*, Amsterdam: Amsterdam University Press, 1978.

Struys, Jan. "Rampspoedige reizen door Rusland en Perzië" in Kees Boterbloem, ed., *de zeventiende eeuw*, Amsterdam: Panchaud, 2014.

Svedeniia o botike dedushke russkago flota za 200 let' s' 1688 po 1888 god', St. Petersburg: n.p., 1888.

Swart, Erik. *Krijgsvolk: Militaire professionalisering en het ontstaan van het Staatse leger, 1568–1590*, Amsterdam: Amsterdam University Press, 2006.

Tilly, C. "War Making and State Making as Organized Crime," in Peter B. Evans, Dietrich Rueschemeyer, and Theda Skocpol, eds, Bringing the State Back in, Cambridge: Cambridge University Press, 1985, 169–91.

Unger, R.W. *Dutch Shipbuilding Before 1800: Ships and Guilds*, Assen: Van Gorcum, 1978.

Vanvugt, E. *Roofstaat*, Amsterdam: Nijgh and Van Ditmar, 2016.

Veluwenkamp, J.W. *Archangel: Nederlandse ondernemers in Rusland, 1550–1785*, Amsterdam: Balans, 2000.

Vlugt, Simone van der. *Wij zijn de Bickers*, Amsterdam: Prometheus, 2019.

Vogel, H. "Arms Production and Exports in the Dutch Republic, 1600–1650," in M. van der Hoeven, ed., *Exercise of Arms: Warfare in the Netherlands, 1568–1648*, Leiden: Brill, 1997, 189–210.

———. "List of Arms Traders 1600–1650) [sic]," in J.P. Puype and M. van der Hoeven, eds, *The Arsenal of the World: The Dutch Arms Trade in the Seventeenth Century*, Amsterdam: Batavian Lion International, 1996, 76.

Vries, Jan de. *The Economy of Europe in an Age of Crisis, 1600–1750*, New York: Cambridge University Press, 1976.

Vries, Jan de, and A. van der Woude. *The First Modern Economy: Success, Failure and Perseverance of the Dutch Economy, 1500–1815*, Cambridge: Cambridge University Press, 1997.

Wagenaar, Jan. *Amsterdam in zijne opkomst*, 13 vols., Amsterdam: Isaak Tirion, 1760-c.1784.

Wagenaar, Lodewijk. *Sri Lanka en Nederland sinds 1602*, Nijmegen: Vantilt, 2016.

Wallerstein, I. "Braudel on Capitalism, or Everything Upside Down," *Journal of Modern History* 2, 1991, 354–61.

———. *The Modern World-System*, 4 vols., Berkeley, CA: University of California Press, 2011.

Wijn, J.W. "Het krijgswezen in den tijd van prins Maurits I," unpublished PhD diss., University of Utrecht, 1934.

Wills, Jr., John E. *Embassies and Illusions*, Cambridge, MA: Harvard University Press, 1984.

———. *Pepper, Guns and Parleys*, Cambridge, MA: Harvard University Press, 1974.

Wolfe, Tom. *The Bonfire of the Vanities*, New York: Farrar, Straus, Giroux, 1989.

3 The Early Modern Dutch and War, Part 2

Morale

3.1 Mindset

A significant component of the early modern Dutch sense of identity was a martial and masculine prowess.[1] We saw earlier how all men were expected to handle a firearm and be ready to fight in case of an attack on the republic. At sea, sailors knew how to use firearms and cold steel. The legend of Kenau Simonsdochter Hasselaar (1526–1588), the redoubtable defender of Haarlem who poured boiling tar from the city walls on the Spanish besiegers, appears to have been cherished, signifying even a readiness among women to take up arms in a crisis, adopting a male and bellicose role.[2] It is germane here to ponder the apparent conviction, fairly widespread in the late sixteenth century among military officers (foreign and domestic, as well as among thinkers such as Justus Lipsius), that the Dutch were lacking Roman-or Spartan-like qualities to make them into credible soldier-citizens capable of defending their republic.[3] Altogether, this perception seems to have been grounded in the sort of traditional noble contempt for the burghers, who made their money through commerce and manufacturing rather than fighting. It sat ill with the *schutters*, the citizen militias, made immortal thanks to Rembrandt's *Nightwatch*, that were armed, maintained public order, and drilled to defend their cities in times of siege, and appears a rather oafish misreading of the burghers' mindset: Effeminate or feeble they were not.[4] On the contrary, their very compassion towards the poor and meek seems grounded in a facile desire to buy off their conscience, when they appear wholly unscrupulous, and perfectly willing to turn to violence, in their business affairs.

As historians have noticed, once the greater professionalism of the armies of Maurice and William Louis became the norm in the Dutch land forces by about 1600, the burgher militias became a comparatively ineffective fighting force, assigned to auxiliary tasks such as guard duties.[5] The *schutterijen* became social clubs, displaying pomp and pride at ritual ceremonies, vehicles to underscore masculinity or virility (even if in Frans Hals's paintings the militiamen's officer corps often looks overweight to us) and command social respect from their social subalterns.

Still, the militia was not just a case of grown-up men playing boys' games.[6] Burgher militias regularly exercised with firearms.[7] They kept the peace within the towns' walls, manned those walls, and posted sentry at their gates. One of the most elaborate accounts reflecting the mindset of the Dutch elite in the middle of the seventeenth century, that of Amsterdam's alderman-in-chief Hans Bontemantel (1613–1688), is eloquent testimony to the survival of the martial mentality among the *schutters*, a century after the most harrowing phase of the Dutch independence wars against Spain.[8]

Schutters commanding officers tended to be part of the city regency, but their lower officers came from among the middle class of merchants, professionals such as doctors or guild masters, while the rank-and-file were made up out of men from the lower middle class and skilled working class (artisans).[9] While a significant part of the male population (the semi-skilled workers, day labourers, or the indigent) was excluded from the *schutterijen*, *schutter* numbers may have been 10,000 in seventeenth-century Amsterdam, which means that some 5 per cent of the city's population served in them.[10] Since one could become a *schutter* only as an adolescent, it can be estimated that one fifth of the city's male population saw guard duty, drilled, or marched as a part of this militia. If one adds several hundreds of regular soldiers who were normally garrisoned in in the city of Amsterdam and the innumerable sailors—capable of wielding firearms and other weapons—who called the city their home (many of whom, of course, were absent for lengthy periods), one may suggest that this was an urban community very much armed and ready to do battle when called upon.[11] The walls and bulwarks surrounding the cities were another constant reminder of the precarious nature of the peace that reigned in the interior of the seventeenth-century Republic.

Bontemantel admitted that the *schutters* had frequently engaged in frivolous pastimes in the immediately preceding years of the year of agony that was 1672 but described how they were at the ready when they were once more called into action to face the looming French threat.[12] He wrote how his *schutters* "have been so much trained in the use of arms and in other exercises during the heavy wars against England and France, that they do not have to yield to any regular units [*lantmilitie*]."[13] Among their Amsterdam officers (members of the city's upper crust), the enthusiasm was more apparent than real, though: When asked to deploy, it was only Bontemantel himself who keenly volunteered to march with his unit to the front. According to a sneering Bontemantel, Louys Trip, who served as captain of the militia and was to be elevated to the city council in the following weeks (replacing among others Bontemantel), stated how he "could not handle [*volgen*] combat . . . [, this] soon-to-be alderman, councillor, mayor and director of the East-India Company."[14] Trip was a scion of the famous family who had made an absolute fortune in the arms trade.

Marjolein 't Hart does indeed perceive in the 1672 call-up of most adult men in the towns and countryside signs of "compulsory military service," albeit "short-lived."[15] The cost of maintaining a well-trained army based on universal male conscription was too prohibitive, whereas long-term service in the militia would have depleted the male labour population in the towns. But the motivation among the ranks serving in the militia in 1672 was as good (or as bad), it seems, as it had been when it fought the Spaniards a hundred years earlier, even if its fighting capacity or efficacy was not.[16]

Serving in war was seen as a likely occurrence for men in the Golden Age Republic. Many Dutchmen (and foreigners) chose to become sailors, who were almost uniformly expected to be able to handle weapons (from cannon to pistols, muskets, swords, knives, and daggers) and almost inevitably saw combat when serving on their ships, whether those of the navy, the VOC and WIC, or those owned by private individuals. Sometimes men took to sea because of insurmountable personal difficulties (especially poverty), but for many, the seafaring vessels and life overseas promised more than a mere livelihood, such as adventure and booty.[17]

't Hart argues that the constant vigilance required from those living in a country under foreign threat "increased [the] duties imposed upon burghers during the Dutch Wars of Independence [and] strengthened the notion of local citizenship."[18] Lipsius notwithstanding, a sort of latter-day armed Greek *polis* was therefore created, even if service in town militias began to lose its military significance in the course of the Eighty Years' War and even when, from the end of the Twelve Years' Truce onward, warfare was kept at arm's length as far as the Republic's core provinces were concerned.[19] A patriotic or civic, indeed nationalist, spirit prevailed among broad layers of Dutch society, which on various crucial occasions clearly trumped any class antagonism. This sort of civic solidarity began to falter only in the course of the eighteenth century, when religious freedom and political autonomy seemed safe, while anti-Catholic, anti-Spanish, or anti-French sentiments waned.[20] Lack of a common enemy weakened nationalist resolve, and the Prussians met very little resistance when they invaded the country during the 1780s.

In how far the Dutch activities were structured by a "messianic imperialism," a widespread identification with a chosen people that fought in the name of a True Protestantism remains moot.[21] One relevant peculiar phenomenon at least deserves to be pondered here: Until 1648, the Dutch government and its armed forces fought with sometimes fanatical determination the battle with perfidious Catholicism in Europe (not just through military operations but also by bankrolling and supplying other Protestant armies), whereas their colonial administrators, soldiers, and even church ministers hardly lifted a finger to bring the Calvinist Gospel to non-Europeans.[22] Such a lack of proselytism was perhaps wise because the Dutch in overseas areas could ill afford to provoke the anger of the well-armed polities with whom they traded (and in whose territories they sometimes founded trading posts and even larger settlements). Provoking violent protest through religious proselytism was thus shunned for tactical reasons: The protracted struggle with the native Americans along the Atlantic coast or the Bantam and Mataram sultanates on Java shows that it was not easy to gain unchallenged military superiority despite technological advantages.[23] Offending religious sensibilities was not very wise if one wanted to capitalise on trading opportunities; if the Dutch may have doubted such wisdom, the fate of the Portuguese and Spaniards, who were banished from Tokugawa Japan, where they came to be seen as part of a global Catholic conspiracy, will have been revealing.

And, soon after the Dordt Synod concluded in 1619, the Dutch Calvinists' effort to Protestantise even their own population became tepid, certainly when compared with the zeal of the Catholic Reformation in Spain. Areas in the east (Twente) and south (north-Brabant) of the Republic, captured late in the struggle with the Spaniards, remained solidly Catholic until deep into the twentieth century.[24] There were a few Catholic martyrs in the 1560s, 1570s, and 1580s, but no Catholic zealot perished for his beliefs afterwards. Concomitantly, Spanish brutality against the Dutch (and Flemish) population declined drastically after Antwerp's fall in 1585 as well.[25] In other words, even if after 1600 the war in the Low Countries remained in theory one to the death between Catholicism and Protestantism, in practice, the violence of the conflict was rather restrained (although less so at sea).[26] The Dutch soon paid mere lip-service to the idea of being a messianic nation, uniquely chosen to rescue true Christianity with fire and sword from the corrupt Catholic church.

Meanwhile, morale was kept up by the burgeoning presses in this centre of European print culture. Undoubtedly, illiteracy remained significant even among the urban population of Holland, but the Dutch also excelled in churning out iconographic illustrations of hostile cruelty against innocent civilians, committed by military serving the Spanish kings in the Eighty Years' War, or Louis XIV after 1672.[27] Such broadsheets found an audience beyond those who could read with ease; in this way, semi-literate or illiterate, the common folk's fury was fuelled. Once again, "[people in the seventeenth century] considered war and violence a fact of life that was inevitable."[28] The Dutch fell victim to plunder but in their turn looted and pillaged as much as any when on campaign. Religious outrage, though, seems muted in much of this iconography after 1600.

To allow for a much greater agency among lower-class Dutch soldiers and sailors in their efforts to benefit from their wielding of rare skills that were in high demand complicates the traditional Marxian understanding of capitalists as strictly speaking middle-class exploiters.[29] Perhaps rather than being (class-conscious) proletarians, after 1600, a sort of capitalist mindset spread among the lower strata of Dutch society. Many people understood how to offer rare skill that was in high demand on the labour market. We should consider early modern rank-and-file soldiers as artisans or skilled workers; indeed, mercenaries may have lived a more adventurous and enjoyable life than the average stay-at-home peasant or unskilled urban worker. In sometimes consummate fashion, they sold their talent for a considerable price, operating like small-scale private entrepreneurs.[30] Certainly, the bunch of Amsterdam and Noorderkwartier sailors and shipwrights who in 1667 and 1668 enlisted for extremely high wages in the tsar's service displayed a good deal of savvy and was keenly interested in turning a handsome profit.[31] It seems no coincidence that this troop's departure for Russia occurred at the very moment the leading Dutch politician Johan de Witt established the world's first marine corps: Dutch sailors were expected to be able to fight.[32] A further logical step towards professionalisation, this was another long-lasting innovation in the way wars were fought.

The question begs whether this militarist-capitalist mindset was a purely male phenomenon, given many contemporary women's close familiarity with war. For women, life in the army was perhaps less unequivocally preferable over staying at home for the women serving in various capacities in the army train than for men. A great number of women in the villages of North-Western Europe, though, seem to have spent their lives in everyday drudgery. While many remained single, those who married concluded unions more often than not on economic grounds (at the wishes of others). Given these alternatives, perhaps the army train was not the worst place to spend one's life as a woman; Bertolt Brecht's *Mutter Courage*, which depicts the utterly ghastly existence of a woman in the army train, is, after all, fiction, written 300 years after the Thirty Years' War; Grimmelshausen's contemporary work about "*Courasche*" on which the Brecht play is based has a different, more satirical, tone.[33] Obviously, in the warfare of the age women rarely saw combat but were rather involved in the train, as sutlers, cooks, housekeepers, *de facto* nurses, prostitutes, or, indeed, wives. Kenau Hasselaar's case was a rare instance of a woman actively joining the fighting.

It can be said, however, that women in the Republic, as Van den Heuvel and others have indicated, had more agency than their contemporaries elsewhere, and that life in the Dutch towns was perhaps more exciting for women than life in a village in Bavaria or the Massif Central.[34] The capitalist spirit was not quite gender specific, one gathers, for many a widow (also of arms traders) took over the business of a suddenly deceased husband who had left them without an obvious male successor; like Hasselaar, some of these women had remarkable agency, such as the publishers' widows Van Meurs or De Groot.[35] In Russia, where Orthodox noble women were secluded, Maria van Sweeden-Ruts managed to persuade Tsar Aleksei to confirm her ownership of many of her husband Jan van Sweeden's enterprises after the latter's sudden death in 1668 and had no qualms about billetting the sailors that were to police the Caspian Sea for Tsar Aleksei.[36] She had the tsarist government pay her for many of the costs her husband had incurred in hiring various artisans, including those Dutch sailors, to serve the tsar.[37] The agency of Dutch women is also apparent from the 1670s petition to the same tsar by *Alenitsa Ivanova dochershika* (Aaltje Jansdochter), the widow of the *Oryol*'s carpenter Dirk Pietersz, for her husband's wages.[38]

Emblematic of female assertiveness was the widow of the "founding father" of one of the mightiest trading houses on Russia, Marcus de Vogelaer sr, Margriet van Balkenburg, who took over his business in 1610, including his seat among the VOC's governing board, the *Heeren XVII*.[39] She was taxed an astonishing surtax of 1,500 guilders in 1631 Amsterdam, which meant that she was estimated to own property valued at 600,000 guilders and thereby well-nigh the richest person in the city.[40] The fabulously successful arms trader Elias Trip was "only" levied 1,200 guilders in the 1631 assessment.[41] To provide some further perspective, Van Deursen estimated the "typical" average annual wage as about 200 guilders per year.[42]

In the absence of any telling egodocuments of women involved in arms manufacturing or trade, one is otherwise left to speculate, however.[43] Women must have shared the conviction that violence and war were a normal part of life.[44] Many women appear to have housed garrisoned soldiers to whom they charged room and board in the seventeenth century, a welcome addition to their income, as Benjamin van der Linde points out for Leeuwarden and Groningen.[45] And the continual state of war did offer sometimes perhaps even better opportunities to women born in abject poverty; one wonders if the tellingly named *marketensters* indeed divined an opportunity for gain not otherwise easily available (despite the *Mutter Courage*–type risks involved in this activity). In general, the opportunities for sex work that came during war either at the front, on campaign, or in the hinterland were rather better than in peacetime, since the authorities lacked the will and ability to really suppress the trade (in the towns, prostitution was in practice often regulated, even if formally prohibited).[46] This was work that was in complete defiance of all principles and rules prescribed in Scripture and condemned by public morality, but little concerted effort was made to end prostitution before the confessionalisation wave that began to gain force towards 1700.

The downtrodden, men or women, who were allegedly people without agency, appear often enough in the sources as *pur sang* capitalists, doggedly pursuing material rewards driven by a belief that the world is makeable, rather than that one is tied to one's divinely ordained station in life. It is moot when exactly this sort of man (and to some degree woman) as *homo faber* became a dominant role model among significant swaths of the population in the Low Countries, but it was a major departure from the medieval conviction that one needed to meekly accept one's fate, awaiting better things in the afterlife.[47] It was probably linked to flourishing urban life in Brabant, Flanders, Holland, and Zeeland that long predated the outbreak of the Dutch Revolt in 1566. And it is certainly true that not everyone had converted to it among the poor in the Dutch towns, let alone the countryside. It is similarly plausible that this capitalist opportunism waned once the Dutch economy ended its phenomenal growth towards 1700, when chances for advancement began to dry up, and that, in the later eighteenth and early nineteenth centuries, this entrepreneurial or capitalist spirit almost vanished among the Dutch working class during the prolonged economic stagnation of those decades.

But this Dutch faith that you can make it if you try, a sort of a proto-American Dream, is undeniable in the Golden Age. Jan de Vries has recently suggested the occurrence of an industrious revolution occurring among the Dutch in the Protestant north, and delayed gratification, or a conviction about the benefits of savings and thrift, offset, or combined with, a spreading consumerist revolution.[48] Perhaps, though, because this was such an early version of the capitalist ethos, it sported rough edges that come across as crude and savage to us who are used to a more "civilised" form of capitalism. Violence was a fact of life not just because of constant warfare but also in settling disputes at a personal level, and the authorities in the Dutch Republic did not shirk from applying the death penalty to convicted criminals, whose bodies were hanging for weeks on the gallows just outside of the city gates, while lesser offenders were mutilated on court orders.[49] And it had been so since times immemorial. The inhabitants of the United Provinces (or of the Seventeen Netherlands) had been accustomed to perpetual warfare, and the Eighty Years' War was in some ways a merely extraordinarily long sustained instance of this grim existence.[50] What was new, however, was the link the population began to make between warfare and the opportunity for profit it created: "*Men maakte van de nood een deugd*," "make a virtue out of necessity," the saying may have been. The wars against the Habsburg Philipses and Louis XIV were defensive, at least in Europe, but not necessarily an unmitigated tragedy. This is even more true for the Dutch involvement in the Danish-Swedish conflicts, Russia's military modernisation, or the Dutch military moves in Indonesia, Taiwan, India, Iran, along the Atlantic seaboard of North America, or in the Caribbean, Brazil, and sub-Saharan Africa, in all of which places the Dutch waged offensive wars. Threatening or using violence was one method that could be used to acquire profit.

A militarily focussed mindset was married to a capitalist ethos, leading to the accumulation of stunning wealth by certain individuals and contributing to a level of affluence across Dutch society that was without par in the seventeenth century. Money could be made from war in unexpected ways, too: Israel notices how the artist Philips Wouwerman (1619–1668) "amassed a fortune by painting hundreds of cavalry skirmishes for which, evidently, there was an inexhaustible demand."[51] Haks suggests that the homefront, even when not in the proximity of a combat zone, was as supportive of the wars their country waged between 1672 and 1713 as it had been between 1566 and 1648, even if during both those lengthy engagements fatigue began to creep in, which was escalating towards the end of each of them.[52] Manning agrees with Haks that resolve remained strong after 1672: Whereas he argues that the Dutch before 1672 had been less prone to join the colours, they provided more soldiers to William III's armies than the English, who could draw on a population twice the size of the Republic's.[53]

Before 1700, a primordial penchant for violence lent a particular ruthless quality to the pursuit of riches on the part of the Dutch and may be part of the explanation of the lack of moral scruples regarding involvement in the slave trade, arms trade, or in battle. But the Dutch *homo militaris* on land and at sea, who lived in a felicitous symbiosis with the *homo faber* in the Low Countries of the sixteenth and seventeenth centuries, undoubtedly disappeared after 1700.

3.2 Dutch Identity

Being Dutch often meant to sacrifice oneself, or lose one's kin, on the altar of national independence. This was a country born in war, and even in the orally transmitted collective memory, a sense of nation forged in the heat of war will have survived. But defending one's own turf, as in 1572 or 1672, is one thing; fighting for one's country in faraway places is another. How firm was Dutch sentimental attachment to their homeland?

Towards the end of his life, the Dutch Protestant minister François Valentijn (1666–1727) wrote in his description of the East Indies, how

> . . . the Dutch [*Nederlandsche*] nation was not only [more advanced] than all the ancient peoples who had been in the East [i.e., Asia], but particularly because of the way they rule in those countries and many monarchies that they possess there, ahead of the other Europeans . . . they show how they have not strayed from their ancient Batavian ancestors.[54]

For Valentijn, it seemed uncomplicated who these Netherlanders were, and perhaps in the Far Eastern VOC factories that he knew Dutchness had been a straightforward concept, encompassing those of European extraction who were on the VOC payroll. The issue of being Dutch in the seventeenth century, however, was much more complicated.

What exactly made someone "Dutch"? To some extent, of course, any identification as a member of an ethnocultural group is subjective and subject to change as the history of immigration indicates. National identity is often "fluid" or even "liminal," using terms often used in discourse about identity.[55] To determine the extent of any shared sense of identity is therefore complicated.[56] As Serhii Plokhy suggests, in the seventeenth century, "ethnonational identities were secondary to other types of identity and loyalty, such as those based on family, clan, social group, region, dynasty and religion, [but] ethnonational identity existed and contribute[d] significantly to the formation of collective and individual self-consciousness."[57]

Of course, early modern people were not enumerated in a census or poll and asked about their identity as modern surveys sometimes do. Passports or identity papers did not exist. Furthermore, the political boundaries of the Republic became firm with the Peace of Münster only in 1648. This was a country that saw every year thousands of people in search of employment arriving from other parts of Europe, settling in without any check of their papers, and so forth, as is the custom today. How long did it take for them to identify or pass as Dutch rather than Hessian, Sephardic, Westphalian, Flemish, Walloon, English, Scottish, Irish, Danish, or French? And did the inhabitants of each of the seven provinces consider themselves first Frisian or Hollander before Netherlander? Or did people even feel first and foremost Haarlemmer, Amsterdammer, or Waterlander before they even felt Hollander? And in how far did they first and foremost identify with the community of their church? A common language did not exist either. The mother tongue in one province was Frisian. In the east, Saxon dialects were spoken on both sides of the border with the Empire. And in the Spanish Netherlands, about half of the population spoke a version of Netherlandic or Dutch, too, but was subject to the Habsburg king residing in Castile.

Despite such complications, I agree with Plokhy, Anthony Marx, or Adrian Hastings that it is too reductionist to argue that broad-based nationalism is a purely modern phenomenon, born in the age of the great French political and British industrial revolutions.[58] As I have suggested previously, among broad layers of seventeenth-century Dutch society a sense of patriotic solidarity can be detected.[59] When few in the Republic proved willing to sign up for service in Brazil (or on the ships that departed for it) around 1650, enough were quite willing to serve in the navy against the English in 1652.[60] Surely, it will have seemed less daunting to fight in waters nearby the Republic, but can that alone explain this remarkable difference? Those who embarked in 1652 must have at least in part been motivated by a desire to defend their country, reflective of a nationalist loyalty.

To establish exactly who was included into this Dutch community and who was not is impossible, for such a conviction was more implicit and ill defined than explicit and clearly demarcated. People's sense of allegiance to the Republic as their "homeland," or fatherland *(Vaderland)*, and their loyalty to the stadtholders was mixed with other identity markers, such as their religious beliefs (and membership of an organised church), a degree of class consciousness (not just among the working classes, but also among nobles and affluent denizens of the middle classes), and a more specific geographically and politically determined loyalty to one's region or city as well as an allegiance to one's guild, firm, or patron, for example.[61] And blood ran a lot thicker than water, as is evident from the family networks of regents and businessmen.

An effort was made to invent a tradition through linking the freedom-loving and bellicose Batavians depicted by Tacitus to the seventeenth-century Hollanders (or all Dutch), but in how far such myths convinced anyone remains moot.[62] After all, not that many people had the money and leisure to read the books in which this ancestry was expounded. As the German chancellor Otto von Bismarck (1815–1898) knew so well, galvanising a sense of collective identity through the demonising of a common enemy is a remarkably effective means of forging a nation; a multitude of Dutch texts from the Eighty Years' War that make the "Spaniards," their king, military commanders, and troops into monsters (including the use of the Black Legend) survive. They attest to the prodigious production of the printing presses of the Low Countries in the late sixteenth and seventeenth centuries as well as the scale of the reading audience receptive to the "us against them" rhetoric they propagated.[63] The plastic arts additionally solidified collective solidarity, not just through depicting heroic moments or Spanish atrocities in painting but also by such things as siege maps that decorated domestic walls.[64] It is noteworthy in this respect, too, that the text of the current Dutch national anthem, the *Wilhelmus*, is a long poem in praise of William I of Orange, which was already diffused in the late sixteenth century (albeit without its current musical score).[65] The anti-Spanish, and subsequent anti-English or anti-French, propaganda seems to have contributed in no small measure to the Dutch seventeenth-century sense of collective belonging. And, obviously, nothing bound the Germans of Bismarck's day more to their country than the growing prosperity that accompanied the first decades of the second German Empire. The Dutch Republic, too, engendered loyalty from its inhabitants through its remarkably high standard of living.

No formally recognised independent Dutch Republic existed before 1648, despite the Union of Utrecht of 1579, or the *de facto* recognition of the country by the French and English monarchs towards 1600. Many of the protagonists in the United Provinces in politics and economic life were born in (Spanish) Flanders and (southern) Brabant. But people thought of themselves as Dutch all the same. In the overseas parts that flew the Dutch flag, most residents from European descent readily identified as

Dutch; doing so offered them protection, privileges, and even comfort in a hostile environment. In other words, while they undoubtedly acculturated, to a greater or lesser degree, to their non-European surroundings and adopted non-European ways, they also acculturated to the Dutch way of handling things and became at a minimum versed in the Dutch language.

Despite clear evidence of discrimination of German or Scandinavian immigrants, the Republic remained a country that was relatively tolerant of newcomers. This was the case not only for the seven provinces that made up the Republic but also for its overseas territories, where many natives of other European countries settled. Those who had not been raised in the Republic, as historians of the European immigration to the Republic have persuasively noted, were lower on the pecking order of Dutch society, even if a remarkable degree of tolerance towards them was exhibited (certainly when compared with the xenophobia that was encountered in other places in the seventeenth century).[66] It is difficult to say when immigrants "passed the bar" of Dutchness, although for some (e.g., those hailing from the southern Netherlands in the 1570s and 1580), this was rather easier than for others; recently, it has been suggested that Huguenot refugees of the 1670s and 1680s, who scholars thought to have experienced a fairly smooth settlement in the Republic, were actually not always welcomed with open arms.[67] Certainly, the military (as can be seen from higher officers such as Johan Maurits of Nassau-Siegen, Kurt Sivertsen Adeler [1622–1675], or Niels Olsen/Cornelis Cruys [c.1655–1727]) and the trading companies seem to have been least discriminating in their perception of who was or was not Dutch.

It needs to be further investigated what exactly happened with foreign mercenary troops in Dutch service, especially when they had served out the terms of their contract or chose to retire from their profession. Around 1700, three quarters of the officer corps of the Republic's army was "Dutch," by which presumably is meant born on Dutch soil.[68] A similar dominance by Dutch officers prevailed in the navy. Haks suggests, rightfully, "looking at these numbers [of the thousands of deaths in key land and sea battles in the wars fought between 1672 and 1713, it] seems evident that the longer the wars lasted, the greater the percentage of the population that knew of a fallen relative or acquaintance."[69] Such sacrifice becomes less painful if it is given the meaning of dying for a good cause, such as that of national independence.

Although undoubtedly religious motives were entangled with feelings of national solidarity in this regard, a strenuous effort was made to liberate Dutch captives from confinement (which was linked with enslavement) by Muslims, such as the Barbary corsairs.[70] Collections to this purpose among Protestant churchgoers were common across the United Provinces, in both towns and villages, and were coordinated by some of the highest-ranking regents, such as Nicolaas Witsen.[71] Such care for one's compatriots in need, too, informed the efforts of the VOC officers in Iran to rescue Jan Struys and his comrades in the 1670s (even if this crew was hired as part of a Russian effort to compete with the VOC!).[72] This suggests that a form of national solidarity, even if mixed with religious concerns, existed in this era.

The behaviour of Dutch expatriates indicates that there was a clear limit to early modern Dutch nationhood's hold. "Renegades" (converts to Islam) are numerous in the annals of Dutch history of this period, whereas others chose to convert to Eastern Orthodoxy (with others emphatically remaining Calvinists) in Russia, "went native" in Asia, or became Englishmen or Hamburgers.[73] Ultimately, though, the fluidity of the Dutch "national identity" does align with my argument that a version of a capitalist or opportunistic mindset was common in the Republic, and, undoubtedly, in other, neighbouring, parts of north-western Europe, where serfdom was disappearing and geographical mobility became ever more common as a result (and for reasons other than an end to legal bondage as well). To some degree, being Dutch meant taking one's chances, actively trying to improve one's life, God helping the man who helped himself; this sort of universal capitalist guise appealed not merely to those who were born in the United Provinces after 1566. And it meant that it was sometimes more rewarding to lose one's Dutch identity.

As being Dutch was not a rigidly demarcated identity in the seventeenth century, the reader may object at times at my slightly arbitrary use of "Dutch" as an adjective and noun. A stark example of this whim may be my appropriation of Louys de Geer as a Dutchman. De Geer was born in the prince-bishopric of Liège, which was not even one of the provinces of the Emperor Charles V's seventeen "*Nederlanden*." De Geer may be dubbed Dutch in my view, because, as a Calvinist, he chose to live in the northern Netherlands (and seems to have preferred to live out his last years in Amsterdam). But what about his extensive service to the Swedish crown, which ennobled him? I consider De Geer Dutch nonetheless because that has been the consensus among historians who have written about him, even if I am not quite convinced myself that this is justified.[74] De Geer's success is emblematic of Amsterdam's flourishing, as Hajo Brugmans explained in his history of Amsterdam.[75] Certainly, even when De Geer was in the middle of expanding his Swedish iron-and-arms enterprises, he was key in equipping and supplying the ruthless Ernst von Mansfeld, one of the main Protestant commanders in the Thirty Years' War, who was primarily subsidised by the Dutch Estates-General; De Geer acted at the time both as financier and as agent of the Dutch government.[76] He had done so well that he could bail out the Dutch government when it was short of ready cash. It seems that his loyalty was throughout to the Dutch (more than the Swedish) as well as the Protestant cause. Meanwhile, the admiration of De Geer's arms trade was great in Holland and his loyalty was rewarded; the Estates-General allowed him to export his weapons to friendly powers such as Sweden without having to pay an excise tax, and he enjoyed various other such perquisites.[77]

De Geer's "Dutchness" was shared by most scions of the noble Nassau family, even if William I and his siblings, as well as several scions of the succeeding generation, had been born in the German parts of the Holy Roman Empire. To give another example of the complication in pinpointing someone's national allegiance, Koenraad van Klenck was the grandson of minor "German" nobleman who had been a courtier of the Nassaus at Dillenburg in the Empire. In the 1660s, Koenraad and his brothers requested the Holy Roman Emperor Leopold I (1640–1705) to confirm the noble title they had inherited, even though the family had evidently relocated to the United Provinces almost a century earlier.[78] This was part of a desire for literal gentrification to which the Dutch mercantile elite was prone, even though the Van Klencks could claim genuine noble ancestry.[79] Still, the Emperor was a Catholic monarch, and the Van Klencks were citizens of a Protestant Republic. Requesting affirmation of their noble status was a curious move. A few years later in Russia, Koenraad van Klenck prided himself on his status as Lord of Lohrheim and Ohrsee (places in the Empire, too), but sheerly for his role as Extraordinary Ambassador of the United Provinces alone he should be considered Dutch.

Finally, it is worthwhile to ponder one more curious case in which someone *ceased* to be Dutch to clarify what it meant to be Dutch. In a petition of 1648, Andries Denijszoon Winius asked to become a subject of the Russian Tsar Aleksei Mikhailovich; identifying himself as a native of Amsterdam, Winius stated, in the somewhat awkward Russian chancellery language of the age, that he had "abandoned his being subject of the Dutch Estates [-General] long ago."[80] A successful merchant and entrepreneur, Winius was a sort of upstart, not unlike a number of his contemporaries who became leading lights in the Dutch economy and society and in its politics between 1590 and 1650. He claimed that he no longer felt himself Dutch in 1648 (when he was in his forties), but he did seem to have thought of himself as such previously. He had started out as an enterprising Dutchman before he switched his allegiance to the Russian tsar: There is little doubt that he was prompted by the expectation of considerable economic benefits that would derive from this move, although anger at not being supported by the Dutch government in his Russian ventures (as some of his compatriots were) may have played its part.[81] It is noteworthy that only several years *after* this change of sovereign Winius converted to Russian Orthodoxy: His 1648 request had not been the consequence of a religious epiphany. The most famous Dutch poet of the age, Joost van den Vondel (1587–1679), lauded Winius in a poem as a sort of ideal Dutch entrepreneur when the merchant returned to Amsterdam as the tsar's key weapons purchaser in 1653 (and he bought some 20,000 muskets on this trip, which added to the thousands of arms the factories at Tula that he founded were turning out).[82] This exercise in vanity seems to reflect Winius's spite about the injustices he had suffered at the hands of the Dutch government, which he had abjured.

Winius's case is a rarity because of its peculiar Russian context, as in Muscovy Western foreigners remained "*nemtsy*," Germanic outsiders, as did Patrick Gordon, the Catholic Scot, or François Lefort, the Swiss Calvinist. The tsars were tolerant of other religions not in the least because of the vast size of their realm and the great variety of peoples under their rule, which made attempts to convert all to Russian Orthodoxy a chimera in this "composite empire."[83] Westerners were not overly pressured to become Orthodox, even though a few did (more often than not as second-generation immigrants, in other words, children already born on Russian soil). But to actually become a Russian subject by way of formally submitting to the tsar was rather unusual for a Western European around 1650. Still, Winius's case does underscore the fluid or liminal understanding of "nationality," which became especially apparent among those whose fortune was largely made abroad. And whereas the nationality of Winius, the Orange-Nassaus, or De Geer can still be determined with some degree of certainty, this is much harder for the Marselis family. After 1620, the various Marselis brothers and cousins were active across all northern Europe, with siblings residing in Holland, Hamburg, Denmark, and Muscovy at the same time.

In other words, national identity (the existence of which is undeniable among the *literate* population of the Dutch Republic in the seventeenth century) was fluid, and it is sometimes difficult to pin down the moment at which a person can be considered (or can consider himself) Dutch rather than Flemish or Walloon Calvinist, French Huguenot, or German. I may have been overly generous in identifying people as Dutch in this book, and thus on occasion have given too much credit to "Dutch" influence or involvement. Still, this was a distinct common identity, and I side with people such as Hastings, Plokhy, Anthony Smith, and others who have argued against the overemphasis on the purely modern quality of nationalism by theorists such as Ernest Gellner, Eric Hobsbawm, or Benedict Anderson.[84] Again, Plokhy sensibly suggests the undeniable existence of a national or shared ethnocultural identity in many pre-modern complex societies. In the remarkably literate Dutch Republic, where in Amsterdam more than half of the grooms could sign their wedding licence in the seventeenth century, this sense of collective identity was fairly widely diffused.[85] This is not to say that other identity markers left their imprint on the inhabitants of the Dutch Republic in the seventeenth century. Religion for many was more important than nationhood: See the influx of southern Netherlanders into the "Calvinist" North in the late sixteenth century and of French Huguenots a hundred years later. Still, it remains moot in how far, or for how long, religious trumped national identity. Some of the refugees from Brabant, Flanders, or Wallonia fled for economic reasons, once Antwerp was blockaded and what is Belgium today turned in to the "battlefield of Europe." Indeed, economic opportunity may have constituted the biggest draw.

Part of Dutch national identity (and possibly the most widespread commonality, judging from the consistent popularity of the dynasty) was an allegiance to the stadtholders,[86] which meant the scions of the house of Orange-Nassau, stadtholders of Holland, Zeeland, Utrecht, Overijssel, and Gelderland, and, somewhat less, the house of Nassau-Dietz, which held the stadtholderate of the northern provinces in the seventeenth century.[87] This appears paradoxical, for the Republic seemed to have definitively rejected monarchical rule around 1580. Nonetheless, William I and his descendants (up to and including his great-grandson William III) proved remarkably popular. The mystique of the monarch was deeply ingrained in the collective psyche, in an age where people in England and France still believed in the magic of the royal touch.[88] The cult of the Orange-Nassau family was nurtured by a deft propaganda, not in the least through the exceptionally large Dutch publishing industry and the visual arts, as the paintings by Gerard van Honthorst (1592–1656) and others prove (as did the orange, white, and blue flag). And their popularity had much to do with their paramount role in warfare.

When the stadtholder Frederick Henry was buried in 1647, it was no accident that his "funeral procession included a strikingly large number of . . . senior army officers. . . ."[89] The Orange-Nassau worship was linked with the military feats of the stadtholders, who were seen as repeatedly having preserved Dutch independence as the country's supreme military commanders. This adoration therefore underscores the pervasive "military mindset" that was common in Dutch society. In addition, as Benjamin Roberts has suggested, other "naval heroes and military men" were "role models" for Dutch youths.[90] Roberts adds, "By the end of the Revolt in 1648 the image of the soldier in Dutch art [reflective of society's attitude] had undergone a major change from their criminal-like status [in the 1560s] into heroes and courtiers."[91] While Roberts may overstate the case about the villainous reputation of soldiers among the general population in the middle of the sixteenth century, the Dutch did worship at the feet of admirals such as Tromp and De Ruyter (while the Orange-Nassaus were revered as field commanders).[92]

But any ideal type of resolute, unwavering nationalism followed by all and sundry who were born within the United Provinces' border did not exist, in fact (nor has it ever anywhere). Fighting in the Dutch war of independence and the subsequent wars in which the Republic was embroiled was clearly not exclusively the effort of those born and raised in the Low Countries. Whereas the Dutch navy employed many Germans and Scandinavians, the land army was composed of soldiers from a variety of European countries, most of whom intended to go home after the campaigns were over, even if some eventually chose to stay in the

Republic after demobilisation (or lost their lives fighting for the Republic).[93] As Roger Manning observes,

> English and Scots soldiers comprised nearly half of the field armies of the Dutch Republic in the age of Maurice of Nassau, contributed significantly to the successful Dutch struggle for independence from Spain and continued to serve in the Dutch army until the beginning of the Age of Revolution.[94]

He adds that this service was often a sort of apprenticeship for the British warriors, a military education that they brought back to the islands in the late 1630s with rather tragic consequences.[95] And English and Scottish officers and soldiers fought in great number in the Dutch armies again from 1672 onward.[96]

In the 1610s, the 3,000 troops recruited by Johann Ernst of Nassau-Siegen to fight in Italy were officered by captains (who in those days did the actual hiring, even if most of the hirelings in this army had to pass the personal muster of Johann Ernst) from various parts of Europe: About half of them were natives of the Low Countries, whereas others hailed from France, Germany, and Britain.[97] More often than sailors, soldiers serving the trading companies overseas tended to be born outside the Republic.[98] In part, it seems, Dutch men were able to calculate whether soldiering far away from Europe was worth the trouble in the light of other opportunities open to them and often declined the option; the wages for such service were low compared with other jobs, especially given the extra risks and length of the sojourn overseas, and many therefore avoided such service.[99] Foreigners picked up the slack, but even then not always: It led at some points to the enlistment of African slaves in the Dutch military, as happened in Brazil.[100]

In the Dutch Atlantic, Klooster notes, Europeans hailing from other countries than the Dutch Republic were numerous, among whom were Sephardic Jews.[101] And the Dutch, like all Europeans outnumbered in Africa, Asia, and the Americas by the local population, struck many alliances in their efforts to establish a bridgehead or maintain themselves.[102] Some of these dalliances were personal and involved (common-law) marriage with native women: In almost all Dutch outposts, very few women resided who hailed from the Low Countries.[103] Such sexual relations were frowned upon by many among the community leaders, but little could be done to stop the practice, given human nature.[104] Meanwhile, many of these liaisons were asymmetrical, of course: Routinely, Dutchmen abused native women in all sorts of manner. And rape was common.

Whereas Isaac (1558–1624) and Jacob (1585–1616) le Maire acquired notoriety for their "interloping" with the VOC in Asia, numerous others did the same with regard to the WIC.[105] The VOC appears to have been reasonably capable of enforcing its monopoly in some of the main regions in which it operated, such as Java and the Spice Islands, and was willing to use ruthless force to do so (as in the Amboina Massacre of British traders).[106] Thus, too, were two Genoese ships (with mainly Dutch crews)—on which Jan Struys may have served—forced to surrender near the Bantam Straits in 1648.[107] But in the Atlantic, the WIC faced much more European competition, not in the least from Dutch entrepreneurs and sailors sailing under foreign flags.[108] Finally, even in Europe, both merchants such as Winius and others switched their allegiance. Among them was "[the Swedish resident] Abraham van Eyk . . . one of the renegades of which [the Republic] had countless numbers in the seventeenth century, to the great detriment of its commerce."[109] So foreigners followed the Dutch flag, while Dutch men (in particular) served foreign paymasters or sovereigns if that seemed more advantageous. Nationalist loyalty, then, remained fickle.

Notes

1. In his master's thesis, David Beeler reiterated the acute anxiety regarding a flagging military that is apparent in Dutch paintings from the early years after the Peace of Münster with Spain in 1648 (see Beeler, "Sobering Anxieties"; see as well Kunzle, *From Criminal*, 579–608). See also Kunzle's criticism of Huizinga's suggestion that war was an alien idea to the Dutch (Kunzle, *From Criminal*, 3). Soldiers are shown to be taken advantage of, and ridiculed in, a variety of masterful paintings, carrying an implicit warning that the Republic could only neglect its defence (or armed forces) at her own peril. Like the ill-fated stadtholder William II of Orange, the artists appear to protest the army cuts imposed by the States-General that accompanied the end of the Eighty Years' War. However, the paintings may reflect a reality: With peace imminent, the Dutch were saddled with large numbers of troops who had to be released; this not only allowed in 1647 the Russian emissary Miloslavskii to hire the Van Bockhoven clan of military experts but also saw large numbers of troops dispatched to embattled Dutch Brazil (Klooster, *Dutch Moment*, 86; see as well ibid., 116). When Brazil was surrendered to the Portuguese in 1654, veterans returned to the Republic from South America and were seemingly omnipresent idling away, which the paintings may reflect (ibid., 91). Doubtless, after all, such veterans already became a common sight in the late 1640s, as more remained in the Republic than went to Russia or Brazil. Jan Struys's (alleged?) service for the Genoese doge in 1647 in an ill-fated attempt to trade on the East Indies appears another sign of the Dutch having to shift gears because of the end of the war with Spain; most of the crew of the two ships was Dutch (see Boterbloem, *Fiction and Reality*, 9–10, 12–13). And in this respect it is noteworthy that Paul-Rudolf Beem and his stepson Lodewijk Fabricius, Brazilian veterans, enlisted in Tsar Aleksei Mikhailovich's armies, albeit in 1660 (ibid., 50).
2. Whereas she existed (and was, in fact, a member of a powerful regent family), some of the more colourful details about her resolute defence of Haarlem have never been definitively corroborated. Beyond doubt is her remarkable agency, which saw her not only succeed in business but also even occupy important government posts in Zeeland. She died on an overseas trip to Norway that she undertook in her sixties. See later in chapter for more on women in Dutch war and society and, for much more on Kenau, see Kloek,

Kenau en Magdalena; Kloek, *Kenau: De heldhaftige*; Van der Vlugt, *Wij zijn*, 46–9. The city of Haarlem had a special place in the iconography of the revolt, rallying the northern Netherlanders around their (new) flag (see Kunzle, *From Criminal*, 187–251).

3. Manning, *Apprenticeship*, 26. I find it a tad ironic (and I wholly disagree with the point) that Manning states "[s]ervice in the army was not only divorced from patriotism and religious sentiment, it was incompatible with Dutch political culture" (ibid., 41). Among examples to the contrary are siblings of Nicolaas Witsen and Koenraad van Klenck who served in the Dutch army as well as the attitude of Bontemantel in 1672 mentioned elsewhere in this book. It may be true that many Dutch military men served in other capacities than as regular soldiers because of their exceptional expertise, as in fortification building, artillery, and so forth; the Van Bockhovens were not unusual as expert drillmasters. Beem, Fabricius, and many fighting overseas show that the Dutch were perfectly capable and willing to soldier. The numbers and references Manning supplies (among which is a non-existing Table 4.2, see 42n5) are of uncertain provenance and seem unreliable snapshots. Manning seems to have fallen victim here to the same bias he notes among the late sixteenth-century English military officers regarding the Dutch as soldiers.
4. For example, note the militia's vain efforts in defending Haarlem in 1572–1573 (Manning, *Apprenticeship*, 31). *Schutters* were often augmented with "*waardgelders*," soldiers who were locally recruited, sort of *ad-hoc*, and usually from lower-ranked civilians than those who joined the schutters (see De Jong, "Militaire hervormingen," 469). They seem to have disappeared after 1650, another sign of the increasing professionalisation of warfare.
5. See 't Hart, *Dutch Wars*, 86, 96; 't Hart, though, suggests that they sometimes played a significant role at least until 1648 ('t Hart, *Dutch Wars*, 83). See also Manning, *Apprenticeship*, 145.
6. For this aspect, see Roberts, "Marlboro Men," 88. My thanks to David Beeler for reminding me of Roberts's intriguing work. See as well Kunzle, *From Criminal*, 579.
7. See Brugmans, *Geschiedenis*, vol. 3, 277–82.
8. For an easily readable transcription of the manuscript, see Bontemantel, *De regeeringe*.
9. They obviously had the added advantage of disciplining the men who served in them and were thus a means of political or social control exerted by the elite. This in part explains the rather toothless quality of the protest movements in the Republic; the regents' dominance was challenged only when rifts erupted among the elite in the 1780s.
10. Brugmans, *Geschiedenis*, vol. 3, 280.
11. More on this below, but see Klooster, *Dutch Moment*, 113–16.
12. Bontemantel, *De regeeringe*, vol. 1., 211–15.
13. Ibid., 213.
14. Ibid., 206. Trip was related by marriage to the arch-intriguer Gillis Valckenier, who was the slickest operator on the Amsterdam city council in this period and no friend of Bontemantel.
15. 't Hart, *Dutch Wars*, 985.
16. Kunzle, *From Criminal*, 585.
17. See Klooster, *Dutch Moment*, 113–14. As Klooster notes, thousands served in garrisons at the Dutch fortresses and enclaves in Africa, Brazil, the Caribbean, and the New Netherlands (ibid., 114–15).
18. 't Hart, *Dutch Wars*, 86. See as well ibid., 97.
19. See as well ibid., 96.

20. In northern Holland, the willingness to defend one's country with arms was very much alive in 1672, see Van Deursen, *Een dorp*, 290.
21. Parker, *Success*, 160.
22. Ibid., 162–3.
23. Ibid., 165–6.
24. Ibid., 162.
25. Ibid., 160.
26. Ibid., 164–5.
27. Haks, *Vaderland*, 38–9.
28. Ibid., 49.
29. As Marjolein 't Hart points out, a rather instrumental attitude towards war can already be discerned among the lower strata of Holland in the heat of the Dutch Revolt during the 1570s, when many applauded the war with Spain as an opportunity to raise the rent of town dwellings (see 't Hart, "From the Eighty Years War," 261).
30. See Davids, "Shifts of Technological Leadership," 341.
31. See Boterbloem, *Fiction and Reality*.
32. On the marines, see Leupe and Van Braam Houckgeest, *De geschiedenis*. Numbering 4,000, they were created by the States-General in late December 1664 (Kernkamp, ed., "Twee 'niet ter drukpersse'," 163).
33. Brecht, *Mutter Courage* [first performed in 1941]; Von Grimmelshausen, *Trutz Simplex*. As Parrott and others suggest, although some of these women were sex workers, many others lived in common-law unions with soldiers or performed other tasks that kept the army going, such as cooking or washing (of course, many of these sutlers played several roles; see Parrott, *Business*, 69, 167, 203–6).
34. Van den Heuvel, *Women*.
35. About women as actors in the economy, see Van den Heuvel, *Women*.
36. See Boterbloem, *Fiction and Reality*, 76.
37. Although she was forced to petition later again for full remittance (*Rossiiskaia Gosudarstvennaia Arkhiv Drevnikh Aktov* [*Russian State Archive for Ancient Acts*] in Moscow *fond* 141 *delo* 371 (1668), *listy* 1–8 [from here abbreviated as 141/371 (1668), ll.1–8] and 159/*opis'* 2/1363 [no later than 1675], ll.1–3). See as well Demkin, *Zapadnoevropeiskoe*, vol. 2, 12 [he errs by a year].
38. *Krest'ianskaia voina*, vol. 4, 135. For a number of similar cases, see Klooster, *Dutch Moment*, 118–20.
39. Veluvenkamp, "Kompaniia 'de Vogelar i Klenk'," 44–5.
40. Frederiks and Frederiks, *Kohier*, 35. The Moens family was taxed at 1,600 guilders, while Balthasar Co[o]ymans sr paid a whopping 2,000 guilders, as did Guillermo Bartolotti (ibid., 42, 60–1). Separately, Marcus de Vogelaer jr was taxed for another 200 guilders (ibid., 55). The richest family was that of the former mayor Jacob Janszoon Poppen (1576–1624), who paid 2,500 guilders (ibid., 61). Poppen's name is among the early Arkhangel'sk traders.
41. Frederiks and Frederiks, *Kohier*, 55.
42. Van Deursen, *Plain Lives*, 7.
43. Rudolf Dekker has calculated that slightly less than 10 per cent of all ego-documents that he and his team have unearthed in the Netherlands between 1500 and 1800 were written by women (see Dekker, "Egodocuments in the Netherlands").
44. For some confirmation regarding this notion, see Montoya, "'Zie hier een vreemde oorlog'."
45. See Van der Linde, *Das Leibregiment*, 88.
46. See Van de Pol, *Burgher and Whore*.

47. See, for a discussion, Van Deursen, *Plain Lives*, 67–78, and, especially, ibid., 76–8.
48. See Jan de Vries, *Industrious Revolution*. And De Vries suggests convincingly that the emergence of this industrious mentality was connected to the sudden reduction of holidays as a consequence of the (Calvinist) Reformation, although it remains a bit of a chicken-or-egg conundrum whether this reduction was imposed by the Calvinist church and only gradually (and perhaps willy-nilly) accepted by the populace, or whether in some ways it aligned rather well to an already pre-existing mindset that privileged hard work over leisure (which chafed against the interminable Catholic saints' days, etc.) in the urban regions of the Low Countries.
49. See Spierenburg, *Judicial Violence*.
50. It seems no accident that neostoicism was popular among Netherlandic intellectuals such as Justus Lipsius and P.C. Hooft and that some of the leading lights "sought to mobilize the people and equip them morally, politically, and in every other way to succeed permanently in the great task of breaking free from Spanish tyranny" (Israel, *Dutch Republic*, 567–8).
51. Israel, *Dutch Republic*, 562.
52. Haks, *Vaderland*, 11. His evidence is especially that of printed works.
53. Manning, *Apprenticeship*, 415.
54. Valentijn, *Oud en Nieuw Oost-Indiën*, vol. 1, "Voorreden," [4].
55. See Van Gennep, *Rites*, 11; Turner, *Ritual Process*, 97–108.
56. Guido de Bruin provides an excellent detailed discussion, see De Bruin, *Geheimhouding*, 28; and, especially, ibid., 580–601. Note as well Peter Burke's remarks on the difficulty of reconstructing popular culture in early modern Europe (Burke, *Popular Culture*, 103–30).
57. Plokhy, *Origins*, 7.
58. Hastings, *Construction*; Plokhy, *Origins*; Marx, *Faith in Nation*. See also Haks, *Vaderland*, 11. Confusingly, the Latin term "*natio*" and its vernacular equivalents were current in the early modern period, but they did mean something different from today (see, e.g., Barendse, *Arabian Seas*, 87–125).
59. See Boterbloem, *Fiction and Reality*, 173–4. See as well Van Deursen, *Een dorp*, 287.
60. Klooster, *Dutch Moment*, 116.
61. On class in the early modern period, see "Natalie Zemon Davis," 111; and specifically for the Dutch Republic, Van Deursen, *Plain Lives*, 3–4. On national identity, see Haks, *Vaderland*, 11, 17–18. On religion, and the nexus of loyalty to the Oranges and the rigid branch of the Dutch Reformed churches (linked to early modern "patriotism," as he calls it), see, for example, De Bruin, *Geheimhouding*, 593–4, 598.
62. See De Glas, *Holland*, 17–20.
63. See, for example, Van Deursen, *Plain Lives*, 213–14.
64. Kunzle, *From Criminal*, 441–506.
65. It was composed around 1570, probably by a Calvinist minister, Petrus Dathenus.
66. See Lucassen, *Migrant Labour*; Van Gelder, *Oostindisch avontuur*; Van Gelder and Roeper, *In dienst van de Compagnie*; Eßer, "From Province to Nation"; Sommerseth, Ekamper and Sogner, "Marriage Patterns"; Van der Linden, *Experiencing Exile*.
67. See Van der Linden, *Experiencing Exile*.
68. Haks, *Vaderland*, 9.
69. Ibid., 9.
70. See Teeuwen, *Financing*, 78–9; Van Deursen, *Een Dorp*, 294, 303–4.
71. See Gebhard, *Het leven*, 169–76; Klooster, *Dutch Moment*, 158–9.

72. Boterbloem, *Fiction and Reality*, 38, 122, 128.
73. As Erik Amburger wrote, by 1639, one quarter of the total income of Hamburg's citizens (its population was about 50,000, but Amburger referred to burghers alone) was owned by those identified as "Niederländer" (Amburger, *Die Familie*, 24). See also his discussion on ibid., 184–5, which is perhaps too much influenced by a twentieth-century concept of nationality that is rigidly circumscribed (he did publish some dubious stuff in the 1930s on the national identity of Germans abroad). Among the expatriates changing cultural allegiance were some notorious Ottoman naval commanders, such as Jan Janszoon van Haarlem (Murat Reis) and his comrades Ivan de Veenboer (Sulayman Reis) and Simon de Danser; see Snelders, *Devil's Anarchy*; Vrijman, *Kaapvaart*; Vermeulen, *Sultans*; Davis, *Christian Slaves*; Wilson, *Pirate Utopias*. Jan Jansen, a Dutch renegade in Ottoman or Tatar service, surrendered to the Russian army under Patrick Gordon at the 1696 Siege of Azov. Excellent on this is Van Gelder, "Republic's Renegades," 175–98.
74. It is significant indeed that the great twentieth-century chronicler of Amsterdam's history, Hajo Brugmans, has an engraving of De Geer displayed as a frontispiece in his third volume (Brugmans, *Geschiedenis*, vol. 3, 2).
75. For example, ibid., 13–14. See as well De Geer van Jutfaas, *Lodewijk de Geer*, 1–2; Romein and Romein-Verschoor, *Erflaters*, 285–306.
76. Breedvelt-van Veen, *Louis de Geer*, 29, 38–9. On Mansfeld, see Kunzle, *From Criminal*, 264–5.
77. Breedvelt-van Veen, *Louis de Geer*, 39.
78. Van Aalst, *Het archief*, 53; Molhuysen and Blok, eds, *Nieuw Nederlandsch*, 467–70.
79. See Schmidt, *Om de eer*, 15.
80. See, for the document, Orlenko, *Vykhodtsy*, 287.
81. Some of the Dutch court painters in England seem to have been motivated in the same way to switch allegiance to the Stuarts, such as Peter Lely, although Lely, like Godfrey Kneller, was actually born in the Holy Roman Empire.
82. Frost, *Northern Wars*, 165.
83. For a good discussion what this concept meant in the Russian context, see Romaniello, *Elusive Empire*.
84. Among the many worthwhile works on this topic, see Smith, *Antiquity*; Gellner, *Nations*; Hobsbawm and Ranger, eds, *Invention*; Anderson, *Imagined Communities*. See, too, Hroch, *Social Preconditions of National Revival in Europe*; idem, *European Nations*.
85. See Boterbloem, *Fiction and Reality*, 130; see as well Schama, *Embarrassment*, 579.
86. This term originally meant something such as deputies or governors, ruling on behalf of the monarch; they were originally *ex-officio* commanders of the armed forces in their provinces.
87. In his marvellous work on popular culture in the early modern age, Peter Burke suggests that any reconstruction of it must remain imperfect, even if in recent decades historians and other scholars have become truly adept at mining sources for evidence of it; it seems, however, beyond question that in early modern Dutch culture—the text of the "Wilhelmus" dates from the late sixteenth century—the house of Orange was wildly popular until the death of William III (see Burke's latest—third edition: Burke, *Popular Culture*). The one moment that this popularity frayed a bit was when William II (1626–1650) occupied the Holland stadtholderate; perhaps William II's championing of the armed forces (which he seems to have wanted to maintain at wartime levels even after the Peace of Westphalia) was (consciously or not) linked to the idea that his status as stadtholder very much improved in warlike conditions.

88. See De Bruin, *Geheimhouding*, 149, 593.
89. Israel, *Dutch Republic*, 546.
90. Roberts, "Marlboro Men," 86, 89.
91. Ibid., 87.
92. For the awe in which Western and Central Europeans held soldiers such as the *Landsknechte*, see Parrott, *Business of War*, 61–2; see further Roberts, "Marlboro Men," 87–8.
93. Certainly before 1609, others, such as Poles and Swedes, participated in the rebel army of William of Orange and his son and nephew (see Frost, *Northern Wars*, 107, 125).
94. Manning, *Apprenticeship*, vii. See also Klooster, *Dutch Moment*, 122.
95. Ibid., 216–18.
96. Manning, *Apprenticeship*, ix.
97. Geyl, *Christoforro Suriano*, 27–32. Some of the troops had likely deserted from Dutch service, probably keen on the remuneration offered by the Venetians (ibid., 33–4).
98. Klooster, *Dutch Moment*, 121–2.
99. Ibid., 125–6. Klooster suggests a basic eight guilders a month for WIC soldiers, which is half of the average worker's wage in the Republic as estimated by Van Deursen (see Van Deursen, *Plain Lives*, 7). Only officers' wages truly outstripped those of workers in the Republic's towns; of course, they were usually scions from higher social strata than that of manual workers (Klooster, *Dutch Moment*, 126). Klooster suggests as well that payment in Brazil was irregular, as there were no solicitors who could advance the wages in expectation of the government's transfer payments to the army (ibid., 138).
100. Klooster, *Dutch Moment*, 241.
101. Ibid., 5, 63–4, 121–2, 215.
102. Ibid., 5–6.
103. Ibid., 216, 235–6.
104. See Blussé, "Cornelia van Nijenroode."
105. See Barreveld, *Tegen de Heeren van de VOC*; see as well Valentijn, *Oud en nieuw Oost-Indiën*, vol. 1, 201–4.
106. Gelderblom, De Jong and Jonker, "Formative Years," 1066–7.
107. Boterbloem, *Fiction and Reality*, 12–13.
108. See Klooster, *Dutch Moment*, 182–7.
109. Elias, ed., "Contract," 386–7.

Bibliography

Aalst, G.M. van. *Het archief van de familie del Court van Krimpen (1506) 1611–1979*, Den Haag: Nationaal Archief, 1986.

Anderson, Benedict. *Imagined Communities*, rev. ed., London: Verso, 2006.

Barendse, René. *The Arabian Seas*, Armonk, NY: M.E. Sharpe, 2002.

Barreveld, Dirk J. *Tegen de Heeren van de VOC: Isaac Le Maire en de ontdekking van Kaap Hoorn*, Den Haag: SDU, 2002.

Beeler, D. "Sobering Anxieties," unpublished master's thesis, University of South Florida, 2014.

Blussé, L.J. "Cornelia van Nijenroode," available at: http://resources.huygens.knaw.nl/vrouwenlexicon/lemmata/data/Nijenroode/en, accessed 18 May 2019.

Bontemantel, Hans. *De regeeringe van Amsterdam, soo in 't civiel als crimineel en militaire (1653–72)*, G.W. Kernkamp, ed., 2 vols., Den Haag: Nijhoff, 1897, available at www.dbnl.org/tekst/bont014rege01_01/colofon.php, accessed 12 September 2016.

Boterbloem, K. *The Fiction and Reality of Jan Struys: A Seventeenth-Century Dutch Globetrotter, Houndmills*, Basingstoke: Palgrave, 2008.

Brecht, Bertolt. *Mutter Courage und ihre Kinder*, Berlin: Suhrkamp, 1949.

Breedvelt-van Veen, F. *Louis de Geer, 1587–1652*, Amsterdam: Paris, 1935.

Brugmans, H. *Geschiedenis van Amsterdam*, vol. 3: *Bloeitijd, 1621–97*, 2nd ed., Utrecht: Het Spectrum, 1973.

Bruin, G. de. *Geheimhouding en verraad: De geheimhouding van staatszaken ten tijde van de Republiek (1600–1750)*, 's-Gravenhage: SDU Uitgeverij, 1991.

Burke, P. *Popular Culture in Early Modern Europe*, 3rd ed., Farnham: Ashgate, 2009.

Davids, Karel. "Shifts of Technological Leadership in Early Modern Europe," in K. Davids and J. Lucassen, eds, *A Miracle Mirrored: The Dutch Republic in European Perspective*, Cambridge: Cambridge University Press, 1995, 338–66.

Davis, R.C. *Christian Slaves, Muslim Masters, Houndsmills*, Basingstoke: Palgrave, 2004.

Dekker, R. "Egodocuments in the Netherlands from the Sixteenth to the Nineteenth Centuries," in Erin Griffey, ed., *Envisioning Self and Status*, Hull: Association for Low Countries Studies, 2000, 255–85, available at: www.egodocument.net/pdf/Egodocuments_in_the_Netherlands.pdf, accessed 17 August 2016.

Demkin, A.V. *Zapadnoevropeiskoe kupechestvo v Rossii v xvii v.*, 2 vols., Moskva: Institut Istorii RAN, 2004.

Deursen, A.Th. van. *Een dorp in de polder*, Amsterdam: Aula, 2003.

———. *Plain Lives in a Golden Age*, Cambridge: Cambridge University Press, 1991.

Eßer, Raingard. "From Province to Nation: Immigration in the Dutch Republic in the Late 16th and Early 17th Centuries," in S.G. Ellis and L. Klusakova, eds, *Imagining Frontiers, Contesting Identities*, Pisa: Pisa University Press, 2007, 264–76.

Elias, J.E., ed., "Contract tot oprichting van een Zweedsch factorie-comptoir te Amsterdam in 1663," *Bijdragen en Mededelingen van het Historisch Genootschap* 24, 1903, 356–400.

Frederiks, J.G., and P.J. Frederiks, *Kohier van den tweehonderdsten penning . . . Over 1631*, Amsterdam: Ten Brink and De Vries, 1890.

Frost, Robert. *The Northern Wars: War, State and Society in Northeastern Europe, 1558–1721*, Harlow: Longman, 2000.

Gebhard, J.F. *Het leven van Mr. Nicolaas Cornelisz. Witsen (1641–1717)*, vol. 1, Utrecht: Leeflang, 1881.

Geer van Jutfaas, J.L.W. de. *Lodewijk de Geer van Finspong en Leusta (1587–1652)*, 3rd ed., Utrecht: Kemink and Son, 1852.

Gelder, Maartje van. "The Republic's Renegades: Dutch Converts to Islam in Seventeenth-Century Diplomatic Relations with North Africa," *Journal of Early Modern History* 2–3, 2015, 175–98.

Gelder, Roelof van. *Het Oostindisch avontuur*, Amsterdam: SUN, 1997.

———, and Vibeke Roeper. *In dienst van de Compagnie*, Amsterdam: Atheneum, Polak en Van Gennep, 2002.

Gelderblom, Oscar, Abe de Jong, and Joost Jonker, "The Formative Years of the Modern Corporation: The Dutch East India Company, 1602–1632," *Journal of Economic History* 4, 2013, 1050–76.

Gellner, Ernest. *Nations and Nationalism*, Ithaca, NY: Cornell University Press, 1983.

Gennep, Arnold van. *The Rites of Passage*, London: Routledge, 1960.

Geyl, P. *Christoforro Suriano, Resident van de Serenissime Republiek van Venetië in Den Haag, 1616–1623*, Den Haag: M. Nijhoff, 1913.

Glas, Nico de. *Holland is een eiland: De Batavia van Hadrianus Junius (1511–1575)*, Hilversum: Verloren, 2011.

Grimmelshausen, H.J.C. von. *Trutz Simplex: Oder ausführliche und wunderselsame Lebensbeschreibung der Erzbetrügerin und Landstörzerin Courasche. . .*, Nürnberg: Felsecker, 1670, available at: www.deutschestextarchiv.de/book/show/grimmelshausen_trutzsimplex_1670, accessed 2 April 2019.

Haks, Donald. *Vaderland en vrede: Publiciteit over de Nederlandse republiek in oorlog, 1672–1713*, Hilversum: Verloren, 2013.

Hart, Marjolein 't. "From the Eighty Years War to the Second World War: New Perspectives on the Economic Effects of War," *Tijdschrift voor Sociale en Economische Geschiedenis* 2, 2014, 261–79.

———. *The Dutch Wars of Independence: Warfare and Commerce in the Netherlands, 1570–1680*, London: Routledge, 2014.

Hastings, Adrian. *The Construction of Nationhood*, Cambridge: Cambridge University Press, 1997.

Heuvel, Danielle van den. *Women and Entrepreneurship*, Amsterdam: Aksant, 2007.

Hobsbawm, Eric, and Terence Ranger, eds, *The Invention of Tradition*, Cambridge: Cambridge University Press, 1983.

Hroch, Miroslav. *European Nations: Explaining Their Formation*, London: Verso, 2015.

———. *Social Preconditions of National Revival in Europe*, Cambridge: Cambridge University Press, 1985.

Israel, Jonathan. *The Dutch Republic*, Oxford: Oxford University Press, 1995.

Jong, M. de. "Militaire hervormingen in het Staatse leger en de opbouw van het wapenbedrijf, 1585–1621," *Bijdragen en Mededelingen voor de Geschiedenis der Nederlanden* 4, 2003, 467–93.

Kernkamp, J.H., ed. "Twee 'niet ter drukpersse bereide' geschriften van Pieter de la Court," *Bijdragen en Mededelingen van het Historisch Genootschap* 56, 1935, 151–214.

Kloek, Els. *Kenau: De heldhaftige zakenvrouw uit Haarlem (1526–1588)*, Hilversum: Verloren, 2001.

———. *Kenau en Magdalena*, Nijmegen: Vantilt, 2014.

Klooster, Wim. *The Dutch Moment: War, Trade and Settlement in the Seventeenth-Century Atlantic World*, Ithaca, NY: Cornell University Press, 2016.

Krest'ianskaia voina pod predvoditel'stvom Stepana Razina, vol. 4, Moscow: Gosizdat, 1954.

Kunzle, David. *From Criminal to Courtier: The Soldier in Netherlandish Art, 1550–1672*, Leiden: Brill, 2002.

Leupe P.A., and F.A. van Braam Houckgeest. *De geschiedenis der mariniers van het jaar 1665 tot op heden*, Nieuwediep: L.A. Laury, 1867.

Linde, B. van der. *Das Leibregiment der friesischen Staathalter*, Berlin: Duncker and Humblot, 2016.

Linden, David van der. *Experiencing Exile*, Farnham: Ashgate, 2015.

Lucassen, Jan. *Migrant Labour in Europe, 1600–1900*, London: Croom Helm, 1987.

Manning, Roger. *An Apprenticeship in Arms: The Origins of the British Army, 1585–1702*, Oxford: Oxford University Press, 2006.

Marx, Anthony. *Faith in Nation*, Oxford: Oxford University Press, 2003.

Molhuysen, P.C., and P.J. Blok, eds. *Nieuw Nederlandsch Biografisch Woordenboek*, vol. 10, Leiden: Sijthoff, 1937.

Montoya, Alicia C. "'Zie hier een vreemde oorlog.' Constructies van emotie in Madame de Sévignés brieven over de Frans-Nederlandse oorlog (1672–1678)," in Lotte Jensen and Nina Geerdink, eds, *Oorlogsliteratuur in de vroegmoderne tijd*, Hilversum: Verloren, 2012, 87–104.

"Natalie Zemon Davis," in H. Abelove et al., eds, *Visions of History*, New York: Pantheon Books, 1984, 97–122.

Orlenko, S.P. *Vykhodtsy iz Zapadnoi Evropy v Rossii xvii veka*, Moscow: Drevlekhranilishche, 2004.

Parker, G. *Success Is Never Final: Empire, War, and Faith in Early Modern Europe*, New York: Basic Books, 2002.

Parrott, David. *The Business of War*, Cambridge: Cambridge University Press, 2012.

Plokhy, Serhii. *The Origins of the Slavic Nations: Premodern Identities in Russia, Ukraine and Belarus*, Cambridge: Cambridge University Press, 2006.

Pol, Lotte van de. *The Burgher and the Whore: Prostitution in Early Modern Amsterdam*, Oxford: Oxford University Press, 2011.

Roberts, Benjamin. "Marlboro Men of the Early Seventeenth Century: Masculine Role Models for Dutch Youth in the Seventeenth Century?" *Men and Masculinities*, July 2006, 76–94.

Romaniello, Matthew. *The Elusive Empire*, Madison, WI: University of Wisconsin Press, 2012.

Romein, J., and A. Romein-Verschoor. *Erflaters van onze beschaving*, 12th ed., Amsterdam: Querido, 1977.

Schama, Simon. *The Embarrassment of Riches*, New York: Vintage Books, 1997.

Schmidt, C. *Om de eer van de familie: Het geslacht Teding van Berkhout 1500–1950: een sociologische benadering*, Amsterdam: De Bataafsche Leeuw, 1986.

Smith, Anthony D. *The Antiquity of Nations*, Cambridge: Polity Press, 2004.

Snelders, Stephen. *The Devil's Anarchy*, Chico, CA: AK Press, 2014.

Sommerseth, Hilde L., Peter Ekamper, and Sølvi Sogner. "Marriage Patterns and Residential Behaviour Among Norwegian Women in Amsterdam, 1621–1720," *Continuity and Change* 2, 2016, 175–209.

Spierenburg, P.C. *Judicial Violence in the Dutch Republic*, Amsterdam: Amsterdam University Press, 1978.

Teeuwen, Daniëlle. *Financing Poor Relief Through Charitable Collections in Dutch Towns, c. 1600–1800*, Amsterdam: Amsterdam University Press, 2016.

Turner, Victor. *The Ritual Process: Structure and Anti-Structure*, New York: Aldine de Gruyter, 1969.

Valentijn, François. *Oud en Nieuw Oost-Indiën. . .*, vol. 1, Dordrecht and Amsterdam: J. Van Braam en G. onder den Linden, 1724.

Veluvenkamp, Ia.V. "Kompaniia 'de Vogelar i Klenk' v gollandsko-russkikh kommercheskikh otnosheniiakh xvii v.," in Iu.N. Bespiatnikh et al., eds, *Niderlandy i Severnaia Rossiia*, St. Petersburg: Russko-Baltiiskii informatsionnyi Tsentr, 2003, 37–73.

Vermeulen, Joos. *Sultans, slaven en renegaten*, Leuven: Acco, 2001.

Vlugt, Simone van der. *Wij zijn de Bickers*, Amsterdam: Prometheus, 2019.

Vries, Jan de. *The Industrious Revolution*, Cambridge: Cambridge University Press, 2008.

Vrijman, L.C. *Kaapvaart en zeeroverij*, Amsterdam: Van Kampen, 1938.

Wilson, Peter Lamborn. *Pirate Utopias*, Brooklyn, NY: Autonomedia, 2003.

4 Sailors, Soldiers, and Arms Abroad, Part 1

Empire

4.1 Reluctant Imperialists

As with the British Empire, there was no coherent imperial strategy or ideology behind the Dutch maritime exploits that began in earnest in the 1590s.[1] Or if there are signs of some sort of plan, it was aimed at winning a war in Europe against the Spaniards, as was the combat on land. Even the Grand Design *(Groot Desseyn)* of the 1620s, which may have been a riff of similar ideas proposed by the French royal advisor the Duc de Sully (1560–1641), had this intention.[2] While some initiatives hint at a coordinated drive to carve out an empire in the Spanish style, they were never sustained. This is true for the projects of Jan Pieterszoon Coen in Asia, the vague early plans of (some inside) the West India Company (and the short-lived occupation of part of Brazil), or the exploits of Rijckloff van Goens sr in India. As soon as costs ran too high (and especially the Van Goens conflict—if it was such—with his colleagues in Batavia makes this apparent), the Dutch extricated themselves from violent conflict. In how far this was based on a detailed or accurate assessment of the costs and benefits (if such could be made at all) is unclear, but the fruitless military campaigning in the Low Countries themselves after 1600 probably provided a useful object lesson.

In the early 1660s, Brazil and Taiwan were given up in part because maritime military expeditions to relieve those embattled enclaves promised to be extremely expensive (in human and financial cost).[3] Concomitantly, Portugal, having gained its independence from Spain again, was no longer any threat to the Republic by the 1660s, while the VOC on its own would never have been able to dislodge the still formidable Ming party that ensconced itself on Taiwan in 1661. Instead, the VOC bypassed Taiwan and sent a number of embassies to Qing Beijing to try to establish direct trade with China and its new dynasty during the 1660s (whose attempts nevertheless proved to be in vain), while Brazil was exchanged for the Guyanas.

Although initially aimed at fighting the Iberian foe in its colonies and trade as much as in north-western Europe, the Dutch overseas (ad-)

ventures soon almost exclusively focussed on the pursuit of profit rather than winning military victories or wreaking havoc on European foes' possessions.[4] By 1590, Dutch merchants had a wealth of experience in trading on the North and Baltic sea shores. While their success outside Europe can in part be attributed to their lack of scruples about the way in which they conducted business, they also displayed a level of tact in their negotiations that set them apart from their European competitors, perhaps because of their experience with maritime trade in European waters. Though often blunt and showing no respect for local sensibilities, they did at times appear less crude than their rivals and succeeded better than them in appearing as trading partners rather than conquerors, using all sorts of persuasion rather than constantly threatening violence. This allowed them to stay in Japan, for example. Dutch success, of course, was in no small way due to their ability to supply their clients with scarce goods, and arms were a key part of that, for African or North American chiefs, Russian tsars, Japanese shoguns, and so on.

Many historians have suggested that the volume of colonial or long-distance trade was small, and that its value was a fraction of that of the Republic's short-haul import and export. Therefore, before we address the sale of Dutch weapons and the activities of Dutch mercenaries outside Europe (which both may have been likewise of a much smaller scale than inside Europe), we will first turn to the European side of the matter, and especially the entrepreneurs who made their fortune in this region. One remarkable example may suffice to remind the reader of the scale of the Dutch arms trade with Europe (and Morocco). In an article published in the German-occupied Netherlands in 1941, the historian G.W. de Boer detailed some of the astounding volume of arms exports in 1639 and 1640, soon after the—possibly decisive—Dutch naval victory over the Spanish fleet at the Battle of the Downs.[5] De Boer sketched how hundreds of thousands of pounds of sulphur and gunpowder and hundreds of thousands of cannonhulls, pikes, muskets, bullets, fuses, and various unidentified weapons were shipped under licence from Amsterdam to England, Ireland, France, Hamburg, Morocco, and other destinations by members of the Trip and Marselis families as well as a number of their contemporaries. This vast volume of trade took place while peace with Spain was still eight years away! Clearly, by then, the Republic had a great surplus of military goods on offer, far too large to be consumed by the endemic warfare conducted by the Dutch army and navy on the country's borders or at sea.

During the heyday of Dutch arms production and trade, the most renowned Dutch merchants of death were the members of the De Geer–Trip clan, whose trade indeed mainly focussed on Europe. It found its roots in a felicitous partnership (and indeed was solidified by many marriages) between a merchant family from Dordrecht and a refugee arms manufacturer from Liège, one of the traditional regions of metallurgy and weapons production in the Low Countries.[6] Following the gradual concentration of most of the largest Dutch capitalist enterprises in Amsterdam, the clan joined the Amsterdam patriciate, intermarrying further with the families of other tycoons. The historian Elias's words of more than a century ago give some sort of idea of the extent of Elias Trip's business:

> [Elias Trip]'s greatest fame was due to his extensive trade in the tools of war: Weapons, bullets, cannon, etc., which he primarily acquired in England and the Liège region. . . . Not only did he supply the Estates of Holland regularly with cannon and saltpetre, since the first contract (up to the price of almost a [metric] ton of gold), which they concluded with him in August 1602, but even from Venice he received in 1617 an order to hire a regiment of foot soldiers and arms, of which he took care together with Louys de Geer. In 1629, Trip signed a contract with the king of Sweden for the delivery of a shipment of arms for the total sum of 189,600 guilders. Six years later, the Estates of Holland allowed him to export 80 pieces of artillery to Russia for the "Grand-Prince of Muscovy." . . . In 1632 the Swedish king owed Trip 1,011,281 [guilders].[7]

Not encumbered by any scruples regarding the morality of their business, the De Geer–Trip family compact flagrantly undermined the Dutch national interest on several occasions, such as when openly competing with the WIC or trading arms on England during the First Anglo-Dutch War (1652–1654).[8] The De Geers received the city of Amsterdam's protection when faced with a judicial inquiry by the Estates of Holland, undoubtedly showing who was boss in the Dutch pecking order.

Ironically, towards the end of their lives among the most formidable competition of Elias Trip and Louys de Geer sr were Elias's nephews (and Louys's in-laws) Louys and Hendrick Trip, the eventual builders of the famed Trippenhuis in Amsterdam.[9] Later, in the 1660s, a quartet of Amsterdam businessmen who competed with the De Geer–Trip conglomerate began to represent Swedish interests in the city; arms fell within their purview and were by far the most lucrative commodities for this partnership, among whom were two Amsterdam regents (Joan Hulft and Cornelis Graafland).[10] The going was so good that close relatives and friends turned into business rivals.

The following sections will sketch some of the characteristic Dutch involvement in various theatres of war across the globe, beginning in Western, Central, and Southern Europe. Then the scene moves further abroad before returning to northern Europe. In some parts of the world, Dutch military men, materials, and merchants made a brief or ephemeral appearance; in others, their presence was sustained and their significance profound. The Dutch military influence on the Swedish army of Gustavus

Adolphus is well known, as is the impact of the Dutch on naval warfare. We will investigate the Swedish and Danish case in somewhat greater detail than that of other areas, and then specifically home in on the Russian case, where the Dutch played a most spectacularly crucial role in every aspect of warfare, helping the Romanovs lay the groundwork for an empire which has survived in various guises until this very day.

4.2 Europe and the Mediterranean

Roger Manning has explored the impact of the military reforms by Maurice of Orange and his relatives on the manner of combat in the British civil wars.[11] In great detail, his *Apprenticeship in Arms* outlines the seventeenth-century Dutch influence on British military practice and, conversely, the significant role of British officers and soldiers in the Dutch late sixteenth- and seventeenth-century armies.[12] Manning rightfully suggests that it was particularly the actual practical experience of serving in the Dutch armies (and subsequently in the various armies fighting the Thirty Years' War) that changed the manner of fighting of the British military. This suggests, too, why in the seventeenth century Dutch military specialists were sought after across Europe and beyond. The significance of books such as De Gheyn's is more difficult to assess than the practical experience of officers who had seen action in the Dutch armies prior to 1640.[13] In the British case, in part because Puritans sympathised most with the Dutch cause, especially Cromwell and the Roundheads appear to have been more influenced by the Dutch military innovations in theory and practice than the Cavaliers. Dutch siege engineers were active in the civil wars.[14] In Britain and Ireland, as elsewhere, the Dutch lead proved fleeting: On land and at sea, the British armed forces gradually began to match and then surpass the Dutch in the second half of the seventeenth century. But the Dutch way of waging war once more left another, and most profound, imprint on the British isles.

While Parker has highlighted the remarkable accomplishment that was the landing of William III's army at Torbay in the autumn of 1688, few lessons about the execution of amphibious operations seem to have been drawn from it by military planners, since the next major such operation may have been the expedition to the Crimea of 1854.[15] In effect, of course, this invasion was the greatest Dutch military feat of all time. The Dutch navy assisted the successful disembarkation of upward of 25,000 troops, and London was occupied by the Dutch army. It involved a feverish preparation by the Dutch arms industry and naval shipyards, and almost the entire highest political leadership of the country had a role to play in its organisation, not in the least that of Amsterdam.[16] The financing of the expedition was expertly organised, with the expedition's soldiers and sailors being amply remunified.[17] And while the city of Amsterdam had been reluctant about the venture beforehand, it was most responsible for the financing of the operation, sending one of its mayors, Nicolaas Witsen, along as its watchdog.[18] The campaign was pulled off without any bloodshed, because of which it may have been overlooked as one of the most successful military ventures ever, given its startling outcome. In this resounding triumph, we can discern at its best the Dutch knack for calculating risks, important in business and warfare. The operation was so well timed and organised that victory was always likely, as long as a "Protestant" wind blew. Still, it was a sort of last hurrah: In the course of the War of the Spanish Succession in the early eighteenth century, British military and naval superiority became indisputable, despite the feats of the Dutch Blue Guard. Still, the Torbay expedition caused William III to leave an indelible imprint on both on British and Irish political history.[19]

In the Thirty Years' War, men from the Low Countries frequently served as military officers.[20] Most famous among them was Jean (Johan) T'Serclaes, Count of Tilly (1559–1632), commander of the Catholic forces in the Thirty Years' War, and perhaps the most famous Walloon mercenary of the early modern age.[21] While younger than William I of Orange, he can be compared to him, as a Catholic counterpart to William's Protestant *condottiere*. The Prince of Orange was acquainted with Tilly's father, who was a counselor of Charles V, while Tilly's mother had been part of the court of Charles V's sister as a lady-in-waiting. Tilly was thus a noble who stood not far below the Oranges among the higher aristocracy of the Low Countries. But raised by Jesuits, Tilly became a champion of the Catholic reformation (Counter-Reformation) as much as his contemporary Maurice of Orange-Nassau was Calvinism's outstanding commander. Tilly's early success in the Thirty Years' War was overshadowed by his infamy as the general who lost control of his men at the brutal sack of Magdeburg in 1631; the following year, he was mortally wounded against the Swedes of Gustavus Adolphus. This ignominious end to his career coincided with the twilight of the Walloon mercenaries' omnipresence on the battlefields of Europe. They did not quite disappear, but they and their reputation declined, at a time when the armament industries of Liège, Namur, and Hainault faded as well, as they were confronted with heavy competition from the former Liègeois De Geer's enterprises in Sweden.

Meanwhile, Hans (Johan) de Witte (1583–1630), a Calvinist from Antwerp, supplied and financed the war machine of the other outstanding Catholic commander of the first part of the war, Albrecht von Wallenstein (1583–1634).[22] De Witte was not alone in this line of business, as several Flemish businessmen seem to have greased the wheels of war on the Catholic side. On the other side, the Dutch government subsidised the Protestant cause and helped it survive before first Gustavus Adolphus and then the French came to its rescue after 1630. Despite Dutch aid, a series of Protestant commanders, from the Winter King, Frederick V of the Palatinate (1596–1632), Ernst von Mansfeld, and Christian of Brunswick (1599–1626), to King Christian IV (1577–1648) of Denmark, all equally failed at winning any significant battles (both Mansfeld and Brunswick had earlier served under Maurice in the Low Countries, from which experience they appear to have learned little); Protestantism might have been swept out of most of Central Europe were it not for the dependability of Dutch financial support, which allowed the Protestant side time and again to raise armies to face the almost infallibly triumphant Catholics on the battlefield between 1618 and 1632.[23] As in the British civil wars, Dutch engineers, predominantly fortification builders, were active across Central Europe in this age, too, such as Johan van Valckenburgh, Johan van Rijswijck, or Henrik Ruse (1624–1679).[24]

In the 1590s, Dutch ships brought Baltic grain to Italian ports to stave off a famine on the peninsula. It signalled the beginning of a much more marked Dutch presence in the Mediterranean. In military terms, this Dutch role is evident in both the Uskok wars we encountered earlier and in the Cretan or Candian War (1645–1667), another struggle between Venice and the Ottoman Empire. De Jonge speaks of several thousands of Dutch sailors serving against the Turks in this conflict.[25] One of them may have been Jan Struys, whose book tells the story of how he joined numerous Dutch sailors, captains, and ships as part of the Venetian fleets that annually sailed for the Dardanelles in the 1650s.[26] Dutch sailors commanded and manned not only Venetian ships but also some of the Turkish fleet.

Indeed, many renegade Dutch sailors already had become notorious as Barbary corsairs. Best known, perhaps, among these pirates is the New Amsterdam settler Anthony Jansen van Salee (1607–1676), who was a son of a Haarlem sailor, Jan Janszoon (c. 1570–c. 1640), better known as *Murad Reis* ("Admiral Murad").[27] Murad Reis raided for slaves as far as Ireland and Iceland and became for a while the governor of Salé (near Rabat in Morocco). Despite his father's notoriety as a Barbary pirate captain, Anthony Jansen married in Amsterdam and eventually settled in New York. There is no doubt that Murad Reis (who had started his privateering by raiding Spanish ships from Dunkerque before the port fell into Spanish hands) made a fortune. And he was not the only one who banked on his advanced sailing skill to become a wealthy renegade and rose to great heights as Muslim searobber: Among them were Simon de Danser (1577–1611) and Sulayman Reis (d. 1620), born in Hoorn as Ivan de Veenboer.

And there were Dutch mercenary soldiers who fought first for the Venetians in the Candian War and then enlisted with the Turks after capture, in exchange for lavish payments (as well as becoming Muslims).[28] Their conversion is echoed in the stories of Jan Struys in *Reysen* regarding Muslim efforts in the Caucasus to convert him, apparently not merely a trope to warn Dutch readers about evil temptations.[29] They were contemporaries of the Russia-bound Van Bockhovens, soldiers equally in search of new opportunities with the wars in the Low Countries, and perhaps Germany, whittling down.[30]

In attempting to ransom Dutch sailors who had been captured by the notorious North-African pirates known as Barbary corsairs, Nicolaas Witsen, who was for some years a key organizer of the effort to buy enslaved Dutch sailors their freedom, suggested that the Moroccan sultan might be best pleased if offered a delivery of arms.[31] As we already saw, before 1650, several Moroccan rulers had been supplied with Dutch weaponry. Witsen's suggestion was likely based on his knowledge regarding their interest in up-to-date arms. Witsen was married to Catharina Hochepied (1654–1728), whose cousin Daniel Hochepied (1657–1723) was the first of a long line of Dutch representatives in the Ottoman Empire (predominantly residing in Izmir rather than in Istanbul).[32] Hochepied's father had been a director of the Dutch Levantine Trade Board, which supervised since the 1620s Dutch trade with the Ottomans. Because of his wife's cousin (who supplied him with curiosities from exotic places), Witsen was probably reasonably attuned to the sensibilities of the Barbary chiefs (who were either Moroccan or Ottoman vassals) and better than most capable of ransoming Dutch captives.

Despite the friction regarding the enslavement of Dutch sailors, the relationship with the Turks tended to be rather good, because the Dutch at first were similarly inveterate enemies of the Spanish king and never joined any anti-Turkish alliances after 1648. In Istanbul, Izmir, or Aleppo, too, their representatives displayed a degree of subtlety that some of their European rivals lacked. Dutch merchants and VOC officials sported a similar sort of circumspection with other potentates in Eurasia, such as the Moghuls, the Chinese and Japanese emperors, and (although somewhat less so) the Iranian shah.[33] This was a more fruitful code of conduct than trying to use blunt force against such powerful empires, of which the Dutch did not have remotely enough, so far away from home.

Notes

1. Armitage, *Ideological Origins*. Jon Wilson's work convincingly details the happenstance nature of British rule in India (Wilson, *India Conquered*). I am not sure if an overview from this angle has yet been written for the similar case of the Dutch in Indonesia.
2. Borschberg, "Introduction," 30–3, 96–7, 108.
3. There were a number of reasons: Distance (even from Batavia) was one of them, although officials' mistakes (including those by Maetsuycker) were as important (see Mostert, "Chain of Command," 67–8).
4. ". . . the VOC was a curious hybrid of Mercury and Mars" (Borschberg, "Introduction," 6); see as well ibid., 119.
5. De Boer, "Een Amsterdamsche 'lorrendraayer'," 48n1. See also Amburger, *Die Familie*, 41. The ties between the De Willems and Marselises to which De Boer refers went at least back to the 1620s (see Lauridsen, *Marselis Konsortiet*, 27). Paul de Willem lived in Amsterdam, his brother Jan in

Copenhagen; Paul seems to have dabbled in the arms trade on Russia as well (see Breedvelt-van Veen, *Louis de Geer*, 75n2). His name, though, does not show up among those shipping goods to and from Arkhangel'sk in the early 1630s (while those of A.D. Winius, Jurriaan van Klenck, the younger De Vogelaers, the Bernaert/Bernard brothers, Karel du Moulin, Nicolaes Ruts, Christiaan and Lambert Massa, Selio and Peter Marselis, as well as Elias and Pieter Trip do appear), see *Notariele Akten, passim.*

6. Even if Van Dillen notes that the founding fathers Elias Trip and Louys de Geer fell out for a while around 1630 and became competitors (see Van Dillen, ed., "Amsterdamsche notarieele acten," 216–17).
7. Elias, ed., "Contract tot oprichting," 362–4.
8. Ibid., 370–2.
9. Ibid., 374–6.
10. Ibid., 383–6. Graafland was an upstart, as his father had sold small iron items, such as nails and locks.
11. See Manning, *Apprenticeship*.
12. Ibid.
13. See, for example, Dunthorne, "Dutch Revolt," 176. For some other books that drew heavily on the Dutch experience, see Manning, *Apprenticeship*, 192.
14. See Reger, "In the Service," 9.
15. A great overview is provided by Parker, see Parker, *Success*, 39–66. Unusually for the Dutch, some impressment of sailors was used (ibid., 58).
16. Ibid., 58–9.
17. Ibid., 60–1.
18. See Wagenaar, *Vaderlandsche historie. . .*, 2nd ed. vol. 15, 424–77. He used Witsen's manuscript account of the expedition, which has been lost since, as a key source. Wagenaar suggests that Appelman, one of the city's four mayors, was left in the dark about the preparations, because he did not support it (ibid., 425).
19. See earlier (and Manning, *Apprenticeship*, 246). Goodman points out that the Birmingham arms industry can be traced to the very first weeks of the reign of King William III (Goodman, "On the Progress," 494–5).
20. See Martines, *Furies*, 38–9.
21. Not surprisingly, especially German historians have written about him. See, for example, Rill, *Tilly*. In French, see Samseon de Gérard, *Le Comte*. We are awaiting a good scholarly English biography of Tilly.
22. His exploits were detailed in brief Redlich, "Military Entrepreneurship"; for an elaborate account, see Ernstberger, *Hans de Witte*.
23. Dutch subsidies increased after a fairly modest initial contribution to the Elector of the Palatinate; at the Battle of the White Mountain, some Dutch contingents saw battle, and a few other units were involved in other early episodes of the conflict. But whereas the Dutch soldiers largely disappeared after 1621 (unless one sees the second phase of the Dutch-Spanish war as a part of the Thirty Years' War), the Dutch subsidies to the Protestant side steadily increased.
24. On the fortress builders in Germany, see Soenke, "Johan van Rijswijck"; Weber, *Johan van Valckenburgh*.
25. De Jonge, *Nederland*, 226.
26. Struys, *Reysen. . .*, 78–9.
27. See, for example, Van Dyke Roberts, "Anthony Jansen."
28. De Jonge, *Nederland*, 230–2; Boterbloem, *Fiction and Reality*, 22–4.
29. Boterbloem, *Fiction and Reality*, 111, 113.

30. See Parrott, *Business*, 45, on the Venetian practice of hiring of foreign *condottieri*.
31. Gebhard, *Het leven*, vol. 1, 303.
32. Peters, *wijze koopman*, 57–60.
33. Some of this was due to a fairly advanced level of interest in (and knowledge about) the various states and cultures which they encountered. Dutch envoys such as Cornelis Haga in Istanbul or Hubert Visnich in Isfahan made an effort to immerse themselves in the local culture, and the study of various non-European cultures by Dutch scholars (such as Golius or Baldaeus) occurred at a fairly sophisticated level.

Bibliography

Amburger, E. *Die Familie Marselis*, Gießen: Wilhelm Schmitz, 1957.

Armitage, David. *The Ideological Origins of the British Empire*, Cambridge: Cambridge University Press, 2000.

Boer, G.W. de. "Een Amsterdamsche 'lorrendraayer' Celio Marselis," *Jaarboek van het Genootschap Amstelodamum* 38, 1941, 37–66.

Borschberg, Peter. "Introduction," in P. Borschberg, ed., *Journal, Memorials and Letters of Cornelis Matelieff de Jonge: Security, Diplomacy and Commerce in 17th-Century Southeast Asia*, Singapore: NUS Press, 2015, 1–138.

Boterbloem, K. *The Fiction and Reality of Jan Struys: A Seventeenth-Century Dutch Globetrotter*, Basingstoke: Palgrave, 2008.

Breedvelt-van Veen, F. *Louis de Geer, 1587–1652*, Amsterdam: H.J. Paris, 1935.

Dillen, J.G. van, ed. "Amsterdamsche notarieele acten betreffende den koperhandel en de uitoefening van mijnbouw en metaalindustrie in Zweden," *Bijdragen en Mededelingen van het Historisch Genootschap* 58, 1937, 211–301.

Dunthorne, Hugh. "The Dutch Revolt in English Political Culture, 1585–1600," in Theo Hermans and Reinier Salverda, eds, *From Rags to Riches*, London: UCL Press, 2017, 173–82.

Dyke Roberts, Hazel van. "Anthony Jansen van Salee, 1607–76," *New York Genealogical and Biographical Record* 1, 1972, 16–28.

Elias, J.E., ed., "Contract tot oprichting van een Zweedsch factorie-comptoir te Amsterdam in 1663," *Bijdragen en Mededelingen van het Historisch Genootschap* 24, 1903, 356–400.

Ernstberger, Anton. *Hans de Witte. Finanzmann Wallensteins*, Wiesbaden: Franz Steiner, 1954.

Gebhard, J.F. *Het leven van Mr. Nicolaas Cornelisz. Witsen (1641–1717)*, vol. 1, Utrecht: Leeflang, 1881.

Goodman, J.D. "On the Progress of the Small Arms Manufacture," *Journal of the Statistical Society of London* 4, 1865, 494–506.

Jonge, J.C. de. *Nederland en Venetië*, Den Haag: Van Cleef, 1852.

Lauridsen, John T. *Marselis Konsortiet: En Studie over Forholdet Mellem Handelskapital og Kongemagt i 1600-Tallets Danmark*, Arhus: Jysk Selskab for Historie, 1987.

Manning, Roger. *An Apprenticeship in Arms: The Origins of the British Army, 1585–1702*, Oxford: Oxford University Press, 2006.

Martines, Lauro. *Furies: War in Europe, 1450–1700*, London: Bloomsbury, 2013.

Mostert, Tristan. "Chain of Command: The Military System of the Dutch East India Company, 1655–1663," MA thesis, Universiteit Leiden, 2007, available at: http://vocwarfare.net/thesis/, accessed 25 November 2018.

Notariele Akten (of Dutch Shipping on Arkhangel'sk), available at: http://resources.huygens.knaw.nl/archangel/app/inleiding?language_of_user=en, accessed 23 February 2019.

Parker, G. *Success Is Never Final: Empire, War, and Faith in Early Modern Europe*, New York: Basic Books, 2002.

Parrott, David. *The Business of War*, Cambridge: Cambridge University Press, 2012.

Peters, Marion. *De wijze koopman: Het wereldwijde onderzoek van Nicolaes Witsen (1641–1717), burgemeester en VOC-bewindhebber van Amsterdam*, Amsterdam: Bert Bakker, 2010.

Redlich, F. "Military Entrepreneurship and the Credit System in the Sixteenth and Seventeenth Centuries," *Kykols* 2, 1957, 186–93.

Reger, W.M. "In the Service of the Tsar: European Mercenary Officers and the Reception of Military Reform in Russia, 1654–1667," unpublished PhD diss., University of Illinois at Urbana-Champaign, 1997.

Rill, Bernd. *Tilly. Feldherr für Kaiser und Reich*, Munich: Universitas, 1984.

Samseon de Gérard, Guillaume. *Le Comte de Tilly*, Paris: Guibert, 1992.

Soenke, Jürgen. "Johan van Rijswijck und Johan van Valckenburgh: Die Befestigung deutscher Städte und Residenzen 1600–1625," *Mitteilungen der Mindener Geschichtsvereins* 46, 1974, 9–39.

Struys, Jan. *Drie aanmerkelijke en seer rampspoedige Reysen. . .*, Amsterdam: J. Van Meurs and J. van Someren, 1676.

Wagenaar, Jan. *Vaderlandsche historie. . .*, 2nd ed., vol. 15, Amsterdam: Weduwe Isaak Tirion, 1770.

Weber, Karl-Klaus. *Johan van Valckenburgh: Das Wirken des niederländischen Festungbaumeisters in Deutschland, 1609–1625*, Cologne: Böhlau, 1995.

Wilson, Jon. *India Conquered: Britain's Raj and the Chaos of Empire*, New York: Simon and Schuster, 2016.

5 Sailors, Soldiers, and Arms Abroad, Part 2

Beyond Europe

5.1 Dutch Activity in the Americas

The Netherlandic arrival in the Americas can be traced back to the early sixteenth century, when sailors from the Low Countries joined Spanish fleets crossing the Atlantic. Only after some years of privateering that occasionally yielded lucrative prizes, however, did genuine efforts come about to establish a bridgehead there on behalf of the Republic as part of the effort to thwart the Spaniards and perhaps cut them off from the sources of their riches.[1] This struggle was costly, in terms of human lives and otherwise, whereas the proceeds remained altogether low before 1700, even if some individuals (such as the Cooymans family or Piet Heyn) hit the jackpot.[2]

Founded in 1621 at the very time of the renewal of hostilities with Spain, the Dutch West India Company (WIC) was created as an instrument to wage war even more explicitly than the older VOC.[3] Its focus was on looting rather than trade. Its success should perhaps be measured according to different standards than the VOC, which after its bellicose beginnings prioritised trade (even if the distinction between honest and less-than-honest trade, all the way to outright robbery, was not clearly observed).[4] Although the WIC has become infamous because of its role as a crucial booster of the trans-Atlantic slave trade, it began to involve itself in this commerce in earnest only after 1648.[5]

Whereas its architects aimed at warfare, it was not clear how it was to harm their Iberian foe most in the Western hemisphere. Under its umbrella (and next to it), inventive types experimented from its early days onward with colonial schemes. Dutch settlement colonies, however, never gained traction in the Americas (unless it was in the morbid way of settling African slaves). Few seemed keen on moving to the Americas. Ultimately, the Dutch activities in the Americas limited themselves to trade and sugar production and remained comparatively low in economic value. But for almost half a century (c. 1621–1667), Dutch land warfare and privateering took place on a considerable scale from Brazil to Manhattan, accompanied by an upsurge in the sale of arms in the Western hemisphere.

The brutal side of Dutch overseas ventures is captured in an ultimatum delivered by Abraham Crijnssen (d. 1669), admiral of the Dutch squadron of eight ships that arrived before Paramaribo (Surinam) in February 1667, to the English defenders of the fortress at the settlement:

> Sir, Being come hither by the command of the High-puissant Lords the States my Masters, to incorporate the fort with your command, this is the reason I send you this drummer with this letter, to the end you may render it, promissing you that in such case your selfe and all the inhabitants of the countrey shall absollutely retaine the entire property and possession of what they have, without loss of the least thing, but in case you refuse it, I am resolved to atack you by sea and land, with the designe of killing all that shall oppose, not giving quarter to any on. You may regulate your selfe here upon, whilst I attend an answer to this letter within one quarter of an hower without any delay.[6]

If it appears as if impatient overconfidence speaks here (the English defenders, who were several hundred strong, including African slave auxiliaries, and wielding some cannon, rejected the ultimatum), Crijnssen's Zeelanders proved they did not bluff by storming the fort the next day and forcing the English to ask for a truce.[7]

Because of its lack of sustained profits, the Dutch West India Company had to be refinanced in 1647 and was overhauled in 1674 and 1675.[8] In part, this was because it lost much of its purpose after 1648 (when peace with Spain was signed) and especially after 1664 (when New Amsterdam was lost, just after a treaty with Portugal acknowledged the loss of Brazil). The WIC's overhead was not worth the investment: The trip by ship between Africa and the Americas or Europe and the Americas was often not much longer than six weeks (especially going westward), not much longer than trips to Russia; given this relative proximity, interloping in the trans-Atlantic and Caribbean trade was more frequent, and competition with foreign countries more intense.

In the West Indies, the cost of a monopoly enterprise was not worth the benefits it might yield in terms of safeguarding commerce. The organisation of the VOC, in contrast, made sense: The degree of risk and difficulty in the trade on Asia was far greater, while the profits reaped from shipping scarce Asian goods were greatly vaster than from transporting the fairly bulky American commodities such as sugar. In southern or western Africa or the Americas, individual entrepreneurs did not need the sort of protective shell as those active in Asia did, at least not after the Dutch gave up on Brazil and the New Netherlands. VOC officials, too, had a great knack at propitiating the various rulers of the territories with which they traded, from Istanbul to Tokyo (Edo). Additionally, the VOC may have been better led than the WIC: It seems to have been much smarter at judging when military operations became too costly to sustain (as it did in India), and thus threatened profits.[9]

The Portuguese, British, or French in Asia were not as strong militarily as the European rivals the WIC encountered in the Western hemisphere. A war of conquest was only briefly envisioned by the WIC governors or the Estates-General, but the 1623 *Groot Desseyn* that aimed to cripple Spanish-Portuguese rule permanently quickly proved to be an overly ambitious project.[10] The organisation operated most successfully as a bunch of searobbers, which was mainly in its first decade or so.[11] Government and merchants (and even the occasional preacher) worked hand-in-glove setting up the American enterprise.[12] The WIC enjoyed its marquee victory in capturing the Spanish Silver Fleet near Cuba in 1629, arguably the most successful case of piracy in history.[13]

Klooster rightfully suggests that the Dutch appear to have modelled much of their trading empire after the Portuguese, establishing fortified trading stations (*factorijen* or factories) rather than setting up larger areas of territorial control.[14] There was one serious attempt at establishing a larger colony at Brazil, but the Dutch presence there did not last longer than a generation. New Amsterdam and the surrounding area seemed more like the Cape Colony in Africa, with the aim of provisioning the more lucrative properties in the Caribbean Sea and on the South American mainland, rather than the American equivalent of the major Dutch hubs at Sri Lanka, the Spice Islands, Makassar, or Batavia.

Brazil, in Klooster's view,

> was seen by many . . . in the Dutch political and mercantile elite as the premier Dutch colony in the western hemisphere—hence the willingness to wage a long and, at times, seemingly endless war that consumed many thousands of soldiers and sailors. In terms of military personnel, Brazil dwarfed all other Dutch colonies and trading posts combined.[15]

Initially, then, the Dutch incursions in the Caribbean were part of a sort of global strategy to spite their Iberian foe, and the conquest of part of Brazil on the Portuguese seemed an important victory. As Klooster writes, "The Dutch Atlantic Empire was forged on the battlefield . . . [and t]he overseas deployment of troops was a[n] . . . extension of the decades-old independence war against Habsburg Spain."[16] Military victory was more important than economic profit. But once 1648 came about, the cost of to defend this outpost seemed no longer justified. This conclusion, however, was reached only by about 1660, when the fall of the Dutch outpost at Pernambuco to the Portuguese in 1654 was accepted.

Klooster suggests that "the war in Brazil was the largest interimperial conflict of the seventeenth-century Atlantic, a fight that historians have underappreciated."[17] That last point is true, but for the Dutch (or

Spaniards), Brazil was a sideshow to their European war. Even though the struggle for its control was a costly affair for both sides, it involved far fewer troops or ships that the fighting in Europe (or on the European seas); indeed, the Dutch sojourn in Brazil lasted for a mere one generation at most (1624–1654), which was brief if compared with the Dutch long-term prodding and plodding campaigning in Indonesia or India. Very little was gained from the Brazilian episode, with the important exception of valuable expertise regarding the organisation of sugar plantations and the knowledge of how to supply them with labour by way of an enslaved workforce.

The case of Brazil (and the New Netherlands) is further proof of the point that, whereas the Dutch were often tempted to establish themselves on a more permanent basis overseas (as indeed they did in the Guyanas and on a few small Caribbean islands), and despite many a display of their great martial prowess and skill, they were unwilling to engage in prolonged military campaigns in the way they did in Europe to accomplish this.[18] When the effort and cost became too great, they cut their losses.[19] It seems telling that Crijnssen's flotilla set course for Surinam rather than New York (New Amsterdam), which had not been yielding much. Similar behaviour can be observed in the Dutch fighting in southern India (and the tension between the commanders of the VOC armies there and their supervisors in Batavia). One can suggest that after 1648, the Dutch restricted themselves to fighting overseas wars if the outcome might yield a profit (for personal gain or the gain of their trading companies). Warfare overseas had limited goals. No campaigns were tasked with an imperial mission for the greater glory of an illustrious fatherland.

A link may be recognised in the equally great reluctance to expand territorially into the southern Netherlands, something still pursued by William the Silent's sons before 1648. This yielded the Oranges strong opposition from Amsterdam, which had no interest in seeing Antwerp return to anything like its former glory. Subsequently, even William III showed little to no interest in acquiring the southern and eastern parts of the Netherlands besides the establishment of the barrier fortresses, which seemed a much cheaper solution than a full-scale annexation of the area (which by William III's time was ruled by an allied Power). The significance or deterrent role of those strongholds is hard to assess, as is the advantage of a buffer zone of a neutral territory inbetween over a common border with France.

On the one hand, the acquisition of Flanders, Brabant, and parts of Wallonia might have yielded more territory to defend for the Republic, but, on the other hand, it would have gained a comparatively wealthy economic hinterland. This, in the long term, might have created a crucially larger country, giving the Republic a better capacity to defend itself towards 1800, with a population not much smaller than that of Frederick the Great's Prussia, and an economy much more thriving than

Prussia's. Similarly, the eastern borders of the Republic were also drawn somewhat randomly and could have been pushed further back; Upper Guelders remained within the Empire (rather than joining the rest of the former Duchy of Guelders), and Münster remained a nasty thorn in its side instead of being clipped. Here it appears as if short-term savings may have led to woeful costs on the long term.

Salvador (Bahia) was captured in 1624 on the Portuguese (ruled by the Spanish king Philip IV), even though it was lost again in 1625.[20] Dutch buccaneers terrorised the Spanish possessions, capturing the Spanish Silver Fleet in the Bay of Matanzas in 1629. Eventually, the Dutch did manage to gain a firmer foothold at Pernambuco (1630–1654), but despite the splendour of Johan Maurits of Nassau's court, displayed little stamina in trying to remain in Brazil when the Portuguese, in part benefitting from the Dutch being distracted by the English in the first Anglo-Dutch War (1652–1654), made a comeback.[21]

The conquest of Surinam in 1667 was a sideshow, then, for the Dutch (and they lost Paramaribo briefly again through an English counterattack soon after), even if Crijnssen briefly showed the English colonists and their auxiliaries who was boss and Surinam was considered a bigger prize than New York.[22] The WIC did not establish or expand any truly lucrative venture in the Caribbean that lasted, although Dutch merchants, planters, and sailors played a role in the slave trade and established a significant plantation society in the Guyanas. But this industry remained comparatively small if looking at the plantation economies of Brazil, Jamaica, Saint-Domingue, Cuba, or the US South.[23]

The Dutch arrival in North America was likely triggered by the Iberian and British cod trade between Newfoundland and Europe on which the Dutch encroached.[24] By 1600, furs were loaded, sometimes acquired from French merchants who traded along the Saint Lawrence river, and sometimes directly from native American traders.[25] But these were episodic ventures until the foundation of the New Netherland Company in the 1610s, which oversaw the establishment of a Dutch fortress in Fort Nassau on the Hudson river.

The Dutch sojourn in North-America spanned less than two generations (1614–1664). It did not yield great benefits and was marked by brutal violence. Thus, in a conflict between the local Indians and the Dutch settlers at Manhattan in 1643, to set an example, European troops hacked infants to pieces and mutilated adults, the opening act of a truly savage conflict.[26] Named after the governor of New Amsterdam, Kieft's War became one of the more notorious episodes of the killing of native North Americans by Europeans. Ironically, the Dutch had undermined their own military advantage by selling firearms on a grand scale to the native communities after 1635, even if the WIC feebly prohibited such trade.[27] Although complaining about their sale of weapons to native Americans, British North American colonists, too, bought their arms from the Dutch in New Netherland before 1664, in particular during the quarter century prior to New Amsterdam's surrender, when the British civil wars interfered with regular trade from Britain.[28] Again, the global dimension of Dutch arms sales is striking: The Republic's merchants delivered at the same time a great number of arms to those fighting in Ireland, Scotland, and England.[29]

The territory of New Netherland was in theory large at first, stretching from the area near what is now Philadelphia to the northern Massachusetts border.[30] But the mapmakers in Europe did not base themselves on any realistic idea of territory in Dutch hands. Eventually, the latitude of the northern border was lowered, and Dutch claims by the middle of the 1620s amounted roughly to the eastern half of today's New York State.

New Amsterdam, like "old" Amsterdam, was a cosmopolitan colony; most of its inhabitants had been born outside the United Provinces. This was not untypical for Dutch overseas settlements, as the same sort of demographic profile prevailed in such a supposedly Dutch bastion as Batavia in the 1670s.[31] Batavia had more Chinese than Dutch inhabitants and far more slaves than Europeans resided in the city. Such population data illustrate how Dutch colonial outposts were rarely populated by Dutch settlers. This was not unusual, meanwhile, for settlement colonies were in general rather the exception than the rule among the seventeenth-century overseas European empires.[32]

The North American chapter of Dutch rule was hardly ever peaceful; a variety of wars made the 1640s and 1650s restless, and by 1664, the colony was given up to the British, with whom previously at most an armed truce had obtained.[33] In 1673, Dutch authority was restored in their former North American possessions, but New York and its environs were given up again without demurring at the negotiation table that concluded with the Treaty of Westminster of 1674.[34] Some compensation was sought in attempts to acquire French colonies, but despite Dutch naval strength, the French proved resilient in hanging on to their overseas holdings. Especially in North America, the Dutch imperialist effort proved a costly failure. True to form, they withdrew, probably relieved to extricate themselves from a losing proposition.

Ultimately, Brazil, the New Netherlands, and New Amsterdam were almost accidental colonies. The Dutch colonial effort in the Americas found its origins in the desire to take the war with Spain further abroad. Once the war with Spain was over, its sense of purpose was lost. Of all Dutch overseas ventures, the American was most fleeting, even if a reliable source of income was acquired by some through Dutch shippers' slave trade on Africa and the exploitation of sugar plantations on the South American mainland as well as the operation of some occasionally bustling trading stations on the Caribbean islands during the last decades of the seventeenth century.[35] The slave trade and sugar plantations worked by African slaves seemed lucrative ventures but needed little to no outlay from the Dutch state to operate (or so it was thought).[36] Klooster argues that "violence was the ultimate expression of what it meant to be Dutch in both a religious and cultural sense" in the Atlantic World.[37] This is not hyperbole. And so little was gained from this savagery.

5.2 Trade Empire: The Dutch in Asia

The Dutch East India Company sometimes receives accolades as being the first modern share-holding corporation, or as the archetype of the multinational, large capitalist enterprise of today.[38] Founded in 1602, it certainly enjoyed a long period of economic success, but if it was so stunningly successful, it should perhaps have lasted beyond 1800.[39] In any event, the VOC's early capitalist success story is one of a peculiar kind: It serves perhaps as an example of the sort of capitalist economic development heavily aided by the state as advocated by Friedrich List, or even of the corporatist capitalism that was tried in Mussolini's Italy. For it was the opposite of an enterprise that tried to defeat the competition in an honest rivalry through offering the buyer better or cheaper products on the market. Instead, it sought monopoly, and used whatever means were necessary to accomplish this.

As in other scholarly discussions of precocious Dutch modernity, the literature underplays the violence, wholly backed and sponsored by the Dutch state, that simmered behind its mercantile and colonial ventures.[40] The VOC was in its first decades similar to the WIC: It unscrupulously combined trade with piracy and other sorts of violence to gain the upper hand, especially over its Iberian foes (mainly the Portuguese in Asia).[41] And afterwards, it turned to violence if this seemed advantageous, as it did on Java, Sri Lanka, or southern India.[42] Some impressive conquests were made, but other ventures proved costly and inconclusive.[43] Undoubtedly, all VOC chiefs were willing to do what was necessary to turn a profit.[44]

The company's leadership, though, prioritised trade over territorial control. The VOC was particularly interested at monopolising the overseas pepper export from the region to Europe, which had been in the hands of the Portuguese since the establishment of their first bridgehead at Goa during the early sixteenth century.[45] While the Dutch acquired a virtual monopoly over the supply of nutmeg, mace, cloves, and cinnamon to Europe, capturing all of the Asian pepper export proved chimerical, however. Pepper was grown in too many different places in South and South-East Asia, and too many competitors were interested in shipping it to Europe. The cost of establishing control over these far-flung regions was too prohibitive for the VOC.

The following is a brief account of the seventeenth-century VOC's bellicose activities in the various regions of Asia where it was most prominent: The Indonesian Archipelago and Malacca; Taiwan and Japan; and

India and Sri Lanka. Here and there, I refer to various other places where the VOC role was more ephemeral (Thailand, Iran, Mocha; South and East Africa, which also fell under VOC purview, will be discussed in the next section). By homing in on several individuals who left a profound imprint on the Company as its senior officials in Asia, VOC operations relevant to our topic come more sharply into focus. Finally, some of the key findings as they relate to the arms trade and diffusion of military innovation will be emphasised.

In the Indonesian islands and at Malacca, the VOC first struck out, led by key pioneers such as Jan Pieterszoon Coen or Cornelis Matelieff (1570–1632), who both tried to develop a coherent strategy to guide VOC operations in this region.[46] The long-remembered Amboina Massacre of 1623, in which British merchants were butchered, starkly displays the violent streak the Dutch even early on might display in their search for profit; meanwhile, the number of English (and Japanese as well as Portuguese) victims of this episode was actually dwarfed by other bloodshed committed against local Asian communities, such as, for instance, the innumerable people VOC soldiers and officers killed on Banda in 1621.[47] As Mostert remarks,

> Violence, in the form of militarily driving out competitors, blockading their harbors, as well as . . . to force monopolies and favourable trading conditions upon local rulers, [were] accepted instruments to influence the market and enhance profit for the VOC.[48]

The deepest imprint on the VOC's *modus operandi* in Asia was probably left by the longest serving governor-general in Batavia, Joan Maetsuycker (1606–1678), who led the VOC from 1652 to 1678. He used brutality in measured fashion: "Maatsuiker was both willing and able to use violence to protect the Company's interests, but did not have the hawkish and self-righteous characteristics of some of his predecessors and successors."[49] He struck a balance that may have been optimal between measured expansion and consolidation, with profits being uppermost in his mind. Thus, he was less of a violent colonial conqueror than his colleague and rival Rijckloff van Goens sr (1619–1682), twice governor of Sri Lanka, and Maetsuycker's deputy (from 1675 to 1678) and successor (from 1678 to 1681), about whom more later.[50]

Next to Maetsuycker and Van Goens sr, Cornelis Janszoon Speelman (1628–1684) may epitomise the VOC spirit.[51] Speelman, for much of his career a bookkeeper and, at the time of his appointment as expedition commander, suspended on accusations of engaging in private trade, conquered the sultanate of Makassar on Sulawesi (Celebes) between 1666 and 1669 in a brutal campaign.[52] An accountant who excelled at cracking numbers, Speelman apparently seamlessly doubled as a ruthless *conquistador*, exemplifying the violent component of Dutch capitalist ethos.

After his victory over Makassar, he joined the Council of India in Batavia alongside Maetsuycker and Van Goens. His stock rose further through another vicious campaign he led against the Mataram sultanate on Java, after which he became second-in-command in Batavia to Van Goens from 1678 and 1681.[53] He succeeded the latter as governor-general in Batavia in 1681, a position he occupied when he died three years later. Speelman as governor-general appears of a type found across European colonial empires, that of the colonial official gone to seed; company lawyer Pieter van Dam (1621–1706) expressed relief that God took Speelman away before the Dutch VOC directorate, the Gentlemen Seventeen *(Heeren XVII)*, had to remove him.[54]

Despite Speelman's victories, the Dutch, "one of the leading fighting nations of Europe," were incapable of comprehensively defeating either the Javanese or the Madurese over the course of a well-nigh 50-year (1677–1723) war fought out on Java, the island on which Batavia was located.[55] The VOC's technological advantage in fighting local rulers was particularly telling in two respects: At sea, warships (and even merchantmen) proved superior—albeit not wholly invincible—to Asian opponents, whereas on land, Dutch fortifications were almost impregnable (and in both cases, the use of artillery had a lot to do with this superiority).[56] But when campaigning on land, the VOC armies enjoyed a much less clear-cut advantage, which those endless Javanese campaigns indicate.

As Ricklefs suggests, "War was as central to the VOC in Java as it was to Javanese society."[57] Not eschewing violence when its use appeared strategic, Maetsuycker, Van Goens sr, and Speelman consolidated the VOC's position in Asia through a variety of challenges (such as the fall of Taiwan, the Javanese wars, and the French war) and laid the groundwork for its continuing flourishing for another century.[58] Of course, not every official was as versatile or bold as Speelman, which brings us to Taiwan. In 1661, the fortress of Fort Zeelandia was besieged by an armada commanded by the Ming general Zheng Chenggong. Koenraad van Klenck's older brother, Herman (sometimes known as Klenck van Odessa, 1621–1699), who was trained as a lawyer and occupied a high position in the VOC directorate in Batavia, was dispatched with several vessels from Batavia to Taiwan to replace the colony's governor Frederick Coyett (1615–1687) in the midst of this siege.[59] Once he descried Zheng Chenggong's vast Chinese fleet, Herman van Klenck decided to abscond, sailing instead on to Japan. This may have been prudent but was likely informed more than anything by cowardice. Van Klenck could at least have probed Chinese strength, as the combat strength of his sailships was far superior than that of the Chinese junks. And any sign of a relief force might have emboldened the defenders inside the fortress.

As said, the Dutch especially excelled at fortress building, which made it hard to dislodge them, unless it was through an interminable siege or blockade, as happened with Fort Zeelandia on Taiwan.[60] Even though no attempt was made to end the siege by rendering assistance from the sea, Fort Zeelandia might have held out, if it had not been betrayed. While Fort Zeelandia fell in 1661 to Zheng Chenggong, only one other significant Dutch-built fort surrendered in a siege between 1600 and 1800.[61] In this respect, the significance of the Military Revolution for the survival of the Dutch maritime empire seems evident.

Rather harshly, Frederick Coyett was blamed for the loss of Taiwan; sentenced to death by the VOC's council in Batavia, his life was ultimately spared; he would write a spirited defence of his conduct after he was allowed to return to the Republic in the 1670s.[62] Curiously, Frederick's son Balthasar (c. 1650–1725) became a "noble" retainer in Koenraad van Klenck's embassy to Moscow around the same time.[63] In Balthasar's printed account of this embassy, no sign of animosity towards Van Klenck can be found.[64] How exactly the lines of patronage ran in the Republic is often hard to establish, but like the Van Klencks, the Coyetts appear to have been clients of the Oranges, as apparently William III was instrumental in allowing Frederick Coyett's repatriation.[65] Nonetheless, intrigue may be suspected: Balthasar Coyett (who had relatives in Russia) might have been added to the embassy in part to keep a watchful eye on Koenraad van Klenck. As far as we know, meanwhile, Herman van Klenck, who remained until the end of his life a VOC employee in East Asia, was not punished for his absconding. But it seems significant that he never made promotion either.

The Dutch boasted of their martial prowess, as Wim Boot suggests in relating a conversation between François Caron (1600–1673), a key trailblazer in the establishment of Dutch power in East Asia, and Japanese interlocutors in 1639; when the latter wanted to know whether the VOC could replace the Portuguese as the trading partner of their country, the Japanese linked success in trade to military strength:

> The first question asked of Caron was, whether the Portuguese and Spaniards would be able to prevent the Dutch from coming to Japan, in case the Portuguese were expelled. Caron replied that it was the Spaniards and Portuguese who feared the Dutch, not the Dutch who feared the Iberians. Dutch squadrons harassed Goa and the Spanish strongholds almost yearly. If the Spanish would have been able to keep the Dutch away from Japan, they would have done so long ago. In Europe, the Dutch had been fighting them for many years and had bested them both on sea and on land.[66]

Projecting military strength, of course, is a tried-and-true strategy. Caron's boasting impressed the Japanese. By 1642, VOC officials had become the only Europeans allowed to trade with Japan. But the Dutch could stay at Deshima only on Japanese terms. Caron's blustering was never backed up by a show of Dutch military strength.

A detailed published account by the Haarlem surgeon Wouter Schouten about his service with Rijckloff Volckertszoon van Goens's forces in southern India and on Sri Lanka attests to Van Goens's ruthless determination.[67] One graphic description by Schouten of the aftermath of a scene of slaughter in 1662 on India's Malabar coast may suffice to give a flavour of the nature of Van Goens's campaigning:

> During the bloodshed about 400 *nairos* [hindu warriors] had perished. The bodies lay in big heaps on top of each other; the walls [of the temple] were covered with blood and splattered with brains. The pagoda, court and surrounding roads were covered with enemy corpses. I saw a man draw his sword and stab a heavily wounded *nairo* until he gave up the ghost. After he was scolded for this, he said to me: "Well, why not, those dogs have cut my nose off," which indeed appeared to be the case. . . . The most intrepid of our people collected . . . a good deal of plunder, from earrings, golden rings, chains, to diamonds, etc. Thus we could observe Adam's children's greed, who quickly and skillfully tore off the earlobes and fingers of the fallen *nairos* to acquire these attractive objects.[68]

Mostert's case study of the conflict between the Portuguese and Dutch regarding Sri Lanka and southern India shows how the VOC deployed large numbers of soldiers in Asia, with more than 1,000 troops arriving annually in Batavia from Europe between 1656 and 1663, while the more than 2,000 sailors who transported them every year to the battlefield of Sri Lanka could be assigned military duty on arrival as well.[69] The ships that carried these forces took along tens of thousands "*melee*" weapons such as swords, pikes, or axes as well as thousands of muskets, carbines, pistols and arquebuses, and countless gun components.[70]

Stationed again in South Asia in the 1670s, it was Rijckloff van Goens sr who oversaw the attack on Louis XIV's Asian squadron under admiral De la Haye.[71] After this fleet had repaired to the fortress of Trinconemale, Van Goens's forces captured both the fortress and many of the French warships in late 1672; allied with the king of Golconda, Dutch soldiers and ships comprehensively defeated English and French forces in 1673 and 1674. After his military campaigns on Sri Lanka and in southern India, though, even Rijckloff van Goens sr concluded that profits were what mattered.[72] On good grounds, Ottow describes Van Goens as no different from other VOC officials in supporting its calibrated sort of trade policy.[73]

Mostert points out that no open war between Asian Powers and the Dutch government ever broke out before 1780; soldiers and sailors who saw combat were in the service of the VOC rather than the Dutch state.[74] Campaigns remained localised and were as much as possible of short duration (even if some wars could drag on for very long, as on Java).

The VOC was a business whose decision-makers were utterly cautious in ensuring that its operations were profitable, using very precise cost-benefit analyses; warfare, normally, was expensive.[75]

On campaign, Dutch commanders and their soldiers (or sailors) used brutality in an often ruthlessly calculated fashion rather than engaging in wild savagery. Mostert rightfully points out that "violence became a legitimate tool to influence the market."[76] But violence is hard to control once it is unleashed and savagery was encouraged by the poor wages paid to the soldiers.[77] While its soldiers frequently raped and murdered people and pillaged their communities, the VOC was just as keen on delivering firearms, powder, and the like to local potentates, to some extent undermining their own chances at military hegemony, similar to the Dutch in North America.[78] While spices were the most precious cargo going to Europe, people and arms formed the bulk of the cargo on the trip from Europe to Asia.[79] Peters and André de la Porte encountered some impressive cannons (cast in Amsterdam and Enkhuizen around 1640) that the VOC gave to the Moghul Aurangzeb; the early Qing were fond of Dutch hand-held firearms as well.[80] This arms dispatch coincided with mass shipments of weapons to Russia, showing the continued high productive capacity of the Dutch arms industry around 1660.

Ricklefs has tried to pinpoint the effect of the Dutch technological advance on Javanese combat:

> The four main innovations in infantry armaments introduced by the Europeans to Java in the later years of the seventeenth century and early years of the eighteenth century were the *snaphaen* (snaphance) flintlock to replace the matchlock musket, the pre-packaged paper cartridge, the grenade and (apparently [after about 1725]) the bayonet. The cumulative effect of these was primarily to increase dramatically the reliability, rate and accuracy of infantry fire and, after the introduction of the bayonet, to make it feasible to dispense with the use of pikes.[81]

But he takes issue throughout his work with the idea that the indigenous chiefs were merely copying key elements of Europe's Military Revolution:

> . . . indigenous fortress warfare in Java was comparable to that in Europe. Trunajaya's fortifications at Surabaya in 1677 and Kêdhiri in 1678 and Namrud's at Mêsir in 1681 seem not to have been inferior to contemporary European fortresses. It is not surprising, then, that Javanese and VOC artillery were comparable. Cannon had been manufactured in Java for some time, . . . The only significant innovation introduced in Java by the VOC with regard to siege warfare was the hand- or *Coehoorn* mortar. This was a light trench mortar for throwing grenades into enemy trenches or fortifications, invented by

> the Dutchman Baron Menno van Coehoorn. It was apparently first used by the Company in Java in the campaign of 1706[.][82]

It is difficult to disagree with Ricklefs's argument, since the "Great Divergence" between Europe and Asia is not quite evident for the seventeenth century, if measured by the degree of European control over Asian territory, which appears negligible, or the paucity of any clear-cut significant military victories by the Europeans.[83] But Ricklefs's assessment should be read against Andrade's argument, who does argue for the Europeans already slightly edging ahead.[84] And Ricklefs's argument is not always wholly consistent: He does suggest that in violent conflicts, the VOC seemed to hold the advantage in terms of discipline as well as strategy and tactics, whereas indigenous forces had superiority of numbers.[85]

Evidently, a technological gap between European and Asian means of war existed, but it could yet be overcome. Undermining any such superiority, the Dutch helped Asian rulers by trading more advanced weapons to them, and even gifting them such arms. With the exception of the larger sailships, perhaps, weapons were still made simply enough that they could be copied by local Asian craftsmen: Therefore, even such gifts could backfire. There is no doubt that European naval supremacy over non-Europeans at sea was nonetheless well-nigh absolute (if we consider the Ottoman Empire as European, too) throughout most of the early modern era, however. Europe's sailships not only astonished the native Americans when they first spotted them, but allowed the Dutch to intimidate both the shah of Iran (in 1645) and India's Moghul, even if they utterly lacked any substantial land army to back up their bombardments and really challenge those emperors.[86] The capture of Fort Zeelandia by Zheng Chenggong may seem to run counter to the argument of Dutch naval superiority, but a mere 14 Dutch warships were faced by an opponent commanding hundreds of ships (estimated at 400!); furthermore, as already noted, the fortress ultimately fell because of treason by one of the local VOC officers.[87]

Perhaps it is therefore all the more unsurprising that Tsar Peter the Great became so extraordinarily obsessed by this overwhelming European maritime superiority, expending incredible human effort on remaking his country into a partially maritime power (the foundation of St. Petersburg and its replacement of Moscow as the Russian capital should be included in calculating its costs). And Peter's attempt to start a navy was not the first by a Russian ruler. His predecessors Mikhail and Aleksei tried to reroute the transport of Asian silk across Russia to Europe.[88] Northern and Western Europeans throughout the seventeenth century were preoccupied by the search for cheaper silk, with transport routes slow and ponderous. Asian silk originated in northern Iran, India, or China; Iran was obviously nearest to Europe, but its silk was shipped to

Europe by way of laboriously slow caravan routes via Aleppo or Izmir, or overseas from Bandar-e-Abbas (Gombroon), with VOC ships usually first transporting it to Batavia before it went to Europe.[89] Shortening the shipping route seemed worth the while, even when Iranian silk was not as highly valued as Chinese. Thus, in 1676, Koenraad van Klenck tried to persuade the Russians to reroute some of the Persian silk exports to Europe through Muscovy by way of the Caspian Sea, along the Volga and on the northern port of Arkhangel'sk, even willing to allow Armenians rather than Dutch merchants to transport the goods across Muscovy. But his timing was unfortunate: Aleksei's own project had collapsed in 1670, and the tsar died before Van Klenck could lay out his plans before him. A wobbly regency took over in Moscow, which was unwilling to take great risks. Van Klenck's efforts were the last of the Dutch attempts to reroute the shipping of Iranian raw silk to the markets of Europe. The northern silk route, even if still later probed by Fabricius on behalf of the Swedish king, never became a going concern.

A ruthlessly rational mindset expressed itself clearly throughout the Dutch drive into Asia. Diplomacy, war, and trade were all used to gain an economic advantage: Weaker opponents were militarily defeated, stronger foes were enticed by trade offers, and all were confronted with diplomatic guile. To coat their own nefarious behaviour with a moral veneer, Dutch duplicity was often projected on opponents, local potentates and their subjects who resented the foreign intruders upsetting traditional trading patterns.[90] Arms were traded everywhere, not in the least with Tokugawa Japan but also with open enemies such as the Javanese rulers.[91] The Dutch navy assisted the Chinese imperial (Qing) navy in the Qing–Ming conflict and made short work of the Iranian fleet in the 1640s.

The Dutch imprint in various Asian locales was long lasting, spanning 350 years on some of the Indonesian islands. The VOC gradually established factories or stationed representatives across Asia, predominantly in ports, but at times also inland. The Asian business was lucrative, both for higher Company officials and for those who served it as sailors or soldiers, even if it was a lethal endeavour at the same time for many of its participants. Van Goor estimates that, whereas almost a million Europeans left the Dutch ports on VOC ships destined for the "East Indies" in the seventeenth and eighteenth centuries, only slightly more than one third managed to return home.[92] This translates into the annual departure of some 5,000 people to the East, which is of the same magnitude as the seventeenth-century departure of British subjects to the Americas and elsewhere. It is reflective of a broad-based desire in the Netherlands to seek one's luck wherever it takes one, an essential component of the capitalist mindset. Although a few chose to stay in Asia, most of those who died, on the trip or in Asia, had planned to go back to Europe to spend their earnings (or indeed the money they would get by selling off the contents of the chest or trunk *[kist]* that they were allowed to bring back to Dutch soil).

Still, wages on VOC ships were not especially high in the eyes of Dutch-born sailors, who preferred also for other reasons short-haul shipping to the Mediterranean or Baltic Sea.[93] A multitude of foreigners, as Van Gelder notes, enlisted with the Company, for work as a VOC sailor or soldier was for them often a better option than staying behind in their homeland in the Holy Roman Empire, Denmark or Norway.[94] In addition, there was the possibility, more imagined than real, of finding untold riches. A fickle loyalty to the VOC or the state that backed it was an element of these daredevils' mindset, whether they were Dutch or not. Ricklefs depicts the VOC servants more as "the disorderly folk of Jan Steen" than the "substantial, upright and pious Calvinists" of Rembrandt; regardless, the Company offered a possible escape from a life of poverty.[95] Of course, the risks were great when serving as a sailor on the Company's ships or as a soldier in the Company's troops, if only one in three of those who left for the East returned to Europe, but it is moot in how far one's lifespan might have been longer if staying in Europe.[96] Marcus Rediker and Peter Linebaugh have suggested that in this same age, Caribbean pirates harboured some sort of proletarian class consciousness; a version of this may have informed the behaviour of many serving in the Company's ranks, in the sense that these were people who believed that they had agency in determining their own fate and might acquire some of the spoils of burgeoning capitalism.[97]

In their campaigns, VOC military units had sometimes very few Europeans in their ranks, and largely relied on Asian soldiers.[98] Apart from soldiers under VOC command, the Company also deftly used Asian allies.[99] If we take into account that the majority of the European soldiers in VOC ranks usually hailed from outside the Republic, Dutch-born men seem to have largely staffed the officer corps of the combat and garrison forces across the VOC empire in Asia.[100] One might suggest that this is further confirmation of the Dutch inclination to ruthlessly exploit the options to get ahead in life, letting others serve as cannon fodder and receiving oneself better pay and perquisites than one's European or non-European comrades.

Within the Company in the initial decades (c. 1600–1650), some even from humble background do seem to have made career, as happened in the Republic itself somewhat earlier, across the half century that saw the replacement of many a Catholic member of the elite by Protestant upstarts (c. 1570–1620), coinciding with the enormous growth of economic opportunity that resulted from the Fall of Antwerp. Eventually, the higher echelons of the VOC became more of a dumping ground for the superfluous sons of the elite and those who had to escape from something, such as Koenraad and Herman van Klenck's oldest brother, Johannes (1618–1672). Johannes van Klenck seems to have become entangled in scandal as professor of Amsterdam's Atheneum Illustre in the late 1660s and absconded to Batavia, seeking refuge with Herman.[101]

One element in understanding the remarkable successes the Dutch achieved in Asia may be hard to measure but seems to have played more of a key role (as it did in Europe) than the use of sophisticated means of warfare: The use of what we now call intelligence or, in other words, detailed information that gave the Dutch an advantage in trading over their European and Asian competitors but also underscored their military campaigns.[102] Not least in importance was their use of maps, of course, the making of which was another craft in which the denizens of the Low Countries excelled. Intensive communication between VOC outposts, Batavia, and the Republic led more often than not to prudent policy; only very few severe defeats were suffered, of which the surrender of Fort Zeelandia was the most glaring.[103] Towards the end of the century, the Dutch board of the VOC (the Gentlemen Seventeen), asked the long-serving company lawyer Pieter van Dam to encapsulate the most pertinent developments in the company's history in a lengthy history, which remained under wraps, merely accessible to higher VOC officials.[104] The information it contained gave the company servants significant advantage over competitors, or so it was believed. Earlier, too, the company had been utterly jealous about its correspondence and reports. Conversely, the Japanese indulged in the Dutch presence at Deshima after 1642 not just for the exotic commodities but also because of the texts about the affairs of Europe and the world they received (known as Dutch knowledge or *Rangaku*).

Although for our purposes, the technology transfer of Dutch arms and military expertise *to* Asia is most germane, it is worthwhile to note that Dutch shipping from Asia (as opposed to within Asia) did not limit itself exclusively to spices from what is now Indonesia, but included chinaware (porcelain), raw silk, and, what is especially interesting, some strategic commodities.

Besides silk, Bengal was an important source of saltpetre, the quality of which was much better if produced in warmer climates than the Baltic area or Russia, where the Dutch had earlier acquired it. In 1675 and 1676, according to Om Prakash, more than 100,000 guilders of saltpetre left Bengal for Dutch harbours, 38 per cent of the total value of the exports from this region.[105] A corollary was the purchase of opium in Bengal, which was sold by the VOC on Java and other Indonesian islands in a cynical practice that foreshadowed the British export of Indian opium to China in the nineteenth century.[106]

Debilitating military conflicts (as on Java) and fruitless efforts to make inroads (as in India) in various places may have begun to affect the initial Dutch penchant to maintain a costly hegemonic military position to back up their economic domination of much of the long-distance maritime trade in Asia. There were no eighteenth-century successors to Van

Goens or Coen. To be fair, none of the Dutch advance in Asia had ever been easy, and rather than accomplishing the subjugation of Asian potentates, a compromise was usually the outcome of Dutch efforts to subdue local states. In Japan, the Dutch had to settle for Deshima, while China kept them altogether out, despite three embassies to the Qing Court in the 1650s and 1660s, and a temporary alliance *de facto* with the Qings against the rearguard of the Ming. Even then Taiwan had been lost to Zheng Chenggong. Rijckloff van Goens sr did succeed in laying claim to all of Sri Lanka, but his forays along the southern Indian (Coromandel) coast yielded no significant long-term gain. Already by 1700, the Dutch began to be overshadowed by the British EIC in South Asia; the VOC's decline was slow, but even before the Dutch surrender to the French in Europe in 1795, Dutch trading posts on the Indian subcontinent had become relics of the past.

While warfare diminished the revenue of the VOC, the Dutch were nonetheless often smart enough to turn a profit. Where necessary, the VOC cut its losses, concentrating its enterprise on the trade in fewer but extremely lucrative items, such as nutmeg, cloves, and cinnamon, over which they had acquired a real or virtual monopoly in the seventeenth century. But Dutch military campaigning, or the Dutch trade in weapons (or in raw materials for arms manufacturing such as saltpetre), disappeared in most of Asia after 1700, surpassed by both the British and French Asian ventures, as they themselves had once taken over from the Portuguese. Warfare was costly in terms of money and men, and some of the military engagements, as on Java in February 1686, between VOC soldiers and Asian (Javanese, Balinese, and Madurese) forces, ended in crushing defeats (albeit of fairly small detachments), showing how the innovations of military technology and other aspects of the European Military Revolution (such as battlefield deployment, volley fire, or heightened drill) gave relatively little advantage to foes who vastly outnumbered the Dutch.[107] Together with Van Goens's fruitless efforts to carve out a territorial hinterland to the VOC factories on the South Indian coast and the surrender of Fort Zeelandia, the limits of early modern European imperialism becomes clear from such exploits.

5.3 South of the Sahara

During the last 30 years or so, a great number of studies have appeared about the Dutch slave trade, most notably those by Johannes Postma and Pieter Emmer.[108] The story of this nefarious enterprise seems not much different from that of British or French slave hauling. Likewise, the Dutch had their sugar plantations worked by African slaves in the Caribbean.[109] They may have played a crucial role, however, as a sort of transmission belt. Many scholars suggest that the Brazilian plantation system was introduced by the Dutch to other areas in the Caribbean, after which the

British and French made the sugar trade into a vastly profitable enterprise.[110] One aspect, though, remains somewhat underexplored: Dutch payments to the African slave merchants in exchange for their human chattel.[111] Dutch slave traders often paid Africans in weaponry, which was in high demand, particularly because firearms gave African slave raiders a great advantage in capturing their human prey.[112] It is symptomatic of the Dutch's declining skill at arms manufacturing (and perhaps of a certain contempt for their African clients) that guns traded on Africa after 1700 proved increasingly defective.[113]

Some of the bloodshed in Africa was due to the fighting that erupted between the Western Europeans. The Dutch and English tried to establish their own fortresses along the coast, rivalling or replacing the Portuguese, who had established themselves there from the fifteenth century onward, and who had founded the trans-Atlantic slave trade. Dutch ships arrived at the African coast in the 1590s, lured by tales of gold and ivory.[114] Balthasar de Moucheron (1552–c.1630)'s ships unsuccessfully attacked the Portuguese factory at Sao Jorge da Mina (Elmina) in 1596.[115] Two years later, his vessels managed to capture an island of the West African coast where slaves worked on sugar plantations, but this colony was soon abandoned. A far more ambitious expedition (counting no fewer than 73 ships) a few years later failed again in establishing a firm foothold among the Luso-Hispanic African coastal possessions. The initial Dutch explorations of Africa south of the Sahara, in fact, usually had other intentions than buying slaves.[116] Elias Trip, for example, hoped to find that all-important gunpowder component, saltpetre, on some of the islands off the West African coast.[117] Dutch merchants did not offer much weaponry in exchange at first, nor did they purchase (m)any slaves before they established their bridgehead in Brazil in 1630. Around 1600, in their everlasting battle with Spaniards and Portuguese, the Dutch struck alliances along the African coast with local chieftains (who sought out their military support), still having to meet the local rulers halfway at least, on a sort of middle ground.[118]

Only after the definitive capture of the Elmina fortress on the Portuguese in 1637 did Dutch slave-hauling in Africa begin to take flight.[119] At first, the destination was Dutch Brazil, but after 1654, slaves, often via Curaçao, were transported across the Caribbean. For some years in the 1680s, the fourth Balthasar Cooymans (1618–1690), whose stepmother was a Trip girl, even held the *asiento*, the monopoly on the slave trade on the Spanish-American colonies.[120] The Dutch slave trade remained significantly smaller than that of their European competitors, but it lasted a long time (from about 1600 to about 1815) and ultimately transported more than half a million Africans to the Americas.

The human commodities were acquired in exchange for highly desired goods among local African slave traders, foremost among which were arms, initially cold steel but eventually firearms.[121] From the middle of the century, a growing territorial enclave in South Africa was protected by Dutch arms and soldiers. East of the Cape, the Dutch also captured slaves on Madagascar. The extent of Dutch involvement on Madagascar (or on the East African coast) in the seventeenth century is moot. One gets the impression that occasionally slaves were bought on its coast but that the Dutch believed that little could be gained from establishing a more permanent presence. According to François Valentijn, a Dutch captain in French service raided the coasts along the Red Sea and Madagascar in the 1660s.[122] The French appear to have been slightly more interested in staking a claim there, but they, too, remained hesitant. Most Europeans altogether avoided the western part of the Arabian Seas, which had few trading goods to offer at any advantageous prices and across which Muslim corsairs cruised in considerable numbers. Along its coasts, the Ottoman sultan's power as well as that of other Muslim polities was significant, while Arabian and other merchants cornered most of the market, not in the least because they were far better informed about the regional commodity trade than the Europeans. For the VOC, it seemed for a while more economical to settle at Mauritius (where the Dutch infamously exterminated the dodo), even if this outpost was abandoned by the 1700s.

The Dutch acquisition of fortresses along the Gold Coast of Africa and their capture of the slave trade from Africa to the Americas almost led to their full domination over this littoral for a brief spell beginning in the early 1660s.[123] Ultimately here, though, increasing English and French competition encroached on Dutch territorial control and the trade in human beings with local African chiefs. That the English were not to be trifled with was brought home by Admiral Robert Holmes's expedition of 1664, which devastated the Dutch possessions on the West African coast.[124] Although De Ruyter would soon restore Dutch authority in many of its West African possessions, the English remained on the offensive, sometimes militarily, but more often economically (even when they were closely allied with the Republic between 1688 and 1714) in the trans-Atlantic world. They clearly began to overshadow the Dutch in North America and the Caribbean after 1650 and saw their ascendancy underscored by acquiring the *asiento* at the Peace of Utrecht in 1713.

But while their role diminished in Western Africa, on the southern tip of Africa, a settler colony survived until the French era (1795–1813) of Dutch history. Such a type of colony was unusual for the Dutch. The Cape Colony was initially created as a sort of foraging station on the long road to the East Indies, on which the crews often severely suffered (and died) from scurvy and other diseases that are caused by long-term lack of fresh fruit, vegetables, or drinking water. The diary of the founder of the Cape Colony, Jan van Riebeeck (1619–1677), once more displays the typical aggressive attitude displayed by the Dutch abroad.[125] Upon arrival in 1652, his little army of sailors and soldiers immediately set to work to build a fortress. A European conqueror overseas established himself in truth only after building (or capturing) a fortress, behind the walls of which he could hunker down if the relations with the indigenous population took a bad turn. Capetown in this sense joined New Amsterdam, Fort Zeelandia, Mauritsstad (Recife), Melaka (Malacca), Elmina, Batavia, or several fortresses along the coast of the Indian subcontinent. Many of these fortresses, given the advanced skill the Dutch had in this regard, were as impregnable for Asian or African soldiers, or even European attackers, as the walls of Leyden or Alkmaar had been for the Spaniards in the 1570s.

By the middle of the seventeenth century, the Dutch skill in this regard was virtually without match. As we saw, they lent a hand to many interested in building (or destroying) fortifications, in Britain, the Holy Roman Empire, or Russia. Only towards 1700, their skill at erecting forts (and siege warfare) fell clearly behind the experts of the age, the French. We saw already that this was one of the key areas of expertise that allowed the Europeans to gain the advantage over others in military terms in the early modern era, as was naval warfare, especially when it involved heavily armed sailships. The Dutch were in the forefront of both developments, perhaps for them rather more crucial, because they sustained their maritime empire. These skills proved more significant than their deft use of countermarch and volleyfire on the battlefield.

Notes

1. Klooster, *Dutch Moment*, 13–16, 21, 25, 29. For a few years around 1600, salt from Venezuela was transported in fairly large amounts, an effort stymied by the Spaniards; salt, too, was later shipped from Tortuga for a short period (ibid., 59).
2. Ibid., 253, 255.
3. "[W]arfare (the main reason why the company was created in the first place)," Antunes, Odegard and Van den Tol, "Networks," 81. See also ibid., 82. For an intriguing comparison between WIC and VOC by way of the examples of Johan Maurits van Nassau and Rijckloff van Goens, see Odegard, "Colonial Careers."
4. Klooster, *Dutch Moment*, 6, 34–5. Klooster very succinctly outlines the recent welter of historiography on the "Dutch Atlantic," of which the great majority of writings tends to focus on the Americas (ibid., 7). Before the 1609 truce with Spain, several expeditions were dispatched on an *ad-hoc* basis to intercept Spanish or Portuguese ships travelling to the Caribbean or back (ibid., 28). Some hostilities, by the way, continued after the truce was concluded (ibid., 29, 31). See, too, Akveld, ed., "Journaal," 90.
5. See for a brief history Den Heijer, "Dutch West-India Company," 77–112.
6. Edmundson, ed., "Verhaal," 242.
7. Ibid., 243–4.
8. Great detail on this is provided by Klooster, see, for instance, Klooster, *Dutch Moment*, 84–6, 136.
9. Odegard, "Colonial Careers," 223.
10. Klooster, *Dutch Moment*, 36–7, 39, 42–3.

11. See, for example, ibid., 43.
12. Ibid., 35.
13. Ibid., 45–7.
14. Ibid., 19.
15. Ibid., 8.
16. Ibid., 3.
17. Ibid.; see also ibid., 33–53.
18. Ibid., 33. As is obvious, I have heavily drawn in these pages on the marvellous survey about the Dutch in the Atlantic world by Wim Klooster, see Klooster, *Dutch Moment*. Klooster's work itself draws on the great amount of studies regarding Dutch activity in western Africa and the Americas, about which I have decided to be rather brief therefore.
19. Klooster, *Dutch Moment*, 84–5.
20. Ibid., 40–1.
21. Ibid., 49–51, 63–6, 88–9.
22. The Dutch has for decades before 1667 been involved in Guyana in search of a stable colony, without settling there for any great length of time (ibid., 58–9, 95–6).
23. See Van Lier, *Samenleving*; Wolbers, *Geschiedenis van Suriname* [originally, 1861], 52–5; Van der Meiden, *Betwist Bestuur*. There was some salt winning going on as well (see above note 1), which led to the Dutch acquisition of Curaçao, after failing to establish themselves on other salt-rich islands off Venezuela (Klooster, *Dutch Moment*, 60–1).
24. Klooster, *Dutch Moment*, 23.
25. Ibid., 23.
26. Henri and Barbara van der Zee, "The Dutch," 499. Indeed, at the very beginning of the arrival of Hudson's expedition (which consisted largely of English sailors serving the Dutch flag), the native Americans had already been treated with brutal violence (see Schulte Nordholt, ed., "Nederlanders," 40).
27. See Greer, *Jesuit Relations*, 13. Puype suggests the true take-off of such sales began around 1635 (see Puype, "Some Notes," 232).
28. On this, see Meuwese, *Brothers in Arms*. This book looks at both West Africa and North and South America. See as well Todt, "Trading," 363–4, 374–5. See further Van Groesen, ed., *Legacy of Dutch Brazil*; Klooster, *The Dutch Moment*, 2; Shaw Romney, *New Netherland Connections*; Schulte Nordholt, ed., "Nederlanders," 54. Enlightening, too, is Puype, "Some Notes."
29. See Williams, "Flintlock Ordnance," 7–8; Klooster, *Dutch Moment*, 147–8.
30. Klooster, *Dutch Moment*, 57–8.
31. For Batavia, see Ricklefs, *War, Culture*, 15. See, for example, Otto, *Dutch-Munsee Encounter*, 5. It remains problematic to state that the more than half of the "European population of New Netherland was [not] Dutch," in the seventeenth century, as Otto and many others point out (ibid., 5; see also Klooster, *Dutch Moment*, 216–19). As I have suggested in an earlier part of this book, there was no consensus on what it meant to be "Dutch."
32. Ricklefs, *War, Culture*, 21. The exception primarily was British and Spanish: Ireland, Barbados, and the eastern American coast were the locales to which British emigrants departed. Even then, this was often through coercion (transport), as was the case for New France, too. Numbers remained low before 1700 in those instances as well. As Henry Kamen has suggested, despite appearances, much of Spanish America was very thinly populated by immigrants from Spain (see Kamen, *Empire*). For most of those seeking their fortune overseas (at least when departing), the dream was to make good

elsewhere and return triumphantly (or at least comfortably) home. In sheer numbers, Chinese emigration, which remained limited to various regions in East Asia, was much larger. In the Chinese case, as in the Russian case with Siberia or several southern borderlands, there was comparatively significant population movement into newly claimed territory such as Mongolia, Xinjiang, and Tibet.

33. Klooster, *Dutch Moment*, 96–9.
34. Ibid., 108–11.
35. See, for a similar appreciation, ibid., 76.
36. Costs remained high at times, because of posses chasing runaway slaves and more elaborate expeditions to combat Maroons ("*bosnegers*"; see Stedman, *Narrative*).
37. Klooster, *Dutch Moment*, 255.
38. For criticism of this idea, see Odegard, "Colonial Careers," 223. Large it certainly was, with already 25,000 employees in 1625 and perhaps 40,000 in 1688 (see Van Rossum, *Werkers*, 16). The literature on it is vast, and I can only suggest a few of the best recent works on it as well as the indispensable Boxer (Boxer, *Jan Compagnie*; Boxer, *Dutch Seaborne Empire*; Parthesius, *Dutch Ships*; Wills Jr, *Pepper*; Ward, *Networks*; in Dutch, Knaap and Teitler, eds, *De Verenigde Oost-Indische Compagnie*). Of course, there is a marvellously digitised early modern history of the VOC available, see Van Dam, *Beschrijvinge*.
39. It is true that some of its remnants were eventually absorbed into the *Nederlandsche Handelsmaatschappij* (founded in 1824), but this transition was comparable to that from the Soviet Union to the Russian Federation in 1991: In other words, very little was taken over by the VOC's successor.
40. See for a correction to this overly peaceful image, Clulow and Mostert, eds, *Dutch and English East India Companies*.
41. Mostert, "Chain of Command," 7.
42. Ricklefs, *War, Culture*, 33; Vink, "Freedom and Slavery," 39.
43. Mostert's remarks regarding the possible superiority of European troops over Asian foes are apposite (see Mostert, "Chain of Command," 19–22). See as well ibid., 37–8. It is a bit odd that in assessing the timing of the "Great Divergence" between Europe and Asia, historians have seemed to ignore this crucial advance of military technology in divining its occurrence or origins, suggesting a more general technological advance instead (which some then especially locate in industrialisation; see, for example, Pomeranz, *Great Divergence*; Van Rossum, *Werkers*, 26–7). Might makes right, in a way: People tend to obey if they are ordered to do something at gunpoint. Firearms were already crucial for Cortes and Pizarro, and a century later in the establishment of significant European enclaves in North America, Africa, and Asia. That made the difference, in my view, long before the industrial revolution. This development had started around 1500, not 1800; machine-gunning native peoples was its culmination.
44. See Ricklefs, *War, Culture*, 33, 48–50; see also for a clear outline of both the Van Goenses' imperialist plans, Vink, "Images and Ideologies," 103.
45. Winius and Vink, *Merchant-Warrior Pacified*, 23.
46. For more on Matelieff, see Borschberg, "Introduction," esp. 131–8. See also Mostert, "Chain of Command," 12–13.
47. Mostert, "Chain of Command," 16. For a recent account that still seemed permeated with English irritation at the ruthless massacre of the ten English merchants, see Milton, *Nathaniel's Nutmeg*.
48. Mostert, "Chain of Command," 11.
49. Ibid., 55.

50. On his belligerent ideas, see Mostert, "Chain of Command," 61; Odegard, "Colonial Careers," 225. Mostert refers in part to Van Goens's 1655 *Vertoog*, a report which he had delivered to the *Gentlemen XVII* (the Dutch VOC board of governors) during a brief sojourn in the Republic. Mostert, "Chain of Command," 62: "Here, then, was a high-ranking VOC official with a Conquistador mentality." See also Ottow, *Rijckloff*. The second part of Ottow's biography exists in an unpublished version. This work shows its age: It is too forgiving and even admiring of Van Goens as a resolute "leader," etc.
51. See Stapel, "Cornelis."
52. For this campaign, see Stapel, "Cornelis," 36–60.
53. Stapel, "Cornelis," 86–113.
54. Van Dam, *Beschrijvinge*, vol. 3, 22–3.
55. Ibid., 32.
56. Mostert, "Chain of Command," 32–3; see as well Andrade, *Lost Colony*, 314–15. In countering arguments that contemporary Asian rulers also wielded cannon, Mostert remarks, "Having a lot of guns is one thing, putting them to good use quite another" (Mostert, "Chain of Command," 33). Of course, he primarily looks at South-East Asia and the southern Indian coastal areas as well as Sri Lanka, not at the shah's, Moghul's or Chinese emperor's use of artillery in battle or siege warfare.
57. Ricklefs, *War, Culture*, 20.
58. For an overview regarding Dutch thought about their Asian empire in the seventeenth century, see Weststeijn, "VOC." See as well Andrade, *Lost Colony*, 327.
59. Van Dam, *Beschrijvinge*, vol. 2, part 1, 714–15; C.E.S., *'T verwaerloosde Formosa*, 174–5.
60. Andrade, *Lost Colony*, 13, 316.
61. Mostert, "Chain of Command," 27–31.
62. C.E.S., *'T verwaerloosde Formosa;* Andrade, *Lost Colony*, 3–18.
63. I have found no evidence that the Coyetts were noble; like with Witsen on the Boreel Embassy, a trio of young men were added as "nobles" to the retinue to embellish its diplomatic heft somewhat in the eyes of the extremely status- and title-conscious Russians.
64. [Coyett], *Historisch Verhael.*
65. See Andrade, *Lost Colony*, 6. I am not sure who Andrade means by Coyett's "younger brother," allegedly "a famous diplomat," while his description of William as "regent of the Netherlands" is a bit unusual (ibid.). Coyett was brother-in-law of François Caron, who switched allegiance to Louis XIV in the middle of the 1660s (see Molhuysen and Blok, eds, *Nieuw Nederlandsch*, vol. 8, 329–30). The Coyetts, too, had enterprising relatives in Sweden and Russia.
66. Boot, "Not Out of Love," 181–2.
67. Breet, ed., *Oost-Indische voyagie.*
68. Ibid., 215–16.
69. Mostert, "Chain of Command," 42–4.
70. Ibid., 46, Tables 2 and 3. See as well for ammunition and tools destined for the gunfoundries and smithies in Batavia, ibid., 49, Table 4. And on cannon, see ibid., 50–2.
71. Valentijn, *Oud en Nieuw Oost-Indiën*, vol. 1, 131–2. As Valentijn points out, Pondicherry, about the only French outpost in South Asia in the late seventeenth century, surrendered in 1693 to the Dutch (even if they returned it later to the French): See ibid., 133–4.
72. In her painstaking investigation of seventeenth-century Dutch activity on the Malabar coast, Meilink-Roelofsz dryly lists the VOC's efforts at carving

out an enclave among the local South Asian states, see Meilink-Roelofsz, *De vestiging*. Marie Antoinette Meilink-Roelofsz (1905–1988) worked for decades as an archivist in the Dutch national archives in The Hague and developed an encyclopedic knowledge about the contents of the VOC archives. Long after her book on the Malabar Coast, she defended her dissertation in Amsterdam, see Meilink-Roelofsz, *Asian Trade*, a still very useful analysis.

73. Ottow, *Rijckloff*, 201.
74. Mostert, "Chain of Command," 5. I am not wholly convinced by Mostert's point, as there was a sea war between the Safavid shah and the VOC in 1644 and 1645. He does make a distinction, though, between VOC and the Dutch Republic (see ibid., 6 as well).
75. See, for a brief overview in English, Gelderblom, De Jong, and Jonker, "Formative Years."
76. Mostert, "Chain of Command," 16.
77. Peters, *In steen geschreven*, 43n29.
78. Ibid., 89n14.
79. Ibid., 53.
80. Peters, *In steen geschreven*, 17; Andrade, *Lost Colony*, 275.
81. Ricklefs, *War, Culture*, 130–1.
82. Ibid., 131. For Van Coehoorn's mortar, see Van Hoof, *Menno van Coehoorn*, 84; Reinstra, *Menno*, 12.
83. Pomeranz, *Great Divergence*.
84. Andrade, *Lost Colony*, 307–29.
85. Ricklefs, *War, Culture*, 38.
86. See, for example, Mostert, "Chain of Command," 18; and the Ming were equally impressed (see Andrade, *Lost Colony*, 36).
87. Andrade, *Lost Colony*, 10, 317, 326.
88. See Boterbloem, *Fiction and Reality*, 89.
89. For more on silk exports from Iran, see Steensgaard, *Asian Trade*, 394–6; and on Russia in this regard, see Glamann, *Dutch-Asiatic Trade*, 118–21.
90. For an overview, see Subrahmanyan, *Europe's India*; of interest, too, are the books by Lach and Van Kley, *Asia*. And for a more specific overview of the Dutch and Asia, especially as reflected in art, see Zandvliet, Blussé, et al., *Dutch Encounter*.
91. It seems not unreasonable, at least, to assume that the data for the eighteenth century are equally applicable to the previous century; see Gaastra, "Verenigde Oost-Indische Compagnie," 251.
92. Van Goor, *Nederlandse kolonien*, 49, table. Some 8,000 Asian European journeys were made by VOC ships from 1601 to 1795; about 973,000 sailors sailed to Asia, of whom about 364,000 returned (ibid., 50).
93. Van Vliet, "Staatse Vloot," 53, 53, Table 2.
94. Van Gelder, *Oostindisch avontuur*.
95. See Ricklefs, *War, Culture*, 15. For the social mobility of some sailors, including the eventual admirals Maarten Tromp and Michiel de Ruyter, see Van Deursen, *Plain Lives*, 26, 76–8; among the higher VOC personnel, the governor-general Antonio van Diemen (1593–1645), a one-time VOC soldier, stands out as a rags-to-riches type (Ricklefs, *War, Culture*, 15).
96. Cf. Ricklefs, *War, Culture*, 17.
97. Linebaugh and Rediker, *Many-Headed Hydra*, 27–8. Undoubtedly, piracy was attractive from a financial viewpoint; in the Anglo-Dutch wars, sailors were keen to join the licensed sea-roving ships, as the pay was decent and could be augmented by (legitimately) sharing in the loot (see Bruijn, "Kaapvaart," 418).

98. See, for example, Ricklefs, *War, Culture*, 138–9, 143; Mostert, "Chain of Command," 22–5.
99. Mostert, "Chain of Command," 25–7.
100. For the non-Dutch Europeans, see ibid., 20.
101. There is some evidence that he may have lost his mind, but the source for this, Isaac Vossius (1618–1689), is not altogether reliable and left the Republic at the same time as Van Klenck; for more, see Van Miert, *Humanism*, 68–70.
102. See Klebusek, "Business"; for the subtle manner in which they organised military campaigns using a great variety of sources, see Mostert, "Chain of Command," 85–90, as well as ibid., 122.
103. A recent detailed account is Mostert, "Chain of Command," 101–9. He draws heavily on Boxer, "Siege of Fort Zeelandia."
104. Van Dam, *Beschrijvinge*.
105. Prakash, *Dutch East India Company*, 200; see as well Mostert, "Chain of Command," 35–6.
106. Prakash, *Dutch East India Company*, 57–8, 145, 148–56. See as well the recent Derks, *Verslaafd aan Opium*. See further Prakash, *Dutch East India Company*, 35, 58–60, 200.
107. Ricklefs, *War, Culture*, 93–9. And even the custom of drilling soldiers that went back to stadtholder Maurice seems to have spread on Java in the early eighteenth century (ibid., 224).
108. Postma, *Dutch in the Atlantic*; Emmer, *Dutch Slave Trade*. See also Klooster, *Dutch Moment*, 159–60, 164. I was once Emmer's student in a graduate program in Caribbean studies taught at Utrecht University.
109. See Mintz, *Sweetness*.
110. Among others, see Greenfield, "Plantations," 119.
111. In part, this has been the consequence of the destruction of the WIC's archives, see Henk den Heijer, "West-African Trade," 151. For a recent study of the British guns-for-slaves exchange with Africa in the eighteenth century, see Whatley, "Gun-Slave Hypothesis."
112. Klooster, *Dutch Moment*, 147–8, 237–8; Den Heijer, "West-African Trade," 154–5.
113. Den Heijer, "West-African Trade," 154–5.
114. Klooster, *Dutch Moment*, 24–5.
115. Ibid., 26–7. The same Moucheron was instrumental in organising the first steps towards the Dutch East India Company (Valentijn, *Oud en nieuw Oost-Indiën*, vol. 1, 168). See as well Enthoven, "Early Dutch Expansion," 17–48, 27, 29, 31, 42–3.
116. There still is more to be done in this respect, especially given that primary sources such as Pieter van der Broecke's work and (although it is not truly a primary source, in a way) Olfert Dapper's overview early on set a high standard in terms of Dutch literature on Africa (La Fleur, ed., *Pieter*; Dapper, *Naukeurige beschrijvinge der Afrikaensche gewesten*; Olfert Dapper, *Naukeurige beschrijvinge der Afrikaensche eylanden*); see as well Jones, "Decompiling Dapper." But see especially Ratelband, *Nederlanders*; Ribeiro da Silva, *Dutch*.
117. Elias, ed., "Contract tot oprichting," 359.
118. Although they needed to learn how to do this; only in capturing Elmina in 1637 did they show themselves truly adept at this (see Klooster, *Dutch Moment*, 67). For the concept of "middle ground," see White, *Middle Ground*.
119. On the capture of Sao Jorge da Mina, see Klooster, *Dutch Moment*, 66. Luanda and Sao Tomé followed in 1641, although the latter was lost again

in the following year, and Luanda in 1648 (ibid., 70–1, 83). Fort Axim was added to the Dutch African possessions, though, in 1642 (see ibid., 72). The Portuguese split with Spain in 1640 made no difference for the Dutch, who proceeded to fight both until 1648, and Portugal on its own, albeit intermittently, until the early 1660s. And the Swedish and Danish African companies were shell-companies for Dutch entrepreneurs who did not want to submit to the authority (monopoly) of the Dutch West India Company in its various iterations regarding the slave trade across the Atlantic (see G.W. Kernkamp, ed., "Een contract," 444–5). It is noteworthy that the Swedish agent setting up the Swedish company was one Laurens de Geer, a son of Louys de Geer (ibid., 446); the Danish venture was for a while led by one of the Cooymanses.

120. Goslinga, *Dutch*, 361–2. If ever there was a clan that was related to every Dutch regent family, it was that of the Cooymanses, who fled Antwerp after its fall in 1585 (see Elias, *De vroedschap van Amsterdam*, vol. 2, 759–67). Cooymans's father was one of the richest people in the Republic (see ibid., 762).
121. Den Heijer, "West-African Trade," 154–5. Note that Olfert Dapper, who wrote an exhaustive description of Africa that was published in 1668, still suggested that the people of Senegal and Gambia imported steelbars and knives and swords; his information was likely a little out of date, but nonetheless did reflect the assortment of trading goods the Dutch brought to Africa in the first half of the seventeenth century (see O. Dapper, *Naukeurige Beschrijvinge der Afrikaensche gewesten*, 352, 360).
122. Valentijn, *Oud en nieuw Oost-Indiën*, vol. 1, 130.
123. Klooster, *Dutch Moment*, 100–1.
124. Ibid., 101–2.
125. Van Riebeeck, *Dagverhaal*, 11–12.

Bibliography

Akveld, L.M., ed. "Journaal van de reis van Piet Heyn naar Brazilië en West-Afrika, 1624–1625," *Bijdragen en Mededelingen van het Historisch Genootschap* 76, 1962, 85–174.

Andrade, Tonio. *Lost Colony: The Untold Story of China's First Victory Over the West*, Princeton, NJ: Princeton University Press, 2011.

Antunes, Catia, Erik Odegard, and Joris van den Tol, "The Networks of Dutch Brazil: Rise, Entanglement and Fall of a Colonial Dream," in Catia Antunes and Jos Gommans, eds, *Exploring the Dutch Empire*, London: Bloomsbury, 2015, 77–94.

Boot, Wim. " 'Not Out of Love, but for Money and Profit': Dutch-Japanese Trade from the Seventeenth to the Nineteenth Century," in Catia Antunes and Jos Gommans, eds, *Exploring the Dutch Empire*, London: Bloomsbury, 2015, 179–202.

Borschberg, Peter. "Introduction," in P. Borschberg, ed., *Journal, Memorials and Letters of Cornelis Matelieff de Jonge: Security, Diplomacy and Commerce in 17th-Century Southeast Asia*, Singapore: NUS Press, 2015, 1–138.

Boterbloem, K. *The Fiction and Reality of Jan Struys: A Seventeenth-Century Dutch Globetrotter*, Houndmills, Basingstoke: Palgrave, 2008.

Boxer, C.R. *The Dutch Seaborne Empire*, London: Hutchison, 1965.

———. *Jan Compagnie in War and Peace*, London: Heinemann, 1979.

———. "The Siege of Fort Zeelandia and the Capture of Formosa from the Dutch 1661–1662," *Transactions and Proceedings of the Japan Society of London* 24, 1926, 16–47.

C.E.S., *T verwaerloosde Formosa. . .*, Amsterdam: Jan Claesz. ten Hoorn, 1675.

Clulow, Adam, and Tristan Mostert, eds. *The Dutch and English East India Companies: Diplomacy, Trade and Violence in Early Modern Asia*, Amsterdam: Amsterdam University Press, 2018.

Coyett, Balthasar. *Historisch Verhael of Beschryving van de Voyagie gedaan onder de Suite van den Heere Koenraad van Klenck*, Amsterdam: Jan ten Hoorn, 1677.

Dam, Pieter van. *Beschrijvinge van de Oostindische Compagnie, 1639–1701*, 6 vols., ed. F.W. Stapel, Den Haag: Nijhoff, 1927, available at: http://resources.huygens.knaw.nl/retroboeken/vandam/#page=0&accessor=toc&source=1, accessed 1 March 2019.

Dapper, Olfert. *Naukeurige beschrijvinge der Afrikaensche eylanden. . .*, Amsterdam: Jacob van Meurs, 1676.

———. *Naukeurige beschrijvinge der Afrikaensche gewesten. . .*, Amsterdam: Jacob van Meurs, 1668.

Derks, Hans. *Verslaafd aan Opium: De VOC en het Huis van Oranje als drugsdealers*, Amsterdam: Atheneum, 2015.

Edmundson, G., ed. "Verhaal van de inneming van Paramaribo (1665) door Generaal William Byam," *Bijdragen en Meededelingen van het Historisch Genootschap* 19, 1898, 231–62.

Elias, J.E., ed. "Contract tot oprichting van een Zweedsch factorie-comptoir te Amsterdam in 1663," *Bijdragen en Mededelingen van het Historisch Genootschap* 24, 1903, 356–400.

———. *De vroedschap van Amsterdam*, 2 vols., Amsterdam: Israel, 1963 [reprint].

Emmer, Pieter. *The Dutch Slave Trade*, New York: Berghahn, 2005.

Enthoven, Victor. "Early Dutch Expansion in the Atlantic Region, 1585–1621," in Johannes Postma and Victor Enthoven, eds, *Riches from Atlantic Commerce*, Leiden: Brill, 2003, 17–48.

Fleur, J.D. la., ed. *Pieter van den Broecke's Journal of Voyages to Cape Verde, Guinea, and Angola, 1605–1612*, London: Hakluyt Society, 2000.

Gaastra, F.S. "De Verenigde Oost-Indische Compagnie in de zeventiende en achttiende eeuw: de groei van een bedrijf. . .," *Bijdragen en mededelingen voor de geschiedenis der Nederlanden* 91, 1976, 249–72.

Gelder, Roelof van. *Het Oostindisch avontuur*, Amsterdam: SUN, 1997.

Gelderblom, Oscar, Abe de Jong, and Joost Jonker, "The Formative Years of the Modern Corporation: The Dutch East India Company, 1602–1632," *Journal of Economic History* 4, 2013, 1050–76.

Glamann, Kristof. *Dutch-Asiatic Trade, 1620–1740*, Den Haag: Nijhoff, 1958.

Goor, J. van. *De Nederlandse kolonien. Geschiedenis van de Nederlandse Expansie*, Den Haag: SDU, 1994.

Goslinga, C.C. *The Dutch in the Caribbean and on the Wild Coast, 1580–1680*, new ed., Gainesville, FL: University of Florida Press: 2017.

Greenfield, Sidney M. "Plantations, Sugar Cane and Slavery," *Historical Reflections/Réflections Historiques* 1, 1979, 85–119.

Greer, Allan. *The Jesuit Relations: Natives and Missionaries in Seventeenth-Century America*, Boston, MA, New York: Bedford-St. Martin's, 2000.

Groesen, Michiel van, ed. *The Legacy of Dutch Brazil*, Cambridge: Cambridge University Press, 2014.

Heijer, Henk den. "The Dutch West-India Company, 1621–1791," in Johannes Postma and Victor Enthoven, eds, *Riches from Atlantic Commerce*, Leiden: Brill, 2003, 77–112.

———. "The West-African Trade of the Dutch West India Company, 1674–1740," in Johannes Postma and Victor Enthoven, eds, *Riches from Atlantic Commerce*, Leiden: Brill, 2003, 139–70.

Hoof, Joep van. *Menno van Coehoorn, 1641–1704: Vestingbouwer, belegeraar, infanterist*, Den Haag: Matrijs, 2004.

Jones, Adam. "Decompiling Dapper: A Preliminary Search for Evidence," *History in Africa* 17, 1990, 171–209.

Kamen, Henry. *Empire: How Spain Became a World Power, 1492–1763*, New York: HarperCollins, 2003.

Kernkamp, G.W., ed. "Een contract tot slavenhandel van 1657," *Bijdragen en mededelingen voor de geschiedenis der Nederlanden* 22, 1901, 444–59.

Klebusek, Marika. "The Business of News," *Scandinavian Journal of History* 3–4, 2003, 205–13.

Klooster, Wim. *The Dutch Moment: War, Trade and Settlement in the Seventeenth-Century Atlantic World*, Ithaca, NY: Cornell University Press, 2016.

Knaap, Gerrit, and Ger Teitler, eds. *De Verenigde Oost-Indische Compagnie tussen oorlog en diplomatie*, Leiden: KITLV, 2002.

Lach, Donald, and Edwin van Kley. *Asia in the Making of Europe*, 3 vols., Chicago, IL: University of Chicago Press, 1965–1993.

Lier, R.A. van. *Samenleving in een grensgebied*, Den Haag: Nijhoff, 1949.

Linebaugh P., and M. Rediker. *The Many-Headed Hydra*, Boston, MA: Beacon Press, 2000.

Meiden, G.W. van der. *Betwist Bestuur: Een eeuw strijd om de macht in Suriname, 1651–1753*, Amsterdam: De Bataafsche Leeuw, 1986.

Meilink-Roelofsz, M.A.P. *Asian Trade and the European Influence in the Indonesian Archipelago*, 's-Gravenhage: Nijhoff, 1962.

———. *De vestiging der Nederlanders ter kuste Malabar*, 's-Gravenhage: Nijhoff, 1943.

Meuwese, Mark. *Brothers in Arms, Partners in Trade*, Leyden: Brill, 2012.

Miert, Dirk van. *Humanism in an Age of Science: The Amsterdam Atheneum in the Golden Age, 1632–1704*, Leiden: Brill, 2009.

Milton, Giles. *Nathaniel's Nutmeg*, London: Picador, 1999.

Mintz, Sidney W. *Sweetness and Power: The Place of Sugar in Modern History*, New York: Viking Penguin, 1985.

Molhuysen, P.C., and P.J. Blok, eds. *Nieuw Nederlandsch Biografisch Woordenboek*, vol. 8, Leiden: Sijthoff, 1937.

Mostert, Tristan. "Chain of Command: The Military System of the Dutch East India Company, 1655–1663," unpublished master's thesis, Universiteit Leiden, 2007, available at: http://vocwarfare.net/thesis/, accessed 25 November 2018.

Odegard, Erik. "Colonial Careers: Johan Maurits van Nassau, Rijckloff Volckertsz. van Goens and Career-Making in the Early Modern Dutch Empire," unpubl. Ph.D. diss., University of Leyden, 2018.

———. *De Oost-Indische voyagie van Wouter Schouten*, ed. M. Breet, Zwolle: Walburg Pers, 2003.

Otto, Paul. *The Dutch-Munsee Encounter in America*, New York: Berghahn, 2006.

Ottow, W.M. *Rijckloff Volckertsz. van Goens: De carrière van een diplomaat, 1619–1655*, Utrecht: Trajecta, 1954.

Parthesius, Robert. *Dutch Ships in Tropical Waters*, 2nd ed., Amsterdam: Amsterdam University Press, 2010.

Peters, Marion. *In steen geschreven: Leven en sterven van VOC-dienaren op de Kust van Coromandel in India*, with photographs by Ferry André de la Porte, Amsterdam: Bas Lubberhuizen, 2002.

Pomeranz, K. *The Great Divergence: China, Europe, and the Making of the Modern World Economy*, Princeton, NJ: Princeton University Press, 2000.

Postma, Johannes. *The Dutch in the Atlantic Slave Trade, 1600–1815*, Cambridge: Cambridge University Press, 2008.

Puype, J.P. "Some Notes Regarding the Evidence of Dutch 17th-Century Flintlocks Recovered from Seneca Iroquois Sites in New York State," in H.L. Visser and D.W. Bailey, eds, *Aspects of Dutch Gunmaking*, Zwolle: Waanders, 1997, 204–35.

Ratelband, Klaas. *Nederlanders in West-Afrika, 1600–1650: Angola, Kongo en Sao Tomé*, Zutphen: Walburg, 2000.

Reinstra, Albert. *Een veldheer in Wijckel, Menno baron van Coehoorn*, Franeker: Van Wijnen, 2009.

Ribeiro da Silva, Filipa. *Dutch and Portuguese in West Africa (1580–1674): Empires, Merchants, and the Atlantic System*, Leiden: Brill, 2011.

Ricklefs, M.C. *War, Culture and the Economy of Java: Asian and European Imperialism in the Early Kartasura Period*, Sydney: Allen and Unwin, 1993.

Riebeeck, Jan van. *Dagverhaal*, vol. 1, (1652–1655), Utrecht: Kemink en zoon, 1884.

Rossum, M. van. *Werkers van de wereld: Globalisering, arbeid en interculturele ontmoetingen tussen Aziatische en Europese zeelieden in dienst van de VOC, 1600–1800*, Hilversum: Verloren, 2014.

Schulte Nordholt, J.W., ed. "Nederlanders in Nieuw Nederland: De oorlog van Kieft," *Bijdragen en Mededelingen betreffende de Geschiedenis der Nederlanden* 80, 1966, 38–94.

Shaw Romney, Susanah. *New Netherland Connections: Intimate Connections and Atlantic Ties in Seventeenth-Century America*, Charlotte, NC: University of North Carolina Press, 2014.

Stapel, F.W. "Cornelis Janszoon Speelman," *Bijdragen tot de taal, land- en volkenkunde van Nederlandsch Indië* 1, 1936, 1–169.

Stedman, John G. *Narrative of a Five Years' Expedition Against the Revolted Negroes of Surinam in Guiana. . .*, London: Johnson and Edwards, 1796.

Steensgaard, Niels, *The Asian Trade Route of the Seventeenth Century*, Chicago, IL: University of Chicago Press, 1974.

Subrahmanyan, Sanjay. *Europe's India: Words, People, Empires, 1500–1800*, Cambridge, MA: Harvard University Press, 2017.

Todt, Kim. "Trading Between New Netherland and New England, 1624–1664," *Early American Studies*, Spring 2011, 348–78.

Valentijn, François. *Oud en Nieuw Oost-Indiën. . .*, vol. 1, Dordrecht and Amsterdam: J. Van Braam en G. onder den Linden, 1724.

Vink, Marcus P.M. "Freedom and Slavery: The Dutch Republic, the VOC World, and the Debate Over the World's 'Oldest Trade'," *South African Historical Journal* 1, 2007, 19–46.

———. "Images and Ideologies of Dutch-South Asian Contact: Cross-Cultural Encounters Between the Nayaka State of Madurai and the Dutch East India Company in the Seventeenth Century," *Itinerario* 2, 1997, 82–124.

Vliet, A.P. van. "De Staatse Vloot in de Tachtigjarige Oorlog," in J.R. Bruijn and C.B. Wels, eds, *Met Man en Macht: De Militaire Geschiedenis van Nederland 1500–2000*, Baarn: Balans, 2003, 44–62.

Ward, Kerry. *Networks of Empire*, Cambridge: Cambridge University Press, 2010.

Weststeijn, Arthur. "The VOC as a Company-State: Debating Seventeenth-Century Dutch Colonial Expansion," *Itinerario* 1, 2014, 13–34.

Whatley, Warren C. "The Gun-Slave Hypothesis and the 18th-Century British Slave Trade," *Explorations in Economic History* 67, 2018, 80–104.

White, Richard. *The Middle Ground: Indians, Empires, and Republics in the Great Lakes Region, 1650–1815*, Cambridge: Cambridge University Press, 1991.

Williams, David. "The Flintlock Ordnance Muskets of William II and Their Supply," *Arms and Armour* 1, 2012, 7–19.

Wills, Jr, John E. *Pepper, Guns and Parleys*, Cambridge, MA: Harvard University Press, 1974.

Winius, George D., and Marcus P.M. Vink. *The Merchant-Warrior Pacified: The VOC (The Dutch East India Co.) and Its Changing Political Economy in India*, New Delhi: Oxford University Press, 1994.

Wolbers, J. *Geschiedenis van Suriname*, Amsterdam: S. Emmering, 1970.

Zandvliet, K., L. Blussé, et al. *The Dutch Encounter with Asia, 1600–1950*, Zwolle: Waanders, 2004.

Zee, Henri, and Barbara van der. "The Dutch in New Netherland," *Bijdragen en mededelingen voor de geschiedenis der Nederlanden* 87, 1982, 489–504.

6 Dutch Activity in Scandinavia

6.1 A Case Study: Louys de Geer

> [Louys de Geer] was born in the Liège region, where the iron industry was [long established and] wielded more technical know-how about iron mining and processing than [his brother-in-law Elias] Trip [knew], whom he soon surpassed as a trader in iron goods. In 1615, he moved, like his brother-in law had done the previous year, from Dordrecht to Amsterdam. With that move, golden years began for him: In the same year he undertook a trip to Sweden to order artillery for the [Amsterdam] Admiralty, which proved decisive for the rest of his life . . . he perceived how enormous opportunities were beckoning. A limitless supply of almost wholly untouched ore could be found in its rocky soil: Ignorance and lack of capital prevented the Swedes from mining these treasures, and the limited amounts of iron and copper that were won yielded only a low price on the market because of the poor processing technology used. . . . Two years later, his efforts to gain Gustavus Adolphus a loan in Amsterdam acquainted him with the Swedish king, who requested him to hire a regiment and arm it. . . . Gustavus Adolphus [was to] greatly appreciate De Geer, whose ironworks and gun manufactories delivered all the arms and cannon, improved according to the King's own designs, that the Swedish armies needed for the war in Germany.[1]

Whereas Louys de Geer likely remains the most famous of all Dutch arms manufacturers, he was one of many. Thus, in the middle of the seventeenth century, the Utrecht gunsmith Jan Knoop (c. 1612–1688) was one of the most popular arms manufacturers in northern Europe, whose products were admired by Danes, Swedes, and Russians alike.[2] Even while the renown of people such as De Geer or Knoop may have been exceptional, a fondness for Dutch weapons was common in northern Europe and shows the high acclaim enjoyed by the Dutch producers of the age. Some became magnates like De Geer, Trip, or Marselis, whereas others achieved moderate fame and affluence. Knoop's renown as a gunsmith in all three "northern" monarchies reflects the importance of Dutch commodities and trade for this region, whereas De Geer's success manifests the sort of copying and borrowing to which the three northern Powers were prone in seeking an advantage in their internecine warfare.

Before we home in on the Scandinavians and Russians, it is germane to say something about that fourth significant Power in north-eastern Europe around 1600: The sprawling state of Poland-Lithuania, the economy of which was closely connected with that of the Dutch Republic.[3] Robert Frost and, somewhat less wholeheartedly, Norman Davies, have made a convincing case in arguing that the *Rzeczpospolita* was far from a spent force in the seventeenth century; it was above all Poland that had the strongest military at the beginning of the century.[4] In the early years of the Dutch boom, much of the iron and copper used in the Dutch manufactories originated in Hungary and Poland and was shipped to the Republic from Danzig, while considerable amounts of these metals went as well to the Holland and Zeeland ports by way of Hamburg and Lübeck.[5] This added to the long-established transport of Polish grain to Amsterdam and other ports, the so-called mother trade of the Dutch. And while the Dutch played an ephemeral role with regard to the internal affairs of Poland-Lithuania, merchants from the Low Countries played so pronounced a role along the shores of the Baltic that Dutch served as the *lingua franca* along its shores in the seventeenth century.[6]

In fortifying Poland-Lithuania's military's might, the Dutch role was largely indirect. This was mainly due to the way war was fought on the huge Eastern European Plain, where population density was low and towns became sparse the further east one went. Because of the vast expanse of the Polish-Lithuanian empire before 1654 (or even 1700), slow moving armies on foot were not as effective in this region's warfare. Relatively few sieges occurred (and if they happened, they were conducted differently than in Western Europe), and Poland had virtually no fleet.[7] The Polish military predominantly fought on horseback, with great skill, carefully innovating if this seemed opportune.[8] Thus, the areas of warfare in which the Dutch truly excelled were of no great consequence to the Poles.[9] Nonetheless, the Commonwealth's military was, to some extent, sustained by the Dutch, who bought the overwhelming share of Polish grain exports. The revenue from the grain sales allowed the Polish army, consisting predominantly of mounted nobility, to fight its wars. The Dutch supplied the Polish armies with weapons as well.[10]

Before 1700, Poland's military problems were usually more than anything rooted in domestic political conflict, which had a corrosive effect on the longer term.[11] After 1700, the road to ruin became ever more inevitable. An ominous sign was Poland's sudden collapse around 1655, when a deluge *(potop)* beset it of Ukrainian (Cossack), Swedish, and Russian military forces.[12] It subsequently recovered in military terms but, beset by internal strife, was forced to swallow the humiliating terms of the 1667 Truce of Andrusovo with Muscovy.

In the region's mayhem after 1650, Brandenburg-Prussia emerged as an ever more significant player, which saw its status confirmed with the creation of the Kingdom of Prussia in 1700.[13] A key moment in its rise was the 1675 victory at Fehrbellin, in which the Prussians defeated the Swedes. The Zeelander Benjamin Raule (or Raulé, 1634–1707), who seems to have fled his debts in the Republic, became the architect of a fledgling Brandenburger navy in the late seventeenth century, but this project was aborted.[14] Prussia's first king Frederick William I (1657–1713) was a great-grandson of William I the Silent and apparently capable of speaking Dutch, as he did when Tsar Peter the Great visited in 1697. Prussia's rise, though, was a development that truly began only after 1700, and the Dutch had little influence on it. Prussia joined Russia in replacing Poland and Sweden as the strongest powers in this region after the (second) Great Northern War (1700–1721). Most of Prussia's renown as a military marvel, though, derives from its military prowess during the eighteenth century.

The Swedish king Eric XIV (1533–1577, r. 1560–1568) already received muskets (or arquebuses) from Antwerp at a time when only one manufacturing plant of firearms operated on Swedish soil.[15] The real take-off for the Swedish arms industry can be pinpointed to the years soon after 1600, with Louys de Geer and Elias Trip being pivotal figures; their northern turn occurred in part because the transport of their goods along the Meuse with Liège was interrupted by warfare.[16] Concomitantly, towards the end of the sixteenth century, the Swedes began to recruit mercenaries in the Netherlands with the permission of the Estates-General.[17] As elsewhere, with technological change and the expansion of campaigns into wars of longer duration (mainly between Denmark and Sweden, which had the first have the upper hand until the 1620s) came increased cost, in part because wars were fought at sea, again an area in which the Dutch excelled.[18] Money and expertise were badly needed, and the Dutch stepped in to supply them.

At a time when the United Provinces observed a truce with the Spaniards, between 1609 and 1621, the young Swedish King Gustavus Adolphus (r. 1611–1632) was keen on the recruitment of officers who had fought in Maurice's campaigns of the 1590s and 1600s. He was an admirer of Johan (VII) von Nassau-Siegen, one of the trio of Nassaus involved in the modernisation of army drill and infantry deployment; indeed, Johan VII had commanded the Swedish army in Livonia in the early 1600s.[19] The Swedish commander Jacob de la Gardie (1583–1652), who went on to lead a campaign into Muscovy in 1609, trained in the art of war in the armies of Maurice of Orange-Nassau.[20] Around this time, ships and sailors were hired in the United Provinces to modernise the Swedish navy as well. Close ties between the two countries were apparent in the southern port of Gothenburg, which had a considerable Dutch community in the early 1600s.

In response to a Swedish *Rikstag* decree of 1604 to have pig iron processed at home rather than having it forged abroad, its native manufacturing industry languished at first. In the mid-1610s, however, Swedish metallurgy began to flourish at Finspong thanks to Louys de Geer, who employed a large contingent of Walloon and northern Netherlandic experts.[21] De Geer, his brother-in-law Steven Gerards, and their associate Willem de Besche realised in the early 1610s that without expert help the native Swedish arms industry could not produce the volume of weapons that they were capable of selling from their base in the United Provinces to a great variety of clients across Europe.[22] Swedish iron proved stronger when it was subjected to the Walloon method of forging, which was better suited for it than the German manufacturing process previously used to make this key material.[23] In Sweden, wood was available aplenty for the ovens, while labour was cheap through the use of local peasants as labourers; many Finns in search of seasonal work as lumberjacks joined De Geer's enterprises as well.

From 1615 onward, De Geer expanded the Swedish arms manufacturing branch by leaps and bounds, as the quotation with which this chapter began suggests. He ingratiated himself with the king by recruiting more than 200 soldiers in the Republic for Gustavus Adolphus to serve in the Baltic against the Russian tsar's military.[24] In early 1617, another 1,200 troops were recruited by the Swedes in the Republic, for whose transport the Republic lent 20 ships to the Swedes; the soldiers were equipped by De Geer, who loaded the ships with additional weaponry to be used by troops already deployed in that theatre.[25] The next year, De Geer shipped more arms to Gustavus Adolphus who was facing another war, this time with Poland: Thousands of firearms and harnesses, as well as powder and fuses, were dispatched. By 1620, De Geer had established himself as the key arms dealer and mercenary recruiter for Gustavus Adolphus. His bills were in part settled by the Republic, which subsidised the Swedish king. Within the next few years, De Geer was delivering weapons to others as well, including Ernst von Mansfeld; the Danish, French, and English kings; and the Venetian Republic.[26] When in the early 1620s Gustavus Adolphus could not pay his bills, he settled his debts with the Dutch entrepreneur by making De Geer and his companions outright owners of the Finspong ironworks, which they had initially leased from the crown.[27] De Besche and De Geer then modernised the works further and moved into large-scale production of arms in Sweden itself.[28]

As Amburger suggested, arms manufacturing is an especially telling form of early capitalist enterprise, for its complex nature necessitates a significant division of labour:

> Casting iron cannon demanded a blast furnace, which together with the foundries were purposely linked to workshops for hand-held firearms, sidearms and harnesses, in other words, [working] with

> mallets, pickhammers [and the like]. For such a combined venture a much more significant capital investment was necessary than for the traditional small shops, or simple foundries. All these [production stages] needed waterpower, be it to propel the machines, be it merely to operate the bellows at the blast furnace. From the sixteenth century onward the mill, the oldest type of factory, became ever more sophisticated, firstly for grinding powder and to propel the hammers, and then in the seventeenth century as paper mill as well; thus early capitalism has been called the classical age of the mills.[29]

This was the sort of complex plant, a combination of iron foundry and arms manufactory, founded by people like Louys de Geer in Sweden, Gabriel Marselis in Norway, or Andries Winius and Peter Marselis in Russia. Of course, powdermills and sawmills, as along the Zaan river north of Amsterdam where they can still be admired, also dotted the landscape of the seventeenth-century Dutch Republic.

As evident from Amburger's quotation, De Geer's forges produced not just iron rods but also muskets, harnesses, cannon, shot, and the like, at first mainly in nearby Nørkoping, and then elsewhere as well.[30] From 1627, De Geer began to personally manage his arms business in Sweden, convinced that his personal attention to the arms and ironworks would improve both quality and quantity.[31] The Swedes reaped the benefits of De Geer's dedication to his business: By the late 1620s, they began to defeat the Poles in battle using armour-piercing, Dutch-made muskets, which lessened the Polish advantage derived from their skillful use of cavalry.[32] De Geer acquired a monopoly on gun manufacturing in Sweden by 1630; his plants' production eventually dwarfed any foreign imports supplying Gustavus Adolphus.[33] Instead, weapons began to be exported in copious amounts: Hundreds of artillery pieces began to find their way to the Republic, some for the use of the Dutch, but many intended for other buyers who purchased their arms in Amsterdam.[34] This city became the staple for Swedish weaponry, receiving the lion's share of the burgeoning production of De Geer's enterprises. As De Geer imported more pieces than the Dutch could use, even in the midst of the Thirty Years' War and the second phase of the Dutch war with Spain, the Estates-General gave De Geer permission to export artillery (albeit not to its enemies). This was big business: Cannon delivered to Rotterdam in 1639 cost the city more than 1,100 guilders a piece, which is four or five times the annual wage of a skilled worker in those days.[35] By that time (1637–1640), De Geer oversaw the production of thousands of guns of all sorts of calibre. Even earlier ". . . [w]hen Gustavus Adolphus in 1630 shipped an army of 35,000 men to Germany, it had been almost wholly armed by de Geer. . . ."[36] The real tycoons involved in this line of business, of course, hedged their bets. De Geer, for example, exploited copper mines of which copper thread and kettles were made as well. This, too, proved lucrative.[37] Louys de Geer left at least 17 tons of gold at his death, the equivalent of about 1.75 million guilders.

Even if less marked than in contemporary Muscovy, the Swedish government, whether led by Gustavus Adolphus, Chancellor Axel Oxenstierna (1583–1654, regent 1632–1644), or Queen Christina (r. 1644–1654) allowed for the hiring of foreign experts to modernise their country in technological terms, as is evident from De Geer's enterprises: French-speaking craftsmen from Liège and Sedan were especially in demand.[38] Most of them arrived between 1620 and 1635, usually travelling to Sweden by way of Amsterdam where they signed their contracts.

Sweden, on one hand, and Russia and Denmark, on the other, were at loggerheads throughout the seventeenth century. After the 1617 Russian-Swedish Treaty of Stolbovo, wars between Danes and Swedes, or Russians and Swedes (despite efforts from Danish kings and Russian tsars, they did not conclude a coalition against Sweden before 1700),[39] did not tend to last long before the Great Northern War broke out in 1700 (which lasted more than two decades).[40] For the Swedes, the wars were frequently complicated through concomitant campaigning in Poland and the Holy Roman Empire. The Danes, who around 1600 possessed not only Norway but also a good slice of what is now southern Sweden (and usually had a stake in Schleswig-Holstein), likewise fought wars on several fronts at the same time. In all of these conflicts, Dutch natives played a significant role as artisans, traders, mercenaries, or manufacturers. The Republic seldom was one of the belligerents in these Northern conflicts, but the Dutch state did not always stay neutral.

The question whether entrepreneurs such as the Marselises in Denmark or the De Geers in Sweden can be considered Dutch at all is intriguing, and may add some more nuance to my earlier reflection on early modern national identity. Especially in terms of their own worldview (that included their strong adherence to Calvinism), the two families appear to have felt Dutch, but this perhaps only goes for the first generation who arrived from the Low Countries in Scandinavia, before 1650; once their offspring grew up in their adopted countries, they probably considered themselves Danish or Swedish before anything else. In Sweden today, the descendants of Louys de Geer sr are still members of the nobility, and several generations of the Marselises were part of the Danish aristocracy.

An illuminating comparison might be that with Andries Andrieszoon Winius (1641–1716), who was raised in Russia; seven years old when his father became a subject of the tsar, and 13 or 14 when he converted with his father to Russian Orthodoxy, he has gone down in history as Andrei Andreevich Vinius.[41] Vinius joined the tsarist bureaucracy in his early twenties and served the tsar until his death in 1716 but, late in life, did seek sanctuary for a few years in Holland (a province he had visited only on a few brief occasions as an adult), showing a curiously lingering identification with the Republic (and he apparently still spoke

Dutch well enough in his sixties). I suggest nevertheless that A.A. Vinius, who ultimately returned to Russia, should be considered Russian. In contrast, Louys de Geer sr, who seems to have been keen to die in Amsterdam rather than in Sweden, or Gabriel Marselis jr (1609–1673), who, despite his vast Danish interests was partial to his magnificent estate near Haarlem, remained Dutch.[42] Unsurprisingly, the key here is economic. As Amburger wrote, "Both the Marselises and Louis de Geer relied on their Amsterdam offices in not merely delivering arms as well as ships and ships' materials, hiring soldiers and trading in grain, saltpetre and salt."[43] Vinius instead had made career and a fortune (even if much of this was confiscated in the 1700s) in Russia, after his father had cut off any contacts with a Dutch home base.

6.2 A Case Study: The Marselis Family

In Denmark and Danish-ruled Norway, the counterparts to De Geer were the brothers Gabriel and Selio (1602–1663) Marselis, who followed in the footsteps of their father Gabriel sr (c. 1576–1643). They involved themselves in enthusiastic fashion in the mining business, digging up copper, iron, and even silver in Norway.[44] And they did not stop at extracting ore: "Through [their Norwegian ironworks, the Marselises] supplied the [Danish king Frederick III] with . . . weapons [and even] exported them, as in 1652 to Holland."[45] Selio (Celio) Marselis made a fortune supplying the warring factions facing off in the escalating British civil wars around 1640.[46] This Marselis, too, lent the exiled Charles II 24,000 *reichsthalers* in 1653.[47] Both Gabriel and Selio delivered copious amounts of arms to King Christian IV of Denmark (1577–1648, r. 1588–1648), who participated in the Thirty Years' War and then fought Sweden in his dotage during the 1640s. Like De Geer, the Marselis men played a vital role, for, similar to Sweden or Russia, Denmark "lacked the experience needed in political and military terms, the technological knowledge, economic skill, capital and international connections to rival the Western-European states."[48] Denmark's heavy dependence on the capitalist efforts of the Marselis family echoes Swedish reliance on De Geer.[49]

Denmark at times threatened to become a satellite in the Dutch orbit, which led to efforts to curtail or contain the Dutch presence. Thus, the long-reigning King Christian IV demanded that the Dutch experts (from artisans to merchants or bankers), who began to arrive in significant numbers in his country in the last third of the sixteenth century, became loyal subjects of the Danish crown.[50] Christian's insistence reminds us of the first Romanovs' stipulation that foreigners who served the tsars needed to train native Russians their skills. In Russia, though, restrictions were even greater: Foreign experts often faced the greatest reluctance on the part of the authorities if they requested to leave Muscovy.

On the eve of his ill-fated campaigning in the Thirty Years' War, Christian IV engaged in a renewed hiring spree of Dutch experts, one of whom was

> Jan Cornelisz Ourog, master guncaster, [who] has told me that he recently cast in Holland 46 extraordinarily good metal cannons of eight feet long that can shoot 18 pounds of iron, that weighed 2200 to 2300 pounds and were sufficiently tested; furthermore, pieces of ten-and-a-half foot long, that shoot 24 pounds of iron, weigh 3200 to 3300 pounds, [and] passed a test sufficiently well. And he took one of the . . . pieces of 18 pounds that had been cast in normal fashion and bored it for 24 pounds of shot, which still passed a test. Furthermore, he has cast smaller pieces of three foot long, that weigh 63 pounds and passed a decent test.
>
> He made a small model that could shoot four or five times before he redid it as a large piece, although he did not test this large piece. This Master Jan Cornelisz. humbly offers his service to your royal majesty, ...[51]

Satisfied with Ourog's skill as described by one of his agents, Christian IV task him to cast cannon "in the English style" at the Norwegian forges.[52] And a similar royal invitation to come to Denmark was given to the arquebus-and-musket-maker Johan Ditersen of Delft.[53] Additional royal licences were issued to another gunmaker and steelmaker.[54]

Amburger suggested that besides his desire to aid the cause of Protestantism in Germany and Bohemia, Christian engaged in a policy aimed at undermining the Dutch dominance of the Baltic Sea and the northern route to Russia but to accomplish this needed "Holland *[holländische]* craftsmen and Holland capital."[55] This included whalers, operating out of Glückstadt, a town in what is now northern Germany, founded by the Danish king in 1617.[56] Eventually, from 1639 onward, the firm of Marselis and Berns began to cast cannon there as well.[57] Efforts to establish overseas monopoly companies for the Danish crown were likewise undertaken by Dutchmen such as Johan de Willem (Willum, d. 1631). But the Danish efforts to compete with the Dutch mercantile empire largely failed. Although the Danish crown received enormous revenue from the Soundtoll, Danish vessels shipped few goods from Baltic ports to the North Sea and beyond.

The arms trade cannot flourish without some connivance from the authorities. The eighteenth-century Amsterdam historian Jan Wagenaar (1709–1773) treats us to a telling anecdote involving the Marselises that highlights this collusion. Although the story was perhaps erroneous (Marselis may not have been guilty on this occasion), it does reflect the clout or reputation of a family of tycoons such as theirs. Besides the cynicism of the Amsterdam regents that emerges, it also betrays the widespread tentacles of the Marselis clan:

> [On 20 April 1638, France's strongman the Cardinal de Richelieu wrote to the French ambassador to the United Provinces that he should] tell [Frederick Henry, the prince of Orange and stadtholder of Holland and Zeeland] he had received news from Amsterdam that, through the mediation of a merchant whose name is [Gabriel Marselis], who is the agent of the King of Denmark, the Spaniards have purchased 300,000 pounds of gunpowder there, which is to be sent to Antwerp. [The ambassador replied on 29 April:] I have spoken to the Prince of Orange about the information you had heard about the merchant Marselis. He [the Prince] told me that he already knew this and had written to the Amsterdam authorities that they should apprehend [Marselis] and put him on trial.[58]

Marselis was questioned by the Amsterdam magistrates, but besides denying any involvement in this trade on the French and Dutch enemy, reminded them that he was the Danish king's representative, and that if they sanctioned him, his monarch might interfere with the Dutch "*moeder-negotie*" of the grain trade on the Baltic Sea, the lifeline for Holland.[59] Denmark at the time still controlled territory on both sides of the Danish Sound, and could close this waterway off (even if that was easier said than done). Ultimately, the Marselis clan managed to assuage Dutch alarm regarding their unscrupulous ventures by delivering guns to the Amsterdam Admiralty.[60]

Wagenaar suggested that "[i]t was sufficiently evident in these times that the enemy was supplied with arms from [our own] lands, including by way of Amsterdam."[61] Indeed, one of the unscrupulous types trading on the enemy in those years appears to have been Andries Bicker, several times mayor and one of the most powerful figures in the city.[62]

As De Boer wrote,

> [through their marriages] [Se]lio and Gabriël [Marselis] became part of a circle of very enterprising merchants, who all were active in the trade in arms. [Their sister] Maria wed in 1626 Samuel Sautyn, merchant and sulphur-manufacturer [who enjoyed a rather duplicitous reputation at the time]; her sister Sara married in 1628 Pieter Trip . . . a nephew of the famous Elias Trip, the great arms trader . . . their in-law Jan van der Straten [Johan van (der) Straeten, one of the richest people in Amsterdam, as is apparent from the 1631 tax assessment] dedicated himself to the same business. . . .[63]

This Pieter Trip joined Louys de Geer and Elias Trip as companion in a business in which the two brothers-in-law mainly concentrated on the sale of arms.[64] Thus already in the 1620s almost all leading tycoons of the Dutch arms industry where linked through marriage. It remains difficult to establish if they ever truly fell out with each other, even in those years during the 1640s and 1650s that saw the Marselises backing the Danes and the De Geers their Swedish enemies. After all, war between the two Scandinavian countries meant good business for both families.

6.3 De Geer Versus Marselis

The Marselises attempted to change Christian IV's misfortunes in a war that beset the aging king in the winter of 1643–1644.[65] In the United Provinces, sympathies in this conflict seem to have been divided, with the majority of the merchants of Holland relishing the humiliation of Christian, whose tolls were an impediment to profits, while Frederick Henry and some of his backers were more pro-Danish.[66] Working through the brokerage of the Marselis brothers and De Geer, both Danes and Swedes hired sailors and bought arms and ships in the Republic (itself still at war with Spain).[67] The two moguls tried to outbid each other in Holland for the services of soldiers and sailors.[68]

First Christian IV and then Gustavus Adolphus (and the regency that succeeded him) had fought the Imperial armies in the still ongoing Thirty Years' War, but in 1643 these Protestant champions squared off against each other.[69] Because it saw two anti-Catholic monarchs fight each other, one suspects that in supporting their respective monarchs the Marselis and De Geer clans' motives may have been before all making money. De Geer's biographer Froukje Breedvelt-van Veen outlines a suspiciously enthusiastic response from De Geer to the Swedish declaration of war, which happily aligned with heightened Dutch mercantile irritation at the tolls levied on ships passing through the Sound by the Danes.[70] She plausibly argues that De Geer did not necessarily always applaud the outbreak of war, as in such a crisis the profits of arms sales might be offset by losses for his other ventures; in this case, however, he had become quite annoyed with the Danish tolls (which had been suddenly levied on his Swedish ships that had previously moved commodities toll free) that had damaged his business. De Geer personally negotiated in Holland for Dutch help to the Swedish cause, directly by approaching the Estates-General for an alliance and indirectly by equipping ships to fight the Danes at his own cost in the Republic.[71] Breedvelt-van Veen adds that De Geer was willing to go to this length in part as he had been feuding a long time with Christian IV: The Danish king had been indebted to him for two decades, never making any meaningful payment.[72]

Louys de Geer's fleet did not immediately distinguish itself: Its commander, Maarten Thijssen (d. 1657), proved rash and suffered a painful setback against the Danish navy in May 1644. The defeat was not comprehensive, but the fact that it was due in part to the superior fighting quality of the smaller Danish fleet could be attributed to De Geer's failure to muster a truly formidable naval squadron in Holland.[73] In Dutch broadsides that soon appeared after Thijssen's loss, De Geer was roundly ridiculed for his failure. Unfazed, De Geer mustered another fleet that sailed under Thijssen, with the admiral given this time the brief to join the rest of the Swedish navy, awaiting the outcome of Danish-Swedish negotiations that had begun.[74] Thijssen, ignoring De Geer's orders, decided instead on a much more aggressive strategy, which ultimately was successful and led to the Swedish victory at sea in this war.[75] In its final stages, this sea war saw De Geer personally monitoring the fighting with the Danes on board of one of the ships.[76] The adventure cost De Geer more than a million guilders, which was paid back to him by the Swedish crown, however, in the following years.[77] And the Swedish terms gained De Geer's ships toll-free transit through the Sound, even when transporting arms or ammunition.[78] Ultimately, then, this war ended as an unmitigated Swedish triumph. It definitively ended Denmark's attempts to become a Great Power, which Christian IV had eagerly desired. Although they supported the losing side, meanwhile, the Marselises did not do too badly for themselves in bankrolling the Danes: After the royal coffers completely emptied out, Christian IV was forced to give one of his crowns as collateral to Gabriel Marselis in 1646.[79] Marselis and his family long after continued to enjoy royal favour. Despite Denmark's miserable record in war after 1620, the Danish branch of the Marselis family ended up with vast estates and was ennobled by the king, reaching a status similar to the De Geers in Sweden.

When war between the two Scandinavian countries broke out again in the late 1650s, the Marselises and two partners paid for half a year the entire cost of the fielding of 10,000 troops who fought on behalf of Christian's successor, King Frederick III (r. 1648–1670), which appears to have cost them about half of De Geer's million-dollar venture.[80] Ultimately in this conflict, it was a Dutch fleet that offered relief to besieged Copenhagen, which could not be taken by the Swedes.[81] For once, the Danes held their own, bailed out by Dutch money and military aid and the fact that the Swedes ended up facing almost all other northern European states at once. Despite its favourable outcome, this was another war that devastated Denmark, and at its end, in 1658, Selio Marselis was tasked to haul grain from Arkhangel'sk to relieve the hungry Danes, thus coming to Danish rescue with other means than weapons.[82]

In their Danish (and partly Hamburg) business, Selio and Gabriel Marselis jr were helped by their older brother Peter, who had settled in Moscow not long before 1630, at a time when, for the first time, shipments of Russian grain had been arriving in Denmark.[83] The Muscovite Marselis became an equally powerful tycoon in his adopted country, involved in setting up the iron forges and arms industry there as well as running the tsar's post office. Peter Marselis, about whom more will be said later, would late in life advise the tsar on economic policy and draft a blueprint for the rebuilding of the port of Arkhangel'sk after it was devastated by a fire.

Denmark and Holland allied once more in the 1670s, with the Dutch supplying the Danish navy with sailors and commanders in the Scanian War with Sweden. Frederick III's successor, King Christian V (r. 1670–1699), hired an entire Dutch navy to fight the Swedes.[84] In May 1676, Christian named Cornelis Tromp admiral of this fleet.[85] Tromp inflicted a crushing defeat upon the Swedish navy soon after. In addition to this armada, the Dutch envoy who had announced that Van Klenck's embassy was on its way to the tsar in 1675, Richard de Reyser, was engaged in December 1676 by the Danish envoy to The Hague, Henning Meyercrone (1645–1707), to recruit six to eight companies of mercenaries, which De Reyser was to command himself.[86] De Reyser was concomitantly promoted from the rank of army captain to that of lieutenant-colonel. Jan Struys, who was part of Van Klenck's retinue that went to Moscow, may have gotten wind of the king's fondness for Dutch hirelings, for soon after he decided to seek his luck as well in Denmark.[87]

The Dutch themselves turned away from their great dependency on the artillery produced by the De Geer works after Louys's death in 1652. Remarkably, in the Republic, guns made by the famous Hemony brothers, who were better known as bell makers (whose marvellous tones can still be admired today in the Netherlands), began to substitute for Swedish-forged cannon.[88] Louys de Geer's death loosened the close ties between the Dutch and Swedish branches of his business, coinciding with a growing political estrangement between Sweden and the Republic.

Notes

1. Elias, ed., "Contract tot oprichting," 364–8. See as well Breedvelt-van Veen, *Louis de Geer*, 10–12; Kernkamp, ed., "Memoriën," 191.
2. Yablonskaya, "Introduction," 17–18. Others were Cornelis Coster (of Utrecht), the Amsterdam-based Van Solingen clan, and Jan Flock of Amsterdam. See, for a more general overview in Dutch of the craftsmanship of Dutch rifle-, musket- and carbine-makers, Puype, "De Glorie." Puype underlines the complex division of labour involved in the production process. He suggests like Amburger that the production of firearms, swords, and armour was an example of a putting-out system, with the main assembler having a sequence of artisans making parts of the musket or sword before putting all pieces together (and testing the weapon). Puype argues that it was Maurice of Orange-Nassau personally who was highly influential in encouraging foreign experts to settle in the United Provinces and expand a fledgling (or locally oriented) industry to become Europe's foremost producer of arms in the seventeenth century.
3. As Norman Davies and others have pointed out (Davies, *God's Playground*, vol. 1, 197–224).
4. Frost is therefore one of many who have criticised the concept of a seventeenth-century Military Revolution, see Frost, *Northern Wars*, 307. But he does not quite reject it (see ibid., 309).

5. De Jong, "Dutch," 41–3.
6. Kreslins, "Linguistic Landscapes."
7. Dutch expertise in fortification was called in at times (Frost, *Northern Wars*, 106). On the absence of a Polish navy, see, for example, ibid., 159. The Poles did nonetheless turn to the widespread use of field artillery (see Reger, "In the Service," 11–12).
8. Frost, *Northern Wars*, 57–63, 311.
9. Indeed, Frost notes how a Polish commander informed a Dutch humanist about the advanced sophistication of Polish warfare in the mid-sixteenth century (Frost, *Northern Wars*, 50–1). See also the defeat by the Poles of a combined Swedish-Russian army in 1610, of which the Swedish commanders had been schooled in fighting in the "Dutch style," to no avail (ibid., 67–8). As a young man, the later *Hetman* Krzysztof Radziwill (1585–1640), a Calvinist, witnessed Maurice's army in the early 1600s besieging 's-Hertogenbosch (ibid., 107). And the Pole Krzysztof Arciszewski (1592–1656) was a high-ranking officer in the Dutch army, who fought in Europe and Brazil in the first half of the seventeenth century, and he was not the only Pole to do so (Klooster, *Dutch Moment*, 63–4; Frost, *Northern Wars*, 244). Contacts seem to have petered out after 1650, when Poland sank into crisis.
10. See Scholten, "Arms Trade," 25.
11. Reger, "In the Service," 11.
12. Frost, *Northern Wars*; Davies, *God's Playground*.
13. Frost, *Northern Wars*, 227.
14. Bruijn, "Kaapvaart," 416.
15. De Geer van Jutfaas, *Lodewijk de Geer*, 9. On Sweden's undeveloped resources in the middle of the sixteenth century, see Frost, *Northern Wars*, 7.
16. De Jong, "Dutch," 53–6.
17. De Geer van Jutfaas, *Lodewijk de Geer*, 13–15.
18. Frost, *Northern Wars*, 36.
19. Ibid., 51; in the 1610s, he began a military academy in Siegen, as we saw earlier.
20. Driessen, "Het Gezantschap," 52.
21. De Geer van Jutfaas, *Lodewijk de Geer*, 16–19. And De Geer kept hiring experts in Wallonia for his other Swedish enterprises in subsequent decades (ibid., 25); Van Dillen, ed., "Amsterdamsche notarieele acten," 300–1.
22. Breedvelt-van Veen, *Louis de Geer*, 13.
23. De Jong, "Dutch," 56. See also see Breedvelt-van Veen, *Louis de Geer*, 12, and elsewhere.
24. Breedvelt-van Veen, *Louis de Geer*, 13–14.
25. Ibid., 14–19.
26. Ibid., 19–23, 27–9, 35–7.
27. Ibid., 17–19.
28. Ibid., 82.
29. Amburger, *Die Familie*, 96.
30. De Geer's descendant De Geer van Jutfaas found in the records of the Estates-General in The Hague reference to De Geer's export trade in a welter of commodities: Iron and copper cannon, muskets, pistols, arquebuses, swords, halberds, pikes, lances, harnesses, curasses, bandeliers, helmets, drums, bullets, gunpowder, fuses, and saltpetre (De Geer van Jutfaas, *Lodewijk de Geer*, 19fn. 4, 24–5; see, too, Van Dillen, ed., "Amsterdamsche notarieele acten," 214).
31. Breedvelt-van Veen, *Louis de Geer*, 19.
32. Frost, *Northern Wars*, 104–5.
33. Breedvelt-van Veen, *Louis de Geer*, 83, 86.
34. Ibid., 84.

35. Ibid., 84, 84n4; Van Deursen, *Plain Lives*, 7.
36. Breedvelt-van Veen, *Louis de Geer*, 91.
37. Ibid., 95–117.
38. Ibid., 124–5, 128.
39. Perhaps the most significant attempt was the effort to marry the tsar's daughter Irina to the Danish prince Waldemar in the early 1640s, which Peter Marselis tried to facilitate.
40. Frost, *Northern Wars*.
41. See Boterbloem, *Moderniser of Russia*.
42. See Wilson, *Geschiedenis*, 52–4.
43. Amburger, *Die Familie*, 25.
44. Ibid., 39–40, 48–9. Amburger suggests that Selio in his younger years must have known about De Geer's mines in Sweden (ibid., 52).
45. Ibid., 52.
46. De Boer, "Een Amsterdamsche 'lorrendraayer'," 54.
47. Amburger, *Die Familie*, 51.
48. Ibid., 24; see as well, ibid., 29.
49. Note that the Marselises and the Trips were related through marriage, as were the Trips and De Geers; they were concomitantly related to the gunpowder manufacturers' family Sautijn (see Amburger, *Die Familie*, 37). See also Lauridsen, *Marselis Konsortiet*, 36–8.
50. Amburger, *Die Familie*, 30.
51. Kernkamp, ed., "Memoriën," 214–15.
52. Ibid., 215.
53. Ibid., 215–16.
54. Ibid., 232–3.
55. Amburger, *Die Familie*, 30.
56. Ibid., 31.
57. Ibid., 39. See, too, Lauridsen, *Marselis Konsortiet*, 47, 50–1. The Berns' ancestors had arrived in Denmark from Groningen.
58. Wagenaar, *Amsterdam*, vol. 5, 25–6. The Marselis here is Selio Marselis (1609–1673), who also lent his services to the Danish court before settling in Amsterdam.
59. Selio rather than Gabriel Marselis; Wagenaar and others rather garbled the story (see De Boer, "Een Amsterdamsche 'lorrendraayer'"; Wagenaar, *Amsterdam*, vol. 5, 26).
60. Amburger, *Die Familie*, 41.
61. Wagenaar, *Amsterdam*, vol. 5, 28.
62. Van der Vlugt, *Wij zijn*, 108–9.
63. De Boer, "Een Amsterdamsche 'lorrendraayer'," 52–3. Selio and Peter Marselis traded on Russia at this time (see Kotilaine, "When the Twain," 109). Jan van Straeten's heirs were estimated as owning goods and money of approximately 200,000 guilders in 1631, which amounts to 1,000 times the wage of the average Dutch worker in those days (Frederiks and Frederiks, *Kohier*, 58). His assessment was only slightly lower than that of the powerful mayor Jacob de Graeff (c. 1570–1638; see ibid., 2).
64. Breedvelt-van Veen, *Louis de Geer*, 39–40.
65. Amburger, *Die Familie*, 44; Lauridsen, *Marselis*, 70–4.
66. Amburger, *Die Familie*, 44.
67. See Brugmans, *Geschiedenis*, 13; De Geer van Jutfaas, *Lodewijk de Geer*, 28, 31–8; Breedvelt-van Veen, *Louis de Geer*, 164–5. The Swedish fleet of more than 30 ships equipped by De Geer was commanded by two Zeelanders (De Geer van Jutfaas, *Lodewijk de Geer*, 33).

68. Breedvelt-van Veen, *Louis de Geer*, 164–5.
69. Frost, *Northern Wars*, 137–8.
70. Breedvelt-van Veen, *Louis de Geer*, 153–4.
71. Ibid., 154–5, 157–67.
72. Ibid., 156.
73. Ibid., 170–3.
74. Ibid., 175.
75. Ibid., 176–7.
76. Ibid., 178–80.
77. Ibid., 187–8.
78. Ibid., 196–7.
79. Lauridsen, *Marselis*, 93–7; Amburger, *Die Familie*, 33, 39–40; Harris, *Marselis-Slaegten*, 41.
80. Amburger, *Die Familie*, 56. Frost suggests that at least 2,000 Dutch soldiers fought on the Danish side (Frost, *Northern Wars*, 182).
81. Amburger, *Die Familie*, 57; Frost, *Northern Wars*, 182.
82. Amburger, *Die Familie*, 56; Lauridsen, *Marselis*, 72–3.
83. Lauridsen, *Marselis*, 67; Harris, *Marselis-Slaegten*, 37.
84. See, among others, Frost, *Northern Wars*, 210, 212.
85. Prud'homme van Reine, "De Republiek," 125; *Hollantse Mercurius*, February 1676, 19. An echo of this can be found in Charles XII's complaint about having to fight a Russian fleet that was all but in name Dutch (see Hooijmaaijers, "Cornelis Cruys," 29). Cruys was a Norwegian by birth.
86. *RA Denmark* [Danish National Archives] 301 Tyske kancelli Udentigske Afdeling (years 1223–1770) Nederlandene Gesandtskabsrelationer 1676 (Henning Meyercrone, July–December 1676), 5 (15) December 1676; *Hollantse Mercurius*, January 1676, 2. This was not the first time that Dutch mercenaries on behalf of the Danish king were recruited in Holland while the Republic itself was at war (see Dekker, *Humour*, 89).
87. See Boterbloem, *Fiction and Reality*, 167–9.
88. Elias, ed., "Contract tot oprichting," 389–90. Hans Falck, too, doubled as maker of clocks and cannon in Friesland and in Moscow.

Bibliography

Amburger, E. *Die Familie Marselis*, Gießen: Wilhelm Schmitz, 1957.

Boer, G.W. de. "Een Amsterdamsche 'lorrendraayer' Celio Marselis," *Jaarboek van het Genootschap Amstelodamum* 38, 1941, 37–66.

Boterbloem, Kees. *The Fiction and Reality of Jan Struys: A Seventeenth-Century Dutch Globetrotter*, Houndmills, Basingstoke: Palgrave, 2008.

———. *Moderniser of Russia: Andrei Vinius, 1641–1716*, London: Palgrave, 2013.

Breedvelt-van Veen, F. *Louis de Geer, 1587–1652*, Amsterdam: Paris, 1935.

Brugmans, H. *Geschiedenis van Amsterdam*, vol. 3: *Bloeitijd, 1621–97*, 2nd ed., Utrecht: Het Spectrum, 1973.

Bruijn, J.R. "Kaapvaart in de tweede en derde Engelse oorlog," *Bijdragen en Mededelingen betreffende de Geschiedenis der Nederlanden* 90, 1975, 408–29.

Davies, Norman. *God's Playground*, vol. 1, New York: Columbia University Press, 1979.

Dekker, R. *Humour in Dutch Culture of the Golden Age*, Houndmills, Basingstoke: Palgrave, 2001.

Deursen, A.Th. van. *Plain Lives in a Golden Age*, Cambridge: Cambridge University Press, 1991.

Dillen, J.G. van. "Amsterdamsche notarieele acten betreffende den koperhandel en de uitoefening van mijnbouw en metaalindustrie in Zweden," *Bijdragen en Mededeelingen van het Historisch Genootschap*, 58, 1937, 211–301.

Driessen, J. "Het Gezantschap van Reinoud van Brederode in 1615 en 1616 naar Rusland," in J. Driessen, W. Roobol and Marc Jansen, eds, *Rusland in Nederlandse ogen*, Amsterdam: van Oorschot, 1986, 51–73.

Elias, J.E., ed. "Contract tot oprichting van een Zweedsch factorie-comptoir te Amsterdam in 1663," *Bijdragen en Mededelingen van het Historisch Genootschap* 24, 1903, 356–400.

Frederiks, J.G., and P.J. Frederiks. *Kohier van den tweehonderdsten penning . . . Over 1631*, Amsterdam: Ten Brink and De Vries, 1890.

Frost, Robert. *The Northern Wars: War, State and Society in Northeastern Europe, 1558–1721*, Harlow: Longman, 2000.

Geer van Jutfaas, J.L.W. de. *Lodewijk de Geer van Finspong en Leusta (1587–1652)*, 3rd ed., Utrecht: Kemink and Son, 1852.

Harris, Poul. *Marselis-Slaegten*, Arhus: Centrum, 1980.

Hollantse Mercurius, January 1676.

Hollantse Mercurius, February 1676.

Hooijmaaijers, E. "Cornelis Cruys, a Dutch Rear-Admiral in Russian Service," in Carel Horstmeier et al., eds, *Around Peter the Great*, Groningen: NOS, 1997, 29–34.

Jong, M. de. "Dutch Entrepreneurs in the Swedish Crown in Copper and Iron, 1580–1630," in Hanno Brand, ed., *Trade, Diplomacy and Cultural Change*, Hilversum: Verloren, 2005, 36–57.

Kernkamp, G.W., ed., "Memoriën van ridder Theodorus Rodenburg betreffende het verplaatsen van verschillende industrieën uit Nederland naar Denemarken, met daarop genomen resolutiën van koning Christiaan IV (1621)," *Bijdragen en Mededelingen van het Historisch Genootschap* 23, 1902, 189–257.

Klooster, Wim. *The Dutch Moment: War, Trade and Settlement in the Seventeenth-Century Atlantic World*, Ithaca, NY: Cornell University Press, 2016.

Kotilaine, Jarmo. "When the Twain Did Meet: Foreign Merchants and Russia's Economic Expansion in the Seventeenth Century," unpubl. Ph.D. diss., Harvard University Press, 2000.

Kreslins, Janis. "Linguistic Landscapes in the Baltic," *Scandinavian Journal of History* 3–4, 2003, 165–74.

Lauridsen, John T. *Marselis Konsortiet: En Studie Over Forholdet Mellem Handelskapital og Kongemagt i 1600-Tallets Danmark*, Arhus: Jysk Selskab for Historie, 1987.

Prud'homme van Reine, R. "De Republiek als grote en kleine mogendheid ter zee (1648–1763)," in J.R. Bruijn and C.B. Wels, eds, *Met Man en Macht: De Militaire Geschiedenis van Nederland 1500–2000*, Baarn: Balans, 2003, 105–39.

Puype, Jan Piet. "De Glorie van de Nederlandse geweermakerij in de zeventiende eeuw," available at: www.militairmagazijn.nl/wapens/armamentaria/artikel/wapens_armas_xml_726ae3c0-d043-4713-b0b1-ce2650d33be7/, accessed 20 January 2019.

Reger, W.M. "In the Service of the Tsar: European Mercenary Officers and the Reception of Military Reform in Russia, 1654–1667," unpubl. Ph.D. diss., University of Illinois, Urbana-Champaign, 1997.

Scholten, F.J. "The Arms Trade and Industry in Groningen in the First Half of the Seventeenth Century," in H.L. Visser and D.W. Bailey, eds, *Aspects of Dutch Gunmaking*, Zwolle: Waanders, 1997, 24–72.

Vlugt, Simone van der. *Wij zijn de Bickers*, Amsterdam: Prometheus, 2019.

Wagenaar, Jan. *Amsterdam in zijne opkomst*, 13 vols., Amsterdam: Isaak Tirion, 1760-c.1784.

Wilson, S.A. *Geschiedenis van Bloemendaal*, ed. C.W.D. Vrijland, Haarlem: Schuyt and Co., 1975.

Yablonskaya, E.A. "Introduction to the Catalogue," in E.A. Yablonskaya et al., eds, *Dutch Guns in Russia*, Amsterdam and Zwolle: Rijksmuseum and Waanders, 1996, 10–29.

7 Dutch Activity in Russia, Part 1

Trade and Technology

7.1 Russia's Modernisation

Unlike that of the Swedes or Danes, who had been a part of western Christianity since times immemorial, the Russian mindset had a strong xenophobic streak, rooted in a long isolation of their country from the rest of Europe. Previously more part of the Byzantine than the Latin world, Russia fell by the middle of the thirteenth century under Mongolian (Tatar) rule, which cordoned it off from much communication with Europe for a quarter millennium. Muscovy had shaken off Tatar rule towards 1500, but suspicion of the West grew in the sixteenth century, when the mighty Polish-Lithuanian state fell in with a militant Catholicism poised to convert Orthodox believers to its creed. The unification of part of the Ukrainian church with Roman Catholicism in 1596 (Union of Brest) reinforced this fear, and the Polish involvement in the Russian Time of Troubles fed it further. In the sixteenth and seventeenth centuries, Western travellers noticed how they passed through villages where the women did not show themselves outside in order not to be contaminated by the sight of heretics, and the Russian elite likewise practised women's seclusion. This has been explained as a holdover from the late Byzantine empire's culture, although for the peasants, the fear of the rape of their women by the armed outsiders who frequently traversed the Russian lands in the sixteenth and early seventeenth centuries may have been a factor.

Neither tsar nor his people were keen on foreigners, then. It might be proposed that they would have liked to do without them altogether, were it not for the absolute necessity of using modern arms in maintaining the independence of their state and society and thus preserving their culture in as unadulterated a form as possible.[1] Thus, whereas the marked Dutch role in pre-Petrine Russia seems paradoxical given this xenophobic environment, it was the result of their indispensable importance for this modernisation in terms of their savvy both at trading and at manufacturing arms and waging war.[2] Frost explains this crucial need for military innovation when he says,

> Contemporary warfare was dominated by professionals, and the major problem facing the Russian government after 1650 was the

> professionalisation of Russia's military elite. It is difficult . . . to give any definitive answer on the extent to which it was successful. Nevertheless, it is clear that much progress had already been made by 1700.[3]

And Reger suggests why an exception was made in the policy to keep the Orthodox away from the heretics, noting how

> . . . mercenaries, once they were ushered into the presence of the tsar, examined for technical expertise with weaponry, and assigned a rank and a regiment, associated freely with the Russian people in their regiments and in the provinces as well as the major towns and cities. The freedom to associate made them unique among the foreigners who lived and traveled in Russia in the 17th century.[4]

In other words, the Muscovites were willing to waive the restrictions they placed on the contacts between Western foreigners and Orthodox believers because military affairs had such a paramount importance in seventeenth-century Russia and trumped any cultural rejection of "others." The tsars, aristocracy, and leading clergy tried to keep Orthodoxy pure or uncontaminated, but this could not be done in splendid isolation from developments in military matters elsewhere. They were forced to make concessions and take the risk to corrupt the creed if an Orthodox Russia was to survive at all.

Around 1600, though, Russian modernisation (which had been haltingly initiated by the last tsars of the Riurik dynasty) was impeded by an intense conflict triggered by an uncertain succession to the throne, which, combined with a massive famine, led to a civil war and foreign invasions. Even while the various contestants on the Russian side in this Time of Troubles (which was at its height from 1603 to 1613) wanted to avail themselves of the most modern weapons that could be bought, few had sufficient means and too often uncertainty was so pronounced that arms deliveries from Western Europe were at best sporadic in this period.[5] The foreign invaders during the Time of Troubles, meanwhile, hammered home to the elite that Russia's survival could not be taken for granted; soon it was persuaded that Dutch businessmen's wares offered a way towards a less vulnerable Russia.

In an odd coincidence, the Dutch (northern-Netherlandic) native arms industry and arms trade was at precisely this time beginning to spread its wings. Once Mikhail Romanov was elected tsar in 1613 and a stable government was able to pay, arms importations from the Netherlands began to become a regular feature. Individual traders involved in the arms trade, such as Karel du Moulin, greased the wheels in Russia. When Russian envoys arrived at The Hague to announce the coronation of Mikhail in 1614, the Estates-General gave the new monarch's emissaries a celebratory gift of which arms and armour were the main component.[6] There was competition from the English, but as with most regions where they tried to compete with the Dutch before the Navigation Acts were introduced in 1651, they could not match Dutch salesmanship.[7] The Dutch were wily enough to dispatch their first official embassy to Moscow in 1630 laden with gifts of arms to pique Russian interest.[8] Later embassies refrained from bringing weapons as gifts, for after 1630 the Russians were purchasing great amounts off arms from the Republic.

Given the expense this importation incurred, it seems logical that the tsars became eventually interested in import-substitution and Dutch entrepreneurs such as Andries Winius, Peter Marselis, Lus Tieleman Akema, and others were permitted to expand the small Russian arms industry into something much larger. Winius and company may have been inspired by the example of Dutch entrepreneurs who set up such works elsewhere (as De Geer had in Sweden), while the Russian government was keen to copy its Swedish and Danish rivals (the role of Julius Coyett may have been significant), aware of such expert Dutch entrepreneurs as De Geer; perhaps crucially, Peter Marselis was the brother of Selio and Gabriel Marselis jr. Even when the Great Northern War broke out in 1700, though, 10,000 muskets were still imported from the Netherlands.[9] Into the first decade of the eighteenth century, meanwhile, the Republic remained the main supplier of "weapons and military equipment" to Russia.[10]

Tsar Peter the Great realised that military modernisation (and therefore Russia's survival) could never quite succeed in stark isolation from changes in other aspects of his people's life. He tried to cast off the xenophobia that had characterised Russian culture in a comprehensive offensive. But, for almost a century prior to his "opening of a window to the West," the Dutch enabled much more hesitant Russians than Peter to hold their own in Eastern Europe and Northern Asia and gradually gain the upper hand in their long-term conflicts with Poland. After the Time of Troubles, Muscovite demand for strategic goods and technology rose because of the tsars' realisation that the recovery of territory lost before 1618 to Poland and Sweden could occur only if their army matched the sophistication of those of their western neighbours.[11]

Perhaps nowhere is the Dutch role in seventeenth-century military modernisation more marked than in Russia.[12] Consequently, the Russian case is a most compelling illustration of the sale of soldiery and weaponry that heavily contributed to the Dutch economic boom. Shipwrights and sailors were involved in a series of projects to create a modern Russian navy and merchant marine, while fortress builders helped the Russians protect their borders and their interior against foreign and domestic foes. Mercenary officers recruited, tested, and trained other mercenaries and Russians and led the Muscovite armies on campaigns. Dutchmen set up Russia's first manufactory of firearms at an industrial scale, and Dutch merchants shipped thousands of muskets and ordnance to help the tsar fight his wars with Poland, Sweden, the Crimean Tatars, and the Ottoman Empire. This firepower allowed Moscow's Cossacks to exert tsarist rule over the Siberian native population, too.[13]

As a consequence, "pre-Petrine Russia underwent significant military changes that, in some respects, were similar to the Military Revolution . . . in the West."[14] Russian interest in Western European arms (and in the Western European production techniques by which these weapons were made) was strong throughout the seventeenth century, and it was the Dutch who unfailingly (as Ambassador Van Klenck pointed out to the Peter's father Aleksei in 1676) supplied them with these strategic goods and this crucial technology.[15] As Amburger noted, "the Netherlanders . . . had been keen to deliver arms" at least from the 1610s, when order was gradually restored within Muscovy, even if wars with Sweden and Poland continued until, respectively, 1617 and 1618, initially interfering with these efforts (and making the Dutch government unwilling to sanction this trade).[16]

The sole port of call for Western European ships in seventeenth-century Russia was Arkhangel'sk on the White Sea.[17] Even though the journey from Holland to Russia (around Norway and the Kola peninsula) was short compared with trips to the East Indies (several weeks rather than six months and more) and often had crews of fewer than 20 sailors, it was not an easy trip. Cold and heavy weather often plagued the journeys, and ships could arrive safely only in the summer months. If too early, Arkhangel'sk might be inaccessible through icefloats in the White Sea, and, if leaving too late, the route might be blocked by ice. But ships reached Russia in considerable number. In 1658, a year in which the Russians kept close track of traffic at Arkhangel'sk, ships arrived from 21 June to 23 September.[18] Of 80 ships in all, 62 were Dutch, ten from Hamburg, and four English. This proportion was typical: Indeed, throughout much of the century, three out of four ships arriving at the mouth of the northern Dvina hailed from the Republic.[19]

In volume, the trade on Russia was not a trade that remotely neared the bulk trade of the Dutch with the Baltic littoral, but it was a vital trade for the Russians. It eventually allowed the Muscovites to gain the upper hand over the Poles, beginning the process that culminated in Catherine the Great's dissolution of Poland in the late eighteenth century. Without the aid of the Amsterdam merchants, it might have been Russia-Muscovy that was erased from the map instead.

7.2 The Russia Trade

In his outstanding *Dutch Primacy in World Trade*, Jonathan Israel suggested that the era of Dutch mercantile flourishing lasted until 1740, which was rather longer than the historiographical consensus had previously accepted.[20] He argued that while Dutch economic paramountcy continued for more than a generation after 1700 (as was believed earlier), the source of its strength shifted from its primary focus on the intra-European overseas trade to long-distance trade with non-European areas. Whether or not previous historians obscured the longevity of the boom, Israel was indubitably right in emphasising how the Republic's trading patterns changed over time. Foreign demand for arms shipped from the Republic changed, too, albeit earlier: Beginning about 1650, the demand for Dutch military expertise narrowed, becoming more and more centred on northern Europe. Indeed, Dutch primacy in this respect experienced a final flourish in Russia around 1700.

While the Dutch role as a sort of midwives of Russia's Great Power status was crucial, the riches the Russia trade brought Dutch entrepreneurs was considerable. Before 1650, almost every leading capitalist family in Amsterdam tried its hand at the Russia trade, reflective of its exceptional promise.[21] Dutch enthusiasm about the possibilities of the Russia trade was so great in the early years of the seventeenth century, that for a brief moment a Dutch version of the English Muscovy Company was contemplated.[22] This initiative, which seems to have originated with Marcus de Vogelaer sr, saw a considerable overlap among its backers with the early directors of the VOC's chambers.[23] Among these merchants were Bickers and Hasselaers, whose offspring were among the leading Amsterdam regents, as well as Balthasar de Moucheron and Gerrit Akema, likely an ancestor of the later chief of the Dutch-led arms manufactories at Tula and elsewhere, Lus Tieleman Akema (d. 1676).[24] There was indeed a direct link between the early East India trade and the forays towards the White Sea and beyond: De Moucheron, at least, was hoping to find a searoute to the Indies through the Arctic Sea north of Russia.[25] Perhaps Marcus de Vogelaer's sudden death in 1610 prevented the creation of a monopolistic northern company, although the utter chaos of the Russian Troubles that reached their climax in the early 1610s may have had many merchants doubt the survival of Muscovy altogether.[26] Business continued to thrive, however, even if a formal monopolistic bundling of forces was never accomplished after 1613: Still, sons and nephews (the De Vogelaer brothers, Andries Bicker [1586–1652], Cosimo de Moucheron, and Lus Tieleman Akema) of all four of the entrepreneurs mentioned had ventures or were active in Russia during the middle decades of the seventeenth century.[27] Others involved in the Dutch trade on early Romanov Russia included George (Jurriaan) van Klenck, Jan Cornelisz. Witsen (1569–1636), Gerrit Witsen (d. 1626), Erdman Swellengrebel sr (1571–1636), Nicolaes Ruts (1573–1638), Isaac Massa (1586–1643), Julius Coyett (d. 1634), and Andries Denijsz. Winius.[28]

Although historians have looked at the marked imprint of the Dutch on early Romanov Russia, the crucial importance of military concerns on the part of Russia's new dynasty has often been overlooked or underestimated as a key contributing factor to this development.[29] After 1585, the

Dutch or northern Netherlandic trade on Russia saw the same extraordinary expansion as the Dutch trade on other areas of the globe.[30] Many merchants reaped the profits from the brisk trade on Russia that commenced from 1585 onward and, despite fluctuations, flourished until the early eighteenth century.[31]

The arms trade, though, began to flourish only at the beginning of the Romanov dynasty's rule, that is, around 1613.[32] The Dutch historians Jan-Willem Veluwenkamp and Eric Wijnroks have in detail charted the dominant presence of the Dutch in the trade between Russia and Western Europe in the seventeenth century, almost coinciding with the heyday of the port of Arkhangel'sk as Russia's often frozen "Window to the West."[33] As Wijnroks convincingly argues, the Dutch trade on Russia was to a significant degree the work of Antwerp merchants who had fled to the Netherlands, coinciding with the real take-off period of Dutch mercantile capitalism that followed the fall of Antwerp to the Spaniards in 1585 and the accompanying exodus of Brabantine, Flemish, and Walloon Calvinist merchants and entrepreneurs to the north.[34]

In 1592, one of them, Melchior de Moucheron, received from the Estates of Zeeland a licence to export gunpowder or sulphur to Muscovy.[35] As far as the evidence suggests at least, the trade on Russia nonetheless was mainly in commodities other than arms before 1613, with ships often sailing in ballast to Khol'mogory and, subsequently, Arkhangel'sk.[36] Despite departing the Low Countries in ballast, money could be made. Captains and their financial backers were interested in loading furs, fish, caviar, saltpetre, potash, and wood in exchange for cash payments.[37]

The initial Russian demand for cash displays how the seventeenth century was a watershed period even for peripheral regions of the European world economy with regard to the use of money. Without its widespread availability and easy convertibility, large organisations such as the early modern states or even the trade companies such as the VOC could not operate. This even became the case for Russia, despite the fact that the overwhelming majority of its population engaged in agriculture and mainly produced food for themselves and their lords. But the tsars needed to field a large army in their incessant wars with Poles, Swedes, Tatars, and eventually Turks. The necessary bullion to pay for up-to-date ordnance, supplies, native musketeer *(strel'tsy)* units, and eventually mercenaries had to be imported from the West. As Kotilaine writes,

> . . . merchants of the West came to play a pivotal role in lubricating the wheels of exchange in Russia. Especially the Dutch enjoyed an unparalleled supply of capital and brought large quantities of it to Moscow. In 1604, for instance, [the equivalent of a quarter million guilders] was brought to Kholmogory.[38]

Even though Mikhail Romanov's throne was shaky after his elevation as tsar in 1613, his accession does appear to have almost immediately led to a stampede of Dutch merchantmen arriving at the Dvina's delta. Muscovy remained at war with Sweden and Poland, whose armies occupied large swaths of formerly Russian land. It is no surprise, then, that the new tsar's regime without delay tried to purchase arms to improve Muscovy's defence.

One of the pioneers in facilitating Russian arms purchases was a scion of a Walloon family, Isaac Massa, who was Jurriaan van Klenck's "*grote tegenstrever*," his great rival, during the first decades of the seventeenth century.[39] Massa emerged as the leading figure in the early years of the contacts between Muscovy and the *de facto* independent northern Netherlands. In a lecture in 1989, G.W. van der Meiden noted how in the 1600s the young Massa showed an unnamed Russian nobleman, "who was interested in life in Holland, its religion, the revolt against Spain and the warlike deeds of Prince Maurits [while] Massa presented him with engravings of the various sieges by this famous general, ..."[40] Thus, he tried to trigger Russian interest in the Dutch art of war, and not without effect.

Many of the same families of refugees exploring the trading possibilities in Asia, Africa, and the Americas traded on Russia, such as the De Moucherons, De Vogelaers, or Du Moulins.[41] Their ships sailed all of the Seven Seas around 1600, after transferring their home port from Antwerp to Dutch harbours. By 1600, their bottoms unloaded all sorts of goods at Arkhangel'sk, the only port of entry for goods shipped by Western overseas companies to Muscovy; by the 1610s, arms shipments began to arrive regularly at the port.[42] The trade balance was gradually restored and cash payments declined when the Russian demand for luxury commodities (such as wine or spices) and arms steadily grew after the worst of the Russian domestic conflicts began to abate by 1613. Besides furs, the Dutch were interested in various strategic goods, such as naval stores, potash, and saltpetre, raw materials that could be used by the Dutch war industry which took flight after 1590. Potash was used for a variety of industrial purposes, not in the least in the making of gunpowder. Before it was shipped primarily from the Bay of Bengal by the second half of the seventeenth century, saltpetre was frequently loaded in Arkhangel'sk.[43] Around 1640, Koenraad van Klenck's uncle, Herman Fentzel, was heavily involved in the saltpetre import from Russia, at times as agent of the gunpowder maker Samuel Sautijn, who was married to a sister of Peter, Selio, and Gabriel Marselis jr.[44]

The Dutch became more interested in providing Russia with weapons at the time of their Twelve Years' Truce. The armistice led to a drastic drop in domestic demand for arms, of which the production really had started to boom in the years immediately prior to 1609. Private traders needed to be circumspect, however, as their government would not readily issue permits for arms export to Muscovy: Sweden was considered an ally, while Poland was the source of much of the grain the Dutch consumed.[45] For the first time in 1616, the Dutch authorities formally permitted a small quantity of arms to be shipped, accompanying Russian envoys on their way homeward from a lengthy trip to Holland and France (and shepherded by Isaac Massa, who in those days in parlays with the Russian government in Moscow postured as the permanent representative of the Dutch government, from which he actually never received formal accreditation).[46]

This official reluctance, of course, says nothing about the clandestine deliveries of arms. They occurred, similar to the Dutch merchants' trade of arms and strategic goods with their Spanish foe in the last decades of the sixteenth century. Government prohibitions were readily ignored, for Dutch merchants stood to make great sums of money, with each musket being sold to the Russian government for three to five guilders, carbines for six to ten guilders each, and pistols for about six guilders a piece.[47] Additionally, considerable amounts of ammunition were shipped to Arkhangel'sk.[48]

And the Dutch government was not against the arms trade on Russia as such. As Jozien Driessen writes, the 1615–1616 diplomatic mission of Van Brederode, Bas, and Ioachimi, which aimed at brokering a peace between Sweden and Muscovy, was instructed to outline to their Russian interlocutors how the Republic produced many essential staples, not in the least for warfare, and to emphasise how the United Provinces had successfully fought for years against a formidable foe at sea and on land.[49] Thus, it was implied, if a peace was signed, the Russians would gain unlimited access to a most sophisticated arms industry.

The Russians were by then, though, well aware of the Dutch ability to deliver war materiel. It is clearly evident that the Russians caught on early in identifying the United Provinces as a place to acquire state-of-the-art arms, for which availability and supply the northern Netherlands began to acquire a reputation only after 1600, as we saw previously. The Russians began to rely on the Dutch as the suppliers of firearms earlier than 1630, the year suggested by Veluwenkamp.[50] Symptomatic of this is the employment by the Kremlin Armoury, where firearms were stocked, serviced, and sometimes assembled, of a Dutch expert overseeing repairs already in the 1620s.[51]

Formal restrictions continued to be placed on the delivery of arms or the recruitment of experts to help the Russians wage war, as Eric Wijnroks points out.[52] But in the late spring of 1618, the Estates-General finally gave permission to ship approximately 40,000 pounds of powder and more than 100,000 pounds of lead to the White Sea port.[53] This was at the time that the Russians delivered a fair amount of saltpetre to the Republic in exchange.[54] Towards 1620, then, a brisk trade in a variety of commodities developed, with the Dutch shipping back furs, potash, tar, timber (including ships' masts), saltpetre, and (occasionally) grain, and receiving all sorts of exclusive rights from the Russians as well, such as the monopoly on the export of caviar (as Jurriaan van Klenck, Koenraad's father, enjoyed for a while).[55]

A catalogue of Dutch-manufactured arms preserves in Russian musea compiled in the early 1990s contains a staggering amount of photographs of hand-held firearms.[56] The survival of so many weapons some 300 years after they were last used appears to reflect a massive level of importation. The documentary evidence, even if anecdotal, seems to bear this out as well. As can be expected, deliveries varied, according to the "threat level." More appear to have entered Arkhangel'sk in the early 1630s, 1653–1654, or 1659–1661, when preparations for military campaigns went into high gear.[57]

It does seem that, whenever needed, the Muscovite government succeeded in placing large orders with Dutch traders for weapons, and that those arms were delivered. The urgency for this was less great during most of the 1620s, when Muscovy was mainly recovering from the deep wounds inflicted on it by the Time of Troubles and the foreign wars, the last of which, with the *Rzeczpospolita*, had been ended in late 1618 by the Truce of Deulino. But this was an armistice, certainly in Russian eyes, and by about 1630, Mikhail Romanov and his boyars believed that their country could gain the upper hand in a new armed conflict with Poland, if properly prepared and equipped. By that time, not only weapons (muskets, carbines, pistols) but also thousands of foreign mercenaries arrived to help Russia fight the war that broke out in 1632.[58]

Importation by Dutch merchants of foreign-made arms reached an enormous volume during this Smolensk War (1632–1634) and the subsequent decades.[59] Among the sellers we find the names of Hendrik van Ringen, Karel du Moulin, Elias Trip, David Ruts, Thomas de Swaen, Paul de Willem (Willum), Jan van Lier, Daniël (1596–1681) and Jan (1604–1678) Bernard, Pieter de la Dale, Hendrik Haeckx, and even of the Dutch ambassadors to Muscovy Albert Burgh and Johan van Veltdriel, who shipped vast quantities of iron, copper, lead, cannon, shot, harnesses, rifles (carbines and muskets), pistols, pikes, bandoliers, fuses, barrels, and bullets to the port of Arkhangel'sk. In the Smolensk War, the first full-bodied Russian attempt to win a war with a Western-style military force failed, as the loyalty of Western mercenaries proved fickle, their integration with traditional units in the Muscovite army poorly conceived, and the use of field and siege artillery clumsy.[60] But in trying to survive as an independent state, Russia had no alternative to wielding advanced firearms in fighting its foes in the west or, eventually, the Ottoman Turks, the overlords of the Crimean Tatars with whom endemic warfare had been raging since the sixteenth century.[61] Thus, four Dutch pieces of heavy artillery played a significant role in breaching the walls of Smolensk in 1654, the key military engagement of the first year of the Thirteen Years' War (1654–1667), which ended with the Russian capture of the city.[62]

The Dutch Estates-General continued to refuse to openly meddle in the wars Muscovy waged against its European foes. In preparation for the Smolensk War, the Russians asked ambassadors Burgh and Van Veltdriel for the Dutch state to license the sending of arms, troops, and funds.[63] The Dutch state was, however, not prepared to take openly sides in the budding conflict between Poland and Russia: Poland was too important a source of especially grain for the northern Netherlands and the Dutch could not risk antagonising it. But the Dutch government was all too happy to encourage its citizens to ship weapons privately to the two foes, and Burgh and Van Veltdriel's mission gifted Tsar Mikhail a slew of firearms and harnesses that showcased Dutch skill in making such products, while the two envoys themselves seem to have sold arms on the side for their own private profit.

The close ties between early Romanov Muscovy and the Republic's citizens are reflected in Jan Wagenaar's eighteenth-century description of the visit of the Muscovite envoys Il'ia Miloslavskii (1594–1668)—soon to be Tsar Aleksei's father-in-law—and the high-level bureaucrat *(d'iak)* Ivan Baibakov to Amsterdam in 1646.[64] This Russian mission was primarily intended to acquire arms and officers to aid Russia in modernising and preparing its army for the wars that were in the offing to rectify the humiliation and territorial losses of the early part of the 1600s. The Amsterdam authorities were clearly aware of the lucrative possibilities and persuaded the Estates-General to lodge, feed, and entertain the Russians, after the Dutch authorities at The Hague had initially treated the emissaries somewhat perfunctorily and refused to accommodate the foreigners from the state coffers. This dismayed the Russians, because in Muscovy foreign envoys were maintained by their hosts. Amsterdam prevailed (and the deadly ill stadtholder Frederick Henry even received the Muscovites personally), and was soon able to capitalise on its propitiating of Miloslavskii and Baibakov. It was this mission that for the first time gained the Estates-General's permission to hire soldiers in the Netherlands, and the ambassadors were joined by Isaac van Bockhoven and his clan as well as several other veterans of the battlefields of Western Europe on their return trip.

Further reflective of the intimate ties between the Russian state and the Dutch is the proud confidence about the reliability of the Dutch supply of military hardware to Russia palpable in the words of the Dutch Republic's Extraordinary grand Ambassador Koenraad van Klenck, during his second official audience with Tsar Aleksei in Moscow in 1676. Van Klenck, dispatched to investigate a possible alliance with Russia against the Swedes, bluntly stated on this occasion that

> whereas it seems that the United Netherlands are located far away from his Tsarist Majesty's territories, they can easily be of help to each other, because of the great and renowned seapower of His High Mightinesses, which allows them to deliver . . . all kind of

> ammunition and other aid without any king, prince or republic being able to halt them.[65]

This was an almost impertinent reminder to the tsar of past services rendered by a variety of Dutch arms dealers, who had included the ambassador himself.[66]

7.3 Winius and Marselis

At a conference of historians in Moscow in 2002, the Russian historian S.A. Nefedov stated how

> . . . toward the middle of the seventeenth century the value of the goods annually exported from Arkhangel'sk amounted to . . . 6.2 million *livres* [when] the value of French exports [before Colbert's protectionism] on Dutch vessels amounted to about 16 million livres. If we take into account that the population of France was three times larger than that of Russia and that France was much closer to Holland, we have to concede that the significance of Dutch trade with Russia was great.[67]

One might quibble about the numbers Nefedov furnishes, but Jarmo Kotiliane's dissertation bears out the gist of this Russian scholar's argument regarding the startling scope of Dutch mercantile activities in Russia.[68] What has been perhaps less understood is that the Dutch did not merely trade on Russia in the seventeenth century, but that they were instrumental in fostering Russia's technological and, indeed, military modernisation.[69] One of the few entrepreneurs who has been singled out for his role as a key conduit has been Andries Denijszoon Winius, the individual most active in setting up Russia's first firearms plant in Tula during the 1630s. Besides him, Lus Tieleman Akema (both the uncle and nephew who shared their name), Jan van Sweeden, and Peter Marselis (father and son with the same name) were of great importance.[70]

Nefedov states that Winius, Peter Marselis, and Akema, who partnered in the 1630s at the Tula works, were the "founders of the first Russian manufactories."[71] This is strictly speaking not true. It was not as if the Muscovites had not made their own firearms before, as Thomas Esper proved long ago.[72] The problem was that their technology fell far behind, with the gunmakers in Moscow at the *pushechnyi dvor'* (Gunners' Court) producing cannon and harquebuses that were both obsolete and insufficient, which informed the great need for the importation of firearms. That is, too, why Jules Coyett, a Dutchman of Walloon extraction, or Hans Falck, a German-born bell-and-cannon caster from Frisia, were invited to come to work in Russia.

The American historian Joseph Fuhrmann counted 57 viable manufactories in pre-Petrine Muscovy, mainly led by Europeans.[73] Virtually all foreign entrepreneurs involved in these businesses were born in the Netherlands, similar to their dominance over the iron and copper mining or arms manufacturing in contemporary Sweden and Denmark. Preeminent was the Dutch consortium led by Andries Winius that began to build a watermill-powered iron blast furnace and arms plant near Tula (200 kilometres south of Moscow), which eventually allowed Muscovy to acquire self-sufficiency in cast-iron artillery.[74] Cast-iron guns were stronger than forged iron guns and could be produced much more quickly than bronze cannon, which made them cheaper.[75] The first weapons-grade iron was forged at Tula in 1636. Fuhrmann writes how "[t]he Dutch Tula factories of the 1630's were technologically advanced by even the most stringent international standards. . . ."[76] Soon, musket and carbine barrels, as well as pistols, were added to their production assortment. Still, as Esper suggests, the Russians lacked the capacity to churn out handguns anywhere near the number they needed for their armies.[77] Primarily Dutch merchants, instead, imported them in copious quantities to meet the demand.[78]

The Tula works began a process of import-substitution and a tradition of making sophisticated arms in Russia. They employed Dutch, Walloon, and Scottish managers and masters who, like the mercenaries or sailors in the tsar's service, were hired in Amsterdam.[79] Winius hired the first experts for his plant in 1632, with aid from Elias Trip in the Republic.[80] Despite the crucial part played by the Dutch and other foreigners in effecting military change, the Russian tsars and their advisors were conscious of the high cost of hiring experts elsewhere and importing arms from abroad. They tried therefore (especially after Aleksei succeeded to the throne in 1645) to ensure that foreign masters taught Russian apprentices in their skills and to replace foreign imports with Russian-made arms. Even if it is difficult to establish at which point in the history of these enterprises Russian apprentices replaced Western experts, it is beyond doubt that within a mere few decades arms manufactories operated in which exclusively Russians played a prominent role.[81] The tsar's government's strategy of obliging foreign experts to train Russians in their skill proved a resounding success.

The Dutch influence on Russian arms production therefore was bound to be transitory; when in 1690 the foreign workers at one of the Marselis plants were enumerated, a dozen Walloons were counted, but a mere one Dutch artisan. Two other Dutchmen appear to have occupied managerial positions (one of them a scion of the Ruts family).[82] This was a significant decrease from the number of Dutch craftsmen who had worked at the Marselis enterprises a generation earlier. Not long after 1700, most of Russian arms were indeed made domestically from local resources. By the end of Peter's reign in 1725, the Russian military was steadily supplied by domestic production. Dutch entrepreneurs had played a decisive role in this transformation.[83]

There was undoubtedly some foreign competition for the Dutch arms traders in Russia: The Swedes provided arms and officers in the early 1630s to the Russians (and in exchange for saltpetre), although the Scot Alexander Leslie bought many arms in Holland, from which he also dispatched mercenaries.[84] Peter Marselis shipped 10,000 muskets from Denmark to Arkhangel'sk in 1641, although a couple of years later, he had curasses and sabre-handles shipped from Holland.[85] And John Hebdon, too, competed with the Dutch around 1660, although he appears to have bought many of his arms in the Dutch Republic, in part from the De Vogelaer and Van Klenck consortium.[86] But before 1710, the Dutch seemed to have been the preferred suppliers. Ultimately, the Dutch merchants were not to succumb to foreign rivals but to the competition of weapons producers in Russia, whose industry had once been founded by Dutchmen.

Winius, Akema, and Marselis's metallurgical enterprises at Tula appeared a "great leap forward" for Russia in technological terms (as in the use of watermills to power the production of iron) and by the 1640s produced a variety of weapons of greater technological sophistication than those made in the armoury of the Kremlin. Frost suggests that more than 30,000 firearms were already made by the new manufactories between 1647 and 1653 (mainly, albeit not exclusively, at Tula).[87]

Initially, Peter Marselis seems to have merely arranged for money to be invested in Winius's Tula iron forges before he himself became a partner in this project somewhere during the 1630s. His family was nevertheless already well established in Russia before 1630. The Marselises' foray into Russia occurred in the same era as when they established themselves in Denmark (and Hamburg). In the later 1610s, Peter Marselis's father, Gabriel, may have helped out in mediating with the Poles to get the tsar's father released from his captivity.[88] Filaret (Fyodor) Nikitich Romanov (1553–1633) had been captured by the Poles during the Time of Troubles, after he had been forced to become a monk by Tsar Boris Godunov (1552–1605) in 1601. He rose high within the Russian-Orthodox hierarchy after Boris's death, before the Poles took him hostage. And soon after regaining his freedom, Filaret was elected Russian patriarch.

For a while in the 1620s, the Marselises used the Amsterdam merchant David Nicolaesz. Ruts as their agent in Russia, but ultimately decided that it was best to have one of their own represent their interests in Moscow.[89] Peter Marselis seems to have settled in Russia in 1629, a few years before Andries Winius.[90] His brother Selio brokered a loan in 1631 in Amsterdam to allow Alexander Leslie to buy arms and hire soldiers to fight for the tsar in the war with Poland that was to break out the following year.[91]

Through marriage, Peter and Selio Marselis were related to Samuel Sautijn, the gunpowder manufacturer, and Pieter Trip, the relative and business partner of Elias Trip.[92] When Marselis married Dorothea Barnesley in 1636 in Moscow, he became related through marriage as well to the Van Klenck family (and Koenraad's uncle Fentzel had been an agent of Sautijn).[93] Such familial ties explain why, after 1610, the foundation of any monopoly company for the trade on Russia like the VOC may have appeared superfluous.

After 1640, Winius fell out with Peter Marselis and Lus Tieleman Akema; when the conflict escalated, the Russian government and even the Dutch Estates-General tried to meditate between the rivals.[94] The dispute seems to have been resolved when Winius withdrew from the Tula enterprise and returned to trading in arms, which became more attractive when the tsar made him a *gost'*, that is, a member of the highest tier of the merchants' estate in Muscovy.[95] In 1653, Winius was dispatched to his native country to purchase arms and ammunition for the impending Polish campaign, on which occasion he was celebrated by an engraved portrait that carried the laudatory poem composed by Vondel mentioned earlier.[96] Vinius soon after his return to Moscow converted to Orthodoxy, as we saw.[97]

Peter Marselis, meanwhile, remained a staunch Calvinist, who employed a private minister throughout his life in Russia. Rather than await a definitive settlement about the ownership of the Tula plant, Marselis and Akema turned to building their own blast furnaces, forges, and smithies elsewhere in Russia. In 1647, all three foreign entrepreneurs definitively lost their title to the Tula business, which was taken over by a Muscovite government allegedly unhappy with the quality of the weapons made and the assortment produced in them.[98] But perhaps the court was rather exasperated by the interminable quarrel, for a mere year later, the Tula works were returned by the government to Marselis and Akema, even if only on the basis of a lease agreement.[99] They soon considerably expanded their enterprises and by 1653 even branched out into the production of gunpowder.[100] David Bacheracht (d. 1671) already had started powdermills, again using foreign masters, many of them Dutch, to lead the production process. While Bacheracht hailed from the Danish enclave of Glückstadt in northern Germany, his main financiers were Jan and Daniël Bernard (Bernaert/Bernart), two wealthy Zeeland-born Amsterdam financiers and brokers.[101] The Bernards had represented Marselis and Akema before the Estates-General at The Hague in 1647 and had a long-standing interest in the Russia trade.

The sums invested in the ironworks by Marselis were vast: In the 1660s, he invested at least 80,000 rubles in the Kashira plant (located along a sideriver of the Oka, between Tula and Moscow); this was the equivalent of 2,000 manual labourers' annual wage in contemporary Holland.[102] He was, in other words, as rich as any multimillionaire today, especially because he owned a welter of other businesses.[103] Marselis replaced Winius (who had died around 1660) as the favourite Western foreigner at the tsar's court in the 1660s. While Winius was sponsored by the tsar's mentor Boris Morozov (1590–1661), Tsar Aleksei's later confidant Afanasii Ordin-Nashchokin (1605–1680) patronised Marselis.[104] It bespeaks Marselis's importance that he travelled on the tsar's orders to Vienna, Königsberg, and Copenhagen in 1665 to seek support for Russian efforts to conclude a peace with Poland.[105] But Peter Marselis fell out of favour when his patron Ordin-Nashchokin took the tonsure in early 1671. Once Artamon Matveev (1625–1682) had become the tsar's new first minister, the young Andrei Vinius (son of Andries Winius) was preferred over Marselis.[106]

From the 1650s to the 1670s, the ironworks that Marselis and Akema ran south of Moscow produced cannon barrels, shot, and hand grenades; sometimes the iron was cast into rods to be further melted and forged for other purposes, such as the making of harnesses or handgun-barrels.[107] And the Tula and Kashira plants made sabres and pikes and other weapons as well. Some of their production entailed pots, pans, nails, and some agricultural tools, but they remained at most a sideshow. By 1675, Peter Marselis jr (the oldest of two sons both called Peter Marselis) was exporting Russian-made weapons to Denmark; the Russian arms industry was taking off.[108]

Between 1656 and 1658, Sweden and Muscovy fought an early version of the Gran Chaco War (or an echo of the Swedish-Danish wars of the period), symptomatic of the heyday of the Dutch arms production and trade and of Dutch capitalist hegemony in general. Both sides were supplied by Dutch arms manufacturers and exporters; the latter intermingled in their personal lives as Amsterdam neighbours, friends, and fellow regents and were often intermarried. Hendrik and Louys Trip had apprenticed in Sweden with their uncle Louys de Geer and supplied the Swedish side, whereas the firm of De Vogelaer and Van Klenck, together with the Dutch expatriates Marselis and Akema, furnished the Muscovites with their hardware.

7.4 Technology and Information

Dutch fortification experts began to serve the tsar soon after 1613 as well. Accomplished engineers such as Cosimo de Moucheron [f. 1620s], Jan Cornelisz. van Rodenburg, and Cornelis Claesz. were among them.[109] They contributed to the strengthening of the southern defensive line that was to stop Crimean Tatar raiding from Ukraine into Muscovite territory, while Claesz. also helped build the fortified walls of the towns of Astrakhan and Terskii gorod near the Caspian Sea.

Muscovite participation in the Military Revolution of the age was not limited to the warfare on land alone.[110] Even if his attempts failed,

Mikhail Romanov already tried to establish a seafaring navy (of sailships) on the Caspian Sea, but the project was as unsuccessful as that of his son Aleksei a generation later. Nonetheless, the effort was renewed under Peter with much greater success. Certainly until Peter's Grand Embassy, it was the Dutch who dominated the building of Russian sailships, working as shipwrights and sailors (and hired through the brokerage of Dutch entrepreneurs).[111]

It is germane as well to note that in the first half of the seventeenth century, Dutch merchants were purveyors of another rare commodity of considerable strategic value in early Romanov Muscovy: Information. That the firm of De Vogelaer and Van Klenck received the exclusive lease on several scare commodities found in Russian territory was partially payment for highly prized information they supplied about Europe west of Poland-Lithuania, an area as little known to the early Romanov tsars as Muscovy was to literate Western Europeans. Van Klenck and others (such as Isaac Massa) brought Western European newspapers to Russia and let themselves be debriefed by the Muscovite Foreign Office *(Posol'skii Prikaz)*.[112] Later, members of various Dutch embassies, and eventually the first Dutch permanent resident in Moscow (who was in residence from 1677 to 1698), Johan Willem van Keller, seem to have done the same.[113] In the 1660s, the Dutchman Jan van Sweeden established a postal service with Western and Central Europe, which responded to the Russian desire to gather more regularly key political and military news.[114] The same Van Sweeden also bought arms in the Republic and hired the ill-fated sailors and shipwrights who built the tsar's naval vessel, the *Oryol (Eagle)*.[115] Van Sweeden may have been inspired by Louys de Geer in developing a broad spectrum of initiatives, while he was certainly familiar with the enterprises of Peter Marselis in Muscovy.[116]

And an intriguing relationship developed between the Amsterdam regent Nicolaas Witsen and Russia. Witsen was the son of an Amsterdam burgomaster and a descendant of a family that made part of its fortune during the early stages of the Dutch trade on Arkhangel'sk.[117] This background may have piqued his interest in the country, and he was offered the opportunity to travel to Muscovy in in 1664 as part of Ambassador Jacob Boreel's suite visiting Tsar Aleksei Mikhailovich. During his sojourn, he interviewed Jan van Sweeden and the Russian patriarch Nikon, who was living in exile on his estate near Moscow.[118] It is likely, even if no definitive evidence has been found to prove it, that he struck up a friendship with the young interpreter assigned to the Dutch embassy by the tsar, Andrei Andreevich Vinius, with whom he afterwards might have maintained contact throughout the rest of their lives (they died within months of each other in 1716 and 1717).[119] Witsen made copious notes in a diary about his visit of 1664 and 1665, which remained unpublished, however, until the twentieth century. But he did use the information he gathered to begin to draft a map of Siberia, a project on which he worked all his life.[120] Not only did he tinker with the map, of which a first version was printed in 1687 (and given to Peter the Great), but he wrote an encyclopedic accompanying text, two versions of which (in 1692 and 1705) were printed for Witsen in a very small run.[121] Again, both books seem to have immediately been dispatched to Peter the Great (and to very few others).[122] Witsen supplied Peter with the first somewhat reliable modern map of Siberia, and Witsen's detailing of the languages, history, and culture of "North and East Tartary" will have added crucial data to the strategic information the tsar possessed regarding his Asian territories (and adjacent regions, such as China or Mongolia). In addition, Witsen had written a book on seafaring, which was keenly perused by the tsar, even if he was disappointed that the Amsterdam mayor could not furnish him with blueprints for the building of sailships.[123]

Witsen and Vinius arranged for the construction of Peter's first seafaring sailship in Amsterdam in the 1690s. In 1694, the *Santa Profetie*, flying the red, blue, and white Russian flag (emulating the Dutch flag), arrived at Arkhangel'sk, where the tsar himself was waiting for the vessel.[124] The ship was loaded with arms and ammunition, while it carried 44 iron cannons. Witsen proceeded to be the organiser of the tsar's stay in Amsterdam in 1697 and 1698. We do not quite know the scope of everything with which Witsen supplied Peter, but it is amply evident that he was pivotal player in facilitating Peter's program to make Russia into a Great Power, and even before 1689 may have provided the Russian government with invaluable strategic information through his exchanges with Vinius (who visited Holland in the 1670s as a Russian envoy, which likely strengthened his ties to Witsen).[125]

By the time of Peter's effective takeover in 1689, the prospect of breaking through to the Baltic shore by defeating Sweden and of forcing back the Crimean Tatars on to the peninsula seemed no longer outlandish (even if Peter proved yet incapable at defeating the Ottoman–Tatar coalition). As Peter's Grand Embassy of 1697–1698 proves, the Russians continued to be willing to learn from the most advanced countries in military-technological terms, the Dutch Republic, and (by then) Great Britain. Russia was on the brink of joining Europe's Great Powers. Peter's policies of stepped-up military-technological renewal through foreign expertise allowed Russia to join this select club.[126]

Notes

1. Von Wahlde's dissertation remains of interest, see Von Wahlde, "Military Thought," 2–6.
2. It is interesting to speculate whether Russian tolerance of the Dutch in the seventeenth century resembles that of Tokugawa Japan: Did the Dutch seem too insignificant to be considered a threat, were they especially good in waylaying any fears of cultural contamination, or did they have so much to offer that it was deemed foolish to banish them (or restrict their activities to the

barest minimum)? I am inclined at least for the Russian case to suggest that the third reason was decisive.

3. Frost, *Northern Wars*, 235.
4. Reger, "In the Service," 143.
5. Wijnroks, *Handel*, 229.
6. Yablonskaya, "Introduction," 12.
7. Ibid., 12.
8. See ibid., 11–12. It was easy to understand the Russian interest, as a large order (for some 10,000 musket barrels) had been placed on the Dutch market by a Dutch agent of the tsar in 1629 (ibid., 13). This Burgh-Van Veltdriel Embassy suggested to pay Muscovy with a huge supply of arms for grain shipments to the Republic (Kotilaine, "When the Twain," 125).
9. Yablonskaya, "Introduction," 15.
10. Ibid., 15.
11. Longworth, *Russia*, 128–38.
12. Despite his well-nigh encyclopedic knowledge, Fernand Braudel omits any mention of the Russian importation of (expensive) firearms, without which Muscovy would not have survived against their Polish, Swedish, and Ottoman foes (see Braudel, *Civilization and Capitalism*, vol. 3, 442–3). Braudel seems to be discussing the sixteenth and seventeenth centuries in suggesting that the volume of Russian trade with Iran and Central Asia must have exceeded that with Europe; Kotilaine has definitively proved that to be wrong, at least for the seventeenth century and at least for the value of the foreign trade (Kotilaine, "When the Twain," 104–42, 1046–122). When one looks at arms importation, this seems more than evident.
13. Kotiliane, "When the Twain," 114–15. The first Cossack forays occurred in the 1580s, but the Russian presence remained shaky the first decades following Ermak's campaign.
14. Paul, "Military Revolution," 11.
15. Kotilaine, "When the Twain," 1–2, 114, 125. The English Muscovy Company traded arms on Russia from the 1550s onward (see Veluwenkamp, *Archangel*, 22).
16. Amburger, *Die Familie*, 70.
17. For a comprehensive database, see the database *Notariele akten over de Archangelvaart*.
18. Demkin, "Rospisi." It is curious to note that this local governor who oversaw the count was Prince Pyotr Prozorovskii, an omnipresent actor in Tsar Aleksei's reign, whose life often intersected with Dutchmen.
19. In great detail, the number of Dutch ships can be found on the database *Notariele akten over de Archangelvaart*.
20. Israel, *Dutch Primacy*; see, for a similar argument, De Vries and Van der Woude, *First Modern Economy*.
21. For the Trips in Russia, see Klein, *De Trippen*, 23; Elias, ed., "Contract tot oprichting," 360–1, 363. See further, too, Brugmans, *Geschiedenis*, vol. 3, 15–16. One of the initially successful Dutch merchants of the early Romanov period was Karel Janszoon du Moulin (Carel Molijn), who had the magnificent Elswout estate built near Haarlem; after falling on hard times, he was forced to sell it to Gabriel Marselis jr (see Amburger, *Die Familie*, 51; and the inventory available at http://noord-hollandsarchief.nl/bronnen/archieven?mivast=236&mizig=210&miadt=236&miaet=1&micode=160&minr=850348&miview=inv2&milang=nl, accessed 28 February 2017).
22. Brünner suggest that already in the mid-1590s an attempt was made (see Brünner, "De ontwikkeling," 361). Even if this did not lead to a formal organisation, there was a sort of loose form of collaboration between

Dutch-speaking merchants on Russia, at least until the end of the Time of Troubles, around 1613 (ibid., 361–3).

23. For a list, see Valentijn, *Oud en nieuw Oost-Indiën*, vol. 1, 188.
24. For Gerrit Bicker, see Van der Vlugt, *Wij zijn*, 58–9; Andries Bicker, who became later one of the city's mayors, was also involved in the fur trade with Russia (ibid., 101).
25. Valentijn, *Oud en nieuw Oost-Indiën*, vol. 1, 168, 176.
26. Veluwenkamp, *Archangel*, 60. The De Vogelaers were related to both the Huygens and Cats families, who included leading political figures of the age.
27. Kotilaine, "When the Twain," 129, 131, and Table 2.4, 135; see as well Amburger, *Die Familie*, 81 and 81n332. As remarked in an earlier note, the amount of Dutch politicians who can be linked to the Russia trade is astounding: Witsen, Van Klenck, Johan de Witt (married to Wendela Bicker), Jacob Boreel, Jacob Cats, Constantijn Huygens jr and sr are all among them, to name only the most conspicuous ones.
28. David Nicolaasz. Ruts organised the transport of a significant amount of grain from Russia to Denmark during Christiaan IV's involvement in the Thirty Years' War in 1626 (Lauridsen, *Marselis Konsortiet*, 28). The 1631 commissioning of Rembrandt to paint the portrait of Nicolaes Ruts (in Russian furs) and (c. 1622) of Frans Hals to depict Massa and his wife Beatrix van der Laan attest to the lucrative quality of these endeavours (the Rembrandt is at the *Frick Collection* in New York City; the Hals at Amsterdam's *Rijksmuseum*). Coenraed Burgh, ambassador to the tsar in 1648, married into the Hooft family, another dynasty of regents. Burgh's father Albert had on a previous embassy gifted Tsar Mikhail Romanov with no fewer than 2,000 muskets; this on the eve of the Smolensk War; Burgh was also a WIC Director.
29. Jarmo Kotilaine convincingly suggests that early Romanov Russia was suffering from a severe shortage of precious metals which made extensive import of bullion necessary, as the country was a "highly monetized society" (Kotilaine, "When the Twain," 1).
30. Only because it already had reached a high volume previously, the longer established trade on Scandinavia and the eastern Baltic did not receive a similar bump between 1585 and 1600.
31. Wijnroks, *Handel*; Gelderblom, *Zuid-Nederlandse kooplieden*.
32. Driessen, "Het gezantschap," 54.
33. Wijnroks, *Handel*; Veluwenkamp, *Archangel*. Meanwhile, although Middelburg in Zeeland played a minor role in this trade during the early days after the fall of Antwerp in 1585, the overwhelming majority of goods arriving from or departing for Russia went through Amsterdam (see Kotilaine, "When the Twain," 107–8).
34. Wijnroks, *Handel*, 200–9. It is noteworthy as well that the sixteenth-century trade between the Low Countries and Russia was not very profitable, as it was mainly one of Russian raw materials in exchange for luxury goods or spices, or even bullion (as noted earlier). Goods such as tar, hemp, or wood could also be shipped from elsewhere to Antwerp or Amsterdam. For further detail, see as well Brünner, "De ontwikkeling."
35. Veluwenkamp, *Archangel*, 47; De Stoppelaar, *Balthasar*, 61–73.
36. There were sporadic deliveries during the Troubles, apparently, see Veluwenkamp, *Archangel*, 69.
37. For the fur trade that took flight after 1600, see Fisher, *Russian Fur*, 184, 190–3.
38. Kotilaine, "When the Twain," 36. See also ibid., 110–11.
39. Wijnroks, *Handel*, 364.

40. Van der Meiden, "Isaac Massa."
41. Klooster, *Dutch Moment*, 18; see also Wijnroks, *Handel*.
42. See Yablonskaya, "Introduction," 11.
43. Amburger, *Die Familie*, 76.
44. Ibid., 78.
45. For Sweden's dependence on the Dutch, see Blom and Bas-Backer, *Op reis*, 31; for the moedernegotie with Poland, see Davies, *God's Playground*, 198–223. From 1614, Sweden and the Republic had an alliance, which lasted in effect almost until the death of Gustavus Adolphus in the 1630s (see Kotilaine, "When the Twain," 115–16, 124–5). Semen Zabarovskii and Stepan Ushakov failed to gain permission for Dutch arms deliveries in 1613–1614 (see Scheltema, *Rusland*, vol. 1, 75). Later, Isaac Massa fruitlessly tried to get the government of the province of Holland more interested in a closer alliance and trading partnership with Russia, but the Estates of Holland turned a deaf ear to his proposals. At best, they gave Massa occasionally the brief to engage in a sort of "fact-finding mission." Already in 1615, a second Russian mission called at The Hague (led by Ivan Kondyrev and Mikhail Nemerov), requesting arms, and, tellingly (as it appears to hint at Dutch soldierly renown), asking the Estates-General to order Dutchmen to leave Swedish or Polish military service (Kordt, "Ocherk," cxxix; Van der Meiden, "Isaac Massa," 6). The Estates-General noted in response that inhabitants of the United Provinces were not allowed to enlist in the military of foreign powers.
46. Kordt, "Ocherk," cxlviii, cxlix; Van der Meiden, "Isaac Massa," 9, 11.
47. Kotilaine, "When the Twain," 116n496. A ruble had the value of five guilders in the seventeenth century.
48. Wijnroks, *Handel*, 233–5. Massa promised the Russians almost unlimited supplies of arms (Kotilaine, "When the Twain," 116).
49. Driessen, "Het gezantschap," 56, 64. The account of this trip by Anthonis Goeteeris, one of the first authentic Dutch accounts about the Russians, was recently republished (see Blom and Bas-Backer, *Op reis*).
50. Veluwenkamp, *Archangel*, 69.
51. Yablonskaya, "Dutch Firearms," 52.
52. Wijnroks, *Handel*, 236–7.
53. Heeringa, ed., "Overzicht," 49.
54. Ibid., 51.
55. See Kotilaine, "When the Twain," 53–86. Selio and Peter Marselis imported a great quantity of rye from Russia in 1633, at a time when others such as Andries Winius also attempted to divert the Amsterdam grain market to Russia, or, more likely, to smuggle the grain to Flanders (see De Boer, "een Amsterdamsche 'lorrendraayer'," 50–1).
56. See Yablonskaya, et al., eds, *Dutch Guns*.
57. See Yablonskaya, "Introduction," 13–14. Yablonskaya is *not* attempting to supply a comprehensive count of imported weapons around 1630, but her example alone adds up to 10,000 firearms imported from the Republic on the eve of the Smolensk War. Meanwhile, the Republic itself was still fighting Spain, and so forth.
58. Yablonskaya, "Introduction," 13–14. Trip may have dispatched 50,000 muskets in 1630 (ibid., 14). Note as well the recruitment of "German" cannonmakers by Arent Arentszoon van Stellingwerff in the wake of the disappointing employment of Julius (Elisei) Coyett in the early 1630s; Van Stellingwerff hired the Leeuwarden clock- and cannonmaster Hans Falck (see Reger, "In the Service," 20). It is likely that Coyett, a relative of Balthasar Coyett (the son of Frederick Coyett) who wrote the anonymous account of

the Van Klenck embassy of 1675–1676, was a native from Brabant rather than "Wallonia," as Reger suggests (see Vitsen, *Puteshestvie*, 247–8n268). Julius's son Otto continued his father's glass-blowing manufactory after his father's death in 1634. Otto died in 1660, after which his son Peter took over the works. In how far they had anything to do with Russian cannon-casting after 1634 is unclear.

59. See Amburger, *Die Familie*, 95–6fn388.
60. Reger, "In the Service," 24. Burgh was a founder of the WIC, see Odegard, "Colonial Careers," 224.
61. The work by Richard Hellie on this remains seminal (see Hellie, *Enserfment*), but works by Brian Davies, Carol Belkin Stevens, and William Reger are also essential reading (Brian Davies, *Warfare*; Stevens, *Russia's Wars*; Reger, "In the Service"). For the Polish perspective, see Norman Davies, *God's Playground*, vol. 1; for the Swedes, see Michael Roberts, *Essays*; Glete, *Fiscal-Military State*; and, for the ultimate Russian victory in the north (-west), Frost, *Northern*.
62. Reger, "In the Service," 91. And note the purchases of 1653, 1654, and 1655 and beyond, see Amburger, *Die Familie*, 117 and 117n591, 118.
63. Kotiliane, "When the Twain," 125, 127–8. The ambassadors were interested in saltpetre and grain as an alternative to the halting Polish supply. The Danes had, through the brokerage of David Ruts and Gabriel Marselis, begun to import Russian grain in 1626 (see Amburger, *Die Familie*, 33).
64. Wagenaar, *Amsterdam*, vol. 5, 60; see for more Boterbloem, "Dutch Mercenaries," 64–7.
65. Coyett, *Historisch Verhael*, 86–7. Parts of Coyett's description seem to be almost literally lifted from the ambassador's report to the Estates-General (cf. *Nationaal Archief, archief der Staten-Generaal SG* 8586, folio 296). Another account (of part of the trip) can be encountered in *Hollantse Mercurius*, January 1676, 13–14, which notes that among the people lining up for the entry of Van Klenck into Moscow were the tsar's foreign officers, of whom a number were Dutch ("*uytlanse Bevel-hebbers*," ibid., 14).
66. Kotilaine, "When the Twain," 1–2, 114, 125.
67. Nefedov, "Reformy," 41.
68. Kotilaine, "When the Twain." "The Dutch, especially, possessed unparalleled capital and technical resources which made them the most competitive group of foreign merchants in Russia" (Kotilaine, "When the Twain," 4, 36–7). For some illustration of the Dutch outdistancing their competitors, see ibid., 76, 83 Figure 2.3, 104, 107–8, 130 Table 2.3, 135 Table 2.4, 142–3.
69. It is of significance that the Dutch in the seventeenth century also supplied most of the *Moskovskie inozemtsy*, a sort of green-card holders or landed immigrants, in Russia (see Kotilaine, "When the Twain," 111).
70. See Fuhrmann, *Origins of Capitalism*; Amburger, *Die Familie*, 97–101, 128–9.
71. The most elaborate discussion about this enterprise (and others these entrepreneurs subsequently founded) in English is Fuhrmann, *Origins of Capitalism*, 51–115. See as well Amburger, *Die Familie*, 97–102.
72. Esper, "Military Self-Sufficiency," 197; see as well Reger, "In the Service," 18–20.
73. See Fuhrmann, *Origins*, 11.
74. Veluwenkamp, *Archangel*, 70; Amburger, *Die Familie*, 97–102; Fuhrmann, *Origins*, 51–90. Elias Trip was one of the investors, as was Pieter, while Selio Marselis served as a consultant in its initial stages (Amburger, *Die Familie*, 100; Van Dillen, ed., "Amsterdamsche notarieele acten," 243–4). Amburger

notes that iron was almost exclusively cast for weaponry (Amburger, *Die Familie*, 102).

75. Esper, "Military Self-Sufficiency," 199.
76. Fuhrmann, *Origins*, 265. See also ibid., 250–1.
77. Esper, "Military Self-Sufficiency," 203. And the manufactories of Winius and Marselis seem to have churned out some but not all of the parts of weapons; other parts often were produced in Moscow, or arms were assembled in Moscow using parts manufactured elsewhere (see Reger, "In the Service," 287).
78. Esper, "Military Self-Sufficiency," 205–6.
79. See Amburger, *Die Familie*, 120–1fn18. See, for an example of such hiring (by Lus Tieleman Akema) of an ironworker, Pierre Priou van Hesdan [a village likely located in Hainault province] in Amsterdam in 1641 (Van Dillen, ed., *Bronnen*, vol. 3, 307–9). Editor Van Dillen noted how Gabriel Marselis jr, too, hired Walloon iron forgers on behalf of his brother Peter in the same year in Amsterdam (ibid., 309n). Isaac Bernard (Beernaert) was usually the intermediary in hiring the smiths for Marselis and company.
80. Van Dillen, ed., "Amsterdamsche notarieele acten," 245–6. It may be significant that Trip was quarrelling with De Geer and the Swedish government at precisely this time (ibid., 216–17, 247–8, 255–6, 261–2).
81. For an overview of the various arms manufactories in the middle of the seventeenth century, see Reger, "In the Service," 283–5.
82. Ibid., 171.
83. See as well Amburger, *Die Familie*, 187–8.
84. Ibid., 74.
85. Ibid., 80.
86. Ibid., 118; Yablonskaya et al., eds, *Dutch Guns in Russia*, 150.
87. Frost, *Northern Wars*, 164–5.
88. Amburger, *Die Familie*, 68–9.
89. Ibid., 70. Ruts later involved himself in efforts to purchase saltpetre on behalf of the Danish king (ibid., 76); he made a fortune, and his descendants were still active in Russia in the 1670s.
90. Ibid., 36, 76.
91. Ibid., 79.
92. Ibid., 37, 78.
93. Ibid., 77–8. Jurriaan van Klenck was married to Geertruid Fentzel, whose brother married a sister of Dorothea Barnesley. Amburger notes that in the heat of the battle with Winius in 1647, Isaac Bernard had the Estates-General recognise Peter Marselis as a Dutch citizen (ibid., 108).
94. See Boterbloem, *Moderniser*, 37–8; Amburger, *Die Familie*, 105–6. Amburger suggests that Winius gained the upper hand with the accession of Aleksei in 1645, because the tsar's tutor was Boris Morozov, who had invested in the Tula works. But Morozov's banishment from Moscow a few years later will have damaged Winius's standing.
95. For Winius's purchase of arms in the Dutch Republic in 1653, see, for example, Amburger, *Die Familie*, 117n591; see also Harris, *Marselis-Slaegten*, 73.
96. See Boterbloem, *Moderniser*, 38–9.
97. In his travel notes, Nicolaas Witsen depicts a general consensus among the Dutch community in Moscow that condemned Winius's behaviour as that of a cynical renegade, who hit his wife to boot (see Witsen, *Moscovische*, vol. 3, 411, and 411n1).
98. Amburger, *Die Familie*, 106–7.
99. Ibid., 109–11.

100. Ibid., 110–13.
101. Veluwenkamp, *Archangel*, 146–7.
102. Amburger, *Die Familie*, 112, 131; Van Deursen, *Plain Lives*, 7–8.
103. This despite the fall-out from the copper crisis in Moscow of 1662 (see Amburger, *Die Familie*, 124). He seems to have made a comeback by successfully currying favour with Afanasii Ordin-Nashchokin, Tsar Aleksei's most trusted advisor from 1667 to 1671 (ibid., 136).
104. Amburger, *Die Familie*, 136, 143–4.
105. Ibid., 136–7. In the last years of Mikhail's reign, Peter Marselis had vainly tried to help conclude a Russian-Danish dynastic marriage (the attempt failed because the Danish prince Waldemar refused to convert to Orthodoxy); it may be that his star was temporarily eclipsed by Andries Winius at the court because of this botched affair. In any event, Aleksei chose upon his accession his own inner circle, different from his father's.
106. Amburger, *Die Familie*, 158–9; for more on Andrei Vinius, see Boterbloem, *Moderniser of Russia*.
107. Amburger, *Die Familie*, 114–15, 151–3, 162–3.
108. Ibid., 163.
109. De Moucheron arrived in 1624 (see Heeringa, ed., "Overzicht," 50). Cos(i) mo de Moucheron was the father-in-law of David Ruts (see Amburger, *Die Familie*, 81n332). See further for De Moucheron and Claesz., De Stoppelaar, *Balthasar*, 69, 92n4. For Rodenburg, see Brian Davies, *Warfare*, 74, 80, 88.
110. It is noteworthy that late Ming officials in China seem to have been awed as well by the Dutch seaships; the Russian admiration certainly lasted until the Great Embassy (see Andrade, *Lost Colony*, 36).
111. See Phillips, *Founding*.
112. Shamin, *Kuranty*, 74–5; Waugh and Maier, "Muscovy," 84.
113. On Van Keller as a source of information for the Dutch government, see Eekman, "Muscovy's." But see how, conversely, he informed Peter about battlefield victories by William III (ibid., 50).
114. Amburger, *Die Familie*, 155.
115. See Boterbloem, *Fiction and Reality*. See as well *Notariele Akten*, 108: From this latter source, it is evident that Van Sweeden may have loaded one or two ships in Amsterdam with arms for Arkhangel'sk in 1660. Yablonskaya's essay appears to suggest that this delivery amounted to no fewer than 35,000 firearms (Yablonskaya, "Introduction," 14); Van Sweeden seems to have partnered with the Swellengrebels.
116. See Breedvelt-van Veen, *Louis de Geer*, 121–23, 135–6, 139–40. Like De Geer, Van Sweeden, too, received strong government support to make his enterprises viable.
117. The dissertation and book by Marion Peters are the standard works for those interested in this fascinating figure (see Peters, *De wijze koopman*; Peters, "Mercator Sapiens").
118. See Witsen, *Moscovische Reyse*, vol. 2, 267–89; ibid., vol. 3, 373–88. The conversation with Van Sweeden was almost as remarkable as that with Nikon, since Boreel was accusing Van Sweeden of malfeasance in his dealings with other Dutch traders before the tsar.
119. Vinius, in fact, was a distant relative of Witsen. Wladimiroff's book is based on the hypothesis that the two carried on a secret correspondence from 1665 onward, but he admits that he has no conclusive proof for his argument; given the stream of information Witsen received regarding Siberia and its environs, he must have had people in Russia supplying him with it; undoubtedly, too, some sort of *quid pro quo* agreement may have existed

with those who worked for the tsar's government, with Witsen informing them about the affairs of his country and its neighbours (see Wladimiroff, *De kaart*, 131, 277).

120. Witsen map. The best (and most up-to-date) overview of Witsen's *magnum opus* is Bruno Naarden, "Nicolaas Witsen en Tartarye."
121. Witsen, *Noord*; Peters, *De wijze koopman*, 172–6.
122. Peters, *De wijze koopman*, 191, 194.
123. Bogoslovskii, *Petr*, 175. Of Witsen's other major work, two editions, this time in a larger print run, were published: Witsen, *Aeloude*; Witsen, *Architectura Navalis.*
124. Bogoslovskii, *Petr*, vol. 1, 176–7.
125. Boterbloem, *Moderniser*, 77–86.
126. For more, see Von Wahlde, "Military Thought," 6–9.

Bibliography

Amburger, E. *Die Familie Marselis*, Gießen: Wilhelm Schmitz, 1957.

Andrade, Tonio. *Lost Colony: The Untold Story of China's First Victory over the West*, Princeton, NJ: Princeton University Press, 2011.

Belkin Stevens, Carol. *Russia's Wars of Emergence, 1460–1730*, London: Routledge, 2007.

Blom, F., and P. Bas-Backer. *Op reis voor vrede*, Zutphen: Walburg, 2014.

Boer, G.W. de. "Een Amsterdamsche 'lorrendraayer' Celio Marselis," *Jaarboek van het Genootschap Amstelodamum* 38, 1941, 37–66.

Bogoslovskii, M.M. *Petr I. Materialy dlia biografii*, vol. 1, Moskva: Nauka, 2005.

Boterbloem, Kees. "Dutch Mercenaries in the Tsar's Service: The Van Bockhoven Clan," *War and Society* 2, 2014, 59–78.

———. *The Fiction and Reality of Jan Struys: A Seventeenth-Century Dutch Globetrotter*, Houndmills, Basingstoke: Palgrave, 2008.

———. *Moderniser Of Russia: Andrei Vinius, 1641–1716*, London: Palgrave, 2013.

Braudel, F. *Civilization and Capitalism*, 3 vols, Berkeley, CA: University of California Press, 1992.

Breedvelt-van Veen, F. *Louis de Geer, 1587–1652*, Amsterdam: Paris, 1935.

Brugmans, H. *Geschiedenis van Amsterdam*, vol. 3: *Bloeitijd, 1621–97*, 2n ed., Utrecht: Het Spectrum, 1973.

Brünner, E.C.G. "De ontwikkeling van het handelsverkeer van Holland met Oost-Europa tot het einde der 16e eeuw," *Tijdschrift voor Geschiedenis* 41, 1926, 353–71.

Coyett, Balthasar. *Historisch Verhael of Beschryving van de Voyagie gedaan onder de Suite van den Heere Koenraad van Klenck*, Amsterdam: Jan ten Hoorn, 1677.

Davies, Brian. *Warfare, State and Society on the Black Sea Steppe, 1500–1700*, London: Routledge, 2007.

Davies, Norman. *God's Playground*, vol. 1, New York: Columbia University Press, 1979.

Demkin, A.V. " 'Rospisi karablem' zapadnoevropeiskikh kuptsov, sostavlennye v Arkhangel'ske v 1658 g.," *Issledovaniia po istochnikovedeniiu SSSR dooktiabrskogo perioda*, Moscow: Akademii Nauk, 1987, 89–113.

Deursen, A.Th. van. *Plain Lives in a Golden Age*, Cambridge: Cambridge University Press, 1991.

Dillen, J.G. van. "Amsterdamsche notarieele acten betreffende den koperhandel en de uitoefening van mijnbouw en metaalindustrie in Zweden," *Bijdragen en Mededeelingen van het Historisch Genootschap*, 58, 1937, 211–301.

———. *Bronnen tot de Geschiedenis van het bedrijfswezen en gildewezen in Amsterdam*, 3 vols., 's-Gravenhage: M. Nijhoff, 1929.

Driessen, J. "Het Gezantschap van Reinoud van Brederode in 1615 en 1616 naar Rusland," in J. Driessen, W. Roobol and Marc Jansen, eds, *Rusland in Nederlandse ogen*, Amsterdam: van Oorschot, 1986, 51–73.

Eekman, Thomas. "Muscovy's International Relations in the Late Seventeenth Century," *California Slavic Studies* 14, 1993, 44–67.

Elias, J.E., ed. "Contract tot oprichting van een Zweedsch factorie-comptoir te Amsterdam in 1663," *Bijdragen en Mededelingen van het Historisch Genootschap* 24, 1903, 356–400.

Esper, Thomas. "Military Self-Sufficiency in Muscovite Russia," *Slavic Review* 2, 1969, 185–208.

Fisher, R.H. *The Russian Fur Trade, 1550–1700*, Berkeley and Los Angeles, CA: University of California Press, 1943.

Frost, Robert. *The Northern Wars: War, State and Society in Northeastern Europe, 1558–1721*, Harlow: Longman, 2000.

Fuhrmann, Joseph T. *The Origins of Capitalism in Russia*, Chicago, IL: Quadangle Books, 1972.

Gelderblom, Oscar. *Zuid-Nederlandse kooplieden en de opkomst van de Amsterdamse stapelmarkt (1578–1630)*, Hilversum: Verloren, 2000.

Glete, Jan. *War and the State in Early Modern Europe*, New York: Routledge, 2002.

Harris, Poul. *Marselis-Slaegten*, Arhus: Centrum, 1980.

Heeringa, K., ed., "Overzicht van de betrekkingen van Rusland tot Nederland tot aan het jaar 1800, door N.N. Bantysj-Kamenskij," *Bijdragen en Mededeelingen van het Historisch Genootschap* 51, 1930: 35–103.

Hellie, Richard. *Enserfment and Military Change in Muscovy*, Chicago, IL: University of Chicago Press, 1971.

Hollantse Mercurius, January 1676.

Israel, Jonathan. *Dutch Primacy in the World Trade, 1585–1740*, Oxford: Oxford University Press, 1989.

Klein, P.W. *De Trippen in de Zeventiende Eeuw*, Assen: Van Gorcum, 1965.

Klooster, Wim. *The Dutch Moment: War, Trade and Settlement in the Seventeenth-Century Atlantic World*, Ithaca, NY: Cornell University Press, 2016.

Kordt, V.A. "Ocherk snoshenii Moskovskogo gosudarstva s Respublikoi Soedinennykh Niderlandov do 1631g.," *Sbornik Imperatorskago Russkago Istoricheskago Obshchestva* 116, 1902: iii–cccvii.

Kotilaine, Jarmo. "When the Twain Did Meet: Foreign Merchants and Russia's Economic Expansion in the Seventeenth Century," unpubl. Ph.D. diss., Harvard University, 2000.

Lauridsen, John T. *Marselis Konsortiet: En Studie over Forholdet Mellem Handelskapital og Kongemagt i 1600-Tallets Danmark*, Arhus: Jysk Selskab for Historie, 1987.

Longworth, Philip. *Russia: The Once and Future Empire from Pre-History to Putin*, New York: Macmillan, 2005.

Meiden, G.W. van der. "Isaac Massa and the beginnings of Dutch-Russian Relations," 3, available as pdf file at https://commons.wikimedia.org/wiki/File:Isaac_Massa.pdf, accessed 9 September 2016.

Naarden, Bruno. "Nicolaas Witsen en Tartarye," available at: http://resources.huygens.knaw.nl/retroboeken/witsen/dutch_intro.pdf, accessed 4 May 2019.

Nefedov, S.A. "Reformy serediny xvii veka: Popytka modernizatsii Rossii po gollandskomu obraztsu," in A.K. Levykin, ed., *Zapadnoevropeiskie spetsialisty v Rossii xv-xvii vekov*, Moscow: Moskovskii Kreml, 2002, 40–3.

Notariele akten over de Archangelvaart, available at: http://resources.huygens.knaw.nl/archangel/app/inleiding?lang.age_of_user=en, accessed 23 February 2019.

Odegard, Erik. "Colonial Careers: Johan Maurits van Nassau, Rijckloff Volckertsz. van Goens and Career-Making in the Early Modern Dutch Empire," unpubl. Ph.D. diss., University of Leyden, 2018.

Paul, Michael C. "The Military Revolution in Russia, 1550–1682," *Journal of Military History* 1, 2004, 9–45.

Peters, M. "'Mercator Sapiens' ['De Wijze Koopman']. Het wereldwijde onderzoek van Nicolaes Witsen [1641–1717], burgemeester en VOC-bewindhebber van Amsterdam," unpubl. Ph.D. diss., Rijksuniversiteit Groningen, 2008.

———. *De wijze koopman: Het wereldwijde onderzoek van Nicolaes Witsen (1641–1717), burgemeester en VOC-bewindhebber van Amsterdam*, Amsterdam: Bert Bakker, 2010.

Phillips, E.J. *The Founding of Russia's Navy: Peter the Great and the Azov Fleet*, Westport, CT: Praeger, 1995.

Reger, W.M. "In the Service of the Tsar: European Mercenary Officers and the Reception of Military Reform in Russia, 1654–1667," unpubl. Ph.D. diss., University of Illinois at Urbana-Champaign, 1997.

Roberts, M. *Essays in Swedish History*, London: Weidenfeld and Nicholson, 1967.

Scheltema, J. *Rusland en de Nederlanden*, vol. 1, Amsterdam: Hendrik Gartman, 1817.

Shamin, S.M. *Kuranty XVII stoletiia: Evropeiskaia pressa v Rossii i voznikovenie russkoi periodicheskoi pechati*, Moscow: Al'ians-Arkheo, 2011.

Stoppelaar, J. de. *Balthasar Moucheron*, Den Haag: Nijhoff, 1901.

Valentijn, François. *Oud en Nieuw Oost-Indiën. . .*, vol. 1, Dordrecht and Amsterdam: J. Van Braam en G. onder den Linden, 1724.

Veluwenkamp, J.W. *Archangel: Nederlandse ondernemers in Rusland, 1550–1785*, Amsterdam: Balans, 2000.

Vitsen, N. *Puteshestvie v Moskoviiu, 1664–1665: Dnevnik*, trans. V.G. Trisman, Sankt-Peterburg: Symposium, 1996.

Vlugt, Simone van der. *Wij zijn de Bickers*, Amsterdam: Prometheus, 2019.

Vries, Jan de, and A. van der Woude. *The First Modern Economy: Success, Failure and Perseverance of the Dutch Economy, 1500–1815*, Cambridge: Cambridge University Press, 1997.

Wagenaar, Jan. *Amsterdam in zijne opkomst*, 13 vols., Amsterdam: Isaak Tirion, 1760-c.1784.

Wahlde, Peter von. "Military Thought in Imperial Russia," unpubl. Ph.D. diss., Indiana University, 1966.

Waugh, Daniel, and Ingrid Maier. "Muscovy and the European Information Revolution," in Simon Franklin and Katherine Bowers, eds, *Information and*

Empire: Mechanisms of Communication in Russia, 1600–1850, Cambridge: OpenBook Publishers, 2017, 78–112.

Wijnroks, E. *Handel tussen Rusland en de Nederlanden 1560–1640: Een netwerkanalyse van de Antwerpse en Amsterdamse kooplieden, handelend op Rusland*, Hilversum: Verloren, 2003.

Witsen, N. *Aeloude en hedendaegsche Scheepsbouw en Bestier. . .*, Amsterdam: C. Commelijn, Broer and Jan Appelaer, 1671.

———. *Architectura Navalis et Regimen Nauticum: Ofte Aaloude en Hedendaagsche Scheeps-bouw en Bestier. . .*, Amsterdam: Pieter and Joan Blaeu, 1690.

———. [map] available at: http://resources.huygens.knaw.nl/retrofiles/witsen/images/map_large.pdf, accessed 4 May 2019.

———. *Moscovische reyse 1664–5: Journaal en aentekeningen*, eds P. de Buck and T. Locher, 3 vols., Den Haag: Nijhoff, 1966–67.

———. *Noord en Oost Tartarye, Ofte Bondig Ontwerp van Enige Dier Landen en Volken, Welke Voormaels Bekent Zijn Geweest*, Amsterdam: François Halma, 1705, available at: http://resources.huygens.knaw.nl/retroboeken/witsen/#source=1&page=13&accessor=toc&view=homePane, accessed 4 May 2019.

Wladimiroff, Igor. *De kaart van een verzwegen vriendschap*, Groningen: INOS-NRCe, 2008.

Yablonskaya, E.A. "Dutch Firearms of the 17th and 18th Centuries in the State Armoury Collection," in E.A. Yablonskaya et al., eds, *Dutch Guns in Russia*, Amsterdam and Zwolle: Rijksmuseum and Waanders, 1996, 51–3.

———. "Introduction to the Catalogue," in E.A. Yablonskaya et al., eds, *Dutch Guns in Russia*, Amsterdam and Zwolle: Rijksmuseum and Waanders, 1996, 10–29.

Yablonskaya, E.A., M.N. Larchenko, H.L. Blackmore et al., eds. *Dutch Guns in Russia*, Amsterdam and Zwolle: Rijksmuseum and Waanders, 1996.

8 Dutch Activity in Russia, Part 2

Merchants and Mercenaries

8.1 Another Case Study: The Van Klencks

From the 1600s onward, the Russia trade made the fortune of many in Holland and Zeeland; a pioneer like Isaac Massa may not have become as rich as some others through his work in Russia, but he had been a *factor* (representative) of the Witsen family, who did gain fabulous riches through a variety of ventures, of which the Russia trade was an important component.[1] Wealth translated into political power; following the footsteps of his father and uncle, both Russia traders, Cornelis Witsen became mayor of Amsterdam. Cornelis's son was the renowned *mercator-sapiens* Nicolaas Witsen, a correspondent of the Royal Society, the author of the first description of Siberia and the history of shipbuilding; he served several yearly terms as one of the four Amsterdam mayors who led the city, and represented Amsterdam at William III's side in London in 1689.[2]

Even before 1614, it dawned upon Dutch adventurers such as Massa that fortunes could be made in Muscovy, a country then still embroiled in turmoil. Such a challenge appealed, too, to George, or Jurriaan, as he seems to have called himself, van Klenck, who became one of those merchants who massively augmented his family's fortune by way of the Russia trade.[3] Starting out as the factor of the De Vogelaer company in Muscovy, Jurriaan was among those exploiting the seemingly boundless opportunities offered by trade with Romanov Russia, even if it exposed him to considerable risk, such as when he was robbed by highwaymen during the Time of Troubles.[4] Subsequently, he was imprisoned in the mid-1620s when he refused to pay a Russian merchant for an unsatisfactory caviar delivery.[5] But such setbacks did not stop Jurriaan van Klenck, and he went on to become a partner with the sons of Marcus de Vogelaer sr and a key operator in establishing a sustained and flourishing arms trade with the tsar after the Time of Troubles.

Jurriaan van Klenck died in 1643 before he had groomed a real successor. His death came at a time when other challenges undermined his company's fortunes. His third son, Koenraad, was still an adolescent, too young to step into his father's shoes. Koenraad's older brothers, Johannes and Herman, might have been old enough, but they lacked their father's nerve and knack for business and had turned to other matters: Johannes was a bookish character who had become a philosophy teacher (he was specialised in Grotius's work) at Amsterdam's Atheneum Illustre, a school of higher learning. Herman studied law and was to become a VOC administrator in the Indies. From his questionable behaviour during the failed attempt to save Taiwan, one might infer that he lacked the pluck of his father or younger brother.[6]

In addition, the business may have seemed an unattractive proposition to Johannes or Herman: During the 1640s, the Russian government reimposed full fees on the goods De Vogelaer and Van Klenck imported and exported; a low point was reached in 1652 when the authorities evicted the company on religious grounds from its house in central Moscow.[7] The premises had lodged company agents and had functioned as a warehouse since the early part of the century.

Muscovy was restless during the first years of Aleksei Mikhailovich's reign, and some of the state's policies donned an anti-Western guise to the detriment of Dutch traders.[8] An effort was undertaken to subdue foreign influence in Russia, in part through religious concerns about the contamination of Orthodoxy by heretical Westerners but also in response to Russian merchants' incessant complaints about Western traders outcompeting them and enjoying unfair advantages. The growing xenophobia (and the closing of the ranks of the elite and tsar around the Russian cause) was expressed in the set of basic laws *(Ulozhenie)* of 1649. In that year, English merchants were comprehensively banished from operating inside of Muscovy, a decision provoked by the execution of King Charles I, which offended Russian sensibilities. Contemplating the expulsion of the Dutch (and their junior partners, the Hamburgers) as well, they stopped short of such a step because the Dutch were indispensable as their major arms suppliers.[9] And although several years later Westerners were forced to leave the city of Moscow itself for a suburb, the company of De Vogelaer and Van Klenck's resurgent trading activities in the 1650s, for example, show that xenophobia could never reign unchecked for long.

Already by 1654, when Koenraad visited Moscow, pragmatic reasons tempered the xenophobic mood that had caused the recent banishment of Westerners to the *nemetskaia sloboda* outside of the city walls. The Van Klenck–De Vogelaer company was rising once again, ever more firmly guided by the lead of Koenraad. It was thriving by 1660, a prosperity that continued undiminished even after Koenraad van Klenck's gradual withdrawal from personal involvement in the Russia trade. The enterprise was taken over by the very savvy Adolf Houtman by the 1680s; altogether, the Van Klenck–De Vogelaer company therefore traded for about a century on Russia, an eternity in business history.[10] Perhaps because he was the paramount figure in the mid-seventeenth century in the trade between Russia and the Republic, Koenraad van Klenck may serve as an ideal example of a Dutch (arms) trader capitalising on the golden opportunities Russia had to offer.[11]

The Van Klencks were of minor noble stock. At the ancestral Dillenburg castle in Germany, Koenraad's grandfather, Johann von Klenck, had been an advisor to Count Jan (VI) van Nassau (1535–1606), brother of William I of Orange.[12] Noble status may have lapsed, but, as we saw earlier, in 1668, the Holy Roman Emperor Leopold I ennobled (or confirmed the noble status of) the brothers Johannes, Koenraad, Ernst, Marcus, and Mattheus van Klenck, while recognising their possession of the ancestral estates of Lohrheim and Ohrsee in central Germany.[13] Among his siblings, Koenraad van Klenck was the only merchant-capitalist, a member of a species that dominated the Dutch empire's creation around 1600 but began to disappear towards 1700.

Far more than the Trips or Louys de Geer, Van Klenck was a merchant and investor *pur sang* rather than a manufacturing entrepreneur. Nonetheless, he maintained a diversified business portfolio and engaged in a variety of ventures, investing in the slave plantations of Surinam and the sugar they produced and owning salt mines in Norway.[14] The mines came to him through his brother-in-law, the Scotsman William Davidson (1614–1689), an agent of Charles II who was investigated by Dutch authorities for his involvement in espionage on behalf of the British crown during the Second Anglo-Dutch War.[15] At that point, Koenraad took over a number of Davidson's properties, evidently as a precaution, for the Scotsman's business stood in danger of being confiscated by the Dutch state.

In addition to his business acumen and his father's legacy, Van Klenck relied on networking. Rather better than his somewhat eccentric older brothers, Koenraad van Klenck cultivated influential and powerful friends and came to belong to the upper crust that divided the spoils in Amsterdam.[16] Van Klenck's addition to the Amsterdam *vroedschap* in 1672 was part of a political purge that saw others enter the council who had strong ties to the armament branch, such as Louys Trip and Gillis Sautijn. The 1672 purge was to a substantial degree orchestrated by the regent Gillis Valckenier (1623–1680), but, as I suggested earlier, the appointment of leading members of the Dutch military-industrial complex hints at the new stadtholder's desire to have what seemed to him natural allies from these circles enter Amsterdam's leadership.[17]

Besides his prominence as a tycoon, then, Van Klenck's appointment to the city council in 1672 should be attributed to long-standing patronage of his family by the house of Orange-Nassau, upon which his father had been able to draw as well. When in 1625 Jurriaan van Klenck was confined in Arkhangel'sk by Russian authorities for breach of contract in the caviar transaction, Prince Frederick Henry—who had just succeeded his half-brother Maurice as Prince of Orange and stadtholder of Holland and Zeeland—personally interfered and persuaded the Muscovites to release him.[18] To celebrate his accession to the thrones of England and Scotland in 1660, King Charles II received from Koenraad's oldest brother Johannes an exquisite (and large) map collection, which "became a showpiece of the royal map collections."[19] A grateful Charles, uncle to William III of Orange-Nassau, thanked Johannes by making him a baronet.

Princess Albertine Agnes (1634–1696), widow of Willem Frederik, the Prince of Nassau-Dietz, was godmother for both sons of Koenraad van Klenck's second marriage with Judith van Son (although Nicolaas Witsen's mother deputised for the princess at the second baptism in 1674).[20] Before he embarked in 1675, the newly appointed ambassador to Russia paid a visit to Amalia van Solms (1602–1675), stadtholder Frederick Henry's widow and Albertine Agnes's mother.[21] In sum, for the newly minted stadtholder William III Koenraad van Klenck must have seemed a safe choice to replace one of the Amsterdam adherents of Johan de Witt in 1672. Van Klenck remained a city council member until his death in 1691.[22] As Kernkamp remarked, "once one had embarked on the government's vessel, one sailed on it until death."[23]

Different from the academic or quasi-aristocratic formation of most of his fellow regents in 1672, Van Klenck was someone who had trained and worked as an actual businessman.[24] Already during the 1640s the teenaged Koenraad van Klenck diligently worked, often for lengthy periods, in Muscovy for the Van Klenck–De Vogelaer company. He honed his language skills and knew Russian well enough to serve, for example, in 1652 for the Amsterdam notary Adriaen Lock as a translator and authenticator of writs issued by Tsar Aleksei Mikhailovich.[25] Koenraad had inherited his father's ambition and drive: By 1654, he appears in written records as partner of the brothers Marcus, Daniël, and Jan de Vogelaer, who were of Jurriaan van Klenck's generation.[26] Evidently, the 26-year-old Koenraad had filled the vacancy left by his father in the firm more than a decade earlier. Like Jurriaan, Koenraad van Klenck had a great talent for business: He even outdid his father in becoming the senior partner in the partnership with the De Vogelaers by 1660.[27]

As we saw, the Van Klenck–De Vogelaer partnership was by no means exclusively geared towards the trade in arms, but they exported massive loads of weapons to Muscovy, if called upon, and if it seemed profitable. During the late 1650s, Koenraad was diligently dispatching ships to Arkhangel'sk that supplied the tsar with strategic goods and endeavoured to widen the assortment of goods shipped back from Muscovy to Amsterdam.[28] The company also lent funds to the tsar's agents to buy weapons in Amsterdam. Van Klenck oversaw in 1660 the sale of 12,800 muskets and 80,000 kilograms of gunpowder to the Russians.[29] In the same year, the firm of De Vogelaer and Van Klenck advanced the Muscovite agent John Hebdon more than 300,000 guilders to purchase additional weapons (this bought about 15,000 additional firearms, 5,000 lances, 2,000 horses, 160,000 kilograms of gunpowder and 3,200 kilograms of copper). As a reward for its aid to the Hebdon-brokered transaction, the tsar restored the trading privileges to Van Klenck's firm that Jurriaan van Klenck had once received from the tsar, but had been rescinded around 1645. Armed with this state-of-the-art weaponry, the Russian army took to the field in 1661 against the Polish army in an attempt to force a decision in the war that had been raging since 1654. The boatloads of muskets, powder, and shot shipped from Holland indeed ultimately helped Russia wear down Poland in the Thirteen Years' War.[30]

Not everything Koenraad van Klenck touched turned into gold: The importation of a massive quantity of rye from Muscovy by Van Klenck and others in 1658 was a moderate failure, as the rye was of poor quality and an insufficient amount was shipped.[31] This venture was probably linked to a decrease in the grain importation from Poland to Holland as a consequence of the chaos caused by the Thirteen Years' War and the conflict with Sweden. Despite such setbacks, a steady stream of documentation in the Russian archives suggests that Van Klenck remained the most prominent Dutch merchant on Moscow from the 1650s until the 1680s.[32] The importance of the house of De Vogelaer and Van Klenck in *Dutch* eyes is underlined by the map of Moscow published by the Amsterdam printing house of Johannes Blaeu in 1662, which shows the location of the warehouse of the De Vogelaers in the neighbourhood called *Kitaigorod*: It is the only house indicated on this map in which Western Europeans (before 1654) resided.[33]

In the 1660s, Koenraad van Klenck's business interests spread into other parts of northern Europe.[34] Van Klenck's diversification may have been a partial response to gradually deteriorating circumstances for trade in Muscovy, where the wind blew once again out of a different corner: A mercantilistic policy was implemented in the spring of 1667, restricting foreign trade and levying higher tariffs.[35] Nonetheless, when the Russian envoys Thomas Kellerman and Vladimir Voronin visited the Republic in 1671 in an attempt to purchase silver for the tsar's treasury, they sold 1,286 barrels of potash and other raw materials used for the manufacturing of gunpowder to the "*inozemets gost' Kondrat' Klink*" ("the foreign merchant [on Russia] Koenraad van Klenck") and a partner in Amsterdam.[36]

While the French armies camped only a few miles from Amsterdam in 1672, Van Klenck served as captain of a unit of the city's militia, which, however, never saw battle. After 1672, he spent far more of his time than previously on governmental and judicial matters. From 1674 to 1689, he served three times as one of the city court's nine aldermen *(schepenen)*.[37] Having served his first one-year term on this court, he became part of the council of former aldermen, the conclave that elected the city's four mayors, and from whom the city's mayors were recruited.[38]

The highlight of Van Klenck's political career came in 1675, when he was appointed by the Dutch Estates-General to lead a 53-man retinue as extraordinary ambassador to Muscovy, in order to persuade the tsar to declare war on the Swedish king.[39] The 1675–1676 embassy was afterwards celebrated in a printed account, illustrated with opulent baroque engravings by Romeyn de Hooghe (1645–1708), probably the finest etcher of his generation.[40] The book depicted how Van Klenck did his country proud, by showing off his well-nigh fabulous wealth, perfectly embodying the horn of plenty that was the preferred and persuasive image the Dutch state projected abroad, for it presented the Republic as an attractive trading partner and political ally to other countries.

In the course of his five months in Moscow, the ambassador diligently explored all sorts of enterprises with Russian government officials, as well as Western European, Russian, Armenian, or Iranian merchants.[41] With an eye on previously unsuccessful attempts by the VOC to establish trade relations with Qing China, Van Klenck asked the tsar permission for a Dutch attempt to send an embassy across Siberia to the Kangshi emperor.[42] But Van Klenck's request was turned down, because a Russian embassy headed by Nikolai Spafari-Milescu (1636–1708) was already making its way across Siberia: The Russian government remained reluctant to allow foreigners extensive freedom of movement in their country.[43]

After his return from Russia in the autumn of 1676, Van Klenck held for some five years the position of maritime commissioner ("*Commissaris van Zeezaken*") in Amsterdam.[44] As such, he was one of five officials adjudicating conflicts that arose at the port at all levels. It is noteworthy, meanwhile, that Van Klenck was never elected mayor of Amsterdam. Perhaps one may attribute this particularly to the fact that even after the fall of De Witt (and his allies on Amsterdam's city council), the city regents were never comfortable with mayors thought to be too close to the house of Orange. Koenraad van Klenck died in 1691, leaving behind a daughter from his first marriage and a widow. He was buried in the magnificent Westerkerk, within a few yards of his house, a typically large canal house on the Herengracht (a preferred place of residence of Amsterdam's power brokers then and now).[45]

8.2 Dutch Sailors and Soldiers in Russia

Most famously, the Russians tried to enlist Dutchmen to create a Russian seaborne sailing fleet. Peter the Great's bilingual seafaring regulations *(Morskoi ustav* or *Zeevaartreglement)* of 1720 were published towards the end of the tsar's life, but these rules remained the guidelines for the Russian navy until the final decades of the eighteenth century, reflective of the importance of Dutch people and culture in Russian maritime life.[46]

Following in the footsteps of Jan Struys or Karsten Brandt, hundreds of sailors and shipwrights were recruited by Peter in the 1690s and 1700s. More tenacious in this regard than his father and grandfather, Peter established a Russian navy and merchant marine that became a going concern.

Far less known is the story of Dutch mercenary officers in seventeenth-century Russia, such as Hendrik van Dam or Isaac van Bockhoven.[47] Before Mikhail Romanov's accession to the Muscovite throne, few Dutch military experts entered Muscovite service, since the Estates-General and the stadtholder forbade the Republic's denizens to fight as foreign mercenaries. This prohibition even prevailed during the truce with Spain (1609–1621). Nonetheless, Baron Adriaen van Flodderhoff (Flodorff/Vlodorp) van Luyt sought employment for himself and some (possibly German) fellow officers in the Russian armed forces in 1612 and 1613.[48] He proved a trailblazer, even when the role of the Dutch as military experts and mercenaries in seventeenth-century Romanov Russia was not as dominant as their virtual monopolisation of the import trade in firearms or their strong presence as manufacturers of cannon, muskets, and pistols.[49] In the Thirteen Years' War, more Scots than Dutch seem to have occupied senior ranks among the officers. It is significant, though, that in one list of officers who boasted of qualities other than being combat experts, Reger provides seven names of "masters of firearms, grenades, or mining," six of which appear Dutch (one of whom seems to be Lodewijk Fabricius's stepfather Paul-Rudolf Beem).[50]

The Dutch were indeed key to certain crucial developments in Russia's methods of land warfare. There is no denying that the example of Maurice and William Louis of Nassau and the reflection of their changes in drill and deployment of infantry in battle exerted a strong influence on the Russian way of waging war in two ways: In the first place, the illustrated manual by De Gheyn (or the Wallhausen adaptation of De Gheyn) was printed in a Russian translation in the late 1640s, the first non-religious book printed in Russian.[51] It was distributed among the so-called new formation units that began to make up the main part of the armies of Tsar Aleksei in the Thirteen Years' War against Poland, whose officers were clearly familiar with its contents.[52] The new regiments, too, followed a number of instructions supplied by Colonel Isaac van Bockhoven in a letter addressed to the tsar's father-in-law, I.D. Miloslavskii, who had personally recruited Van Bockhoven in the Dutch Republic in 1647.[53]

Second, many of the foreign mercenary officers who trained and commanded the Russian units from the Smolensk War onward had fought in the Dutch War of Independence in the armies of Maurice or Frederick Henry.[54] Some of them were Dutch, others were not. The most intriguing among them are the Van Bockhoven clan, who are encountered as senior officers in army-related Russian documents from 1647 through the 1680s, while two women of this family married Patrick Gordon (d.

1699) and François Lefort, Peter the Great's favourite foreigners.[55] That alone seems to indicate that Van Bockhovens were pivotal figures among expatriates living in Muscovy between the late 1640s and late 1670s.

Meanwhile, even in the closing stages of the heyday of Dutch paramountcy as capitalist pioneers and military innovators, foundational Dutch works on land warfare continued to be translated, such as that on fortification by Menno van Coehoorn, while someone like François Lefort first earned some stripes on the battlefields of the Franco-Dutch wars of the 1670s.[56] In 1675, together with a number of "Dutch" officers, Lefort exchanged the battlefields of the Low Countries for those of Russia.[57] Once he arrived in Russia, he concluded a very advantageous marriage with a Van Bockhoven girl and entrenched himself among the community leaders of Moscow's foreigners' suburb.

Lefort or Van Flodderhoff seem to have been part of a steady flow of adventurers during this age who arrived at the border of the tsar's empire invited or not. They sought their luck in Russia, attracted by the prospect of munificent rewards.[58] From the 1580s until 1713, many English, Scottish, and Irish soldiers made their way to Muscovy, including the Scots Alexander Leslie and William Bruce. Bruce, father of Russia's first native scientist Iakov Brius, arrived with the Van Bockhoven team on Dutch ships at Arkhangel'sk in 1647. When the fighting in the Netherlands waned by the early 1640s, many British and Irish mercenaries moved back to the British Isles to participate in the civil wars that engulfed the three kingdoms. Once the Parliamentary side triumphed, royalists left, some for political or religious reasons, while many departed in search of employment. Scots, in particular, can therefore be found in significant numbers as officers of the Russian army in the Thirteen Years' War. For a Catholic such as Patrick Gordon, who first served the Poles and then switched sides to the Russians, money trumped religious zeal: The Russian terms offered were too good to decline. Gordon was only one of many British and Irish soldiers of fortune who joined the tsar's military, the first wave of which had been the thousands recruited by Leslie and Van Dam, mainly in Amsterdam, in the early 1630s.[59]

The opportunities seemed breathtaking: Lefort, Bruce, and Gordon reached the very upper echelons of the ranks of the army or even the Russian court. And even for those belonging to the rank-and-file of the army or among the sailors aboard sailships, opportunity beckoned. Jan Struys became a rather well-off (and well-known) figure, a prosperity that was triggered by his service in Russia, as did his colleague Karsten Brandt. Lodewijk (Ludvig) Fabricius (Fabritius/Faber) was another outstanding example of someone seeking his luck in Russia, about whom more below.[60] It is too reductionist to identify such (p)luck as a singularly Dutch essence, especially since some of the most successful upstarts were not Dutch (even if both Gordon and Lefort seem to have moved in Dutchified circles in Moscow's foreigners' suburb and to have understood the Dutch language). It does nevertheless seem that an infectious attitude by which one did not resign oneself to one's station in life was prevalent among the many mercenaries and other foreign workers in seventeenth-century Russia. We saw how this outlook or mindset was widespread in the Dutch Republic and was common among not only many Dutch natives but also those who moved to the prosperous Republic in its Golden Age (or served in its armies or on its ships). Like many of the ancestors of the regents and tycoons of the Golden Age Republic around 1650, this later generation was a crowd of often modest background who sought their fortune in inventive and, if necessary, ruthless ways.

Elsewhere, I have investigated at considerable length the lives of Jan Struys and the Van Bockhovens, typical representatives of that other exemplar of the Dutch militaristic-capitalist ethos, the mercenary. In the case of the Van Bockhovens, the bold step of relocating to Muscovy paid off, even if their "success [was] never final," adopting Geoffrey Parker's usage of the phrase. The trio all reached the rank of colonel, the highest possible for foreigners in the Russian ranks. Cornelis van Bockhoven's career in tsarist service spanned three decades, but he fell against the Turks at Chyhyryn in the 1670s, while Isaac van Bockhoven perhaps never even saw action against the Poles (disease may have seen him off on the eve of the war). The third of the Van Bockhovens who disembarked at Arkhangel'sk in 1647, Filips Albert, though, even if spending some years in Polish captivity, may have died of natural causes after decades in the tsar's armies, and some of his offspring served as officers in the tsarist army. Of course, one Van Bockhoven daughter married Patrick Gordon and another François Lefort. It reflects how careful the Dutch at home and abroad were in concluding marriages; they sought unions that confirmed or enhanced their status and might make them part of an influential network. Wedlock was another avenue to get ahead in life as well as maintaining or increasing one's wealth and standing.

Jan Struys, as far as we know, died as a fairly affluent man in a Dutch enclave in Holstein in the 1690s, while his companion Karsten Brandt returned to Moscow after his harrowing escape from the Cossacks in 1670 to find a comfortable enough existence in the foreigners' suburb. Ultimately, he was a pivotal figure in maintaining young Peter the Great's interest in seafaring, refitting the little sailboat Peter found abandoned in a warehouse in 1688 that had once belonged to his uncle Nikita.[61] Even today, the *botik*, which Brandt first sailed himself around a lake near Moscow, is still on display as the first prototype of the modern Russian navy. Soon after Brandt's demonstration, Peter the Great sailed himself his first vessels near Moscow.[62] Peter's mock naval exploits coincided with stepped-up military exercises of his play regiments *(poteshnye voiska)*, in which he was assisted by Patrick Gordon and François Lefort.[63]

By the second half of the 1680s, the young tsar was then immersed in gaining a sort of comprehensive education in the art of war. In addition to his soldiering and sailing exercises, the Dutch expatriate Frans Timmerman (1644–1702)—who had started out as a factor for some of the richer Dutch traders on Russia during the 1660s—taught Peter mathematics and physics, with the tsar particularly keen on finding out about ballistics.[64] He was perhaps as fond of gunnery as of sailing, eventually reaching the rank of *bombardi[e]r*, or gunner, in his own army, a promotion allegedly rewarding his outstanding artillery skills. Different from other illustrious military commanders of the early modern period such as Maurice of Orange-Nassau, Peter did not read much military theory; given his poor command of written Russian and his handwriting, he may have suffered from dyslexia.[65] But his powers of observation were exceptional, and he compensated by way of his practical lessons in sailing or commanding troops in mock battles. And he was a great admirer of William III, whose exploits against Louis XIV he closely followed in the early 1690s.[66] In 1693, the tsar visited Arkhangel'sk, seeing the northern seaport for the first time for himself; the Grand Embassy of 1697 and 1698 was one final step completing his preparation for the comprehensive military modernisation of his country.[67]

Gradually, the Russians turned to the Holy Roman Empire to recruit military experts (e.g., gunners) and officers, which became a hotbed for innovations in the art of war around 1700. Native Dutch specialists were increasingly occupied with the lengthy wars with France that began in 1672; the country's population base was small, and few professional warriors could be missed and allowed to fight elsewhere. That was less so in terms of sailors, which may explain why Peter the Great had no great difficulty in enlisting seafarers during and after the Grand Embassy (which happened to coincide as well with the brief respite of the 1697 Treaty of Ryswyck). Despite his fondness of the Dutch and their accomplishments, the tsar was perceptive in observing the decline of Dutch pre-eminence in naval warfare even before his journey to Holland and preferred English advances in shipbuilding over the veritable traditions of the Dutch.

8.3 A Case Study: Ludvig Fabritius

Struys and Brandt met on their travels several remarkable characters, such as the Frisian surgeon Jan Termundt, who eventually became part of Peter the Great's motley crew, or the gunner Lodewijk or Ludw(v)ig Fabritius/Fabricius (1648–1729). Fabritius's biography epitomises early modern Dutch mercenary nerve at its finest. Besides his appearance in Struys's book (and VOC documents), we know a lot more about Fabritius than about most of his contemporaries, because late in life he was asked to write down his reminiscences on the request of Peter the Great, around the time of the conclusion of the Peace of Nystadt in 1721. These memoirs have been preserved in Swedish archives and have been published in their original German as well as in Russian and English translations.[68] In addition, we have fairly detailed accounts of Fabritius's visits to Iran in the 1680s, where he first served as unofficial and then as a formal envoy of the Swedish crown in an effort to establish a trading partnership. Two men in his retinue, Engelbert Kaempfer and J.G. Sparwenfeld, wrote about these travels, as did Fabritius himself.[69] From all these sources, Fabritius's life's astounding trajectory becomes apparent.

Fabritius was born in Dutch Brazil in 1648 as a son of a medical doctor, who apparently was the head surgeon of the Fort Oranje fortress (near Recife in Pernambuco) and appears to have died there.[70] His mother, Elisabeth Fuchs, remarried an artillery officer, Paul Rudolf Beem, with whom young Lodewijk arrived in the Dutch Republic in the 1650s, after the Dutch surrender of Brazil to the Portuguese.[71] Lodewijk and his stepfather departed for Russia to join the tsar's service around 1660, when Russia was in the midst of the Thirteen Years' War with Poland.[72] Under the command of Prince Iakov Kudenetovich Cherkasskii (a redoubtable Caucasian general in tsarist service, d. 1666), Beem and Fabritius saw action in Ukraine against the Lithuanian *hetman* Pac, recovering several towns on the Poles, in what seems to be the 1663 campaign season.[73] Fabritius, not 15 years old yet, was appointed adjutant of the artillery (likely as his stepfather's aide) and was subsequently promoted further in rank, even if he remained in effect Beem's aide-de-camp.

Stepfather and son fought in these borderlands for three years. Dispatched to Astrakhan at the Volga mouth in 1667 (and arriving there only in 1668, after spending the winter at Saratov), they were both captured by rebellious Don Cossacks at Chernyi Iar on the Volga in 1670.[74] Fabritius somehow, through ruse and subterfuge and with the help of acquaintances who took pity on him (possibly, the Cossack appreciation of his great skill at using cannon played a role, as well as his fluency in Russian), managed to survive Cossack wrath: His stepfather and all other foreign officers with whom he served seem to have been killed at Chernyi Iar. After Stepan Razin's capture of Astrakhan at the start of summer in 1670, Fabritius bided his time there for a while, lying low during several months of Cossack rule that saw a number of savage episodes. Together with Karsten Brandt, Fabritius managed to escape the city in the late summer of 1670 and made his way to northern Iran.[75] He returned to Muscovy in 1672 and served as officer in Russia until 1677 or 1678, when he departed for Stockholm.[76] In 1679, Fabritius was already back in Russia, in the capacity of Swedish envoy to Iran (after persuading the Swedish king, Charles XI, of the merits of such a mission, albeit at first paying his own way) and returned twice to the shah's court at Isfahan during the 1680s. He became a colonel in the Swedish army in the 1690s but seems to served worked more often as a diplomat than a soldier in the 1690s and 1700s, visiting in this capacity Iran, the Dutch Republic, and Istanbul.

In Fabritius's account, we find a sort of counterpart to Louys de Geer's story. While De Geer represents the businessman so instrumental to the

Dutch *Wirtschaftswunder*, Fabritius, who died at a time when the Dutch Republic's status as a Great Power was sinking fast, represents the other key type instrumental to this startling Dutch boom, that of the intrepid mercenary. An opportunistic and seemingly fearless Low Countries' soldier, he exemplifies Dutch early modern capitalist gumption, at times thanks in no small measure to what resembles an animal survival instinct. Eventually, he made it big in Sweden, like his counterpart. Both De Geer and Fabritius were ennobled by the Swedish crown. Noble status was the ultimate prize even for rich capitalists, as it guaranteed a sort of elite membership in perpetuity, something that trade or business rarely guaranteed across the generations. In other words, De Geer and Fabritius had "made it."

It is noteworthy as well that for both men, national allegiance to the Republic crumbled before capitalist or careerist considerations. For De Geer, sentimental attachment to the Calvinist republic that had been his place of refuge and allowed him to restart his business still outstripped his Swedish ties towards the end of his life (though not for many of his children), but for Fabritius, who had spent only a few years in the Republic during his long life, becoming a naturalised Swede was not that difficult a choice to make, even if he wrote his memoirs at the end of his life in a mangled German rather than Swedish.

8.4 Vanishing Act

> Above this poor cottage/Holy angels fly./Do reverence, great prince!/Here is the cradle of your Empire,/Here Great Russia was born.[77]

The wars with Louis XIV's France that began in 1672 ended by 1713 in a sort of pyrrhic victory for the Dutch Republic. Louis was checked, first with regard to his attempts to make the Republic into a French satellite (or even annex the country altogether) and then when trying to lay his hands on all of the Spanish prize (the southern Netherlands became Austrian in 1713, thus keeping the French at a remove from the Dutch borders). But the Dutch Republic was exhausted at the time of the peace signed at Utrecht. It was true that the French wars still witnessed episodes of breathtaking Dutch military genius, as in the sea battles fought by De Ruyter and Cornelis Tromp in the 1670s, the siege-and-fortification high jinks of Menno van Coehoorn in the 1680s and 1690s, or William III's invasion of England in 1688. But the Dutch advance over economic competitors or political foes diminished after 1672, and the Dutch skill at manufacturing arms was beginning to be outmatched by German and other manufacturers located elsewhere. At sea, British warships surpassed the quality of their Dutch counterparts towards 1700, and, at least in the field of siege warfare, Van Coehoorn may be considered more as a Dutch response to Vauban's genius than an original innovator.

Already by the time of the Second Anglo-Dutch war (1664–1667), British shipwrights were building warships that beyond their larger size were superior to those produced in the Republic in other respects, but the Dutch reputation as the foremost experts of naval warfare remained intact for several more decades. On land, the Dutch military advance was concomitantly beginning to wane as well (of which the first beginnings can already be encountered in the second half of the Thirty Years' War), but the army's obsolescence was almost imperceptible at first. In his overview of Dutch warfare as reflected in early printed texts, Olaf van Nimwegen suggests that even in the War of the Austrian Succession in the 1740s, Dutch troops still punched above their weight, as they had since the grim days of 1672.[78] Still, as we saw from the dissatisfaction of the Africans with whom the Dutch traded for slaves in the first decades of the eighteenth century, Dutch arms were no longer state of the art.

In hindsight, it seem evident that, whereas the northern Netherlands remain today, more than three centuries later, among the leading capitalist countries in terms of gross domestic product or volume of import-and-export trade, and often belong to the top ten of international arms exporters, their role significantly diminished after 1700, when especially Great Britain economically overtook them (with some help of Dutch trading and financial expertise that migrated in the wake of the Glorious Revolution).[79] First more comparative than real perhaps, the decline of Dutch military power was swift and completed within a generation after 1700. It became irreversible because the long conflict with Louis XIV that came to a close in 1713 proved even for a country as rich as the Republic too much to bear. For the Dutch state, warfare as such became unaffordable, the result of an economy-of-scale process. Twenty million French people simply could sustain a much larger armed force than two million Dutch, even if the latter continued to have a better financing system to support their military. Like Sweden, the Dutch Republic had too small a population base to sustain armed forces that might have allowed it to remain a Great Power in the eighteenth century. Of course, in that century, Prussia proved an exception as a smallish country fielding a vast army, but all of its inhabitants contributed to its military machine, while the Prussian king declined to maintain a navy at the same time.

From the Thirty Years' War onward, the size of armies had gradually begun to grow, as had that of ships, and the cost of eighteenth-century warfare became prohibitive for a country with fewer than two million inhabitants.[80] As Olaf van Nimwegen writes,

> During the War of the Spanish Succession the Dutch Republic would employ an army of 120,000 men. The greater war effort had enormous consequences. Government expenditure skyrocketed and losses in human life rose to alarming heights. In 1675 and 1676, Holland had to pay 17 million guilders per year on average for her share in the Dutch war effort. In the 1630s and 1640s, this had been 10 to

> 11 million guilders. In the battle of Nieuwpoort (1600), 1000 Dutch and 3000 Spanish soldiers perished, next to 700 and 600 wounded respectively. Seventy-four years after, French casualties in the battle of Seneffe totalled 8000 to 10,000 men; allied losses amounted to 10,000 to 12,000 dead and wounded, possibly even 15,000. At the battle of Malplaquet (1709), the French dead and wounded numbered 17,000 and those of the allies a staggering 20,000.[81]

Such wars of attrition could not be indefinitely sustained. The advantages that its compact size might have yielded the Republic when armies and navies were smaller (especially because the Republic proved efficient at harnessing its resources to finance its military) now became a handicap. In a variety of ways, Britain, France and Russia began to draw more efficiently on their far larger populations in bankrolling their war machines, with the United Kingdom hewing closest to the Dutch capitalist model. And somehow the Dutch innovative genius, with which the seventeenth century was replete in terms of the art of war and of other arts, vanished. The reasons for this technological stagnation remain opaque: Was it complacency, exhaustion, or something else? One gets the impression that other countries both began to beat the Dutch at their own game of military professionalisation (Prussia perhaps being the starkest example) and proved more adept at harnessing the burgeoning crowd of scientists who might underscore military modernisation, if one looks at Iakov Brius's military academy in Russia, the French Academy of Sciences, or the Royal Society. No such apex of Dutch scholarly and scientific endeavour was created. And it is difficult to continue to stay ahead or on top the competition, if one considers the history of capitalism in more general terms. Britain's reign as the supreme capitalist hegemon lasted longer but eventually came to an end by about 1914, as it seems, has that of the United States in the early twenty-first century.

But until the end of the War of the Spanish Succession, the Dutch role in the international arms trade remained vastly important, especially for the new budding giant in northern Europe, Russia. The Dutch were instrumental in ushering Russia into the circle of the Great Powers of Europe in other ways, too, as in underscoring its territorial claims. Nikolai Kopanev suggested that

> the publication in Holland of S.U. Remezov's 'Siberian draught-book' and the draughts about Siberia by [IJsbrandt Ides] were necessary for the Russian monarchy to underline its rule over this vast territory opened and investigated by Russian explorers in the seventeenth century [and] Holland was selected [for this], as it had been in 1614, when it had been guarantor of the Romanov dynasty's legitimacy by international law.[82]

Likewise important, as we saw, were Witsen's map of Siberia and its accompanying text.

On 14 August 1696 a permit was issued by one of Peter's chancelleries to allow the transport from Arkhangel'sk to Moscow of 4,000 German [or Dutch, for *nemetskii*]-made muskets and Scottish-made locks to the Dutch merchant Daniel Hartman.[83] Hartman was a dominant figure among the Dutch traders of the 1690s. Importing arms, he tried to export ship's masts from Arkhangel'sk, among other things.[84] Hartman often partnered with Heinrich (Andrei) Butenant, who had taken over the Marselis iron forgeries in the 1670s.[85] Butenant (von Rosenbusch) was for a considerable period the Danish resident in Russia and not only continued Peter Marselis's enterprises but considerably expanded this business, opening iron and copper mines in the north.[86]

In the following years, Jan Lups and Christoffel Brants (1664–1732) emerged as the leading Dutch arms dealers on Russia.[87] Zakharov suggests that still at the time of the Battle of Poltava (1709), more than half of the needs of the Russian army were met by foreign imports. He found that between 1705 and 1710, Lups and Brants transported four fifths of the 63,000 rifles and rifle barrels and the same proportion of the 72,000 swords and sword blades imported into Russia.[88] Seven out of ten pistols were also shipped by the same Dutch merchants. In addition, they had thousands of saddles, stirrups, and other equipment for the Russian cavalry unloaded at Arkhangel'sk. The examples of Hartman, Brants, and Lups suggest that the Dutch role continued to be significant. After 1700, though, Dutch experts no longer enjoyed a virtual monopoly over the arms trade to, and manufacturing in, Russia.

On 25 August 1697, the City of Amsterdam's mayors staged a spectacular fireworks display for an august visitor to the city, Tsar Peter the Great, who happened to be rather fond of such pyrotechnics, as they knew (one of the city fathers was Nicolaas Witsen).[89] In many ways, this orgy of booms-and-bangs can be seen as a symbolic farewell to the Dutch dominance of the budding global market in advanced arms sales and expert soldiers. In awe of Dutch military genius, Peter personally honed his skills as a shipwright on the wharves of the VOC in Amsterdam in 1697 and 1698. The tsar returned from his Grand Embassy to Europe with hundreds of Dutch experts, most of whom were to help build and sail Russia's first navy. In Holland, textbooks were printed for the naval academy of Peter the Great, established in 1701.[90] While Russian maritime vocabulary retains many Dutch terms *(shturman, matros)*, the number of non-maritime Dutch-derived words *(briuki, forpost, olstr, kontora, kran, matra[t]s, parikmakher, riumka, stal')* in Russian is remarkable, attesting to a powerful Dutch cultural influence at some point in time.[91] They mainly seemed to have been adopted before 1725.

In recent years, scholars have been inclined to emphasise the cultural and scientific pollination of Peter's Russia by the Dutch Republic and its denizens.[92] Peter, a poor writer of Russian who lacked linguistic talent, nonetheless made a spirited effort to learn Dutch in the decade of his greatest infatuation with Dutch culture and Dutch maritime prowess (1688–1698) and dabbled in the language until his last days.[93] While the tsar certainly enjoyed flirting with the Dutch language or the way of dressing of its peasants and sailors, he was foremost interested in learning from the Dutch about any innovations in waging war. By the end of his embassy to Western Europe, he no longer doubted that the Dutch were falling behind the times.[94] While he did maintain his admiration for the enormous capacity of the Dutch to sustain a huge military machine through their trade and manufacturing, Russia began to hold its own in terms of arms production and founded its own military academy soon after 1700, in which a considerable role was played by the immigrant sons Iakov Brius and Andrei Vinius.[95] Vinius had some inkling of mathematics and ballistics, it seems, but was a rank amateur compared with the much better schooled scientist Brius, a key military pedagogue.

Brius can be linked to lingering Dutch military influence on Russia in another way, through the production one of the earliest secular Russian books in print. The Russian printing presses had not exactly been churning out the polemological books and pamphlets since Wallhausen and De Gheyn's drill book in 1647, and the translation of a book on fortress building *(Nieuwe vestingbouw)* by Menno van Coehoorn (which had originally been published in 1685) is therefore noteworthy.[96] Published in Moscow in 1709, the book had been translated from the Dutch by M (?). Shafirov and Iakov Brius.[97] Van Coehoorn's reputation as a trailblazing military expert survived his death for a while, and the Russian interest in his work is therefore unsurprising, particularly as the Russians were fortifying their new port (and soon to be capital) of St. Petersburg.

Iakov Brius, meanwhile, was a favourite of Peter the Great, and can be considered Russia's first homegrown scientist, as Valentin Boss has suggested.[98] Brius succeeded Andrei Vinius and Frans Timmerman as Peter's technological and scientific advisor. Following in the footsteps of his father, Vinius had helped setting up arms manufactories in the Urals and Siberia as head of the Siberian office, contributed to the foundation of the artillery school, and helped the Russian army recover from the initial severe defeat at Narva in 1700 against the Swedes.[99] Faced with a dire deficit of cannon, which had fallen into Swedish hands at the battle, Peter ordered Vinius to melt down church bells to cast several hundred pieces of artillery to replace them. But the aging Vinius of the 1700s seems to have fallen behind the times, not unlike Dutch technology at this very same moment in history. The future belonged to others.

Notes

1. See Wijnroks, *Handel*, 363, 367n36; Veluwenkamp, *Archangel*, *passim*. Jan Witsen had assets amounting to 85,000 guilders in 1631 (Frederiks and Frederiks, *Kohier*, 60).

2. See Peters, *De wijze koopman*.
3. Veluwenkamp, *Archangel*, 59–62, 81–91, 125. Most of the loading bills for Arkhangel'sk he had notarised in Amsterdam identify him as "Jurriaan." It is interesting that in the 1631 tax assessment in Amsterdam his wealth was estimated a modest 1800 guilders, a mere trifle indeed when compared with his business partners, Marcus de Vogelaer's widow and sons (Frederiks and Frederiks, *Kohier*, 43). I am not sure how to interpret this curiously low assessment, but a number of reasons can be suggested: Jurriaan van Klenck had been amassing debt (or overextended himself), was temporarily in dire straits, his assets were primarily considered as not within the purview of the Amsterdam assessors, or he faked it.
4. Veluwenkamp, *Archangel*, 62; Veluwenkamp suggests that "George" van Klenck became the representative of the already established house of De Vogelaer in 1607 (ibid., 59); see, too, Wijnroks, *Handel*, 13.
5. Wijnroks, *Handel*, 370.
6. C.E.S., *'T Verwaerloosde Formosa*; Veluwenkamp, *Archangel*, 125, 128. About the third son Jurriaan nothing is known: He may have died in childbirth (Loviagin, "Vvedenie," xii; Veluwenkamp, *Archangel*, 204; Elias, *De Vroedschap*, vol. 2, 564).
7. See Lahana, "Novaia," 84–7, 95–8.
8. See, among others, Lahana, "Novaia," 84–100.
9. Kotilaine, "When the Twain," 44.
10. For Houtman's role, for example, Kotilaine, *Russia's Foreign Trade*, 84, 89, 261.
11. Kotilaine, "When the Twain," 33, 58–9, 108–9, 114, 117–18, 129, 131.
12. "Vvedenie," xi–xii; Veluwenkamp, *Archangel*, 59, 204; Molhuysen and Blok, eds, *Nieuw Nederlandsch*, vol. 10, 467–70.
13. Herman van Klenck is conspicuously absent from this list. When Koenraad was identified as lord of the Imperial (German) lands of Lohrheim and Ohrsee in 1675, Johannes was dead, but Herman was still alive. Did Koenraad get title over these properties because Herman lived in the Indies and had forfeited his rights to them?
14. Wolbers, *Geschiedenis*, 52–5; Van der Meiden, *Betwist Bestuur*, 31, 35, 39; *Stadsarchief Amsterdam Notary Archive* 3410, folio 210 (27 April 1666); *Stadsarchief Amsterdam Notary Archive* 3410, folio 301 (4 June 1666).
15. De Bruin, *Geheimhouding*, 465–71. The young Anthonie van Leeuwenhoeck worked for Davidson.
16. See Boterbloem, *Fiction and Reality*, 32–3; Adams, *Familial State*. "The apparent diversity of the field was deceptive, however, given the numerous kinship relations among the Amsterdam elite" (Kotilaine, "When the Twain," 107).
17. Elias, *Vroedschap*, vol. 1, cxxii.
18. Veluwenkamp, *Archangel*, 87.
19. Wallis, "Banquet," 3.
20. Molhuysen and Blok, eds, *Nieuw Nederlandsch*, vol. 10, 469–70. Willem Frederik had ruled the lands in the Empire that belonged to the House of Nassau, in which the Van Klencks had their estates.
21. [Coyett], *Historisch Verhael*, 5.
22. Elias, *Vroedschap*, vol. 2, 564.
23. Kernkamp, "Inleiding," xxviii.
24. Van Aalst, *Het archief*, 53; Molhuysen and Blok, eds, *Nieuw Nederlandsch*, vol. 10, 467–70.
25. *Stadsarchief Amsterdam Notary Archive* 2193, fol. 310 (21 October 1652); *Stadsarchief Amsterdam Notary Archive* 2193, fol. 349 (17 October 1652).
26. *Stadsarchief Amsterdam Notary Archive* 1893, fol. 153 (17 February 1654); Veluwenkamp, *Archangel*, 125.

27. On De Vogelaer's importance in the Russia trade around 1600, see Kotilaine, "When the Twain," 108–9; see as well Wijnroks, *Handel*, 186–7.
28. For example, see *Stadsarchief Amsterdam Notary Archive* 904AII, folios 304 and 306 (25 May 1657).
29. Amburger, *Die Familie*, 118, 118n506; Kotilaine, "In Defense," 77.
30. Massive arms deliveries continued afterwards, as is evident from Ambassador Jacob Boreel's intercession on behalf of Erdman Swellengrebel in 1665; Swellengrebel had not been adequately reimbursed by the Russians for delivering thousands of rifles, muskets, pistols, and carbines—much of the pay was to be by way of potash (*Nationaal Archief, Archief der Staten-Generaal* 8523 [*Verbael*], 466–71).
31. *Stadsarchief Amsterdam Notary Archive* 2205, fol. 786 (26 November 1658); *Stadsarchief Amsterdam Notary Archive* 2206, folios 19–20 (3 January 1659).
32. See Demkin, *Zapadnoevropeiskoe*, vol. 1, 50.
33. Goss, ed., *Blaeu's*, 44–5. The map appears in an edition of an earlier Russian-language map produced somewhere during the 1600s or 1610s. Clearly, the Van Klenck family patronised these renowned map makers (see later and Wallis, "Banquet," 3).
34. *Stadsarchief Amsterdam Notary Archive* 3410, folio 210 (27 April 1666); *Stadsarchief Amsterdam Notary Archive* 3410, folio 301 (4 June 1666).
35. Boterbloem, *Fiction and Reality*, 57–60.
36. Van Klenck had been given the honourary title of *gost'* by the tsar in the early 1660s (this is different from A.D. Winius's title, for there was a sort of special title of *gost'* for foreign merchants that came with fewer privileges and obligations; Winius was considered Russian by the time he was awarded this rank); the partner is called "Roman Shvant" in the Russian document, who I could not identify further (see "Dlia popolneniia," 6). Kellerman or Kelderman was Dutch-born.
37. Bontemantel, *De regeeringe*, 239.
38. Kernkamp, "Inleiding," xxiv.
39. The Russian bureaucratic record for this visit is lengthy and can still be found in the *Rossiiskaia Gosudarstvennaia Arkhiv Drevnikh Aktov* [from here: *RGADA*] in Moscow (see *RGADA* 50, no. 9 [1675–76]). Whereas this file bespeaks careful record keeping (the progress of the ambassadorial suite is carefully monitored, keeping score of the various expenses made by regional authorities and the central government offices), it says nothing about the Russian government's motivation behind its official responses to the Dutch proposals, including Van Klenck's own *démarches*.
40. [Coyett,] *Historisch Verhael*.
41. Ibid., 103–4, 115–16.
42. See earlier, as well as Blussé, "No Boats."
43. Will review of *Russia and China* by Mankall.
44. Veluwenkamp, *Archangel*, 129.
45. Ibid., 132; Elias, *Vroedschap*, vol. 2, 564. Koenraad van Klenck's estate and any family or company archives have since disappeared in the mist of time. The family line in the Netherlands appears to have become extinct (see Loviagin and Tsepkov, eds, *Posol'stvo*, 12). His daughter and son-in-law inherited most of the fortune he had amassed. This daughter, Geertruida (1664–1720), was born in the year her mother Martina Reepmaker, Van Klenck's first wife, died (see Molhuysen and Blok, eds, *Nieuw Nederlandsch*, vol. 10, 469–70). Geertruida married twice, first to Jacob Blom (1656–1691), with whom she had two daughters, and then to Jacob de Wolff

(1655–1701; Van Aalst, *Het archief*, 51–2). From this union, she had two sons and a daughter (Elisabeth) who survived into adulthood: One of these sons was named Coenraat Clenck de Wolff (d. 1760), probably indicative of her affection for her father ('s estate?). At least some of the family inheritance ended up in the hands of the descendants of the De Graaff–Bicker clan (see Van Aalst, *Het archief*). A portrait of Van Klenck survived among the possessions of the Del Court van Krimpen family in the twentieth century (Raptschinsky, "Het gezantschap," 148).

46. *Kniga ustav' morskoi.*
47. See, however, Hellie, *Enserfment*; Boterbloem, "Dutch Mercenaries."
48. Driessen, "Het gezantschap," 52–3; Nozdrin, "The Flodorf Project."
49. Even if deciphering all the Russianised names of the officers listed in Reger's dissertation is impossible, one gets an impression of the origins of the Western officers in Russian service around the middle of the seventeenth century; clearly, different from their dominance in foreign (arms) trade (or the navy), there are far fewer Dutch natives among them; it remains unclear how many had been taught the art of war in the "school" of the battlefields of the Low Countries (see Reger, "In the Service," Appendix 5, 323). The list, meanwhile, is far from exhaustive; from other sources, it is clear that Cornelis van Bockhoven was continually in Russian service from 1647 until his death in 1677, for example.
50. Reger, "In the Service," 208–9.
51. For their print history in the Russian context, see Reger, "In the Service," 144–8. And for the role of mercenary officers in training the Russians in the "Dutch Model," see ibid., 27.
52. As Reger suggests, "The importance of this military literature is too often disregarded because of its limited dissemination but, in light of the centralized nature of the Muscovite state which allowed all aspects of military decision-making to be shaped by the chancellery officials and the tsar himself, all of whom certainly had access to these texts, western [sic] military texts entered Russia at precisely the level of society at which they would have the greatest effect. The principles of organisation in these books were subsequently disseminated through many of the government's communications with the army" (Reger, "In the Service," 154–5).
53. Reger, "In the Service," 159–61.
54. On Maurice as mentor of military instructors, see Reger, "In the Service," 146.
55. Apart from my article (Boterbloem, "Dutch Mercenaries"), see, for example, Reger, "In the Service," 157–61.
56. See Myshlaevskii, "Vyezd."
57. Ustrialov notes how most officers in Lefort's company identified themselves as "Prussians" from Danzig, although the names of two of the leaders begin with "fan" rather than "fon" in the transcribed Russian; he likely served in the mercenary unit of the later duke of Kurland, Friedrich-Casimir Kettler (1650–1698), in the war with France (1672–1678; Ustrialov, *Istoriia*, vol. 2, 8–11; see as well Myshlaevskii, "Vyezd," 638, where it says that there had been no fighting in 1675 in Holland; Kettler apparently went home in the fall of 1675). Ryzhenkov suggests that the Dutchman "van Frosten" recruited Lefort (see Ryzhenkov, "Frants Lefort," 58; his first name was Jacob, which could be either Dutch or German, and his last name appears both as "fon" and as "fan" in Russian documents, see Myshlaevskii, "Vyezd," 636; he claimed himself to be a Prussian native from Danzig, ibid. 638, but so did, falsely, Lefort, see ibid., 639). They arrived, it seems, at the same time as Van Klenck's embassy, likely having been part of the same flotilla sailing to

Arkhangel'sk; some of Lefort's companions were threatened with extradition after a long process in which both the Arkhangel'sk governor and his administrative secretary *(d'iak)* and the authorities in Moscow tried to establish how these uninvited foreigners had arrived in Russia; some were eventually hired by the artillery office, but Lefort (according to his own account) fell ill and missed therefore complying with the extradition order that befell the others (Arkheograficheskaia komissia, *Dopolneniia*, vol. 9, 97–8). In August 1678, Lefort declared that he neither could go back with those who had been sent packing nor join those recruited by the *Pushkarskii prikaz* (artillery office). By then, he had married a "relative" of general-major Filips van Bockhoven, with whom he seems to have resided in the *nemetskaia sloboda*. In the *Posolskii prikaz* (foreign chancellory), the *d'iak* Emel'ian Ukraintsev signed the document of the investigation of Lefort's curious behaviour; Ukraintsev had been an envoy to the Netherlands a few years earlier, and became at some point an in-law of Andrei Andreevich Vinius, the versatile bureaucrat of Dutch heritage (see Boterbloem, *Moderniser*). Because of his good connections with the expats, it may have been Ukraintsev who shielded Lefort.

58. See my remarks about this, Boterbloem, *Fiction and Reality*, 74–5; Mishlaevskii, "Vyezd," 636.
59. Reger, "In the Service," 24.
60. See Boterbloem, *Fiction and Reality*, 50, 75, 86, 88–9, 93, 98–103, 108, 123–4, 127–9, 165, 171, 173, 178.
61. Bogoslovskii, *Petr I*, vol. 1, 55–6.
62. Ibid., 80–1, 90, 105–6.
63. Ibid., 80–1, 109–10.
64. Ibid., 54–5. In his early days in 1663, Timmerman had been arrested in Arkhangel'sk (and placed in leg irons) by the Russians for alleged malfeasance in trading with the Muscovites, and transported to Moscow, where he spent seven or eight months in prison (*Nationaal Archief, Archief der Staten-Generaal* 8423 [*Verbael*], 442–51).
65. See De Bom, *Geleerden*, 290–1.
66. Bogoslovskii, *Petr I*, vol. 1, 131, 136.
67. Ibid., 143–51.
68. They are available at: www.vostlit.info/Texts/rus5/Fabricius/framepred.htm, accessed 3 February 2019. For a transcription of the original German manuscript, see Man'kov, ed., *Zapiski inostrantsev o vosstanii Stepana Razina*, 14–45, and for Fabritius's memoirs regarding his Iranian travels, see ibid., 137–44.
69. Man'kov, ed., *Zapiski*, 137–44; Kaempfer, *Amoenitatum*, fasciculi 5; this Latin treatise was translated first into German as Kaempfer, *Am Hofe*; Sparwenfeld, *J.G. Sparwenfeld's Diary*. See as well Matthee, "Ludvig Fabritius"; "Ludvig Fabritius," the biography available at https://sok.riksarkivet.se/sbl/Presentation.aspx?id=15592, accessed 30 December 2018. Finally, see Konovalov, "Ludwig Fabritius's Account." Fabricius also appears in Struys, *Reysen*.
70. I mainly follow the Swedish biography ("Ludvig Fabritius") here but suggest a few changes when it seems a rather unlikely account. The Swedish account seems largely based on Fabricius's own memoirs, which were undoubtedly hazy about certain details, when he tried to remember his early years more than half a century later. In addition, he seems to have been prone to embellishment, if judging from some of the actions he undertook in his attempts to curry favour with the Swedish king in the 1680s.
71. Most sources suggest that this was in 1660, but it is not clear where Beem and his family resided between 1654 and 1660.

72. This was at the time of the massive arms deliveries by Dutch traders in preparation of a renewed Russian offensive. Fabricius writes that Hendrik Swellengrebel was the agent who hired them (see www.vostlit.info/Texts/rus5/Fabricius/frametext.htm, accessed 3 February 2019). But the dating of these events is difficult; Fabricius writes that he fought first in Ukraine under Cherkasskii against Pac (either Michal or Krzysztof); this cannot have happened prior to 1663. 1660, then, seems too early as the time of his arrival in Russia.
73. On the Cherkasskiis, see Bushkovitch, "Princes Cherkasskii."
74. See Boterbloem, *Fiction and Reality*, 98–9. I am not sure what to make of the Swedish account that he was captured earlier by Cossacks, sold as a slave to an Iranian merchant, and then ransomed on 6 June 1670, a date which in no way aligns with the events at Astrakhan in 1670.
75. Boterbloem, *Fiction and Reality*, 102–3.
76. Here, I follow A.G. Man'kov, the Russian editor of Fabricius's memoirs, who seems more accurate than the Swedes (available at: www.vostlit.info/Texts/rus5/Fabricius/framepred.htm, accessed 5 May 2019).
77. The Russian poet V.A. Zhukovskii, after visiting Peter de Grote's *huisje* in Zaandam with his pupil, tsarevich Aleksandr Nikolaevich, the later Tsar Alexander II (see Hughes, "'Nothing'," 647).
78. Van Nimwegen, "Army," 100–6.
79. Perhaps the reader objects to such a linkage, but there is no doubt that the Dutch throughout the last four or five centuries continually have explored and exploited the business opportunities war offers. Not only the activities of recent international arms traders such as Kouwenhoven prove that point but also the activities of an early airplane builder such as Anthony Fokker, or in recent decades the *Philips* subsidiary *Holland Signaal*.
80. A "Prussian turn" is conceivable, of course, with everyone serving a war machine, as in eighteenth-century Prussia. But even Prussia had three times as many inhabitants as the Republic by 1740, and it is hard to imagine the Dutch, who associated their identity with a concept of liberty, submitting to a government as regimented as the Prussians.
81. Van Nimwegen, "Army," 109.
82. Kopanev, "Gollandskie," 247. On the importance of the map by Hessel Gerritsz. for the Romanov claim to Muscovy, see ibid., 243–4.
83. Arkheograficheskaia komissiia, *Dopolneniia*, vol. 12, 46–7.
84. Ibid., 142.
85. Veluwenkamp, *Archangel*, 140.
86. Ibid., 141. Butenant proved incapable of supplying Peter's armed forces with the arms the tsar desired in the aftermath of the disastrous battle of Narva in 1700.
87. See Zacharov, "Jan Lups," 79–80.
88. Ibid., 80–1.
89. Witsen first came to Peter's attention through his map of Eurasia, which he had dedicated to Peter in 1687 (see, e.g., Kopanev, "Gollandskie," 245).
90. Ibid., 249–50.
91. Van der Meulen, *Nederlandse*.
92. See Cracraft, *Revolution*; Bushkovitch, *Peter*; Hughes, *Peter*.
93. By far the best overview of his flirtation with Dutch was written more than a century ago by a Dutch scholar (see Van der Meulen, "Peter").
94. For a more in-depth impression of Peter's fascination with Dutch culture, see Drissen et al., eds, *Petr I*. After the debacle in 1700 at Narva, Peter directly linked the lack of military successes against Sweden to the unavailability of useful, scientific, books in Russia (see Kopanev, "Gollandskie," 251).

95. Boterbloem, *Moderniser*, 186–7, 190–1, 197, 214.
96. In 1700, the Dutch merchant Jan Thesingh, whose brother had sold previously considerable quantities of arms to Russia, was given a monopoly on the printing of (most) secular Russian books in Amsterdam (Kopanev, "Gollandskie," 246, 248; for the document, see https://archief.amsterdam/stukken/handel/monopolie/index.nl.html, accessed 3 June 2019). Despite Peter's decree, Thesingh, who died in 1701, was not the only one printing books at the behest of Peter the Great in Amsterdam during the 1690s and 1700s.
97. Kugorn, *Novoe*. The Dutch original is Coehoorn, *Nieuwe*. For William Bruce, see Boterbloem, "Dutch Mercenaries," 66–7; Van Hoof, "Nieuwe manieren," 546; Sindeev, "Rossiiskii Briusy." The printing of secular works in Russia was still managed at this time by Dutch printers (see Kopanev, "Gollandskie," 250–1).
98. Boss, *Newton*, 33–44.
99. Fuhrmann, too, noted the younger Vinius's role in guiding the Russian boom in iron manufacturing around 1700 (see Fuhrmann, *Origins*, 261–2).

Bibliography

Aalst, G.M. van. *Het archief van de familie del Court van Krimpen (1506) 1611–1979*, Den Haag, 1986.

Adams, Julia. *The Familial State: Ruling Families and Merchant Capitalism in Early Modern Europe*, Ithaca, NY: Cornell University Press, 2007.

Amburger, E. *Arkheograficheskaia komissia, Dopolneniia k aktam istoricheskim*, vol. 9, St. Petersburg: Imperial Printers, 1875.

———. *Die Familie Marselis*, Gießen: Wilhelm Schmitz, 1957.

———. *Dopolneniia k aktam istoricheskim*, vol. 12, St. Petersburg: Prats, 1872.

Blussé, L. "No Boats to China: The Dutch East-India Company and the Changing Pattern in the China Sea Trade, 1635–1690," *Modern Asia Studies* 1, 1996, 51–76.

Bogoslovskii, M.M. *Petr I. Materialy dlia biografii*, vol. 1, Moskva: Nauka, 2005.

Bom, Erik de. *Geleerden en Politiek: De politieke ideeën van Justus Lipsius in de vroegmoderne Nederlanden*, Hilversum: Verloren, 2011.

Bontemantel, Hans. *De regeeringe van Amsterdam, soo in't civiel als crimineel en militaire (1653–72)*, ed. G.W. Kernkamp, Den Haag: Nijhoff, 1897.

Boss, Valentin. *Newton in Russia: The Early Influence, 1698–1796*, Cambridge, MA: Harvard University Press, 1972.

Boterbloem, Kees. "Dutch Mercenaries in the Tsar's Service: The Van Bockhoven Clan," *War and Society* 2, 2014, 59–78.

———. *The Fiction and Reality of Jan Struys: A Seventeenth-Century Dutch Globetrotter*, Houndmills, Basingstoke: Palgrave, 2008.

———. *Moderniser of Russia: Andrei Vinius, 1641–1716*, London: Palgrave, 2013.

Bruin, G. de. *Geheimhouding en verraad: De geheimhouding van staatszaken ten tijde van de Republiek (1600–1750)*, 's-Gravenhage: SDU Uitgeverij, 1991.

Bushkovitch, Paul. *Peter the Great: The Struggle for Power (1671–1725)*, Cambridge: Cambridge University Press, 2007.

———. "Princes Cherkasskii of Circassian Murzas: The Kabardinians in the Russian Boyar Elite, 1560–1700," *Cahiers du Monde Russe* 1–2, 2004, 9–30.

C.E.S., *T verwaerloosde Formosa. . .*, Amsterdam: Jan Claesz. ten Hoorn, 1675.

Coehoorn, M. *Nieuwe Vestingbouw, Op een natte of lage Horisont. . .*, Leeuwarden: Hendrik Rintjes, 1685.

Coyett, Balthasar. *Historisch Verhael of Beschryving van de Voyagie gedaan onder de Suite van den Heere Koenraad van Klenck*, Amsterdam: Jan ten Hoorn, 1677.

Cracraft, James. *The Revolution of Peter the Great*, Cambridge, MA: Harvard University Press, 2006.

Demkin, A.V. *Zapadnoevropeiskoe kupechestvo v Rossii v xvii v.*, 2 vols., Moskva: Institut Istorii RAN, 2004.

———. "Dlia popolneniia ego velikogo gosudar'a kazny," *Istochnik* 4, 1999, 3–9.

Driessen, J. "Het Gezantschap van Reinoud van Brederode in 1615 en 1616 naar Rusland," in J. Driessen, W. Roobol, and Marc Jansen, eds, *Rusland in Nederlandse ogen*, Amsterdam: van Oorschot, 1986, 51–73.

Drissen, Iozin, et al. eds. *Petr I Gollandiia*, St. Petersburg: Evropeiskii dom, 1997.

Elias, J.E. *De vroedschap van Amsterdam*, 2 vols., Amsterdam: Israel, 1963 [reprint].

Frederiks, J.G., and P.J. Frederiks. *Kohier van den tweehonderdsten penning . . . Over 1631*, Amsterdam: Ten Brink and De Vries, 1890.

Fuhrmann, Joseph T. *The Origins of Capitalism in Russia*, Chicago, IL: Quadrangle Books, 1972.

Goss, J., ed., *Blaeu's the Grand Atlas of the 17th-Century World*, New York: Studio Editions, 1991.

Hellie, Richard. *Enserfment and Military Change in Muscovy*, Chicago, IL: University of Chicago Press, 1971.

Hoof, Joep van. "Nieuwe manieren, sterke frontieren. Het bouwconcept van Menno van Coehoorn en zijn aandeel in de verbetering van het verdedigingsstelsel," *Bijdragen en mededelingen voor de geschiedenis der Nederlanden* 4, 2003: 545–66.

Hughes, Lindsey. "'Nothing Is Too Small for a Great Man': Peter the Great's Little Houses and the Creation of Some Petrine Myths," *Slavonic and East European Review* 4, 2003, 634–58.

———. *Peter the Great: A Biography*, New Haven, CT: Yale University Press, 2004.

Kaempfer, E. *Amoenitatum exoticarum politico-physico-medicarum, fasciculi 5*, Lemgo: H.W. Meyer, 1712, available at: http://diglib.hab.de/wdb.php?dir=edoc/ed000081&distype=start&pvID=start, accessed 29 December 2018.

———. *Am Hofe des Persischen Großkönigs, 1684–1685*, Tübingen-Basel: Erdmann, 1977 [Leipzig, 1940].

Kernkamp, G.W. "Inleiding," in Hans Bontemantel, *De regeeringe van Amsterdam, soo in't civiel als crimineel en militaire (1653–72)*, eds, G.W. Kernkamp, Den Haag: Nijhoff, 1897, iii–ccxxxiv.

———. *Kniga ustav' morskoi o vsem' chto kasaetsia dobromu upravleniiu, v' bytnosti flota na mor'*, St. Petersburg: Sankt'piterburgskaia Tipografiia, 1720.

Konovalov, S. "Ludwig Fabritius's Account of the Razin Rebellion," *Oxford Slavonic Papers* 6, 1955, 72–101.

Kopanev, N.A. "Gollandskie izdateli-knigotorgovtsy i delo Petra Velikogo," in I. Drissen et al., eds, *Petr I i Gollandiia*, St. Petersburg: Evropeiskii dom, 1997, 243–60.

Kotilaine, Jarmo. "In Defense of the Realm: Russian Arms Trade and Production in the Seventeenth and Early Eighteenth Century," in M. Poe and E. Lohr, eds, *Military and Society in Russia*, Leiden: Brill, 2002, 67–95.

———. *Russia's Foreign Trade and Economic Expansion in the Seventeenth Century*, Leiden: Brill, 2005.

———. "When the Twain Did Meet: Foreign Merchants and Russia's Economic Expansion in the Seventeenth Century," unpubl. Ph.D. diss., Harvard University Press, 2000.

Kugorn, M. baron von. *Novoe kriepostnoe stroenie na mokrom ili nizkom gorizontie . . .*, eds. M. Shafirov and I. Brius, Moscow: Tsarist Publishing House, 1709.

Lahana, Martha L. "Novaia Nemetskaia Sloboda: Seventeenth Century Moscow's Foreign Suburb," Ph.D. diss., University of North Carolina, Chapel Hill, 1983.

Loviagin, A.M. "Vvedenie," in A.M. Loviagin and A.I. Tsepkov, eds, *Posol'stvo Kunraada fan' Klenka k' Tsariam' Alekseiu Mikhailovichu i Fedoru Alekseevichu*, Riazan': Aleksandriia, 2008 [originally, St. Petersburg, 1900], iv–clxxvi.

Loviagin, A.M., and A.I. Tsepkov, eds. *Posol'stvo Kunraada fan' Klenka k' Tsariam' Alekseiu Mikhailovichu i Fedoru Alekseevichu*, Riazan': Aleksandriia, 2008 [originally, St. Petersburg, 1900].

"Ludvig Fabritius," available at https://sok.riksarkivet.se/sbl/Presentation.aspx?id=15592, accessed 30 December 2018.

Man'kov, A.G., ed. *Zapiski inostrantsev o vosstanii Stepana Razina*, Leningrad: Nauka, 1968. [Russian version available at: www.vostlit.info/Texts/rus5/Fabricius/framepred.htm, accessed 5 May 2019].

Matthee, R. "Ludvig Fabritius," *Encyclopaedia Iranica*, available at: www.iranicaonline.org/articles/fabritius, accessed 29 December 2018.

Meiden, G.W. van der. *Betwist Bestuur: Een eeuw strijd om de macht in Suriname, 1651–1753*, Amsterdam: De Bataafsche Leeuw, 1986.

Meulen, R. van der. *Nederlandse woorden in het Russisch*, Amsterdam: Noord-Hollandsche Uitgeversmaatschappij, 1959.

———. "Peter de Groote en het Hollandsch," *Onze Eeuw* 13 (3), 1913, 117–38.

Molhuysen, P.C., and P.J. Blok, eds. *Nieuw Nederlandsch Biografisch Woordenboek*, vol. 10, Leiden: Sijthoff, 1937.

Myshlaevskii, A.Z. "Vyezd v Rosiiu Frantsa Leforta (Sovremennaia perepiska)," *Russkaia starina* 3, 1898, 635–49.

Nimwegen, Olaf van. "The Army of the Dutch Republic and the Military Revolutions," in Louis Ph. Sloos, ed., *Warfare and the Age of Printing*, 4 vols., vol. 1, Leiden: Brill, 2008, 84–109.

Nozdrin, Oleg. "The Flodorf Project: Russia in the International Mercenary Market in the Early Seventeenth Century," in Brian Davies, ed., *Warfare in Eastern Europe, 1500–1800*, Leiden: Brill, 2012, 109–18.

Peters, M. *De wijze koopman: Het wereldwijde onderzoek van Nicolaes Witsen (1641–1717), burgemeester en VOC-bewindhebber van Amsterdam*, Amsterdam: Bert Bakker, 2010.

Raptschinsky, Boris. "Het gezantschap van Koenraad van Klenk naar Moskou," *Jaarboek Amstelodamum* 36, 1939, 148–99.

Reger, W.M. "In the Service of the Tsar: European Mercenary Officers and the Reception of Military Reform in Russia, 1654–1667," unpubl. Ph.D. diss., University of Illinois, Urbana-Champaign, 1997.

Ryzhenkov, M.V. "Frants Lefort. Drug i nastavik Petra Velikogo," *Voenno-Istoricheskii zhurnal* 3, 2007, 58.
Sindeev, V.V. "Rossiiskii Briusy," in V.P. Leonov et al., eds, *Kniga v Rossii xi-xx vv*, 21, St. Petersburg: Biblioteka Rossiiskoi akademii nauk, 2004, 163–88.
Sparwenfeld, J.G. *J.G. Sparwenfeld's Diary of a Journey to Russia, 1684–87*, ed. U. Birgegard, Stockholm: Kungl. Vitterhets Historie Och Antikvitets Akademien, 2002.
Struys, Jan. *Drie aanmerkelijke en seer rampspoedige Reysen . . .*, Amsterdam: J. Van Meurs and J. van Someren, 1676.
Ustrialov, N.G. *Istoriia tsarstvovaniia Petra Velikogo*, 6 vols., St. Petersburg: Imperial Printing House, 1858–1863.
Veluwenkamp, J.W. *Archangel: Nederlandse ondernemers in Rusland, 1550–1785*, Amsterdam: Balans, 2000.
Wallis, Helen. "A Banquet of Maps," *The Map Collector*, September 1984, 2–9.
Will, Pierre-Étienne. *Review of Russia and China: Their Diplomatic Relations to 1728*, by M. Mankall, in T'oung Pao 1, 1973, 314–23.
Wijnroks, E. *Handel tussen Rusland en de Nederlanden 1560–1640: Een netwerkanalyse van de Antwerpse en Amsterdamse kooplieden, handelend op Rusland*, Hilversum: Verloren, 2003.
Wolbers, J. *Geschiedenis van Suriname*, Amsterdam: S. Emmering, 1970.
Zacharov, Viktor. "Jan Lups: Der Handelsagent Peter des Ersten," in Carel Horstmeier et al., eds, *Around Peter the Great*, Groningen: NOS, 1997, 78–91.

Conclusion

One of the reasons for the Dutch resilience was their remarkable talent to make the best out of a bad situation, exhibiting a ruthless entrepreneurial spirit. It helped them to avoid the debilitating consequences of the seventeenth-century crisis that devastated Spain, Italy, Germany, and Poland. Of course, the Age of Crisis has been linked to many other causes than interminable warfare alone, but it remains remarkable (or puzzling) how well the northern and southern Netherlanders were able to overcome the especially gruesome decades of the civil war that raged from 1566 to the mid-1590s. They showed astonishing aptitude at turning an otherwise destructive human pursuit into a productive one. The Thirty Years' War in Germany laid much of the Holy Roman Empire low for at least a century; the 30 most devastating years of the Dutch Revolt made the northern Netherlands into a polity and an economy the likes of which had not been seen in terms of its riches and general standard of living. The previous pages have tried to show how exactly warfare itself contributed to that fabulous prosperity.

Such a turnaround by a stimulation of arms production or the arms trade is by no means unique in the history of capitalism. A famous example of this is Germany in the 1930s. The economy of the Russian Federation during the last quarter century has rarely failed to meet expectations in this sector. And this branch of the US economy has continued to perform well despite the 1973 oil crisis or the 2008 financial and economic collapse.

Arms manufacturing for the domestic market and export, and often the sale of scarce military expertise, has remained a constant part of the capitalist success story, I propose, at least from the seventeenth century onward. To a considerable degree, the Dutch weathered the worst of the economic downturn in that crisis era by their activities as arms manufacturers and traders and, at times, by offering their services as military experts (as officers, as rank-and-file mercenaries fighting on land, and as sailors) to those who could afford them.

I do not agree with Pepijn Brandon that, once the other powers could truly challenge its primacy, the "death-knell" for Dutch Republic's success sounded; Brandon contradicts himself in stating how "even if it managed to hold out against the onslaught for a few more decades."[1] Brandon's argument rejects the nineteenth-century historiographical consensus that after 1700 the Dutch elite rested too much on its laurels or had become complacent, as pensioners *(renteniers)* who lived off the dividends of their investments, shy of any further risk-taking. This flabby attitude came back to haunt it when the Prussian army restored the stadtholder William V by force of arms (1787) and the Dutch navy was given a drubbing in the Fourth Anglo-Dutch War (1780–1784) and then with the defeat in comprehensive fashion when the French occupied the country during the 1790s.

Different from Brandon, I tend to support a modified version of this "old" hypothesis, in the sense that I suggest that after 1713 the country's uncompromising military ethos underwent a fundamental modification, with war becoming something uncouth, a form of savagery that was to be pushed aside, even forgotten about, according to the growing norms of "civilised" behaviour (in the sense of Norbert Elias) of the Dutch elite. One might add the possibility that the confessionalisation that occurred in the course of the seventeenth century may have made people less inclined to consider harnessing violence for one's material betterment: Pious sermonising and vigorously reading the Gospels may have had its effect in blunting people's primal violent inclinations on the long term. Off stage, fortune-seekers could still indulge in violence and warfare in search of riches overseas after 1713, whether in the slave trade, the plantation economies of the Caribbean, or in Asia. But those acts took place out of sight, with most of Dutch society no longer conditioned to life in the shadow of war.

The Dutch might still have been at the grown-up table of the European Powers later in the eighteenth century if they had pursued a sort of Dutch version of the Prussian route, with possible territorial expansion into the southern Netherlands to acquire more of a hinterland (a sort of Dutch Silesia), but the lust for warfare had evaporated. Instead, the Dutch hid ever more fearfully behind their curious line of fortresses near the French-Austrian/Netherlandic borders, more and more a relic from the age when such forts were well-nigh impregnable and the Dutch celebrated many a military triumph.

The Dutch had been in the forefront of military innovation at sea and on land during the one and a half century (from 1566 to 1713) of almost incessant warfare in which their seven provinces were involved. Their expertise in warfare and manufacturing skills in producing arms was a key part of the flourishing of Dutch capitalism. The exact significance of the Dutch arms trade can never be established, but the Republic's spending three quarters or so of its annual budget on war was a vast stimulus for the economy of an ever richer country (per capita easily the wealthiest in the world at the time). A wave of innovations nourished this boom, such as in army drill, the use of firearms, siege warfare, fortress building, marines, battleships, or the wielding of mortar and bayonet. As with the British Industrial Revolution, a felicitous coincidence of circumstances made the Dutch moment in world history possible, but as with the British boom, it was ultimately finite. The breakthrough to a truly mechanised production process was never made, despite the use of wind power or peat to operate sawmills and fuel other manufactories or processing operations; printing presses were sophisticated machinery but were operated by hand. And success may ultimately breed complacency. It cannot be entirely coincidental that it was a Dutch historian, Jan Romein, who spoke of a "law of the handicap of a head start," as exactly such a phenomenon can be observed engulfing the country of his ancestors in the eighteenth century (and, as he thought to have witnessed, Britain in the twentieth century).[2] Dutch businessmen continued to trade in arms, of course, but the business of war became a niche trade, rather than a countrywide, or perhaps even national, enterprise.

One needs to reinvent oneself or innovate to stay ahead in the game of capitalism, as the United States did in the IT boom of the 1990s. The Dutch were for the first time confronted with the threat of obsolescence in the First Anglo-Dutch War, when the British navy of special warships proved technologically superior over the Dutch fleet that was still in large part composed of refurbished merchantmen.[3] They did manage to catch up and stay on top for a while longer, not in the least thanks to the genius of people such as Van Coehoorn, De Ruyter, Johan and Cornelis de Witt, and William III, who all contributed to the Dutch survival as a Great Power until 1713. But other countries sluiced their economic potential ever more effectively into their military, which allowed for the deployment of vast field armies (as France could muster by 1700) or navies (as in the case of Great Britain). Tellingly, Visser and Bailey remark how towards 1700 in terms of Dutch gunmaking, "innovation was largely replaced by imitation."[4]

The fondness for Dutch military skill and weapons rapidly vanished after the hiring spree of Dutch experts linked to Peter the Great's Grand Embassy. In Russia, its last hurrah may have been the artillery school connected with Andrei Vinius (with which he was only briefly involved).[5] And the Dutch role as centre of the European arms production and trade equally quickly disappeared after 1700. No economic branch evolves as quickly as the manufacturing of arms, it seems, as is so clearly evident in global history since 1850. Fascist Italy boasted of the most advanced military in the world in 1930, which was found woefully obsolete, however, in 1940. This was the story of the Dutch, even though at a less frantic pace, in the seventeenth century.

The Dutch were too much used to living in a country in which freedom was respected and tolerance the norm (of course, measured against the standards of the age, for they did not live by the principles of the UN

Charter of Human Rights of 1947) to reorganise themselves as a sort of barracks-state as the rulers of Brandenburg-Prussia were able to do. War was too costly, peace too tempting after 1713; the Dutch preferred to rest on their laurels. Collective resolve in the face of foreign threats dissipated in the course of the eighteenth century, probably in part because the elite in the Republic became a closed stratum, to which newcomers were no longer welcome. Had the rentier-regents of the eighteenth century been able to mobilise more of the population in defence of the realm, perhaps the Anglo-Dutch War of the 1780s might have been less than an unmitigated disaster, the Prussian troops that came to the rescue of William V and his spouse might have been stopped, or the French might not have succeeded in occupying the country in the middle of the 1790s. Of course, Dutch decline was slow and relative, and the country's standard of living remained high until the French era and even after when compared with that of other countries during those years. Whereas a sort of second Dutch empire arose in the course of the nineteenth century in East Asia, it was not really the result of Dutch military or capitalist genius but far more of British benevolence and the vast technological advance of all European countries over non-Western regions.

With regard to seventeenth-century arms trade and production, a parallel with the Dutch role as conduit for the diffusion of the slave-holding plantation complex in the Americas, or the related Triangular Trade, suggests itself. The Dutch phase provided an essential stage in the growth of global capitalism, which as I have tried to show was not unrelated to the development of Western (or European) military primacy in the world. But, ultimately, the Dutch were overhauled in both respects, not unlike how they were increasingly bypassed as the staple of the European global trade towards 1700.[6] The Dutch role had been in many ways that of a "diffusion country," as Frijhoff and Spies suggest: "It . . . adopted . . . innovation[s] from elsewhere, made [them] into a success and then passed [them] on," a transmission belt, perhaps, using another metaphor.[7]

"Success," though, depends on the criteria by which it is measured. The Dutch showed how profitability is not of itself moral. What works in capitalism does not have to translate into an improvement of the common good. Indeed, the lesson that could be drawn from the Dutch efforts seemed that moral scruples were more of a hindrance than a help. This, of course, was all the more so the case in terms of the international arms trade and large-scale weapons production.

The Dutch went to work in calculated fashion in engaging in war and the arms trade, after the all-hands-on-deck opening stages of the Revolt. In land warfare, we see Dutch experts as weaponmakers, as engineers of fortresses and practitioners of siege warfare, as artillery specialists, far more often than as battlefield commanders, let alone rank-and-file, as their role as Western officers in Russian service indicates. Of course, the population of the Republic was small and its desperation far less severe than of those born in the barren or devastated regions of Scotland, Ireland, Wallonia, or the Empire, so the temptation to take up arms for the commoners was less enticing. The Dutch lower strata could disregard the promise of a more adventurous existence and a comparatively decent and regular wage which the army seemed to offer to some of Europe's poor in other countries. Even in the Republic, proportionally fewer soldiers came from Holland than from the poorer and more battered eastern provinces or northern Brabant. Dutch sailors preferred the fisheries or the short-haul runs to the Baltic over the endless (and often lethal) journeys to the East Indies: The Dutch preferred to have others do the dirty work in war, as Louys Trip (whose personal wealth approximated a million guilders, or the average annual income of 5,000 Dutch artisans, when he died in 1684) did in 1672. In addition, Dutch genius was expressed by a remarkable talent to keep the warfare that buttressed its economic success for generations outside of the country's core *(De Hollandse Tuin)*, and often enough the country avoided war's severe devastation while reaping its vast profits.

In sum, as the previous pages have tried to outline, the dirty secret of Dutch capitalism is that far too few historians, economists, or politicians have connected its flourishing to this deplorable side of its manifold ventures. The profits of this nefarious industry and trade, too, gave the world the beautiful canal houses and timeless paintings admired by millions of visitors today in the Netherlands. More research needs to be done, but one may surmise that the flourishing of the British economy during the eighteenth and nineteenth centuries, or the German and American economies after 1865, was equally in considerable measure a consequence of such a military stimulus. The Dutch Golden Age unfolding amidst a European-wide economic crisis was to a significant degree built on the vast profits that came from the country's profound entanglement in matters military.

Notes

1. Brandon, *War*, 5; to be fair, on ibid., 7, he does mention the "aristocratisation of the elite" as a contributing factor.
2. See Romein, *onvoltooid verleden*, 9–64.
3. Snapper, *Oorlogsinvloeden*, 114.
4. Visser and Bailey, "Introduction," 17.
5. Boterbloem, *Moderniser*, 187, 192, 197.
6. On this entrepot function, see De Vries and Van der Woude, *First*, 690–2.
7. Frijhoff, Spies, *1650*, 21.

Bibliography

Boterbloem, Kees. *Moderniser Of Russia: Andrei Vinius, 1641–1716*, London: Palgrave, 2013.

Brandon, Pepijn. *War, Capital and the Dutch State (1588–1795)*, Leiden: Brill, 2015.

Frijhoff, W., and M. Spies. *1650: Bevochten Eendracht*, 2nd ed., Den Haag: SDU, 2000.

Romein, J. *Het onvoltooid verleden: Kultuurhistorische Studies*, Amsterdam: Querido, 1937.

Snapper, F. *Oorlogsinvloeden op de overzeese handel van Holland, 1551–1719*, Amsterdam: Ellerman Harms, 1959.

Visser, H.L., and D.W. Bailey. "Introduction," in H.L. Visser and D.W. Bailey, eds, *Aspects of Dutch Gunmaking*, Zwolle: Waanders, 1997, 14–19.

Vries, Jan de, and A. van der Woude. *The First Modern Economy: Success, Failure and Perseverance of the Dutch Economy, 1500–1815*, Cambridge: Cambridge University Press, 1997.

Appendix

On Kondratiev Waves and Dutch Capitalism

The reader may have missed an in-depth discussion of the economics of the Dutch Republic in the previous pages. This lacuna exists because, on the one hand, the general outline of Dutch economic development in the sixteenth and seventeenth centuries has been well enough charted by economic historians in the last half century, among whom especially Jan de Vries and Jonathan Israel deserve pride of place.[1] On the other hand, solid numbers for overall economic growth, employment, import and export, the balance of payments, or even such things as population numbers have never been conclusively recovered even by the best economic historians, for anything resembling comprehensive macro-economic statistics were not maintained in the United Provinces. At most, estimates can be given, many of which are certainly plausible.

Of course, even in our own days, many consider economics a dismal science, so perhaps any such numbers might not help us understand Dutch capitalism and the role of the arms sector within it all that much. Not having trained myself as an economist (even if I was treated to a few courses in economic history as a student and the Soviet Union's history cannot be interpreted without an understanding of Marx), I have refrained from suggesting anything concretely about the weight of the arms industry and trade within the Dutch economy (although the 5 per cent suggested by Frijhoff and Spies seems impossibly low).[2] Still, upon reflection, I do think one curious observation deserves to be made regarding the Dutch economy from the middle of the sixteenth century to the early eighteenth century.

Oddly, given my own academic trajectory, that observation is grounded in the economic ideas of Nikolai Kondrat'ev (whose name is spelled Kondratiev or Kondratieff in Western languages; 1892–1938), executed on Stalin's orders near Moscow during the Great Terror.[3] I encountered Kondrat'ev's theories more than a generation ago; like many, I have always been somewhat sceptical about his theory about business cycles that ultimately seems to be Pythagorean in its essence. But Kondrat'ev has been taken seriously by highly regarded scholars such as Joseph Schumpeter or Eric Hobsbawm.[4] Kondrat'ev's suggestion of recurrent economic waves stretching out for about half a century, meanwhile, mainly applied to the global, modern industrial economy. Thus, Kondrat'ev identified one's wave's cresting around 1815 (reaching an ending in 1849), a second one in 1873 (ending in 1896), and, obviously, a third one in 1929 (ending, one presumes, around 1950).

Economists in interpreting Kondrat'ev (and he himself) appear to have been a little loose in applying any exactitude of the waves; 50 years is more or less their timespan, as the aforementioned years show, rather than precisely. Possibly, the earlier waves developed more slowly because of the lower level of industrialisation. At the same time, Kondrat'ev perceived some sort of a nexus between economic phases and political crises. Thus, he proposed that during an upswing, the worst wars occurred: The Napoleonic Wars fit that pattern, although the German unification wars, US Civil War, and Crimean War were less all-encompassing during the next upswing; the First World War and its aftermath do fit the third upswing period. The Second World War, though, the most devastating in history, came on a downward wave.

Despite all these caveats, it is remarkable how well the Dutch phase of the European world economy can be made to fit a Kondrat'evan pattern. At first sight, this may not seem all that evident. I suggest that a first upswing begins in the 1590s, reaches a high point around 1620, after which a downturn commences, accelerated perhaps by the 1637 Tulip Craze, and ends around 1650, when both the Münster Peace and the Navigation Acts accentuate a nadir. Soon, though, another upswing begins, which reaches its turning point during the 1670s, with the wave hitting another low point around the Ryswyck Peace and Tsar Peter's visit to Holland in 1697. A new upswing then begins that ends around 1720 (the speculation-bubble crises in Britain and France), with a nadir somewhere in the 1740s (during the War of the Austrian Succession).

If we take into account the fate of the Dutch arms industry and exports, which were, with the printing presses, perhaps the most modern branch of the Dutch economy in the seventeenth century, the Kondrat'ev waves seem much more in evidence: Growth from 1590s–1620 (even during the Twelve Years' Truce, arms found a ready market, as we saw, especially abroad), decline after 1621, low point around 1648 (mercenaries depart elsewhere, too, right at that time), renewed growth until the 1670s, followed by a sustained decline when the combined efforts of British shipwrights, French fortress-and-siege experts, or German and Swedish arms manufacturers begin to overtake the Dutch. Peter the Great's conclusion that the Dutch were past their prime as the European leaders in shipbuilding fits this pattern. A renewed growth nonetheless, stimulated by the War of the Spanish Succession and the still high demand of especially the Russians for Dutch expertise and arms, starts around 1697, although its high point may come rather early, by 1714 or so. This follows Israel's thesis, who believes that Dutch trading success finally ended by 1740.[5]

But this last Kondrat'evan wave (1697–1740), as I suggested in the previous pages, was less closely linked to the arms trade. So waves can be identified from 1590 to 1648, 1648 to 1697, and 1697 to 1740, amounting to a fairly decent alignment with the 50-year patterns Kondrat'ev discerned. Jan de Vries indeed suggested that another upswing of the Dutch economy becomes apparent in the second half of the eighteenth century.[6] By the end of that century, finally, the Dutch economy aligns itself with the trends of the industrialising European economy, as identified by Kondrat'ev himself.

Finally, the upswing periods of all three waves can be linked to major warfare, but clearly other things had to fall in place for such mayhem to become a real stimulus. By the 1590s, the existential crisis of the first decades of the revolt (1566–1588) was over, and the economy of Holland, Utrecht, Friesland, Groningen, or Zeeland could develop itself, safely removed from the frontline and being spared the worst consequences of warfare; by the late 1640s and into the 1650s, a major alignment was necessary (away from the carrying trade on England and France, more towards industrial production for areas that were more remote, with whom trade intensified), as was the case in the 1690s. The growth of the scale of warfare (certainly evident in the warfare at sea with Britain after 1651 and on land in the 1670s) still may have provided a stimulus, as did the further growth of warfare's scope towards 1700, but war alone cannot explain the upswing. Indeed, Kondrat'ev himself was not this reductionist. Several economists suggest that Kondrat'ev rising waves are the result of a complex or varied set of stimuli, such as the growth in inventions, technological innovations, the finding of new supplies of raw materials, the opening up of new trade routes and markets, or the development of new production methods. This only strengthens the case for the early modern Dutch economy following the wave pattern.[7]

Notes

1. See De Vries and Van der Woude, *First Modern Economy*; Israel, *Dutch Primacy*. Neither work refers to Kondrat'ev.
2. Frijhoff and Spies, *1650*, 18.
3. See, for example, Kondrat'ev, "Bol'shie tsikly"; Kondratieff, *Long Wave*.
4. Hobsbawm, *Age of Extremes*, 87, 268; Schumpeter, *Theory*; Rostow, "Kondratieff"; Thompson and Zuk, "War."
5. See Israel, *Dutch Primacy*, 377–98.
6. De Vries, "Decline."
7. Schumpeter already suggested this (see Schumpeter, *Capitalism*, 68). See, for a recent discussion, Korotayev, Zinkin and Bogevolnov, "Kondratieff Waves." The authors look at patents, which were not yet widely used in the seventeenth-century Republic.

Bibliography

Frijhoff, W. and M. Spies. *1650: Bevochten Eendracht*, 2nd ed., Den Haag: SDU, 2000.

Hobsbawm, Eric. *The Age of Extremes: A History of the World, 1914–1991*, New York: Vintage, 1996.

Israel, Jonathan. *Dutch Primacy in the World Trade, 1585–1740*, Oxford: Oxford University Press, 1989.

Kondratieff, N.D. "Bol'shie tsikly kon'iunktury," *Voprosy kon'iunktury* 1, 1925, 28–79.

———. *The Long Wave Cycle*, New York: Richardson and Snyder, 1984.

Korotayev, Andrey, Julia Zinkin, and Justislav Bogevolnov, "Kondratieff Waves in Global Invention Activity (1900–2006)," *Technological Forecasting and Social Change* 78, 2011, 1280–4.

Rostow, W.W. "Kondratieff, Schumpeter, and Kuznets: Trend Periods Revisited," *Journal of Economic History* 4, 1975, 719–53.

Schumpeter, J. *Capitalism, Socialism, and Democracy*, 3rd ed., New York: Harper, 1942.

———. *The Theory of Economic Development*, Cambidge, MA: Harvard University Press, 1934.

Thompson, W.R., and L. Gary Zuk, "War, Inflation and the Kondratieff Long Wave," *Journal of Conflict Resolution* 4, 1982, 621–44.

Vries, Jan de. "The Decline and Rise of the Dutch economy, 1675–1900," in G. Saxonhouse and G. Wright, eds, *Technique, Spirit and Form in the Making of Modern Economies: Essays in Honor of William N. Parket*, Greenwich: JAI Press, 1984, 149–89.

Vries, Jan de, and A. van der Woude. *The First Modern Economy: Success, Failure and Perseverance of the Dutch Economy, 1500–1815*, Cambridge: Cambridge University Press, 1997.

Index

For Product Safety Concerns and Information please contact our EU
representative GPSR@taylorandfrancis.com
Taylor & Francis Verlag GmbH, Kaufingerstraße 24, 80331 München, Germany

www.ingramcontent.com/pod-product-compliance
Ingram Content Group UK Ltd.
Pitfield, Milton Keynes, MK11 3LW, UK
UKHW022001180926
475701UK00003B/140
9781032087030